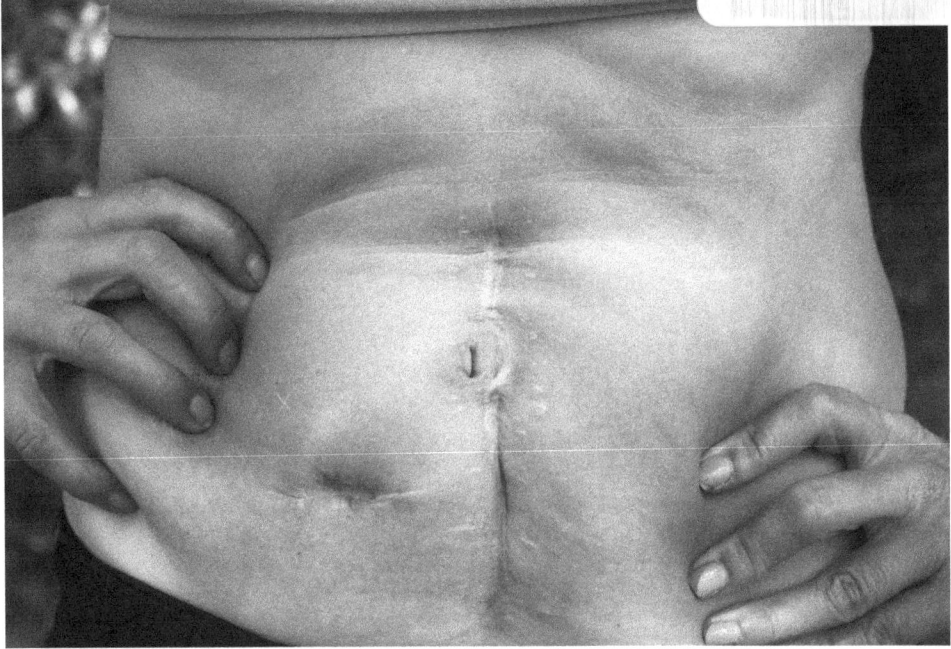

You Got No Guts

Vision Quest for Nontoxic Schools

Zana K. Elin

NEWMAN SPRINGS PUBLISHING
320 Broad Street
Red Bank, NJ 07701

First originally published by Newman Springs Publishing 2024

Artwork by Violet Elin

ISBN 978-1-68498-993-5 (Paperback)
ISBN 978-1-68498-994-2 (Digital)

Printed in the United States of America

To my family

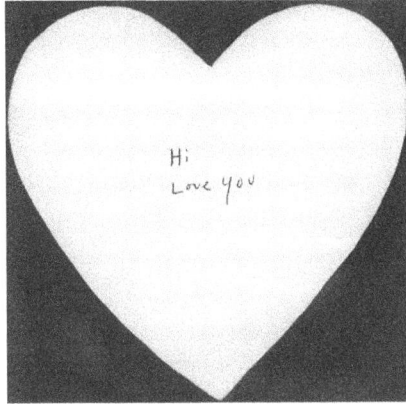

You see us as you want to see us.

—*The Breakfast Club*

Contents

Ten Lessons That Bullying Teaches

History Lesson
Retro Rewind

It's September from days gone by.

> I am woman, hear me roar
> In numbers too big to ignore
> And I know too much to go back an' pretend
> 'Cause I've heard it all before
> And I've been down there on the floor
> No one's ever gonna keep me down again

—Helen Reddy

Cue the Music:
"I Am Woman" by Helen Reddy
"You're No Good" by Linda Ronstadt
"I Will Survive" by Gloria Gaynor

Fun

FU she writes on the desk. Confronted by her teacher, the middle-schooler says she was just writing the word "FUN." Fly immediately guessed that the assistant principal must have heard that a million times before, so Celeste was charged with serving her time in lunch detention with the administrator in the AP's Office. Mortified as her mother, even more as a school-teacher, that Fly's own child would do such an abomination as to write anything on a school desk, let alone whatever was meant by FU and did not get to the letter N. Celeste confesses later: that the girl in class was bullying her, and she was trying to take a stand and make a statement. She becomes the punished, once by the student and then again by the adults.

Three years later, she screams, approaching a Y-shaped intersection, "No! Drop me off at the front of the school, not the back!" Fly's daughter exclaimed as the car swerves left instead of veering right, fishtailing and accidentally running a red light in the pouring rain. They both gasp, hearts racing, hands shaking, and then deep breaths of relief. Fly's daughter saw Totally Tall Skinny Macchiato Val Gal being dropped off at the back of the school several days ago and is terrified to see her again, little did Fly know. Celeste says the harsh words online do not bother her, but her glare and physical presence are particularly brutal and terrifying. The mere thought of the possibility that Totally Macchiato Val could be there again providing an "accidental" run in creates a lingering sense of despair and taunting. How does one person possess the ability to push such attacking behaviors upon another for reasons that are not even completely clear? Bullying and harassing behaviors begin directly with the insecurities of the person initiating these hurtful tactics and are often riddled with one seeking power over another. Totally Macchiato Val was the most self-indulged teen Fly had ever seen even in all her years of teaching or being around teenagers. How dare she flick all her fake plastic hot pink sparkle nails off and toss them all over Celeste's house one day hanging out while they were still friends. Celeste put up with a lot, but the friendship abruptly ended when nude sexting photos of Totally Tall Skinny Macchiato Val Gal ran rampant on kid's cell phones in the schoolyard. Gag me with a spoon!

In kindergarten, Little Celeste was threatened by Peanut Butter Betty as she waved an anaphylaxis sandwich in her face, knowing she was allergic and had to always have an Epi pencil in her backpack and another at the nurse's office. This attack-waiting-to-happen taunting went on and on despite the separate designated "allergy" table and the teachers knowing which students had severe food allergies. She and the other Peanut Butter Allergy Boy would meekly eat their lunch in the corner of shame, knowing the peanut butter sandwich would be waved in their faces over and over again. Worse, they were also separated and isolated from classmates during field trips when they had to sit in the front seat of the bus with the school nurse just in case. They would have preferred sitting in the back of the bus with their friends laughing and joking around just being kids.

In second grade, Angelica Heart Thief Girl bent over to pick up a necklace that Celeste Bag of Donuts accidentally dropped on the classroom floor, as Celeste was often known to be messy and clumsy. Perhaps schmutzy girl suited her best or as Fly's husband coined the nickname Celeste Bag of Donuts as she always seemed to have crumbs all over the place as well as her person. Celeste would pretend to have an invisible crumb box, open the invisible top, pull out the invisible and irritating crumbs, and sprinkle them all over Mama Fly just to annoy her. Angelica decided that rather than hand the necklace over to Celeste, she blatantly took it right in front of her face and put it in her pocket. She told the teacher that Angelica Heart Thief stole the "Daughter" half of the Mother-Daughter heart necklaces Fly and she had gotten for each other and was claiming it was hers. It was only a cheap necklace from the teen junk jewelry store but was very special to them. Disgusted with disbelief, Fly immediately wrote a letter to the teacher and even sent a photocopy of the "Mother" half so she would be able to see that the hearts matched like two puzzle pieces and it surely belonged to Celeste, not Angelica. There was no response, no action, no repercussions as if Celeste was not taken seriously or believed; the "Daughter" half-heart charm necklace was never seen again, lost to the dark vast tumultuous sea like that of the old lady who tossed the sparkly jewel necklace off the back of the Titanic. Fly was crushed by the system and lack of care and action; still holding in her hand today is the "Mother" half of the heart with its lonely jagged edges, wondering why Angelica Heart Thief was no angel and would steal a personal object from someone else. Celeste still recalls this event to this very day as she reflects squinting her laser beam eyes and whispers in a deep demonic voice that sums it all up, "An-gelll-i-caaaaa..."

Little does Celeste Bag of Donuts know that in second grade, her mom, Little Fly, too was picked on. A group of Popular Preppy Girls flushed Little Fly's clothes and shoes into the toilet during gym class and she had to wear her ugly '70s gym shorts, those '70s shin-high socks, a borrowed evergreen school logo tee shirt, and her sneakers the rest of that cold winter day. Little Fly was stunned one could even attempt to flush such large objects down a toilet. Across the room, her clothes were drying ever so slowly on the classroom radiator, drawing attention to it as it mockingly hissed with hot air for everyone to see as the girls snickered and glanced back and forth at each other, affirming what they had gotten away with, as there was secrecy in the girl's locker room; shielded from being witnessed by the adults in the school. A few months earlier, at the Halloween Parade, as Little Fly made her way hesitantly through the spooky maze in the auditorium, darkness loomed and kids were scattering all around; the lights were out and the maze was designed to trap, scare, and confuse at the turn of every corner as the scary haunted house music played and strobes flared. The smells from candy galore, chocolate, and bobbing for apples loomed in the air. Then out of the darkness from behind the red velvet stage curtain, a slightly older boy silently tiptoed up behind Little Fly and shoved a half-eaten slimy apple in the hood that lay open of the red sweatshirt she was wearing disguised as Little Red Riding Hood. He swiftly crept away into the darkness just as quickly as he approached, and she could hear his muffled evil gotcha sound fading away from her. Feeling confused by the unexpected weight on her back and tug of the sharp metal zipper choking at her neck, she twisted, writhed, and struggled to retrieve the gross eaten apple rotted brown on the edges.

Little Fly was mortified, perplexed, and then disgusted, and she remembers it as if it were yesterday, especially every time she tries to eat an apple.

How could it possibly get worse than toilet water on clothing? Well, Little Fly fell one day on the bathroom vanity. She was standing up near the sink and was either reaching for something high up in the medicine cabinet or possibly standing on the counter getting a full view assessment of her wretched body, which was just slightly pre-teen pudgy, not anything obese, when she lost her footing, slipped, and fell. To this day, Fly cannot reach anything up high. She can be seen at the Targe', stealthy as a ninja rock climber, scaling the shelves, using long objects such as plastic wrap as a sword to wrangle products from the top shelf as she sweeps it to the edge, and it tumbles land sliding into the shopping cart. Success as she refuses to get help from the tall man passerby. So Little Fly falls, and of course, class picture day was that Monday where, being the small one, she had to sit up front with her big black eye. Sometime later, she had a birthday party where she had to invite all of the girls from class. Unable to explain the atrocities to her mother, Fly complied that everyone including the Popular Preppy Girls was to be invited. The two elitists of the Popular Preppy Girls thought it to be hilarious to show up to Little Fly's party with penciled-in matching black eyes. Perhaps it was charcoal, but nonetheless, Fly wondered why none of the moms did not say anything at how unusual it was.

It's hard when no one believes what someone is saying, as if a Bigfoot encounter happened. Once, Patches the outdoor cat was disgruntled for some reason and flew off the tool bench in the garage and attacked Little Fly. Her family insisted she was never attacked. Fly's future husband got beat up all the time by girls at the bus stop, chased down, and pummeled. She asked him, "Did you ever get bullied?" He matter-of-factly responded, "Sure." Fly was waiting for an explanation. "Oh! You mean you want details? We just got our butts straight up kicked all the time."

In fourth grade, the girls were so nasty to Little Fly because she dressed differently and was new to the school; that was her guess anyway as to their rationale. Knowing no one in the new school, she just took it and internalized her fear. After all, her family had moved for her older brother so that he could get the special educational needs that were on the cutting edge of educational equality for students with disabilities. It didn't really bother her to escape the cruel Popular Preppy Girls from her other school, plus she signed up for an after-school baking class where she learned how to make Kiss Surprise Cookies and really liked her fun art teacher where she got to express herself. With school stress, however, she packed on a few more pudgy pounds and, while not fully grown yet, developed a pudgy pot belly for sure emphasized by the rainbow crayon pocket on her mustard-colored puffy sweatshirt attempting to camouflage it.

One day, the classroom teacher abruptly pulled the two lines of students over to the right side of the long empty fluorescent-lit gross green-colored hallway, pointing at the group, using her finger as a directional to move over now. Little Fly was startled and flinched at the commanding voice as she hated getting into trouble and strived for perfection and thought herself to be a decent, truthful, and kind person. There was one boy line and one girl line in short to tall height order which Little Fly hated, and it really bothered her to be categorized in this manner. Always almost being the coveted "Line Leader," she had no control over her fun-sized body. She was put in charge of moving the line, stopping the line, going fast or slowly, turning corners, keeping the line quiet in the halls and other instructions given by the teacher. Little Fly had never heard a teacher yell so loud at a group of kids, and the teacher scolded them for their behavior toward Little Fly or perhaps they were just being unruly and loud in general, Little Fly was not sure. Is this what you get switching from private to public school? Little Fly didn't even know what was happening as she tried to ignore and deflect the loud words and taunting from her fellow classmates, but the teacher heard something all loud and clear. She scolded them for being nasty to Little Fly. These were the same kids who picked her last for gym teams and that one day when the dodgeball came at her so fast, she did not even see it coming. It hit her in the gut and knocked the wind out of her so badly she fell to the shiny squeaky gym floor writhing in pain. Embarrassed but unable to breathe, she spent the rest of the week in the nurses' office.

Later that day after the hallway incident, Little Fly was told to sit at Miss Protector of Evil teacher's desk to eat lunch with her while the other students sat at their individual desks. This teacher was very tall, slim, wholesome, and kind and ate healthy apples, which made Fly cringe a little bit, and had to shoot herself with a needle throughout the day. Little Fly had no clue what the shot was about, but she sympathized as it appeared painful and was happy to be removed from the group and not go along with whatever they were doing. She didn't care or so she thought. Little Fly's mom's favorite question she would ask all the time was, "If everyone else jumped off the bridge, would you too?" In which Little Fly would always respond with a sad drawn-out "No..." and her little brother would always sarcastically exclaim, "Yes!" followed by eyeball rolling from Fly and her mom.

Decades later, paralleling her mother's experience, Celeste Bag of Donuts was trick or treating with a group of clicky Basic White Girls as Celeste called them, soon-to-be Totally Vals. All of the helicopter Mommy Vals followed behind the daughters as they were just slightly too young to go alone wandering the neighborhood, even in a decent-sized group. Fly patiently listened to the gossip ensued by the Mommy Vals; they tried to one-up each other with their stories as to who was the popular PTA mom, who had breast cancer, who had other soon-to-be fatal diseases and could not trick or treat, who had the best Halloween decorated house, who gave out the big-sized chocolate bars on the block and so on. They spoke in whispers at times as though to conceal their conversation topics from others around them. Some of the Mommy Vals tried to look like they were also in middle school with their cuffed-up tight jeans faded at the quads with their portly bodies like stuffed sausages and banana clips in their straightened and professionally high-lighted streaked hair. Wasn't middle school dreadful enough once but to want to revisit via attire was beyond Fly's comprehension? Fly thought that she wore banana clips like in sixth grade and what a fashion faux pas for the current time. They were all walking in a parade of sorts when in an instant, Shabby

Val Gal tripped accidentally in front of all the Totally Val Gals, spilling her precious collection of candy all over the harsh gravel road, scraping her knee, and everyone gasped and leaned in to help her get up. But trying to look cool rather than clumsy, she immediately blamed it on Celeste Bag of Donuts who was striding alongside her. Shabby Val was on the fringe part of the Totally Val Gal gang, same as Celeste, although many of the girls secretly wanted to be like her because she marched to her own beat. In an instant like a crowd of brainwashed Tween Zombies, they all turned their back on Celeste and were chanting and pointing fingers with their smirky, angry faces. The Mommy Vals were instantly persuaded that it was the truth because their daughters would never lie. Disgusted and outcasted, Fly insisted Celeste wrap it up and get out of there, free themselves from the cookie cutter Totally Vals and bigger version Mommy Vals. Fly was there and saw what happed so why did this girl have to blame an accidental stumble on someone else? It was a tween mob mentality. Celeste would secretly begin a Burn Book hidden in the deep dark depths of her slovenly bedroom.

One time, Fly was cleaning up and found a scrap of paper in Celeste's backpack that she wrote in high school. The police recommend that parents should, on occasion, go through their kid's rooms to see what's going on with them and notice any red flags. So in essence, Fly was actually snooping, not cleaning. Those were the worst years for Celeste Bag of Donuts, leading her to hate school: students, teachers, corruption; "Dirty Rats" or "You Doityyy Ratzzzzzz" she would call them all in her most villainous deep mobster mimicking voice similar to her demonic "An-gelll-i-caaaaa," as she recalls the thievery. She would crinkle her face and eyes as if to shoot them down with her laser beams. On the crumpled note was written:

> September: My eyes close as I bite my nails
> in an overheated classroom. Trembling as my
> teacher is thinking about who to pick on.

During those teen years, Celeste had been shoved against the lockers by Locker Grunge Girl, almost thrown out of a car on the highway by a supposed boyfriend Dirt Bag Dude, more like boy-fiend. He videotaped her doing something with another boy—okay, it was vaping, and she claimed she only did it once in a back room in school, and he sent it to the administrator as an act of jealous revenge leading to her punishment of In School Suspension and her first suicidal breakdown. Vaping was at its infancy, and they all tried to get their hands on the devices that fooled teachers by appearing as memory sticks, their eerie doppelgangers. Even one of Celeste's friends at the time would go to Targe' and make an insignificant purchase on her parent-guarded debit card just to get cash back so her parents would not know she was buying vaping materials. So Celeste Bag of Donuts spent an entire grueling day in ISS and like in *The Breakfast Club*, they had to write pages by hand on loose-leaf paper about their actions and who they thought they were. Their cell phones were locked up in a box, and they even had to line up in the hall like criminals to go one at a time to the bathroom for all other students walking in between classes to witness and snicker at. Fly will never know what she wrote in her confessional letter, but the manly ISS health teacher was moved to tears crying like a little baby at the end of that dark day as he read her eloquently moving statement. Also, Celeste Bag of Donuts defiantly stole the laminated ISS Rules paper as Fly found it later on in her room during a snoop session.

Celeste came home a few days prior and was mortified and flailed herself against the living room closet, dropping to the floor screaming in inconsolable hysterics. Fly did not know what happened for her to be so frenzied, and she was so concerned it broke her down, but she tried to be strong on the outside for her daughter. Fearing she would be found dead in her closet after school as many children were doing to escape violent bullying and vicious behaviors in school, Fly took off from teaching the next day because she thought Celeste was going to kill herself. Mostly because she was screaming that she was going to do so. Celeste was acting like she was having an out-of-body experience, hysterical and mortified by the fact that Dirt Bag Dude would do such a humiliating thing to her, catching her in the act of taking a puff, and worse, ratting her out. She could never show her face in school again or go to the bus stop. One of Fly's darkest nights, as she sat crying on her bed on top of the covers, was having the courage to call the 1-800 suicide hotline for help and guidance as to what to do. This was definitely not in the Parenting Manual or in any of the "World's Best Moms" books she had read, and Fly would do anything to help her child. From then on, Celeste was terrified to go to the bus stop where Dirt Bag Dude would be waiting in the predawn darkness for the bus or to show her face to schoolmates or in the schoolyard, and Fly pleaded to her teachers via email to be informed and ask for their understanding but no response. Fly surmised that she may have had her body and mind violated at some point in tenth grade, but Celeste was tight-lipped and kept whatever teen dating abuse happened to herself. The following year, Celeste would get strong and embrace the karma that was owed to this boy by turning him into the very same administrator as the guilty one who placed an inappropriate object in the teacher's desk. When she was little, she would chime these words to a tune while clapping her hands, "Inappropriate! That is inappropriate! Inappropriate! That is not okay. Hey!" She took action, and for once, there were consequences. Fly bet that teacher was mortified when she found that pleasure device in her desk drawer. He was suspended and never went back to school that senior year or was allowed to step on school property. He never found out who turned him in, but she felt avenged for his abuse and volatile actions and satisfied that his bad behavior had a cost however short-lived. Long after Dirt Bag Dude was long gone and out of the picture, this would have a lasting effect on her well-being for years to come.

Days came and went and Celeste kept encountering so many Totally Val Gals and more Dirt Bag Dudes that floated in and out of her life like two ends of a magnet attracting and repelling depending on the current drama and gossip. One day, Fly became furious when Celeste came home saying that her coach, not the kind of coach like a young person hired from outside the district for after-school sports, but an actual physical education teacher from her very own school no less, said that Celeste's sports jersey was "a waste of fabric." Sure, did she stand in the outfield looking for four-leaf clovers as she waited for the ball to potentially come her way? Sure, she wasn't a great sports player but a great team player who brought the boom box to get the girls motivated to run laps around the field to pumped-up music, but no one deserves a humiliating comment as to being a waste of a jersey. The team even went to a peanut oil–fried fast-food restaurant at the end of the season knowing full well she would not be able to attend. Mama Fly said, "It's okay, Celeste. Come on. Let's go home." And they left that last game alone, off the bus, shunned and disgraced into the night. Fly remembers seeing that Coach at her beloved kickboxing gym the following year. It was her safe space and one to get healthy at and take out the stressors in life. Fly pretended to not know her and vice versa and saw her as invisible as she stood there at the punching bag across the gym. Fly had written a complaint email to the PE Director but decided not to send it. As their bags faced each other, Fly looked right through her and power-punched her bag so hard with a striking jab-cross-hook-hook-uppercut to the gut as sweat poured down her forehead in anger and disgust that a female would say something like that to another female, teacher to student.

It was hard for Fly to stand by watching her Little Celeste be prey to bully girls like the Totally Vals, the Dirt Bag Dudes, the Struggle Is Real Snobs, and Character Copy Cats. Her body had been pushed and shoved, she was cursed at, her cell phone stolen, locked outside of school, peer pressured to do things, taunted in cyber space, isolated from classmates, and humiliated by adults. This is what children in schools face these days? Schools and schoolyards are supposed to be safe. Outside the schoolyard is another story, beyond the school property and liability. Fly understood the cruel world Celeste had encountered several times: a man in a car slowly drove up to Celeste and her friend she was walking with outside the pharmacy and flashed his private parts. They ran screaming. The friend's dad was a cop so they reported the clear description of the man's physical characteristics and his car in case it happened again to some other innocent girls. Celeste said she almost did not know what she was looking at because she never saw one before. They were scared to death that it would happen yet again when they were caught off guard. Fly would joke to her husband sarcastically that she wanted to get flashed, not realizing the lasting negative effect it had on her daughter being prey to man. First, it's staring, then cat calling, then flashing, following, stalking, then escalating to unspeakable atrocities upon women. The following year, Celeste was walking to the deli alone during her lunch period disregarding her parent's rules about going off school property alone. Fly always said, "Safety in numbers!" A man crept up in a van, opened the window, and asked if Celeste needed a ride. He continued to attempt to lure her into the vehicle driving alongside her ever so slowly. Terrified, she ran into the deli hysterically hyperventilating, screaming, and crying, but where luckily a school secretary was getting a sandwich and was able to get her safely back to school. This incident was also reported to the police through the school district this time, as Celeste memorized the out-of-state license plate, color, make, and model of the van. Fly was furious because her Follow Friends App was not working and she was firm with her child to never go alone again because if he had put her in that van, she may never have been seen again. To this day, Celeste Bag of Donuts has trained herself to learn makes and models of cars for future encounters outside of school grounds. Little did she know the male gaze would plague her for the following decade of her life.

Fly thinks, as she tries to suppress her own past experiences in schools as secret stories she hides from her daughter. She had hoped things would have changed, but with the addition of technology, things have only seemed to have leveled up. Unlike some teens who may sadly take their own lives from having to face head-on and overcome taunting and torment from schoolmates, Celeste's skin is thick and her pen filled with permanent ink. She draws and paints and writes and writes and writes. She protests in marches with a tampon raised high above her head like the Statue of Liberty. Her mouth is like a truck driver and her sharp tongue will cut you. While driving in the car, Little Celeste would always suggest the music. "Hey, Mom, play Fergie Track 4." Duped more than once, Fly would comply and hit the 4 button on the CD player and "Oh, Shoot! Oh Shoot!" would scream loudly as "London Bridge" would rap and she would quickly skip to the next track because they didn't say "shoot." Little Celeste would give a gotcha giggle, pleased that she outwitted her Mama Fly. She was always like that. Once when she was only two feet tall, Little Celeste exclaimed, "Hey look, Mom. Full moon!" as she ran down the long hallway naked, shrieking and laughing hysterically. Mama Fly was simultaneously mortified and amused at her wild moon child, just the same reaction as when she painted with strawberry yogurt up and down the same hallway. Rather than combat and correct her rough exterior, Fly ignores the bad language and cursing so that Celeste can protect herself from the ugly predators in this Great American society and in our Great American schoolyards.

While unwanted and unwarranted attacks on others seem to have been around since the existence of humanity, there are now laws and increasing awareness that protect our children in schools. But what really does come of this? How can children be further protected in schools? And what about protection for the adults in public schools? Adults in any workplace for that matter? Why are citizens being ignored and incidents brushed under the carpet? Administrators turning a blind eye to atrocities? Why is it totally legal to bully in schools and the workplace? Gag me with a spoon again!

Motivation

The Crumpled Paper

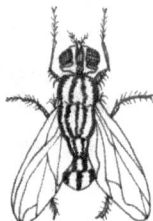

It's January.

The approach
The demand
The force of a hand.

A simple letter to solidify tenure and a job
for life. No traits too great or terrible.

"Proficient yet unremarkable."

—Special Agent Leroy Jethro Gibbs, *NCIS*

No outstanding achievements or performance.
American mediocrity at its best.

Cue the Music:
"Push" by Matchbox Twenty
"Just a Girl" by No Doubt
"Message in a Bottle" (Sending Out an SOS) by the Police

The Crumpled Paper

It all began with a crumpled piece of paper. The decisive moment in a reign of terror kicked off the day Principal Don Voyage came into Ms. Fly's office "Mansplaining" how it was going to be. He was angrily shaking in his hand a piece of paper, leaning his other hand on the edge of her desk as if to balance himself, nodding back and forth, assuming the negative position. She waited as he took his time grunting and visibly sharing his disagreement with her. This piece of paper was the memorandum Ms. Fly had written to him as to the reasons why this third-year teacher should not receive tenure: poor performance, not meeting deadlines, not performing teacher duties, confusing lessons, not following curriculum guidelines, an obscene amount of inaccurate paperwork, odd behaviors, poor communication skills, complaints from students and staff, reporting No Good News ever. The bad outweighed anything good for sure, and this letter stated the overarching facts. And it was like he had falsely advertised his credentials at his initial interview and even his resume seemed to not be in alignment with what was promised in his classroom performance over the two and a half nontenured years. Mr. Paul was indifferent about it, and in fact rather, pompous and overly self-assured, perhaps totally unaware of his deficiencies. After all, he was a popular coach with a boys' team and as Ms. Fly was told by the principal, "People *like* him," even as she forged her concerns over time. In Fly's mind, they only knew Mr. Paul as the coach, the club manager, or a member of the Young Yuppie-Mediocre Millennial Teachers Clique and he was proud he had achieved in life all that he needed at thirty: a job, a car, and a condo. Fly noticed he said "job," not career, passion, or calling and thought it odd yet only possessions he had conquered and acquired.

To the untrained eye, the standard onlooker, not knowing what "good art education" is supposed be, he probably looked like a pretty decent teacher—after all, he was a coach to an aggressive sports team, so he must be good at teaching art. Here, we are not even talking about outstanding art education. But these people did not evaluate his work as Ms. Fly had to or perform inspection reports or share the workspace and class-rooms and storage closets and rely on accurate paperwork and correspondence as she had to do. If he was a physical education teacher and set up for the kids to play baseball in the fall and football in the spring, or to one up that, put footballs on the baseball field and baseball bats on the tennis court and so on it might have been crystal clear to the naked untrained eye. But people don't know much about art; they just see pretty colorful pictures and "happy little trees," as Bob Ross would say as he painted the blank canvas. It would be like looking at the *Mona Lisa* and stating it was a rainbow abstract landscape, which makes no sense as it is in fact a semi-realistic, muted color portrait. His lessons made no sense, and it appeared that only Ms. Fly could blatantly see it; examples of rainbow art which he labeled as "contrast" or "repetition," not "color theory," or the unit that was so confusing it had opposite concepts like "close-up" and "landscape," which is actually usually far away not up close. She tried to fight back as Don had already been altering inspection reports in Paul's favor by scribbling changes all over them like poorly written English papers. The worst was when Mr. Paul labeled the color-coordinated bins incorrectly, like labeling the word "blue" on the orange supply bin and "red" on the green bin and all of them were mixed up with the intent to confuse. She even heard the student's confusion during an inspection; it was all so ludicrous. Fly thought maybe everything was Opposite Day. And as students should be the priority focus of any school, she had to speak up in this notice to the principal of her professional opinion.

So then at that moment, standing in her cute little artsy office, Principal Don Voyage vigorously crumpled up the paper in Ms. Fly's face, grimaced, and angrily tossed it into her trash basket and, with a grunt, stormed out the door, loudly closing it behind him. She was in disbelief that her continuous concerns were not taken seriously and, in fact, ignored and shunned. All he saw was the fake "nice guy" exterior. Not only that, she had been directed to write Mr. Paul's teacher tenure letter because Principal Don Voyage let her know he was writing her very own at the same time. She felt trapped and threatened, as if she would not be granted tenure if she did not do this task and she had already given up her tenure as a teacher to become a middle administrator in this new school district. Both of the tenure letters, Fly's and Paul's, would be reviewed simultaneously at the very next Board of Education meeting with One Line Louie.

Here is the "Crumpled Paper" Lesson Plan created by an anonymous source, but relived by performance and act-out groups all over the globe. Advocates for anti-bullying campaigns share the truth about bullying in schools all around the United States as well. The story exemplifies the emotional scars that a bully can create on another person and it goes something like this:

> A teacher once used the crumpled paper exercise to show her students the lasting impact that antisocial and cruel behavior and bullying can have. She told her kids to each take a nice flat and clean piece of copy paper and told them to crumple it up and stomp on it, but not to rip it. Some students thought it was silly, but they did it anyway. Then she asked them to carefully unfold the paper and smooth it out. Some of the children remarked that it couldn't be smoothed out and it was dirty and scarred. She then asked them to tell the piece of paper that they were sorry for messing it up like that. Some of the students laughed, feeling silly once again for talking to a piece of paper, but the point was made that even though they had apologized to the paper and tried to fix it, the scars would never go away no matter how hard they regretted what they'd done. Even if there is a heartfelt apology, the scars can stay with that person forever.

Apology smology. No one ever apologizes, Fly would come to recognize. That would be an indicator of wrongdoing and guilt.

Flashback a few years. When Ms. Fly was first becoming a middle administrator, a promotion from teaching and a step up the food chain ladder, she was put in charge of nonetheless soon-to-be Principal Don Voyage's niece, Ms. Totally Terrible Petunia. Talk about nepotism, but the person that Ms. Fly replaced retired and did not have the guts to simply "let her go" the year before. And everyone knew it but kept silent. Ms. Fly was left to begin this new career with a terrible legacy of dealing with Ms. Totally Terrible Petunia, and she wasn't even certified or fully schooled in Educational Administration yet. Petunia trash-talked about the other teachers awkwardly right in front of them as she ate lunch in the classroom with other members of the Young Yuppie-Mediocre Millennials Teacher Clique, dumped other teacher's supplies all over the storage closets, created lessons that looked like for elementary school–aged kids, not high school teenagers. She literally almost set the library on fire at the XXXL Art Integrity Inauguration Ceremony. But people did not see that or understand artistic development and growth, they just saw cute wicker baskets and her red thong blasting above her white jeans. She was kind of like that young woman in that terrible teacher movie. She rarely did basic teacher tasks normally or on time, like lesson plans, attending meetings, and other duties contractually required. Even though retirement was pending, the then principal saw the writing on the wall and after being pulled into a meeting in Mrs. Principal One's office, Petunia was seen running down the bland dark school hallway to the storage closet crying and remained in school even though she was allowed take the rest of the day off. She was let go. Fly and the department members had to awkwardly deal with her backlash behavior for the remainder of the school year, a whole three months. It was rumored that Mrs. Crinkly Old Curmudgeonly Art Hag who also recently retired had previously locked Petunia in that closet during one of her lessons, so maybe she thought she could do just the same toward others. Ms. Fly was happy she never had the pleasure to meet the mean retired teacher, but she could tell by the still life objects of wine bottles and other oddities she left behind that she must have been a piece of work.

So Ms. Fly was put in a position to decide upon a new hire after the then Assistant Principal Don Voyage's niece was denied tenure. With budgets dwindling, it was encouraged to find the "diamonds in the rough." It was slim pickings, and Ms. Fly was not even certified to be an administrator yet; she was a mere person in charge for about an earnings of $1.50 per hour for all administrative responsibilities. She would deeply regret listening to District Director Coupon Suzy when she said that it might be good for the senior teacher Mr. Johnart to "have a man around." Fly thought that to be an odd comment and politically incorrect. One interview candidate pulled out all the bells and whistles like a laptop with circulating visuals and did a stellar demo lesson, and all the supervisors fell for it. New hire Mr. Paul had problems throughout the first year, but not significant enough for Mrs. Principal One to not ask him back; he was after all an athletic coach, and she was a huge fan of sports as her sons played the very sport he was asked to coach. He gladly borrowed and used lesson plans from the other teachers without bothering to alter them or personalize to his liking and was coasting by as he rode the coattails of the other teachers. And all the while, Ms. Fly was doing much of the work for him as she could because she would not forward his incorrect records and paperwork to her bosses. He must have felt like teaching was pretty darn easy as he let the other department members lead the way by doing most of the work. Mrs. Principal One once stated to Ms. Fly at lunch after they passed Mr. Johnart in the hallway, "Yea, Mr. Johnart showed up drunk at one of the district art shows a few years back...Teacher of the Year, right?" she proclaimed sarcastically.

This newbie teacher had come highly recommended by a fellow Yuppie Millennial teacher, but later, Ms. Fly questioned maybe the other district was just trying to get rid of him. She should have known the signs like why he was only there for two years on his resume, but as a new middle administrator didn't know better. She did not even go to the demo lesson because no one even told her she was supposed to, so she took the advice of the other supervisors as to the candidate of choice given there was a need for someone who could teach the new computer class. She had tried and tried so many different strategies that she had learned from the educational leader-ship courses to help this teacher learn the craft of teaching and improve, but sometimes, "You can lead a horse to water, but you can't make them drink." Ms. Fly heard this phrase before in her previous workplace, and it really bothered her so much, she left to find a school where people respected their leaders and could figure out how to get to the water and actually drink it so as not to dry and shrivel up from dehydration. And as long as it wasn't Kool-Aid all was well. This water phrase was said by her former director as he stated this matter of fact about his own teachers he hired, trained, and mentored himself and just shrugged it off. He stopped fighting for what was right.

Then after Mrs. Principal One retired, AP Don Voyage got promoted and became the new principal. There were serious red flags with Mr. Paul, but Principal Don Voyage was quick to overlook and dismiss as Don strived to obtain the coveted status of tenure since every time a job title gets altered, educators have to wait three more years to gain tenure yet again, no matter one's age or how long one has been in education. That is also when an educator is at the end of their career usually and they will retire at the height of the salary scale. But despite the fact that Mr. Paul had a stack of memos written to him regarding student safety, curriculum alignment, and basic work performance, paperwork accuracy and attention to deadlines and requests, about department goals and incentives, and school and district policies and procedures and rules, these items got lost down the crack during the changing of the guards. And then, starting Mr. Paul's second year, he began having an outrageous amount of incidents from both within the department and outside as well. Fly was not sure if he even knew what an incident was, but he sure had a lot of them! People from the building would email or visit Ms. Fly in her office and complain about stupid or inconsiderate things Mr. Paul was doing in other parts of the building and she was mortified. She thought she could just wait it out and hope there may be an incident just bad enough that he could be removed or something would happen to him so he would go away. She didn't understand why Don crumpled that paper that day. Ms. Fly had made her voice heard and shared the ongoing problems to Don verbally and then the following year in a written complaint begging for assistance as this teacher was too much to handle. Without using the "L" word, she was trying to suggest that he was a potential liability to the district. He had been doing things like selecting inappropriate artists for teenagers and then lying about it, which just made things worse. He would say that he removed the inappropriate artist from his handout, yet it would be sitting there in the classroom in black and white unaltered. A true lie only Ms. Fly saw. To follow up on her plea memo, Principal Don Voyage had told her in a meeting in the principal's office that if Mr. Paul did not follow directions and meet deadlines and figure out how to "juggle a lot of balls," he would not get tenured. He told Ms. Fly that the priority for him must be to the department and he must follow his supervisor's commands. She had some hope that the right choice would be made soon, but what happened that summer?

That's when Ms. Fly went back to his resume two or three times because items presented on paper during the interview process were clearly not evident in his teachings, work performance, and knowledge base. Perhaps Principal Don Voyage saw Fly's department as petty "arts and crafts" and not important whatsoever, and he needed to focus on state scores of the core departments like Math and Science, English and Social Studies. Fly's dad even used to call it tongue in cheek "artsy fartsy," so maybe that was just his perspective. He would ask Fly when she was a teen, "So what shade of black are you going to wear today?" Maybe it was the fact that Don's niece, Ms. Totally Terrible Petunia, was let go, and he blamed Ms. Fly as a Villainous Tenure Slayer rather than blaming the retired supervisor who should have completed the daunting task earlier. Ms. Fly found left behind a clear memo in standard 12 point Times New Roman font to Dear Ms. Petunia, dated the previous June, stating, "In order to receive tenure, the following issues must be addressed," and it goes on to outline fourteen bulleted items she must adhere to when Ms. Fly took over in September. Fourteen items. Ms. Fly saw the incompetence firsthand at the XXXL Inauguration Ceremony that one night when Ms. Petunia lit the five creativity candles dangerously close to the library curtains. Fly thought for sure the library would go up in flames in front of her own eyes. It would have made it easier to let her go had there been a fire with parents and children running and screaming for their lives from the school. But all people saw was that she had the teens make baskets and puppet crafts, so that looked good and fun on the surface. Fly didn't even know Ms. Totally Terrible Petunia when she went to that new school and had nothing to do with the performance of his niece. But in the end, Fly heard that because of her being fired, or rather "let go," there had been a nasty falling out between the families and Don brewed with steam and resentment. Maybe it was that he had his eye on retirement after working his way up the food chain ladder for decades from teacher to supervisor to assistant principal and then, with three years as principal, he can retire at the top notch. Nepotism and self-serving at its finest at the taxpayers' expense.

The Boy's Club

Four weeks after Principal Don Voyage crumpled that piece of paper, there was a district art show one evening with students and families and music and light snacks and refreshments, just days before the Board of Education meeting, which would solidify the fate of both Ms. Fly's and Mr. Paul's tenure status. She remembered Ms. Petunia's student work from the previous year which had a wine bottle and fruit, in particular a banana with nuts and berries, clearly in the shape of male anatomy and just quietly exhaled disappointment and shook her head about the whole issue. Just then, Superintendent One Line Louie stormed up to Ms. Fly amidst all the happy art students and proud moms and dads and siblings as he stealthily weaved his large body in and out of the crowd and asked abruptly and sternly under his breath so as others could not hear, "We're not going to have a problem with Paul...are we?" But as his large hunched shadowy figure in the boxy dark suit loomed over Little Fly, consuming her personal space in the tight quarters, and with his demonical tone and demeanor, it was more of an intimidating statement than a question. First off, superintendents do not usually associate with people way lower down on the food chain ladder if there are other staff who can intervene so she was taken aback. But then just a few moments later, Fly glanced over her shoulder only to witness Mr. Paul chuckling and chumming it up with soon-to-be Super DaNile down the line one day. Soon-to-be Super DaNile was patting Paul on his shoulder, smiling, and chuckling away with him as if to say, "Good boy." Frozen and unable to respond, Fly stared back as one joyous moment turned into to one of dark intimidation, her jaw slightly opened with disbelief. Supers don't mingle freely with teachers, they just don't.

In those five seconds, it was crystal clear that the Boy's Club was birthed and was working against her and she was not allowed in. Fly remembers a book she read as a child and she found it in her garage one summer while cleaning out, *The Against Taffy Sinclair Club*; Fly knew too well what was happening, the same as when the Totally Val Gal trick or treaters and their Helicopter Mommy Vals in their banana clips all quickly blamed Celeste Bag of Donuts for an assumed intentional tripping of Totally Shabby Val even though she did not. She stood accused, and it became a "fact" to the group; a mob mentality shines once again. The Taffy Clubbers' grand plan constantly backfired and the bully mentality was infectious. The crumpling and aggressive toss of the rejected piece of paper that had described in detail why this person was simply not doing his job as expected was the final say. Principal Don Voyage had mansplained the way it was going to be and that should have been a premonition that her fight for what is right and decent was over. Everything she had learned in her Education and Leadership Diplomas thrown out the window. Five years of graduate schools and additional courses and pre-dissertation writing all disregarded and all decency ignored. This was despite the fact that she had a plethora of evidence and examples reflecting why this person should not be granted tenure, and it was like when there is the flash of a napalm bomb going off on the television set and you feel only impending doom for the entire perimeter in all directions coming your way. The bomb hits, explodes, and there is no stopping its fury in its outward trajectory consuming and demolishing everything in its path of destruction. It was the gun flare that goes off at the beginning of a marathon race to initiate the running. Fly did not sign up for a marathon, and she would only be caught running if she were being chased by a wild animal.

Not only was his performance questionable, but Mr. Paul had also made some disturbing comments to Ms. Fly over the three years that were difficult to share with her administrators because while seemingly trivial apart were starting to become compressed and compact to Fly's eye. She was able to start synthesizing all the random tidbits into a fully painted picture dark in hues. Ms. Fly had sometimes heard the "Every Excuse in the Book" routine from students, but not too often like when "The dog ate my homework" or "My younger sibling dropped and broke the widget" or "My soda spilled all over my art and ripped it" and so on, but Mr. Paul had all those kids beat. Fly asked him once why he did not bundle the final exams like the others had done and every other teacher in the building was requested to do, and he came back with a piercing stare and ridiculous statement, "I couldn't find string." Fly thought, there is string right there in the main office for everyone, and hello, you literally work in an art room abundant with guess what? String! Another time when he was being inspected by Don and Fly, he was asked why he did not summarize the lesson and why the bell rang in the middle of his sentence as the students just up and walked out as if not to care about his words he spoke. Mr. Paul responded that it was because his watch battery had died. Fly thought he must not be able to tell analog time since there was an enormous clock right there above the doorway in the classroom. Once in a meeting, when Ms. Fly kindly asked Mr. Paul to try to do a little better, he responded, bobbing his head affirmatively with a crocodile smile, "Haha, okay, I'll be sure to cross my i's and dot my t's!" and then comically and maniacally laughed as if that were an accident, yet it was only an ominous foreshadowing of what was to come. It sent chills through Fly's body in disbelief and fear because of what he had already done to be just enough proficient yet unremarkable and worse, destructive.

Three years were met with the challenge of facing incompetent work over and over again; many times, multiple confusions and errors on an ongoing daily basis. Every single day, there was a barrage of incidents and misinformation, hyperlogging into websites and constantly getting locked out, confusing lessons, incorrect curriculum content, intentionally ignoring deadlines, intentionally interrupting Ms. Fly's classes while she was teaching, worse, sliding in as if on an invisible skateboard and then sliding right back out, stealing other teacher's handouts or using fellow teacher's student artwork without permission, not participating in department incentives, rubrics that literally didn't mathematically add up, not addressing inspection report recommendations repeatedly, in fact doing the opposite of what was suggested, mis-ordering of supplies, miscalculating budgets, students off the property during class time, students rough-housing as if out on the turf, boys slapping each other on the behinds in class for which Ms. Fly had never seen before, but she was guessing this was a man-greeting. It just kept going on and on forever irrationally like pi—3.14159...

And then there were hideous texts out of nowhere like, "I am taking a sick day as I was dry heaving all night." Disgusted by the details, Fly brushed it off with a response, "Who's this?" as faculty did not commonly correspond via personal devices at the time. Fly already had printed countless emails he had sent riddled with erroneous dates for upcoming events, complaints from coworkers and outside guest speakers about incidents, chronic mix-ups with local art events for students, not following the food chain ladder for student-related disciplinary issues and on and on. It became incredulous to the point Fly could not tell anyone because it all seemed unbelievable and each on their own somewhat appearing trivial. Ms. Fly shared the following email with a colleague, Supervisor Mrs. Parabola, for advice because of how absurd it was, not to mention Mr. Paul emailed it from the next room over when he could have just walked over to Fly's office to clarify the information a mere five weeks into the school year:

> Subject: Federal Forms
> Hi, Fly, (seemingly friendly greeting as always)
> I started to fill out my forms today and I have a question. I asked Johnart and he said

we should fill out 5 total codes for each class that represents the semester.

The form says that if you teach more than 9, lump them together? So since I teach a total of 11 sections through the year, do I lump them together for all the Fine Art Classes, all the Observation Art Classes, and the Mixed Mass Media Arts.

So would I fill out only 4 codes with attendance totals for both semesters? Or 5 codes that represent semester 1?

(And always a cordial closing statement.)

Thanks and have a great weekend!

Paul

Mrs. Parabola was a mathematical expert and always stated things right to the point with precision, matter-of-factness, and even tone. Pi was always 3.14 and on and on steady as a rock. She was the voice of reason and she would never let a math teacher insist that Pi was 4.13 and ended there. Even Mrs. Parabola was so confused at the confusion that she could not even come up with an explanation to help comprehend what was written or what even the question was. Things just didn't add up. In addition, Ms. Fly would run by Mr. Paul's rubrics and miscalculations of grades to Mrs. Parabola for a second opinion just to be sure she was seeing what she was seeing correctly and for sure, that math was always incorrect. Worse were the documents that had negative impacts on the students such as this sent from a local college professor to Ms. Fly regarding one of Mr. Paul's students:

Subject: Selected Student

Thank you for your participation in the Annual High School Exhibition at the University. I regret to say that we can only accept work from grades 9 to 12. Your student Melanie Show submitted a mixed-media work entitled, "Values," but being that she is in seventh grade, she will need to wait two more years before submitting work to this exhibition. "Values" will be held in the closet of the Gallery until the reception night when it can be picked up.

Similarly, but with a darker twist that stretched out for several upcoming school years, Ms. Fly took all of the matted department artworks to hang at several district art exhibitions. Any trained exhibitor or gallery-savvy person knows that one hangs a work of art in either the orientation that is displayed by an arrow on the back, the way it is placed into a frame with hardware or the manner in which the student or artist's name and information is written. Like "Melanie Show, Grade 7, Mixed Media Art, Mr. Paul, UP arrow." So there Mr. Paul was at a district art show once again with soon-to-be Super DaNile not far off in the distance, posing with his smug grin in front of the artwork with one of his male students for all to see and admire. Ms. Fly found out the following year, it was hung upside down. How did she find out? Somehow, Mr. Paul must have "bad-mouthed" the situation to a group of his Sports Club Lost Boys who were at the same time in Fly's Widgetry Class as they mocked and ridiculed her right in front of her face that, "You hung Jo Jo's artwork upside down," as they ganged up on her like lions circling their prey. The accusation was hideous and to rile up impressionable young men was clear and disgusting to Fly. She thought it to be abuse of power of a teacher over their students. Why not Paul simply fix the problem on the spot and flip the frame around rather than begin manipulating the Lost Boys? Principal Don Voyage never did believe her that a group of teen boys repeatedly treated her with such ridiculous disrespect and group torture. Paul would eventually also start walking around with his personal expensive widget, taking the happy photos of students with their teachers and families, yet Ms. Fly would come to realize the pattern that he started to intentionally leave Ms. Fly out as she was busy at these events with administrative duties such as organizing the refreshments, music, certificates, and balloons or greeting families as they entered the art exhibition. He made sure he photographed the Board of Education members though, and even though One Line Louie was long gone and forgotten, he made sure to schmooze with all the head honchos including soon-to-be Super DaNile.

And then there were the strange and odd behaviors such as his weird body movements, stares and glares or looking like a deer in headlights when asked simple questions, self-assigning or "mentoring" male students closely who were not enrolled in his classes. Getting fed up, Ms. Fly tried yet another strategy to get Mr. Paul to help himself reflect and grow as a teacher, which is the most important thing a young teacher should be guided to do, especially a Young Yuppie Millennial. She had tried this method before without success but made one last attempt without having to just spell it out for him to understand. So rather than tell him there was something wrong with his slide presentation and what exactly it was, she asked to briefly meet with him and asked him to figure out what was incorrect. She simply asked him a question, "What is wrong with this presentation?" as they both reviewed twelve slides on a piece of paper. And after searching the images he put into the slide presentation, looking a bit confused, he responded by pointing to a photograph with several children of different races posing and pointed to the one boy and replied, "Because he is black?"

What the heck! Fly thought, stunned at the response. Mortified that was not even close to the idea Ms. Fly was referring to and being totally shocked at the clear bias, she swiftly had to revert to "telling him" and spelled it out to him that his response was an incorrect answer. How he interpreted the curriculum in the slide presentation was not in alignment and that the lesson was about black and white portraiture, but the examples were using the color wheel defeating the purpose of the visuals. In addition, he illustrated the composition technique slide with a mule running through a field of green grass, not a portrait of a person, not black and white. Confusing.

This was clearly a person who did not understand what the field of education entails which is not like a factory line worker doing repetitive tasks, but a continuous learning experience needing constant reflection and improvement and adapting to changes and intense demands. There is nothing wrong with factory line work for some people; in fact, Fly liked the show *Laverne and Shirley* growing up. Some people just like to work in a beer factory and not bring work home with them and, at the end of the day, watch their glove fly away on the conveyer belt. "Schlemiel! Schlimazel!" One spills the hot soup. One gets hot soup poured on them. But there was something more deviant going on like in the *I Love Lucy* episode where Lucy is working in a candy factory and she cannot keep up with the increasing rate of speed of the conveyer belt so rather than admit her faults, she consumes and hides the speeding chocolates in her mouth, hat, and pockets. But teaching simply is not designed to be employment like flipping burgers at the fast-food restaurant, which Fly's husband did once in college and did not even last a week. No wonder, teachers need the summer off; to regroup from the intensities of each school year and to learn and reflect on changes they can make to better themselves for their students. That is always an interview question: "If you were told you had to teach XL class in September, what would you do over the summer to prepare yourself for it?" If the candidate responded that they would do nothing, they would not be hired.

But it was as if Ms. Fly was not only doing her job, plus teaching, plus supervising, it was like doing his job as well because of his incompetencies. Everything he emailed or submitted to her had to be fixed and that took additional time. The first year, Ms. Fly was even asked to complete his teacher modeling hours because the trained, assigned, and paid once Teacher of the Year Mr. Johnart couldn't handle him and gave up. Mr. Paul was always "too busy" to complete the district requirement. It was all too much. Mr. Paul was granted tenure for the following September under the agreement by Principal Don Voyage that Ms. Fly would have to continue checking his detailed lesson plans, slide presentations, rubrics, exams, and artwork examples as if nontenured. More work! This would prove to be a slap on the wrist. And included with Mr. Paul's "Tenure Package," Principal Don Voyage thought it would be great to even give him a hefty stipend and thousands of dollars in technology equipment to oversee a new club whom he needed a club manager for, and at the same time, he would give Ms. Fly the equipment and computers that the department so desperately needed and never ended up sharing in the long run. Not only did this lead to double-dipping with his sports coaching and a new club meeting at the same times after school, it was as if to reward his poor performance like this would make him improve.

One of Principal Don Voyage's favorite mottos was the KISS Principle, "Keep It Simple Silly." But rather than keep it simple, he made a complex situation extremely more complex instead. This school year, Ms. Fly learned that a simple crumpled piece of paper could be the start of a path of devastation. Artists are very particular about their papers, what kind, for what media, what color, how thick, what texture, and surely, they never crinkle it! Unaware, this will foreshadow an overflowing bucket of crumpled papers to come Fly's way for many years, year after year.

America the Beautiful—American Mayhem

America is disgustingly beautiful and beautifully disgusting, pitifully heinous and sometimes sprawling and breathtaking. Nauseatingly destructive yet somehow bountiful and plenty. The land of "the struggle is real" and other first world problems. Temper tantrums erupt at the coffee shop when the minimum-waged worker makes your large skinny, no fat, hot, no whip, vanilla lite latte incorrectly or when they do something wrong with your cuticles at the nail salon as if looking down on the workers as they tend to your tired feet. If Fly hears one more disgruntled teacher who happens to be the teacher union navigator say while scurrying down the crowded hallway between periods, "Livin' the life!" in a sarcastic tone with rolling eyeballs, she might just lose it. Fly loves teaching and interacting with her students. We can't get our iced pumpkin spiced triple shot espresso with extra-fat whip coffees fast enough and do we use plastic bags, paper, or reusable? Plastic, paper, or metal straws? We feel guilty or not if we use the plastic cup or plastic grocery bag rather than bring a reusable item to help save the planet, but then some of us are germophobes. Can one person really make a difference compared to the damage created by major corporations? Some of us Americans feel unknowingly entitled. They do not need to use the pre-existing Bluetooth devices in their new BMZ's and rather would drive distracted like maniacs, indifferent to others and causing traffic chaos, and they are the same people who walk straight into you at the grocery store because they are so connected chit-chatting on their phones and they are more important than everyone else around them as if we want to hear their loud personal conversations from their earpieces or, worse, on speaker mode as they hold their device in front of their big mouths. American idiots. Oblivious to others is our current state of being. Secretive data slaves to their technology devices, addicted and insensitive; it owns us if you allow it, and it is smarter than us.

We are the land of the free and barely free from the land as it burns forests and grounds ablaze, spreads drought leaving us thirsty for water, brews devastating and demolishing hurricanes, spins endless tornadoes across the south and west, and rages river floods up and down the gateway from Canada to Mexico. The land is full of hope and full of hate. The beautiful landscape and man-made infrastructure burns, cracks, and crumbles around us. Potholes suck your car in and spit you out in pieces. Hate and anger, this quest for power shape-shifts into many forms. In this mighty vast land there is an abundance of violence just out there for all to see in public spaces: road rage, robberies, and robo calls; stalking and unspeakable abductions and abominations to women and children; issues at homes we can barely afford, on the crumbling infrastructure we are given to transport ourselves on to travel or get to work, random violence at merchandise establishments, malls, and warehouses, grocery stores, at entertainment arenas such as stadiums and clubs, vacation locations, our educational institutions, and in the place of our livelihoods; the great American workplace of desired occupations and side hustles. People get hurt simply jogging, biking, or crossing the street. People get hurt simply going to school or work. People get hurt simply because others around them are oblivious, indifferent, distracted, selfish, entitled. All the while people are literally dying to come to America to have the rights and freedom and we Americans take it for granted.

And there are serious implicit biases against women and girls in particular, from birth and birthing rights to death because of suicidal thoughts, from being hardworking moms or being stay-at-home moms. Fly once heard her doctor's colleague say that rather than the doctor almost killed her and Celeste during birth instead claim, "He *saved* your lives." A total opposite reaction to an almost fatal mishap. She saw her daughter be blamed for that girl tripping, and then an instant gang erupted, she was there when her daughter wanted to harm herself—she would not leave her sight for a moment, and Fly, in a stressed out meltdown, wanting to drive her car off the bridge rather than go into work and face her harasser. Bullies, privilege, and entitlement are ruling and are able to manipulate the people in charge in order to create an altered reality.

Fly stood at her twentieth high school class reunion, which she vowed to never attend again, boldly in between two six-foot tall white men still begrudging her as to why she was selected to be Drum Major that senior year. They argued at the reunion, as if they kept it all inside for twenty years, as to why they were not picked. One had been preparing to go to an Ivy League college and the other wanting the prestigious title. Why did they feel entitled? Why stew over it two decades later? Fly was dumbfounded at the pent-up aggression. Were they practicing inclusion tactics because girls were not normally Drum Majors back then or was Fly so fly, she was actually more qualified to earn and maintain this elite leadership position having been a drummer and Flag Line Captain prior? She refused to be called Drum Majorette; just call her Major. They stood on either side of her like large looming bookends arguing and still feeling defeated by a girl.

A most glorious cold damp night in late 1980s still lies vivid in Fly's memory when she wants to think of one of her most achieving moments in her life. She conducted the large over 150 band members who looked to her for cadence and instruction as to when and how fast or slow to play their next notes and where to go on the football field as she swung her arms stretched just as high as they would reach into the dark spot-lit sky filled with the cold breath of the students. It was if she were stretching herself to be ten feet tall. She and her underdog partner, who unbeknownst to future Fly would go on to do this as a career, practiced and nailed their eight-count personalized marching salute to the judges and audience encompassing the local university's college stadium. Their lasting frozen end pose with chins up, snapping right hands firmly to their corner eyebrow in salute pleased the crowd as they went wild with excitement from their command. Later, when it was their band's time to perform, in odd unison, after Fly shouted from the depths of her gut, "A-ten hut! (Pause and wait for undivided attention here. All eyes on connected.) Forwarrrrrd…march!" as if to lunge into face to face combat being led by Warrior Fly, the band members in their awkwardly tailored polyester uniforms and plumed hats rapidly and stiffly marched left-right-left-right to their places marked on the field by yard lines creating the opening shape. She often thought that she did not know anything about football except for the yard lines and where center was located along with the perimeter markings.

She hustled to the front of the enormous football field and with a swift about-face and stern look into the eyes of her peers, with her arms swinging high and with the defining nod to initiate the performance, there was a brief moment of dead silence that could raise the hair on one's arms and neck. Then as Warrior Fly swiftly became ready after commanding horns up, she clapped her hands four times and shouted, "Mark, time, mark, and one…two… three…and" and just exactly at that moment, the music blared in unison from all the different instruments of these teenagers across all the yard lines. They had "A Slice of Americana" curated to their repertoire of three vastly different songs that would surely wow the judges in black, dodging in and out of the swiftly marching students changing formation at every count of the beat. They whispered into their tape recorders as this was the last and most reputable and defining competitions of the season. She and her fellow Drum

Major took turns conducting the group. They had spent count-less summer sessions and training to do so. It was Warrior Fly's turn once again to complete the sequence and nail the finale. She thought about Stevie Nicks in the music video "Tusk" where she identified with whimsically and with command taking over the field and onlookers yet marching to her own beat her way. Knees high and self-assured. Fly's mom even had her Drum Major outfit hand tailored by the local seamstress. Warrior Fly absolutely refused to wear the male couture and demanded she wear a uniquely designed more fitting and flattering com-manding outfit made from chiffon and satin flowing and undu-lating in the cold wind that night. She even wore a black velvet choker necklace with a cameo which was unheard of to do but fashionable in her mind. Her white gloves flailed purposefully through the air high up on the podium as the cadence shifted from slow to swift and the drumline rocked the audience. Her body danced with every beat resonating with the crowd. The finale ended with a gigantic American flag spread out over the field by the Color Guard, her loyal following. Fly owned that field with respect and dignity.

The moment of truth came later as the Regional Awards were distributed. Deep down, she knew the Green Machine always won every year as they were bigger and more power-ful. The time came, and Warrior Fly did not know that her dad had to leave because he was not feeling well and had diffi-culty breathing. It was her division. The judges counted down third place, second place. At that point, they knew they either bombed it or the only other possibility. Could it be? Best Drum Major Award to the Marching Band conducted by Warrior Fly! Taking a deep breath in and maintaining a chin up straight unchanged stone face, she and her partner conducted once again as a closure their unique eight-count salute to the judges. At that final salute, the crowd exploded, and even though fro-zen stiff from the late November coldness, Warrior Fly was unex-pectedly rushed by the entire band coming from all directions and hoisted in the air with a levitation of pure teenage joy and elation. She was able to then burst into a euphoric smile and gratitude for all the hard work. There was only success with each individual member working together as a whole. Victory was hers and theirs combined for there is no I in Team. The crowd cheered at the underdogs brought finally to triumph in their last performance as she heard in the tapes the following day, "She's got it! She's got them!" indicating total in synch unison. She owned the moment and had thousands of people hanging on to her grip. This epic day ended with a huge trophy and an extremely loud back of the yellow bus ride home to Beastie Boys' "Brass Monkey."

Put down that cell phone, America, and take a look around you. Remember the times of passing paper notes in class and compiling a mixed tape for a friend? Remember writing letters and thank-you notes and even saying please and thank you? There is something in disarray here in America; few have manners anymore, good character qualities, dare it be mentioned a shred of kindness.

Word Wall

"intimidate" *verb* in•tim•i•date
1. to make timid or fearful: frighten
2. to compel or deter by or as if by threats, or especially in order to make them do what one wants.
synonyms: coerce, frighten, menace, terrify, scare, alarm, terrorize, overawe, awe, cow, subdue, discourage, daunt, unnerve

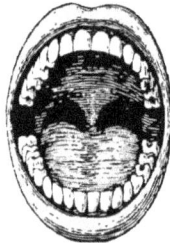

Notable Quotables

Do you have the patience to wait until your mud settles and the water is clear?

—Lao Tsu, Teo Te Ching

To look is one thing.
To see what you look at is another.
To understand what you see is a third.
To learn from what you understand is still something else.
To act on what you learn is all that matters.

—Taoist saying

Lesson Learned

This school year, Fly learned to take the KISS Principle with a grain of salt because things are not as simple as they seem.

Gutless

Act Out!

Activity: Tear out the following blank page and complete the Crumpled Paper activity. You can do this alone or with a friend. Discuss how it made you feel.

Chapter 1

The Lesson Plan

It's September.

Work
Weak
Hate

All are four letter words. Livelihood, career,
passion, dedication, and leadership are not.
F-O-U-R Letter words are a love/hate relationship.

Cue the Music:
"I Knew You Were Trouble" by Taylor Swift
"Lost Boy" by Ruth B.
"Shark in the Water" by VV Brown

Spring Break

Phase 1 of Paul's revenge plan must have gone like this: I will give my supervisor something so undeniably insensitive and hurtful that in her fragile state, she will not even know what hit her. The boys are all on my side in alliance. I will maliciously make angry snarls her way in secret while I smile with a Joker-like maniacal grin ear to ear to others as I stroll up and down the hallways among the other Young Yuppie-Mediocre Millennial Teachers whom I have bad-mouthed about her to in the teacher's lounge. But at the same time to create confusion, I will also walk into school every morning from the teacher parking lot looking like a sad puppy dog with head slumped downward, walking slowly, dragging my feet as if I am the victim. I will be the only one watching her crumble before my eyes. I will continue to submit lesson plans to my boss, even though the contract states otherwise. I will listen to my fellow teachers and realize I can become untouchable, invincible. I will wait and wait until opportunity strikes, and I will pounce with quiet fury.

It was September and Ms. Fly was compelled to start a logbook of noting the ongoing issues with Mr. Paul. A simple date and phrase recording an issue or note about an incident. She already had a huge pile of memos and emails that were not normal of a regular employee or what would be expected performance and behavior especially for the teaching profession, at least that was what Fly had learned about from numerous notable authors, educators, and leaders in her years of taking classes, workshops, and professional development seminars. There are clear publications and lists of "What Great Teachers Do" that make them great as to encapsulate characteristics of decency, high but reachable expectations, and showing kindness toward and caring for others.

So noticing this was not the case, she just jotted down a blurb or direct statement or quote such as when he told her he would be sure to "cross his i's and dot his t's." Perhaps there would be more printouts of an email or copy of a complaint. Ms. Fly put them in chronological order in a three-ring binder.

After months of quasi-substandard unremarkable performance by Mr. Paul, it was finally spring break and Fly could breathe in peace, escaping away from the stupidity and increasing incidents of this now tenured coworker. Newly tenured, perhaps Mr. Paul tried hard to do the best he could even though he was a not-so-great teacher, but then he began to be even more and more careless knowing he could never, like 99 percent, get fired no matter what. Fly thinks an elder teacher, perhaps Mr. Johnart, may have whispered in his ear at a faculty meeting one afternoon as they sat in the back row, "You know, you can get away with anything as a teacher, you're tenured now." Being not the sharpest tool in the shed, he must have pondered this with his confused look, his cocked head like a dog wondering what their pet parent was saying, eyes looking up and to the left questioning, searching for an answer in the air, not knowing what this person is telling him, and absorbing this information like a sponge over months, unlike information and instructions disseminated at department meetings. Waiting and waiting to fully absorb ever so slowly over time like how long it takes for something to grow and morph. Several pages have now been filled of documenting incidents and complaints in Fly's lilac legal pad. She disliked the normal putrid yellow notepad everyone else used and got free from the main office. It was about to be her fortieth birthday over spring break so at least she wasn't at school dealing with the privileged Peter Pan Zombie. Putting the notepad away, Fly was finally able to escape for a long week with her mom and dad, as her father was growing increasingly ill due to COPD and related complications.

When Fly's dad became ill and done with work a few years prior, her parents decided to up and move across the country to the cute little town in which they originally met in the 1960s. Though leaving their grown children and growing grandchildren behind, how can one not think that is the most adorable transition, back to love at first sight where the memories can flourish in one way as they diminish in yet another. They met with hot-rod cars and curlers in their hair without a care in the world about initial appearances. Throughout the week, Fly, Fly's mom, and daughter Celeste, the three generations, had a blast. They went shopping where Fly's mom always spoiled them with unnecessary clothes, purses, trinkets, and room décor; well, it was after all Fly's Fabulous Big Birthday Week! She bought her diamond earrings for her special day that her dad picked out which he had a hard time getting around so they were very special; this was a milestone number. They found a salt rock that holds a tea light and all three of the generations immediately were like, "We have to get that for Pops!" It was made out of the specialty material of his once family-run business. They went to the movies and ate tons of candy and buttery popcorn and Fly's mom was able to snore away and take a nap due to the child-geared animated film that lulled her to sleep. They ate out almost every meal, splurging on strawberry margaritas, fried foods, and filet mignons that Fly could never afford a day on the town like this from her own wallet as a teacher. Fly always thought teachers should make so much more money than they were given since they put their whole heart and soul into their livelihood: an extension of their very being and self reflected in the classroom in her opinion. She often spent more time with her students than her own Little Celeste so was grateful to solely focus on her and her family this week. Fly's dad only made it once to one of the fancy dinners as he then chose to rest the remaining time. His photo taken at that special restaurant concealed a secret no one would realize for days. Fly was shocked to see he needed a wheelchair ramp to maneuver into the restaurant. The three generations visited art galleries and science museums getting sucked into the gift shops upon exiting, buying up every cute ridiculous souvenir to be found in order to remember this very special week.

After a few days of the birthday splurge, Fly's mom took Little Celeste to the grocery store and Fly was left to care for her dad. They had purchased a large cushy recliner-style chair for next to the queen-sized bed, ornamented with their original wedding bedpost and furnishings, so that he can sit up at the breathing machine and watch television. The oxygen machine was as large as R2-D2 and it was quite loud. Favorite show? *Cops*, "Bad boys, bad boys, whatcha gonna do?" and maybe in close second place, *NCIS*, the original with Gibbs. Fly's dad loved the forensics girl character, probably because it reminded him a little part of Fly, quirky and smart, sometimes funny and sarcastic but always sincere and honest. Definitely with a side of perfectionism and a dash of innocence. This perfectionism as well as the nature of an artist made her prone to being hyper aware of her surroundings, analytical in life, and supersensitive to her world. Alone with him, she sat on the edge of the bed, telling him about all the fun things they did that week, and then he wanted to move to the chair. Fly was hesitant because he was now much larger than her and was afraid he would fall. For the first time in her life, she can never recall telling her very own dad a firm but caring "no!" in a teacher-like fashion using her teacher voice. She was scared. After bringing out her super-human strength, she mustered the energy to where at least he moved safely the three feet to the recliner without falling and getting hurt moving only an inch at a time scooching across the carpet. They watched TV, laughing and joking, and he then stated he did not feel so good and something was wrong. He looked sad and confused.

Fly's dad had a hard upbringing; in fact, his parents dis-liked him immensely and only focused on his younger yuppie sister and for whatever reason they may never fully compre-hend. The sister was born with a silver spoon in her mouth, and it was like Fly's dad was born with a sharp fork in his mouth. The sister acquired all the wealth while sitting on her behind while Fly's dad did all of the backbreaking work in the office twelve hours a day. Throughout the week, he played the new hit song "Jar of Hearts" over and over a million times like when a teen-ager finds a new favorite song and hits repeat. What was going on in his mind that week, no one truly knew or understood, but that song had a message he needed to hear: "Who do you think you are? Runnin' 'round leaving scars. Collecting your jar of hearts." Fly thought it resonated with his upbringing, perhaps his evil mother.

Fly's grandmother always claimed she was twenty-nine years old, which was confusing because she was wrinkly and always smelled like mothballs. And when Fly was little, she was certain her parents were around that age, so it didn't make sense to her. Her grams was so mean, she didn't even need mothballs to keep the moths away; she could just look in their direction and they would fly away with warp speed. She was so mean, she never took a sick day because she was too mean to get sick, or at least that is what Fly's mom always told her. She was so mean the company workers would run the other direction when they saw her BMZ car pull into the office parking lot. She was so mean that if you were literally down on the ground and needed help, she would step right over you in a scurry and keep going. She would probably intentionally spill her hot, light, and sweet coffee on you as well just to make it extra painful. She was so mean to Fly's dad and Fly's brother at the family business all of those years that Fly could not tolerate it anymore. The only good memory of her was that she taught Fly to do a mean polka.

The last time Fly ever saw her was at a distant elder relative's funeral. She was rich with money but so cheap, she asked to have the shared hors d'oeuvres wrapped to take home with her in a doggie bag…from a funeral luncheon! Then, Grams viciously grabbed Little Fly by the arm and began shaking her appendage rapidly upon exiting the luncheon, physically gripping her very being from moving forward out the door. Fly was taken aback at the pure brute strength of this seemingly frail, tiny, wrinkly ninety-year-old woman that it left marks on her arm. Her grams commanded sternly with fierce anger in a rehearsed drawn-out statement in the form of a question, "You write to me, you hear?" similar to the tone of One Line Louie's threat. Calmly, seeing that Grams was caught in her own trap, Fly asked, "Okay, do you have an email address?" to which her grandmother replied, "No." Fly broke free from the grip of hatred and walked away, stating, "Oh well then." Fly never looked back from that parking lot as she and her mom sped away to safety. She never did see her ever again, and her dad's sister claimed she did not have Fly's address or phone number or anyone's for that matter to let them know when she passed away. So Fly never even was informed when she passed, but she is sure she could feel a cold windy smell of mothballs in the air and a little less anger and hatred in the world that day.

When Fly was twenty-nine, she felt like quitting teaching. She didn't even want to be twenty-nine forever like her rich mean grandmother who constantly gave her such thoughtful gifts, such as Tyffani's *Book of Etiquette for Girls*. Yuck! She read through that book and did not feel like she needed to know how to properly set a fine dinner table with multiple forks and spoons for different entrees and purposes. One time, she chugged a beer from a bottle in front of her grumps and he commanded that it was not lady-like. Stunned, Fly just looked him dead in the eyes and took another swig. These were people who thought she should be a lawyer. Art was not a profession. They may have well wanted her to be a phlebotomist because there was nothing further from any profession she would be interested in such as these. But she guessed it was all about the making of the money and driving fancy cars and going on lavish vacations. At twenty-nine, Fly contemplated why the world was spinning so fast spiraling out of control. It was expected that everyone had to acquire and use cell phones, email, voice mail, call waiting, and dial-up internet. Fly looked at her new husband as he tried to explain the Interweb to her and asked perplexed and disappointed, "You mean we don't have to go to the library anymore? I like the library. What about the encyclopedia sets?" She had been teaching for just a year or two deep in the inner city trenches and could barely afford a new pair of shoes or a bag of groceries. They call this initiation into teaching war duty. She had cried hysterically four times in the first month of her new teaching job that she thought perhaps she needed to reevaluate her life before she got too old and didn't accomplish anything substantial, let alone to achieve the basic human right of any American: "life, liberty, and the pursuit of happiness." But she entered her first art room and nary a scissor to be found. They were considered weapons so could not have them in school, so she ruled out the collage project immediately. These kids were surely not going to do torn paper collage. She tried to find contact numbers to call home to parents when the middle-schoolers were acting up only to find some were either in jail or selling their bodies on the street corner. She was scared because kids had guns in their lockers, and there were armed city cops in the school. But they did let the contained kids go out for art class. Lucky Fly. These were the baddest of the bad and were not afraid to place the sharp metal point of an open compass at a classmate's neck as he was held face down on the desk. A thirteen-year-old asked Ms. Fly what it was like to be pregnant, which scared her as she was only a mere child. At least she wasn't the gym teacher who got assaulted by trying to break up a fight. She went naively into teaching to "make a difference" even for one student. What a cliché bunch of malarkey, she thought at the time. Watching the presidential debate, the candidates even stated how teachers were treated with low status and not funded appropriately for the work they do.

For a hundred bucks a day, she could have waited tables and not brought work home with her doing lesson plans and grading tirelessly all weekend rather than recuperating from the stressful teaching week or just enjoying life with her new spouse. Fly reflected on her years of teaching when she found a handwritten journal note describing her experience while cleaning out the garage:

> The new teachers of my generation do not want to deal with the crap and psychosis of your children, your personal family crisis, and the bureaucracy of the public school systems. Your children watch too many violent shows and play too many violent games, and this is reflected in their art and behavior in the classroom. It is not my job to teach your child manners. Just not too long ago, students would not dare to be disrespectful and mocking toward their teachers. It is an everyday occurrence in today's confused society. And now students in trench coats are shooting and killing innocent people in their own school? I will not come home crying because a nine- or thirteen-year-old has treated me like a subhuman worthless individual. I don't know why there are so many children today that are so needy because of familial, social, physical, and/or psychological reasons. I refuse to be an art teacher that is a mean old hag, rather I hear the students tell me I am "too nice." What could that possibly mean, and why should I pay the price for being a person who enjoys smiling and laughing on the job?

"Bad boys, bad boys, whatcha gonna do? Whatcha gonna do when they come for you?" was playing in the background and they were hardly paying attention to it. Fly tried to cheer her dad up by saying that her aunt and uncle would be there soon and that they would be having an evening of fun. Two of Fly's mom's siblings, her godparents, had reunited across the country for a not-so-surprise celebration. They were to be there shortly for cards and games, and Fly tried to keep her dad's spirits up as they laughed at *Cops* and how ridiculous it was and how stupid the criminals were, and when they were drunk or high, they were extra stupid. He always was coining his favorite phrase about things that happened in life, "You just can't make this stuff up!" Only he never said the word "stuff." Just then, he asked for a towel because there was a pool of water on the floor and that he must have spilled something. Fly quickly scurried around the condo, looking in all the cabinets, and finally found a towel from the linen closet and knelt down next to the recliner to assess the situation. She could not find a spill but a puddle and searched for where the water was coming from as there was no glass of water nor leak from the ceiling or anywhere. It wasn't a spill at all; his legs were dripping fluid, and as the blood rushed out of her head, she could not believe or comprehend what exactly was happening. He was the water cascading to the floor beneath.

Even with that, Fly's dad, while having been increasingly ill for many years, was having the time of his life with all the company later that night. And what a wonderful surprise for Fly to have loved ones all around. The following day, Fly woke up and that was it! She hit the Big Four-Oh! While not terribly thrilled, she was going to make the most out it no matter what. Like she had a choice? The morning of her Big Day, Little Celeste and Fly put on these silly glittery and sparkly matching tee-shirts they got from a girly tween store since she could fit into the child-sized 16 clothing. The shirts had sparkling rainbows with dancing sprinkled cupcakes donning party hats and musical blowers stating, "Let's party!" Fly used to match clothes with her niece, like Halloween or Fourth of July shirts, but she outgrew Fly, so now, it was her daughter's turn. They pranced into the kitchen in their own birthday parade, just the two of them marching to their own drum beat, when just then, they noticed Fly's mom pacing in the kitchen nook frantically on the phone, calling someone to come immediately and check on him. Something went direly wrong during the night and a visiting nurse needed to come to assess his condition right away. Was it a stroke? Was it oxygen deprivation? What was it? Huge elated smiles instantly in 0.5 seconds turned to concerned frowns and quivers of the lip as they halted their parade. Just the evening prior, they all had an over-the-top fun family gathering around the kitchen table with jokes and drinks and chips and games. They all got chip-faced for sure. The nurse who arrived was checking to see if there was a stroke or something in the night. Then the doorbell rang. Fly rushed to quickly answer it, but as it opened, her godparents beaming with elated smiles and happiness for the special day at the same time loudly exclaimed as they burst through the threshold, "Happy bir…" which they probably rehearsed the whole way over from the hotel. They saw Fly's face and did not even end the well-wishing phrase everyone hears on their birthday morning.

He endured years in and out of hospital care and painful reviving, so on the morning of Fly's special day, he made a decision that would haunt Fly forever, especially on her birthdays. The ambulance pulled up and took him away with her mom by his side as they all convoyed behind him in their cars. Before he entered the ambulance, he whispered that he decided to go to hospice, not to the hospital that fateful day. This was not the gift she was expecting whatsoever. Stunned, she exclaimed, "Wait…what do you mean?" terrified of knowing what "hospice" meant but not believing. Can you change your mind once you get there? Surely this was a mistake. He really did not just decide to go to hospice on Fly's fortieth birthday? Maybe by the time the ambulance pulls into the hospital, he will have changed his mind and go to the hospital part. It is right there, just turn right, turn right! They did not and the ambulance made an abrupt unstoppable left turn into the part of the building clearly labeled Hospice. Fly felt like she hit a wall and was numb from shock, seeing only blackness. There he was laying there barely able to gasp breaths of air needed to survive. Fly's mom sternly stating to him as he lay in the bed, but with caring love whispering that he was not die on Fly's birthday, "Don't die... don't die! Not *today!*"

Despite this turn of events, that evening, Fly's mom had a blingy dinner bash at a fancy restaurant for under twenty friends and family, despite her dad held up in hospice. Fly had a difficult time, but tried to keep her chin up. All of the guests had on the pre-planned silly sparkly funny sun glasses and leis to wear for the dinner. They did not know what to do, so for the four hours, decided to try to go on as planned; everyone has to eat anyway, they thought. Wrapping it up promptly, they returned to her dad's room. Celeste and Fly had plane tickets to fly home the next day and re-enter into the reality of work and school. She tried to sit there calmly and hold his hand, as each breath was shallow and slipping away. Eyes closed as if tired from his journey. Little Celeste was making a drawing on the nurse's dry-erase board. "Get well, Pop Pop." It was late and they had a flight in the morning; the visit was cut short and it was time to go home. It was as if all of the fun they had that week was a distant long gone memory and instantly altered.

Fly cried uncontrollably all the way home, knowing she would never see her father again. The poor businessman in the seat next to her was quietly annoyed, but never said anything. Maybe he knew about the story where you never know what someone else is going through, what kind of baggage they are carrying. Fly heard it once. Someone yelled at a man getting off the elevator for not paying attention, bumped into him accidentally or something to that nature, and yelled angrily, "Hey, watch it! What the hell is wrong with you?" It was a trivial annoyance, but after being yelled at by the stranger, the man simply replied, "I am so sorry to bother you, sir...my wife just died." Little Celeste and she flew back on the plane and placed their luggage just inside the door of their home right before midnight. The bags just sat there at the front door as she could not muster up the energy to move them one inch more. Less than three hours later fast asleep, in the darkness of night, the phone rang. Fly sprung out of bed in the pitch-black darkness fearing the worst. She knew at the first ring. She sat on the floor in the corner in the living room, quivering in the dark, unable to accept but knew what was coming. It was the very same corner future Celeste would collapse in a fit of hysterics and rage from her future Dirt Bag Dude sabotage. It was the coat closet area closest to the exit, but still remaining in the safety of one's dwelling but wanting to escape to somewhere, anywhere. He was gone one day and one hour after her birthday. The book he was reading on the nightstand now frozen in time on the page where he placed his bookmark mid-chapter. Fly keeps this open sci-fi book as a treasure frozen in time of the last words he must have read.

That morning, Fly arose and sat on her back patio numb, staring at the clouds moving by in the light blue sky. It was a beautiful spring day, as it often was around her birthday. Perfect temperature, low humidity, you could wear a sweater or not and be just as fine either way. As she cracked open a cold beer, she contemplated what to do next. She was two thousand miles away and had two tickets to take her teenage niece to Lady Gaga on the day her dad just passed away. She sat there for hours on end all day contemplating what to do as she stared at the shapes the clouds made, trying to make sense of the world. Staring at the quietly drifting clouds, she reflected on the pain he must have endured for years and at the end, with her mom holding his hand, whispering in his ear about all of the wonderful times they had together, on vacations and parties and the life they had created as he slipped away with shallow breath. Fly appreciated all his hard work so they could have fond memories, and she remembered when they drove across the country probably modeled after National Lampoon's Vacation when she got her first period that summer, her younger brother got strep throat, and her older brother almost fell out of the boat while white water rafting. Or when everyone went to Disney for Y2K in December of 1999. Since the world was going to end, they all decided they might as well be having fun if the planes were going to be falling out of the sky at midnight. Fly's dad joked that if that were to happen, all you would have to do at that point was bend over and kiss your ass goodbye. But mostly, she admired his kindness, humor, and attention to detail and was proud that he had several patents for his inventions. He was awe-inspiring.

It was supposed to be her niece's first concert ever and that rockin' aunt never let down. But she had to make a decision to go or not. Fly's dad loved Lady Gaga. She brought him hope and yes, a little dance when her music came on the radio. He loved pop music as much as the oldies and he loved singing "Paparazzi" just as much as "Mustang Sally." When that song came on the radio, he broke out singing the main lyrics with Gaga and making up a little Dad dance, swinging his arms to the beat, "Papa-paparazzi!" He knew his precious daughter always broke out into a laugh because he sounded so ridiculous and funny. It might as well been him singing to Roxette in the driveway in the '80s and '90s, and he knew she didn't like Roxette's songs, but his love for catchy tunes shone bright. He liked people that were unique and different as he may have felt as a child treated like a piece of crumpled paper year after year, being second fiddle to a sibling. After hours and hours of blankly staring up at the universe, the clouds told Fly what to do. They shape shifted and morphed over and over into various objects and familiar forms, and her vision quest for the day was complete. What a great concert it was; she even bumped into some of her students.

The CD

Fly returned to work for a few days after he passed which was the next regular school day. She probably should not have gone in, but the funeral was going to be about a week away, so everyone could get there and arrange travel plans. Fly only had enough time to wash the same clothes packed from spring break and put them back in the luggage, only adding black funeral gear with her burgundy jacket and nice shoes. At work, as a supervisor, Ms. Fly extended several end of the school year deadlines for items since she would be taking the allotted bereavement days as per contract. Upon return, all the teachers submitted the requested items for their annual reports, including art shows, student contests, extracurricular activities, and special lessons per class in which were new or they felt were exemplary.

Within the piles of paperwork and teacher submissions, Mr. Paul handed in a supplemental shiny silver compact disc. No one else had handed in anything more than the worksheet, so it appeared as a mini gift of sorts. It was labeled as a group video project from the new computer class. Intrigued and excited for going seemingly above and beyond with such a document, Ms. Fly placed the CD into her laptop and hit Play. She watched and once again, a smile of hope in 0.5 seconds turned to a frown of disgust. She began shaking and sweating, mouth gaped open with a gasp, or maybe she wasn't even breathing, then tears floated down her face in disbelief as she viewed the contents of the CD. There, he decided to select a graphic video created by his students that vividly displayed gruesome examples of death by smoking. Overly skinny pale women with black teeth falling out, black decrepit lung x-rays, looming death and despair. It began, "One thousand Americans stop smoking everyday...by dying," in bold red letters on a black background fading into the distance like the original 1977 opening crawl in *Star Wars* with photos of people in horrific health conditions, disfigured, lost limbs, blacked-out lungs shrunken and deflated, and the like. Fly briefly flashed back to the movie theater the day that movie came out, standing in the long line with her dad and brothers to see the epic sci-fi on the big screen. This may have been the longest three minutes and thirty-four seconds of Ms. Fly's career. The video went like this:

> One thousand Americans stop smoking every-day...by dying.
> Here are a few ways in which smoking affects your body: lung cancer, heart disease, stomach ulcer, emphysema, bleeding gums, stained teeth, tongue cancer, impaired taste, chronic bronchitis, stroke.
> Yes. Smoking does all these things, however this is just a cartoon, here are some real cases... (graphic images)
> Mouth cancer. An estimated 30,200 new oral cancer cases will be diagnosed this year. (graphic images)

15

Lung cancer. Lung cancer is the largest single cause of cancer deaths in the United States. (graphic images)

Brain tumor. The chemical formaldehyde found in cigarettes increases the chance of brain cancer. (graphic images)

Throat cancer. This year 35,000 people will be diagnosed with throat cancer. This will cause about 8,000 deaths in the year. This means almost one death per hour of the day.

Stop and catch your breath!

Be smart…quit smoking today.

She was horrified, shocked, and confused at the blatant and specific choice of student artwork sample. She mentioned it to Mrs. Parabola in passing, but it was unfathomable like no one could wrap their head around it, but also no one really cared or knew what to do. This type of instance or interaction with teachers was not written anywhere in the leadership manuals and textbooks. It was not under the "difficult employee" section, just nowhere. After re-grouping the following week, Ms. Fly eventually sent it inter-office to the District Director Coupon Suzy for her opinion to ensure she was not just overreacting in a state of mourning. Not even two weeks had gone by since the funeral. Ms. Fly also reported it verbally to Principal Don Voyage during an Annual Assessment Meeting in the Principal's Office, who pretended not to hear what she was saying and simply kept talking about other mundane education-related items like showcases and end of year gatherings. He did not even acknowledge her words, he just kept talking about basic school stuff. A few days later, a teacher came to see Ms. Fly in her office and Fly broke down hyperventilating, explaining what was on the CD and hysterically exclaiming, "Why would he do that?" The fellow teacher who was friendly with Mr. Paul was at a loss for words, concerned, but also a colleague who stood by and did nothing. It was the beginning of the end. A permanent scar ripped into her, images that cannot be unseen, personal lines crossed. Fly was so angry at the indifference, she stayed in the classroom scrubbing down everything she could before the summer vacation when Don Voyage came to find her and asked if she was going to join everyone at the luncheon where she simply replied, "No."

Re: Items

Dear Mr. Paul,

Was your cruel intention a deviant response to Ms. Fly's constant corrections of your poor work performance? Was it the memo in the fall regarding student safety which was reported to the assistant principal that your students almost got hit by a car parallel parking as they took pictures in the street as you stood in the classroom doorway with a large self-satisfied smug look on your face and a huge sigh out...ahhhh, as if you were teaching something amazing, stupendous, and enlightening? Hello...this is a fairly obvious one here: your students are in the neighborhood off campus while you are standing in the classroom by yourself during class time! Did you get mad at your supervisor because she had to point this out and that it is not permissible for students to be off school grounds during your class? Perhaps it was when you didn't hand in all of your paperwork on time in September and maybe you got annoyed that she had to repeatedly ask you for it after the deadline. All of the other teachers didn't have a problem submitting the work accurately and on time, and if they did they would explain why they needed time or help. Or when you went to the male dean with discipline issues rather than Ms. Fly as per policy and food chain ladder, or the student artwork that you labeled to be hung upside down in the gallery for the entire year, then manipulated the gaggle of male upperclassmen to berate Ms. Fly for the next two years until they graduated, mocking her relentlessly that it was her fault the fellow student's artwork was hung upside down? Transference behavior at its finest. You stood right there next to it for a photo op and never said it was upside down nor bothered to mention it or change it. You just stood there with that stuff-eating grin on your face for the photo. She simply hung the art the way you labeled the back. One thing was for sure, the school year was ending and you would not have to present full lesson plan units soon which was an extended agreement of your confused lessons and questionable performance. For example, this hideous dark video camouflaged by the shiny flawless CD exterior, in addition to being callous and cruel, was of extremely poor artistic quality and irrelevant to the curriculum and best suited for a mediocre health class. The true lesson you attempted to teach and your plan to implement has become quite clear. As for District Director Coupon Suzy's response to your CD, Ms. Fly simply got a handwritten message on a cheap three-inch square scrap of paper returned inter-office and attached to it: "*Very* Sorry." The word *Very* was underlined twice aggressively with a period. And if it wasn't heard the first time, this CD was like another shotgun going off *bang!* to start a marathon, but Fly was unaware she would be running in it; it would be a long drawn-out race with no end in sight. Just one week later, the incompetencies continued with more and more small but important errors such as with the student district final exams. This is now going on four years of the exact same exam questions, so Fly just kept it short with all of the mistakes and, on a sticky note, returned it to him with a message to the point:

> Paul,
>   Sorry but please double-check your work. These are Mixed Mass Media Arts questions, not Fine Arts. Please revise for future testing and re-submit.
>
>   Thank you,
>   Fly

Until spring break this school year, Ms. Fly really tried to use her leadership skills in a variety of ways to help Mr. Paul improve. When that someone must have whispered in his ear, "Don't worry, you can do almost anything and never get fired!" it had now definitely resonated and sunk in. Not the sharpest tool in the shed, but this tool he finally understood how to utilize. Ms. Fly and Mr. Paul had weekly meetings, albeit no common time off; they discussed the required "Good News" items that were to be documented for the district, which often he did not bother to have. She called it "No Good News." A teacher who never has any good news to report? Nothing? And yet Mr. Paul continued to blatantly express to Ms. Fly that he gets confused with multiple courses or multiple room assignments or multiple things to do by multiple deadlines, which is actually called teaching. She was becoming drained by the constant mending of his lack of appropriate use of English which was his primary language. After a few years of reading his emailed sentences that included the word, "abit" as in his chronic admission that "He is abit confused," at this or that, Ms. Fly finally corrected him replying, "abit is not a word." Please stop. The same confusion ensued when Mr. Paul jumped on board with Coupon Suzy's directives of using a hot new deep art and literary analysis term called "close reading," as in one is closely reading text or looking at a work of art, yet rather he kept calling it ironically, "closed reading" which she thought to be the exact opposite. It was like from *Mean Girls* that there must be something that he is good at and he must have ESPN or something. And then the last day of school came and Mr. Paul had irresponsibly curated an impossible lesson plan as to have these innocent students create decoupage art with sticky white glue shellacked all over personal objects they brought from home, in which they were too wet as the bell rang that the children were unable to take their dripping and sopping wet creations home that hot sticky day. Fly, as an artist, teacher, leader, mother, daughter, and wife all balled up into one wearing so many hats simultaneously, was disgusted and infuriated and her lips pursed as she tried to keep her mouth shut picking only the big battles. Her jaw became clenched and sore day after day. These students would never see their artwork again.

Mr. Paul, what do you want from Ms. Fly? Perhaps a different career would be better if you can't handle the challenges of teaching and inspiring students. You prefer kicking someone on the ground when they are already down? Is this simply a case of the Peter Pan syndrome and you refuse to grow up and you have become the leader of the Lost Boys? How could you *not* know what happened with your immediate supervisor in such a small department when she was away for a week at her dad's funeral? What did you think happened when you signed the group sympathy card? There is no way you did not know, and given the hundreds of examples you could have selected from an entire school years' worth of art projects, *this* is the one you chose to give to Fly? A CD—cold and shiny, disguised as a gift that perhaps you improved finally by the end of the school year, but alas, mere salt in the wound. For such a silent movie, the message was heard loud and clear. She turned on the radio speeding her way home to begin the summer vacation and screamed from the top of her lungs, "Papa-paparazzi!"

America the Beautiful—American Mayhem

Psychotic gifts at their finest: Death by Cigarette Propaganda defined by those horrific commercials of smokers who are now gone, e-cigarettes, and vaping. The Marlboro Man, handsome and rugged. Makes you want to smoke? It's like giving sunblock to someone who was just diagnosed with skin cancer, or giving donuts to someone who just started Pound Pounders, or stating "Happy Father's Day" to someone who lost their dad, or stating at a hospice fundraiser "Hospice, you're killin' it!" which Fly and her husband actually witnessed and heard at a summer event speech. Or saying to Michael Phelps in a news interview on TV, "I'm dying to see your movie on suicide," as Fly sits there on the couch in the summer watching the morning news in disbelief. Principal Don Voyage, your retirement will definitely not be bittersweet when it comes.

Ten Lessons That Tenure Teaches

Turning diamonds in the rough into a
Superstar or Supervillain

Pros	**and**	**Cons**
1. job security		1. job security
2. hardworking		2. hardly working
3. inspirational		3. indifferent
4. marvelous		4. mediocre
5. visionary		5. blinding
6. dedicated		6. disregarding
7. entertaining		7. entitled
8. creative		8. corrupt
9. master teacher		9. master manipulator
10. teacher of the year		10. teacher of tears and fears

Word Wall

"offensive" *adjective* of•fen•sive
1. to disturb persistently; torment, as with troubles or cares; pester; persecute; to trouble by repeated attacks, incursions as in war or hostilities
2. causing someone to feel deeply hurt, upset, or angry
3. actively aggressive; attacking

synonyms: hostile, attacking, aggressive, combative, threatening, warlike, belligerent, insulting, rude, derogatory, disrespectful, hurtful, wounding, abusive, objectionable, displeasing, annoying, exasperating, irritating, vexing, galling, provocative, provoking, humiliating, impertinent, impudent, insolent, personal, discourteous, uncivil, impolite, unmannerly, unacceptable, shocking, scandalous, outrageous, crude, vulgar, course, indecent, improper

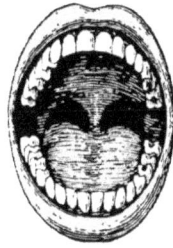

Notable Quotables

The arrow cannot hit the target at which it is not aimed.
—Zen saying

Fast Fact

Before Massachusetts introduced teacher tenure
in 1886, women were sometimes dismissed for
getting married, becoming pregnant, wearing
pants, or being out too late in the evening.
—Teachertenure.procon.org

Is teacher tenure good or bad for American public schools? Teacher tenure is a career status and safety net obtained usually after three years of service and is a highly debatable topic in education. It is put in place to create a level of job security for a variety of reasons, however, makes it virtually impossible to fire a teacher or educational administrator for even conduct unbecoming to the profession. While there are many pros and cons, one main pro is that it protects teachers from being fired or penalized by a district for reasons, including salary scale level, creativity in the classroom, and advocating for student rights. However, a major con is that it is that teachers can become complicit, and it becomes very difficult to fire inept teachers, leaving them in the classroom for decades. Laws and policies vary from state to state.

Lesson #1

This school year Fly learned that sticks and stones will break her bones and words actually do hurt.

"DANGER ZONE"
All Mixed up Playlist #1

A DATE ____ OYES ONO
N R

Mr. Know it All - Kelly Clarkson
Hot n Cold - Katy Perry
Intuition - Jewel
Trouble - Taylor Swift
Spiderwebs - No Doubt
Stressed Out - 21 Pilots
Lost Boy - Ruth B
True Colors - Cyndi Lauper
Lips are Movin' - Meghan Trainor
Rude - Magic!

You're so Vain - Carly Simon
Who will Save your Soul? - Jewel
Right Round - Flo Rida
I'm Just a Girl - NO DOUBT
Everybody wants to
RULE the World - Tears for Fears

Danger Zone - Kenny Loggins
Pressure - Billy Joel

B DATE ____ OYES ONO
N R

That's All - Genesis
Land of Confusion - Spandau Ballet
Communication - Spandau Ballet
One Thing Leads to Another - Fixx
Is There Something I
Should Know - Duran Duran
Killing Me Softly - Fugees
Big Girls Don't Cry - Fergie
Little Lies - Fleetwood Mac
Would I Lie to You? - Eurythmics

9 to 5 - Dolly Parton
She Works Hard for the
Money - Donna Summer
Everyday I'm Shufflin - LMFAO
I Should Have Known -
Foo Fighters
Found Out About You
- Gin Blossoms
The World I Know
- Collective Soul

That Takes Guts

Act Out!

Activity: Music can be a powerful healing tool and help with emotional support. List songs that help you get through tough times at the hand of another or something out of your control. Create a playlist on the following page. Share with others you trust. You can do this alone or with a friend. Discuss how the songs make you feel. Look up the lyrics or analyze the music video. Listen and sing along to the song; it's okay if you are tone deaf. Scream from the top of your lungs, "What's going on?" like 4 Non Blondes. How do you interpret the contents differently than the musical artist who created the song? What phrases have meaning to you and why?

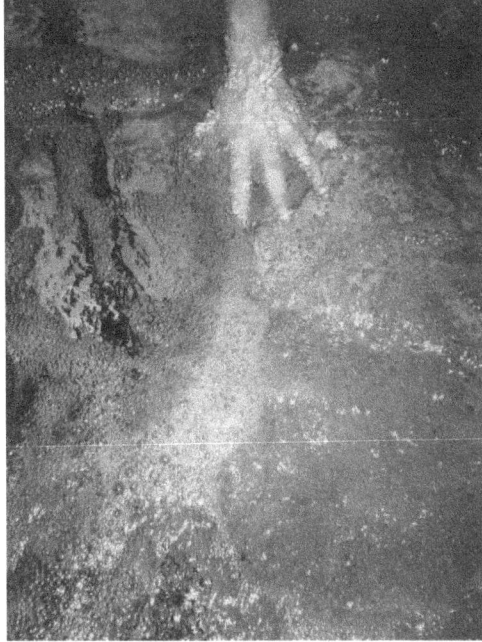

PART 1
Wrath

Art is not what you see, but what you make others see.

—Edgar Degas

Chapter 2
Toxic Zombie Apocalypse

It's September.

I'm making a list of the things I must say
for politeness
And goodness and kindness and gentleness,
sweetness and rightness:
Hello
Pardon me
How are you?
Excuse me
Bless you
May I?
Thank you
Goodbye
If you know some that I've forgot,
please stick them in your eye!

—"I'm Making a List" by Shel Silverstein

Cue the Music:
"Toxic" by Britney Spears
"Zombie" by the Cranberries/ Bad Wolves
"Brain Stew" by Green Day
Bonus Track: "Pumped Up Kicks" by Foster the People

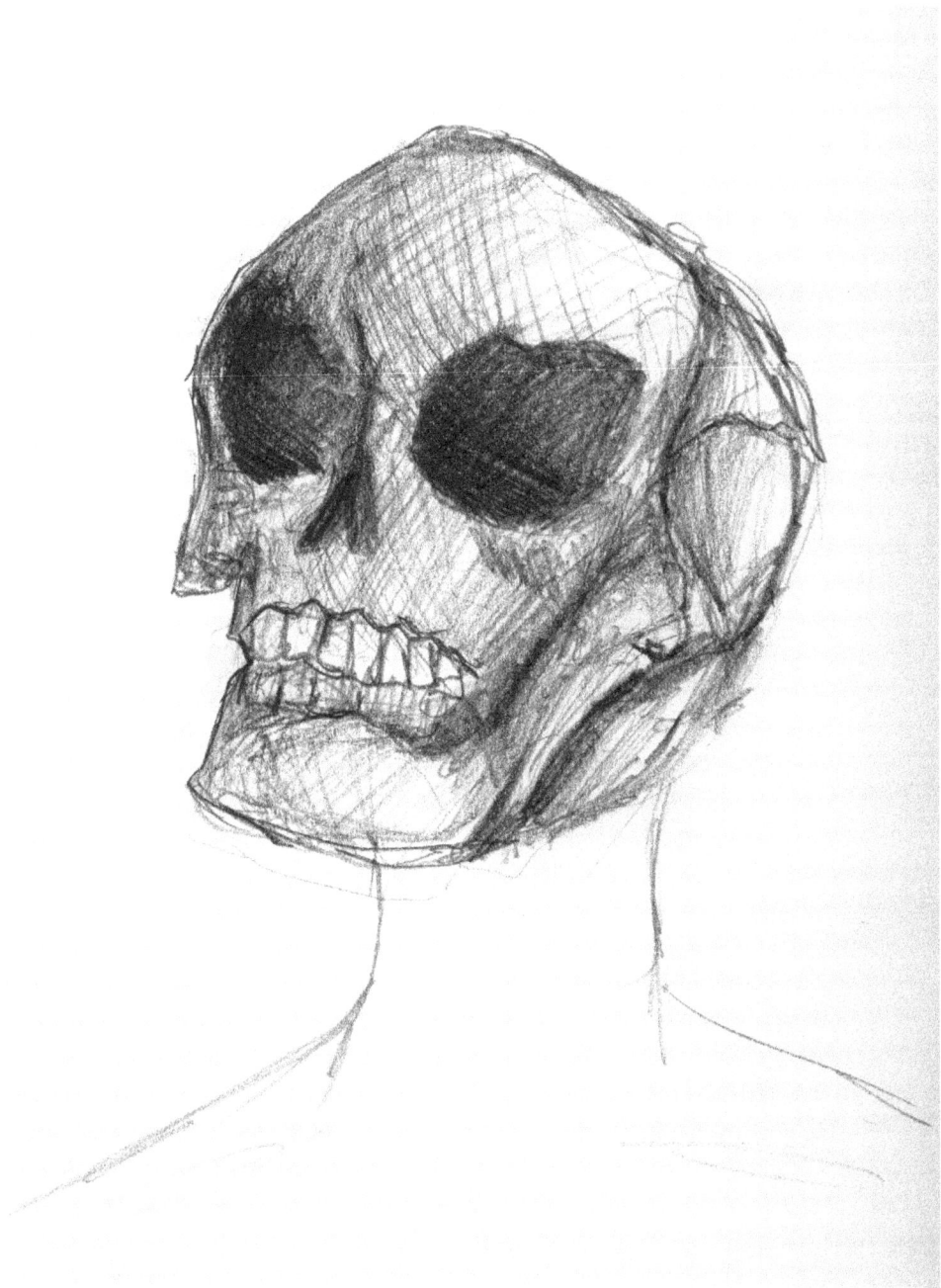

Use Small Words

There has been a revival of zombie movies once again reflecting the global state of being and the human condition. In the 1980s, it was all about the hairy alpha werewolves howling at the full midnight moon prowling in the dark for their victims. In the 1990s, it was all about the sleek, sunken-cheek, well-dressed, and alluring pale vampires vanishing and instantly appearing before your eyes, ready to hypnotize and suck your blood, leaving you cold and pale. But in the current state of America with global warming leading to dramatic weather events, terrorist threats, addictions to pills, alcohol, gaming and technology and random gun violence, monsters can creep up anywhere and anytime with unexpected attacks. One can't even hear them because of the onslaught of earbuds, caring less about what is going on in one's surroundings. There is an obsession with zombies as Americans must feel as such. Zombie moms, zombie dads, zombie kids, zombie consumers, and zombie workers.

"To me, the best zombie movies aren't the splatter fests of gore and violence with goofy characters and tongue in cheek antics. Good zombie movies show us how messed up we are, they make us question our station in society…and our society's station in the world. They show us gore and violence and all that cool stuff too…but there's always an undercurrent of social commentary and thoughtfulness" (Robert Kirkman)

A zombie is essentially one who is brain dead with a terrible attention span, is impulsive and has an unquenchable hunger for the flesh or brains of the living. Some notable characteristics which Ms. Fly thought to be parallel with Mr. Paul are odd physical movements, mindless and unconscious behavior, following with a singular desire to find victims, strong but slow, not self-aware, immune to painful injury, cannot talk but usually grunt. And he just keeps coming at Fly over and over again, never learning what teaching is about. While these characteristics may be slightly exaggerated for a human to occupy, they are not far off for some individuals and there have actually been some recent cases of zombie attacks all over America. Naked men dragging their feet on the city sidewalks, then surprising

31

unsuspecting victims and attacking them, feasting on their flesh as they try to escape the unexpected terror. Cases of being at the wrong place at the wrong time. But with Mr. Paul, a grunt would be even more of a response than the lack of a simple please and thank you, let alone the silence of no response to questions or correspondence at all. Just the blank stare deep into Ms. Fly's soul. Ms. Fly would go to conventions and bring back samples of the latest nontoxic art supplies and goodies to her department teachers and everyone would be thrilled at new art samples, but never a response from Mr. Paul. She would bear gifts at the holidays for everyone and treat the faculty to end of the year luncheons and again, never a simple thank you nor look of excitement from Mr. Paul ever, and he acted almost angry that she was so thoughtful and helpful. Fly picked up a Sock-a-Zombie kit at the local bookstore when she was out shopping for a book one day. It was a miniature inflatable zombie about four inches tall, and she blew it up with her breath and kept it on her desk next to framed postcard of *The Brooding Woman* by Paul Gauguin. The zombie bag had his arms raised out in attempt to conquer what lay ahead. It was adorned with cuts, scratches, and blood randomly on his body, an eyeball popping out of his brain, clothes tattered, and a worm protruding from its ear. Every time Fly went to her office and needed to relieve frustration from Mr. Paul's shenanigans, she simply gave the zombie bop bag a good right cross punch exhaling a "grrrrr…" as she would do in kickboxing class. The problem: the zombie always popped back up into its relentless stance to keep coming at her. One punch, ten punches, or a hundred, this brainless zombie would just keep coming back, so she knew she had to start becoming a prepper for the apocalypse.

Ms. Fly again requested assistance to help handle this employee by the principal and assistant principals. Depending on the incident, problems got reported to a different person in charge: school safety, school events, student discipline, curriculum, testing, and so on. The soon-to-retire Principal Don Voyage reviewed a selection of items of great concern that Ms. Fly had written in a plea memorandum for assistance; that it was too much for a teaching supervisor to take on solo as she had not approved in favor of the tenure debacle. Principal

Don Voyage said he did meet with Mr. Paul and Fly stated, "I could tell," because he acted differently, like being watched and vigilant, for a just few days before reverting back to his usual antics. Ms. Fly was sure they sat in the principal's office as a formality and probably just discussed the game he coached that Wednesday afternoon, and then sent him on his way with a pat on the back. Emerge…a wolf in sheep's clothing.

There was an obscene amount of incidents again starting from the first week of school. It was only September and she sat in her office, exhaling a great sigh of disappointment and frustration. Fly thought it was clarified in an annual report meeting before the long hot summer vacation that he would have the time to reflect, prepare and improve. What is it with these Young Yuppie-Mediocre Millennial Teacher Cliques that are unable to complete simple tasks and makes it harder on everyone else? This was rampant in the building in several departments. This appears to be a generation that is disconnected and desensitized, perhaps from chronic overuse and addiction to ever changing technology and social media, Fly was not sure. His behavior and actions were clearly a huge monkey wrench in an otherwise well-oiled machine.

She sat in her office chair remembering the best thing that happened to her over the long, hot mourning summer. Fly's smile had been broken last spring, and it was about three months before she was able to crack even a small smile and laugh a little. Her best friend said that they should meet halfway at the Casino Posh to celebrate their joint fortieth birthdays in July. They always had fun together. They had good times at Band Camp flying the flags in the Color Guard, and one time in high school, Fly was new to driving and went a little too fast over the railroad crossing hump and the car went airborne as if she was driving the General Lee from *The Dukes of Hazzard*. Scared and amused, they paused in disbelief, then burst into hysterical laughter. Fly never gambled but thought they should definitely do something to celebrate. Diamond Heart Vana was her childhood friend since birth, each other's maids of honors, and always had triple the sparkle. Their brothers were born on the same day in the same hospital room and their moms became instant lifelong friends as did they. Both of her parents were physical education teachers and they taught with dignity and professionalism back in their teaching days, and they were reasonably compensated for their genuine caring and hard work. It was a different generation of instruction when they were growing up as kids. So they escaped from reality for just a day, from the chaos of home life and life in general. They met in the casino parking lot, checked in to the posh room, and after resting their feet and catching up with conversation, headed down to the casino floor. The casino filled the entire dimension of this luxury palace and was filled with sounds of victory, posh music, and neon blinging colors. It was visual overload, but they were loving it. Each twist and turn kept the mystery alive, and in the darkness, time stood still.

Taking turns at the slot machines, Diamond soon came to realize Fly only brought a total of $30 and she looked at her with a "for real?" attitude and laughed. Fly tried to justify her naivety, saying $10 for her husband, $10 for Celeste, and $10 for herself but that was completely unrealistic little did she know. Fly did not know the paper bills would go so swiftly getting sucked into the machine, kidnapped by the one-armed bandit. The house always wins. So they laughed, and after finding out that Diamond brought about $300 with additional birthday bucks she was given from her family, Fly went to the ATM and the annual tradition was born. Later that night, they went to the Club Posh and just listening to the band when two gangster-looking men came up to them and asked, "Hey, ladies, would you like to go out with us on our boat?"

Diamond and Fly politely declined their insane offer and laughed until they couldn't anymore. Sure guys, on your boat in the middle of the dark spooky lake at midnight? Sure, you can chop us up into bitty pieces for no one to find. The morning came too quickly, and before they parted ways, they began a tradition that the person who had the most wins bought the breakfast sandwiches the next morning so everyone left a winner.

And toxic behaviors were experienced elsewhere throughout the building. What was even up with that mean secretary or the curmudgeonly lunch lady? The secretary would just chit-chat on the phone with her family, knowing Ms. Fly only had five minutes between bells to get something accomplished. She would just sit there and blatantly keep talking as if her weekend BBQ plans were being interrupted. Then, Ms. Fly would be in line with Mr. Mapfold, and for the same $5.50, he would get twice as much food served on his plate than Fly and they laughed about it. Some things are implicit, but when it became a running joke about inequitable portion size related to body size, one realizes it's everywhere. Ms. Fly often corresponded with the district director about Paul's self-proclaimed confusion and incoherent lesson plans and compulsive emails riddled with incorrect, confusing, or false information that rambled on and on "abit." Coupon Suzy simply stated that she only dealt with curriculum, but otherwise Ms. Fly should, "Use small words like Yes and No." What was this, kindergarten? Did she listen to Peter Gabriel's '80s hit "Big Time," coming from a "small town, they think so small, they use small words?" Fly was smarter than that, and her big mouth, though quiet and sincere, refused to utter a response. It was clearly becoming increasingly more difficult to do her job and the fact that it was professionally suggested Ms. Fly speak to him like a child while he earned a decent salary was obscene. As the singer would say, this was "so much larger than life." Administration would always state that the teachers in the district made a competitive wage for the time and location and need to reciprocate with services rendered. Fly already had a child at home, and actually, Celeste acted more mature than Mr. Paul at times and he was making a lot of money in this particular district unlike the other surrounding districts. On several occasions, Fly and Little Celeste had play dates with Suzy and her daughter since they were about the same age and they enjoyed hanging out together at the regional art shows. They went several times to parks and playgrounds and the local amusement park and the kids were forced to be work-based buddies. This might have proven to be a mistake to mix work with being social, but what did Fly know; the kids seemed to enjoy each other's company.

But being a person who needs answers as to "why?" Ms. Fly began trying to figure out or identify what the problem with Paul could be even though she was told by Coupon Suzy herself not to research the psychology of employee behavior and that was not her job but to simply live with it. Regardless, Fly researched online articles and finally stumbled upon something called "Passive-Aggressive Personalities in the Workplace" and that seemed reflective of what was going on here. Yes, she agreed with the examples listed online and seemed to parallel what she was experiencing:

> Communicating via notes to avoid personal contact: Yes
> Like an elephant never forgets and slowly builds a mental list until they blow: Yes
> They punish you by silently stewing and blaming: Yes
> Constantly say it's fine or okay when it is not: Yes
> They constantly one-up you: Yes
> They are always playing the victim and withholding with toxic resentment: Yes, yes and yes.

Ms. Fly had concrete concerns: Did this person need help or have a learning disability issue that would excuse the incompetencies? Was it drugs? Alcohol? Anxiety or other disorders that made his brain impenetrable? A special need that Fly should be made aware of? Family problems? Medical or mental issues? But alas, no one is permitted to ask these questions. Normal colleagues usually express normal stresses and things happening in one's personal life even if it is minuscule so that others know what one is going through, but not here. It was a true mystery. One of the other art teachers who highly recommended Mr. Paul said he was in chronic pain, so initially, she felt sympathetic that maybe that was the problem. But upon Ms. Fly asking if he was okay one day, he looked confused and had no idea what pain she was talking about. Or was it this so-called passive-aggressive behavior? Or was he indeed a secret zombie? Fly was told by Coupon Suzy that it was none of her business, but Fly thought it would help give an explanation. Fly grew up with a brother with CP and was usually very patient, respectful, and understanding of people's special needs and differences. Everyone has something going on, so if there is awareness, there can be better relationships and communication, better workplaces and livelihoods.

Creeper

Fly's brother was born with cerebral palsy; they thought from lack of oxygen at birth, as well it was also the doctor's first baby he delivered so, "rookie mistake?" That's what Paul would keep stating when he messed up things in the beginning, with his maniacal laugh-it-off attitude. "Haha. Okay. Rookie mistake." When does it stop being a rookie mistake? After one year, two? A few years? Never? Fly was not really familiar with that sports phrase but understood that the mistake should probably only happen once and everyone is sort of all right with it and shrug it off like you simply did not know any better, but normally, it does not ever happen again because you learn from that mistake or lack of initial knowledge. Live and learn. Fly really liked to learn something new every day and would use that in her lessons with her students when *they* taught *her* something, "Well, you learn something new every day!" she would exclaim to the class.

Fly's brother had a metal brace on one leg growing up and so one can see how he was different. He walks with a pretty noticeable gait, and if he gets stressed or angry which did not happen very often as he has a kind soul, his one eyeball would wander off and he would be talking to you or the person next to you and Fly would be like, "Oh, are you talking to me?" as it appeared he was looking elsewhere. And they would chuckle at his unique qualities and proceed with the conversation. Fly's family moved districts several times so that he could get the special education that was the up and coming movement: small classes, personal attention, inclusion, mainstreaming, and finally ended up in a particular school district, the very same where Little Fly had to eat at the teacher's desk with her presumably diabetic teacher she admired for her strength and the fact that she was one of the handful of people her entire life who "saw it" and "did something." One must wonder what is the percentage of individuals who react appropriately to the phrase, "If you see something, say something." How many people are going to out of their way to find someone in charge, say at the airport or train station, to claim there's a suspicious backpack on the floor that seems to be without a person, and then possibly can be blamed for it since they reported it. Then they miss the train and are late to work or vacation or wherever and it is not worth their time to do the right thing. For Fly, it was probably a very small percentage, but perhaps she should have consulted Mrs. Parabola with the numbers.

Fly survived middle school, but her brother always struggled. Elementary school was a nightmare and really impacted Fly's mom daily, those dreaded middle school years which are hard enough for any kid, and then the roller coaster of high school. Fly actually enjoyed those high school years, unlike Celeste, because she was creative and flourished and participated in a lot of different events, clubs, and opportunities. She excelled, became Drum Major, Art Club president, editorial staff, and member of the Honor Society and Art and Literary Magazine, but in turn for being an extroverted-introvert, she was very sick all the time, especially senior year as she may have overdone it with achievements. She had a 102 fever during state testing on an 80-degree day in an un-airconditioned room and still got an A. Celeste was in high school one day and kept going on about her friend Jen Z. and how they were so gripped by all the new apps and their phones that finally one day, Fly asked her, "Who's Jen Z.?" Celeste broke away from her device and exclaimed, "Generation Z!" It clicked as the children of the Gen X. Celeste was also extremely creative, but maybe by her Gen Z videogame and phone-addicted teenage zombies generation, things had changed a lot. School wasn't what it used to be. For Celeste's generation, many students can easily talk back to their teachers, are completely disconnected from the classroom, and lack decent social skills to communicate with their classmates and peers. Some days, Ms. Fly would stop the class and model what polite behavior was or how they should speak with one another. When a student would barge in late, interrupting the lesson without uttering a word, she would stop the class and say, "Good morning, Ms. Fly. I am so sorry I am late, but my mom had car trouble. How are you today? May you please hand me a piece of paper and I will catch up. Thank you!" That student would swiftly copy and apologize. With the onslaught of cell phones, teachers had become afraid that they could be videotaped, nay recorded and one up posted to social media if they yelled at a class or did something wrong. Ms. Fly even had one kid bring a Big Boy Beer to class, and it wasn't even 9 o'clock in the morning! A girl at his table ratted him out at the bell, and of course, Ms. Fly reported it immediately and he was busted by period 3. Ms. Fly was shocked at the audacity at lack of care for education, but at least he was in school and not truant.

Fly remembers one day walking down the main hallway in her high school and about five students were walking behind her brother in front of her, and they were mocking and making fun of him because he was much slower than the others. Sometimes, it reminded Fly of the scene from *Young Frankenstein* where the servant states, "Walk this way," and proceeds to give Gene Wilder his cane as he cascades down the staircase with his hunchback that would move from his right to left shoulder randomly. So Fly walked his walk; slow and steady wins the race. But in that long dank hallway, she was furious at this gang of teens making fun of him, and it imprinted in her psyche. Fly was about to say something when they abruptly entered classrooms. Fly wished she was like Mrs. Parabola when it came to saying something swiftly back at someone on the spot, but she was more of a sulker, as she preferred to brood over something as it settled into her inner self until she thoroughly thought about a resolution. Then one day, Fly remembered her mom flying off the handle as she picked up the yellow phone, the one with the thirteen-foot coiled cord so you could move around the kitchen and she was yelling at the administration or someone at the high school. She slammed down the phone, threw on her coat, and stormed over to the school instantly to confront the teacher or maybe it was the administrator or maybe even the elusive principal. She had spent her entire life dedicated to ensuring her son get the help he needed to succeed and be a decent human being and American citizen. They moved, he had physical therapy and emotional support, and she worked relentlessly to help him be an upstanding young man. But the crusty science teacher decided it was a fine idea to nickname him "Creeper." This teacher probably had nicknames for every student, which by today's standards would send you to the rubber room, being impossible to get fired, however inappropriate. Fly was never sure what happened after that encounter with her mom, but Fly got that same teacher the following year in Science Lab and he asked with a drawn-out slippery tongue, "Are you Creeper's sister?" with a dramatic lingering voice and accusatory eyeball lean in. Fly knew what her mom was mad about and Fly just glared back at him with a stink eye. With no response as to why that was relevant, Fly intentionally let that frog eyeball explode during lab that one fine day in class after she was told not to.

Fly's brother ended up on the track team excelling in shot put, and he also took a liking to break dancing with friends, which was pretty cool to watch him at that time do such challenging things. That is good, sound physical education. Just like art, anyone can do it, one just has to get over the initial fear or intimidation factor and express oneself. To hold open arms for every student at all levels, get teenagers to move their minds and bodies and understand the benefits of physical health and personal expression. He is the kindest, gentlest person Fly knows and people need to have patience and respect each other no matter what. But in the end, he was sometimes naïve and on the last day of school, exuberated that it was over for at least the two summer months, he threw all his binders and composition books out the school bus window. Of course, his name was on every single one of those loose-leaf pages, so he was banned from driving on school property the following school year. So Fly followed his car, so he could park around the corner, and before she drove him into the school parking lot, they would get donuts, coffee, and tea at the nearby Sack of Donuts. They got the same order every day as it was not like there were a million flavor combinations and choices like now. Chocolate glazed and strawberry frosted, no sprinkles, and off to the school parking lot they went. Little did they know that's where Fly herself learned to do donuts in the snow!

Like a zombie, Mr. Paul presented items to Ms. Fly that were increasingly creepy and disturbing or so she analyzed as such being her area of expertise. First off, she was trained and certified to be an "inspector," a keen observer of goings-on, so therefore found it odd that administrators kept dismissing her findings and reporting of such. But also, artists are natural keen observers and are highly analytical of things around them and societal changes that shape the world and are thus reflected in art of the times, which are called "Art Movements." There is a whole History of Art, and many versions of Histories of Art, mostly however skewed by Western culture as it may be, that most people do not know about, but it exists. Fly never figured out why her History of Widgetry class in college only focused on white male artists, even though most of the professors were woman at the time, but later as the times changed ever so slowly like molasses, came to realize that widgetry was mostly a man's career, unless women came from money or prestige. She came to find the hidden female artists that resonated with her better with regard to subject matter and personal expression. Artists pay attention to detail and are visual by nature, dissecting every nuance presented to the viewer. Colors, patterns, focal point, lighting, subject matter, placement, composition, intent, symbolism, meaning, and so on. After all, the four steps of art criticism that every teenager is taught in art class is first, describe factually what you see; second, analyze the components of how something is put together compositionally; third, interpret what you think the artist is trying to say; and fourth, judge whether you like it or not and support why with detailed explanations.

So one day, Ms. Fly was reviewing teacher's lesson plans as she did every week and was taken aback by a disturbing self-portrait example that Mr. Paul had made for one of his courses. It was a monster mash-up of several photographs: one self-portrait looking down, eyelids softly closed, in that notable sad puppy dog look, the other was a "contrasting emotion" to which Mr. Paul was mouth wide open in an enraged maniacal frozen scream expression with one eye wide open in terror. Ms. Fly got the chills upon viewing the aggression. He appeared to have an unusual bright red skin color juxtaposing the bland washed-out colors on the sad face side. The papers were torn and re-assembled in a Frankenstein-like fashion. The student handout he distributed clearly stated written by Mr. Paul himself, "Effective portraits convey the emotions of the model or subject." As an artist, Ms. Fly clearly understood what was going on here, but then the layer of incompetence was added by stating this project was "in the style" of a particular well-renowned female photographer so ended up being completely off target and untrue based on physical evidence by simply comparing his Franken-Photo to the one of the famous artist's. These portraits were nothing alike, not even close. Sleek, dramatic celebrity portraits of famous actors and musicians are not the same as this rough, poor quality, blurry, disturbing Franken-Collage. Ms. Fly had to just stick to the facts and state that this is not even close to being "in the style" of the artist Mr. Paul insinuated. She off the cuff asked fellow art educator Coupon Suzy for her blind opinion on the teacher artwork and replied, pointing to the typography integrated into the artwork which was cut and pasted like a ransom note, "You mean besides the fact that the word *Conquered* is misspelled?"

Liar, Liar Pants on Fire!

The previous June, Ms. Fly, at the suggestion and recommendation of several fellow supervisors, colleagues, and union navigators she had been consulting since the crumpled paper incident, met with Mr. Paul and came up with a list of things that Paul should focus on to improve for the upcoming school year and it was not even as numerous as the memo given to Ms. Petunia from the retired supervisor. Her experienced and knowledgeable union navigator, knowing now what happened with Principal Don Voyage helped her articulate the contents. The memorandum included things related to lessons and curriculum, care of equipment and student safety, student achievement, time management, but most importantly, following school policies and improving communication and to ask for help when needed to prevent issues. After all, those were the official rules for teaching, and Ms. Fly was a rule follower for the most part. She even tried to commute to work one day without using a blinker and she couldn't do it. This was reviewed with strategies and ideas on how to accomplish these aspects of teaching. September came and game on! Ms. Fly, ever the optimist, was hoping after that long hot summer, she could proclaim with joy and embrace a "Let's see what you've got!" attitude just to try yet another strategy and viewpoint. They even discussed starting over with a clean slate, leaving the past behind them.

Well, it only took less than one week for the atrocities to begin being noticed, and Fly, with a disappointed sigh, took out her lilac legal pad and started documenting "just in case," not knowing where this was all going. She dated the school year on the top. Mr. Paul had now been a member of the department for a few years, so how can one not retain basic information from the previous September? Fly was stumped. Every department in the school and every school in the district did the same tasks at the same time year after year after year. It was like Groundhog Day: Pete and Repeat. There is the same opening ceremony with lukewarm coffee and stale bagels until the budget declined then even that went away, teacher time for setting up of the classrooms and bulletin board displays, looking at the rosters to see who is in the new classes, creating seating charts, the dreaded expensive back to school luncheon of cardboard sandwiches and fake, "How was your summer? OMG, welcome baa-aaack!" conversation in the sweltering hot cafeteria with huge fans just blowing the hot air around, the September paperwork that needs to be filed with the secretaries, the legal data federal student enrollment forms, the scheduled department and faculty meetings, then the first announced inspections, Halloween spooks, daylight savings sleep disruption, resetting all clocks, Parent–Teacher meet night, Professional Development Day on Election Day, get out and vote! And finally the grueling first quarter and massive report card grading is over just as teachers finally learn all of the student's names. The last part took place all in one week which became known to Ms. Fly as "The Bewitching Week." Maybe by Christmas, you learn their last names as well. And then there was the curriculum catch up around Thanksgiving as school had been shattered with all the holidays off and kids forgetting information, and then with great relief from teaching exhaustion finally comes Christmas, Chanukah, Kwanza, and a New Year. Sometimes, things changed because of laws or policies, and that still is always the worst for teachers, because while most teachers love to "be lifelong learners" and to grow and evolve, they still like consistency and routine somewhere in their school day and school year.

It was truly perplexing to Ms. Fly. Before school started, she sent him an email forwarded from the District Director Coupon Suzy about new curriculum, and he would reply in a "two-thumbs-up" tone, which had become commonplace:

> Subject: New Curriculum
>
> Hi, Fly, (deceptive cordial greeting)
>
> Thanks for the email. I had actually found it last week in the documents online, down-loaded it, and looked through already. Good Stuff! (Self-praise, You're welcome)
>
> I am going into school tomorrow morning to start and set up abit of the computers and rooms and such. Janeart said the courtyard construction materials were delivered, so I will be careful to work around them. (So nice of you to go in on your day off and thanks!)
>
> Hope your summer is going great! (deceptively nice closure)
>
> Thanks, (he was never really thankful)
>
> Paul

As Fly contemplated missing the lukewarm coffee and stale bagels, what actually would have been great would be if he implemented the information he so clearly downloaded and looked through as stated in such a peppy manner on his own time over the summer he had to stress subliminally. Again, Ms. Fly had hopes for summer rejuvenation and all her colleagues seemed to think he would come back as a renewed person each September. They would say, "Well, maybe if he gets married, he'll improve." And Fly would be like, "What the heck are you talking about? Is she going to give him the strength to teach?" As the course was new for Mr. Paul to teach, Ms. Fly being the administrator and educational leader, thought it appropriate to lesson share which teachers do all the time if they agree to share. Usually though, teachers will take the main concept or lesson and tweak it to their personal liking and interests or create a variation of the plan. Like a recipe, you do not always have to follow the plan 100 percent, you can sometimes substitute and add whatever vegetables you would like to have in your soup. You can use vegetable, chicken, or beef stock as well. So many choices and possibilities. You can add meat or make the soup vegetarian or vegan. You can add a half-sandwich if you really want to go crazy and have soup and sandwich combo. But no, Mr. Paul simply took all of Ms. Fly's curriculum handouts and used her lessons and handouts she had shared verbatim. Although she had hopes that he would create his own take on the lessons, he simply changed the fonts on the handouts and added "Mr. Paul." She suspected this is what also happened in his first few years taking lessons from the other teachers to make things easier, but in the end, there is no ownership or creativity, you are simply following someone else's recipe.

The emails came every day where Ms. Fly sat at her desk with a look of disbelief at the confusion. Despite ironically volunteering for the "Professionalism" Committee, he did volunteer to be in charge of some new school-wide activities. So every time she opened an email from Mr. Paul, there was a glimmer of hope that he was improving. The glimmers began to slowly become extinguished, like that summer fire pit when you are done for the evening of looking at the stars in the dark warm night surrounded by fireflies and fireworks enjoying the rest and peacefulness of the back yard. The fire still smoldering with embers, not allowing for change from the full-flamed logs. The Casino Posh seemed so far away in the past.

> Subject: Dates for School Activities
> Hi, Fly,
>   I followed the schedule from last year and modified the dates for this year and I wanted to see what you thought. If they sound okay,

I can go ahead and update the memo for distribution.

10/31

11/15

12/21

2/14

3/15

4/20

Thanks,
Paul

This seems like a very nice correspondence, but Ms. Fly had to reply that these were impossible dates and she thought, *What calendar exactly was he referring to, the Mayan Calendar?* It might as well have been because this was the north and south poles instantly magnetically flipping and destroying all existence as we know it. One of the dates he selected, the students would be donned up in ridiculous teenage costumes and makeup full of spooks and hormones flying everywhere; he was going to be on a field trip on the next date; another date was spring break; and yet another was the big XL Art Exam he was proctoring in, which would put him in two places at once on all of these days. But then, double-dipping was not new to him. Every single date he put for the entire year was impossible and incorrect. She should have just been able to read the email and go, "Great!" as she did with all of the other teachers but no. So basically, she thought it sucked if he really wanted to know. So Ms. Fly fixed and changed all of the dates herself to forward to the school administrators, adding a "please do not forward to the entire school, thank you." After all, Mr. Paul was being kind enough to volunteer for this activity, and actually, teachers were not permitted to email the entire faculty because that could and did sometimes easily get out of hand. One time, two teachers were going at it about parking spaces in the building group email chat, and the building faculty all witnessed the cruelty right there for everyone to read and yet nothing ever happens to these disgruntled employees. Then in retaliation, one of those teachers parked sideways across several spaces. But Mr. Paul did start to communicate a little better as outlined in yet another email, but in an unexpected area of the school-yard, not the department:

> Subject: Yesterday
> Hi, Fly, (in which he really meant Die Fly)
> I just wanted to let you know that after school before yesterday's game, I was lightly hit on the head with a ball. I am fine, just a small headache for abit, but just wanted to communicate about the incident. I was advised to fill out an injury report with the nurse just in case. But again, all is well. (Darn, no concussion? Um, also not my department, so I don't care)
> Thanks, (But no thank you)
> Paul

Each month, a new entity arose from the depths and abyss of education Ms. Fly had no awareness could exist. She rubbed her courage bracelet her Mom gave to her after her dad passed, to give her strength to survive. It was a New Year and a long, cold, relentless winter was forced upon Ms. Fly. The New Year was met with Mr. Paul starting to get caught in his own web. He enlisted the help of Linda the Librarian in teaching the students a unit on artists that they could research and create an artwork in the style, a lesson Fly had shared and was excited he had begun altering the content to his liking. But then, Ms. Fly gets a visit from sweet innocent Linda stating there was a problem! What was it that made her eyes so large with fear? Naked men with all parts including their rear. She was frantic and visibly shaking that she posted Mr. Paul's handout on the online database for the students to research, and she had clicked on one of the artists and realized the artist was not filtered on the internet and was shocked when she viewed the artwork because of its sexually explicit and charged content and nude nature. This is an amazing artist but too controversial and inappropriate for teenagers. She was the one who posted it and did not want to get into trouble. Literally that morning, Ms. Fly had emailed some good things Paul was attempting to Coupon Suzy, but then recoiled as this incident erupted like a zombie digging out of the earthen grave.

"Oh well, good feelings gone again," Ms. Fly emailed Suzy.

Worse, Ms. Fly was walking through the shared art room, and after Mr. Paul, with his widened eyes like a deer in headlights, claimed he had removed the artist from his student handout, it was clearly there in the student's binders lying all around the room for all to see that he had indeed had not done so. This was a disappointment to Ms. Fly as these artists were in her historical and educational repertoire, and it was clear that this teacher was either desensitized, had no clue, or perhaps revealed his liking of the mature subject matter. He began his reign of lies one after another after another and she wondered if he lied to everyone or just her.

When Ms. Fly didn't think things could get any more complicated about this lesson plan and she tried to put it behind her, a random artist contacted Ms. Fly about this research project and forwarded the email correspondence:

> Re: New Client Inquiry
> Random Artist: What can we help you with?
> Mr. Paul's Student: I am working on a research paper for my art class and I have chosen you. I have tried to find a biography about you, but I wasn't very successful. So if it wouldn't be too much of a trouble, I would like to request your information.
> Random Artist:
> Student,
> Thank you for providing me with your teacher's name. I called your school, and they transferred me to the department. With the outgoing message on the department voicemail, I couldn't tell if I was supposed to leave a message there or call the other number they suggested for staff. So I called back at the school's main number and asked for your teacher, Mr. Paul. They put me through to his own voicemail. Only problem is, his outgoing message says that

if I want to leave him a message, I will need to call yet *another* number. I'm sorry but I don't have time for that kind of runaround. Especially when these are all long-distance calls for me.

I'm flattered that you would choose me for your project, but I will not be able to assist you at this time. Given the fact that your request included a request for images of girls, of course, I need to look into these matters thoroughly before handing over any information to you. Your work in the style poses legal matters with the models you would be using. Your one-day turnaround request makes all of that impossible. Good luck with your assignment. Hopefully, someone else will be able to assist you on such short notice.

Random Artist

What exactly was going on in the classroom one may never know except for the two lessons inspected by administration each year. What could he have said that made this innocent student feel like they could reach out via email to a stranger, an unknown artist, and have communication with him or her? This was not safe at all, and it is bad enough teens are lured by adults and predators all the time via social media, let alone in the supposed safety of their school.

The next month, Mr. Paul finally saw what the other teachers were doing each year and each month and volunteered himself to drop off for one of the dozens of annual art shows. Again, the same art shows around the same time every year with the same criteria. How can this possibly go wrong as they were done every year? That is why it is called "annual." It could have been easily rectified, yet it was amplified by the incompetency portrayed in his attempts to communicate with Ms. Fly better:

Subject: Art Show drop off
Hey, Fly, (now more casual greeting than ever)
Sorry to bother you, but I just wanted to give you an update on the Art Show. When I got

there today, they only had us slotted for twelve pieces of artwork, three per category. We had one too many of each drawing and painting, so I called Janeart and we took two out.

But then I had to choose only three of my six Mixed Mass Media entries? They said that the Mixed Mass Media category was more "printmaking and such..."? (And they weren't nice about it either.) So I had to remove three artworks as well, saying that all six were in the Fine Arts category. One person said that Stan's typography artwork could enter as Fine Arts, but then the head woman said it could not. I ended up entering Stan's instead of Dan's in the long run when I had to decide. I took out Ann's digital widgetry piece because they said it wasn't digital, but a widgetry entry.

Then they didn't want to accept Fran's artwork, saying it should be in the Widgetry category, not the Mixed Mass Media. I pointed out the hand coloring, so she said she will "let it slide this time..."

Again, sorry to bother you with this, but I wanted to let you know that we only entered nine instead of fifteen artworks. I felt like I was getting an attitude abit about the categories and such. I apologized several times for the mix-up before I left, but they said the Mixed Mass Media category was abit confusing, and they agreed.

Have a nice weekend, (please
Dear God leave Fly alone)
Paul

Honestly, he didn't read the instructions and could this not have waited until Monday morning? It wasn't even about the artwork being removed, as there were plenty of other opportunities for the students for the upcoming several months. Kids are resilient. It's that the adult in the room could not figure out how to organize and submit work for an annual event that blocked student participation and achievement. Mr. Miyagi from *The Karate Kid* once said that there is no such thing as a bad student, only bad teacher.

And then Ms. Fly observed the clear biases like talking to the student with Down syndrome like in a creepy baby voice or trying to pronounce an Asian student's name with a stuttered mocking Asian accent like "I don't understand how to say your name" tone repeated three times, like when someone is ordering from an exotic cuisine menu and does not know how to pronounce the entrée. Ms. Fly would hear this from her office and cringe with disgust of the biases. There was no reaction from Don Voyage as she plainly stated this behavior previously. Intolerable and disgusting! A form of hate that starts with a person's name or disability.

Several times, there were extracurricular events after school that some of the teachers and Ms. Fly would conduct. More than once, Mr. Paul could see that assistance was needed; too many students or not enough hands-on deck for the activities happening as the students were excited for fun after-school activities and a chance to socialize outside of class. Ms. Fly witnessed Mr. Paul pop his head out of the office, assess the situation, see that his coworkers needed help, give a proud smiling sigh as if he was part of something amazing, and then just walk out, leaving the other teachers to struggle. This really got under Ms. Fly's skin, and it happened several times. It was not like a normal person's response to a situation like when he got scared during a sheltering drill and left the students behind. He could have just said, "Hey, sorry I would love to help, but I have a game to go to," or "I have a hangnail," or "I have to go home and do bills, sorry," or "I have to go swim with my team in the ocean with the sharks, maybe next time." Anything, please! But rather, he would give off a noticeable air of proud achievement when he actually did nothing but leave his colleagues high and dry; possibly unnoticed by them but completely observed by the keenly skilled supervisor over and over. He even put on the annual goals to add sculptures from his fine art students for the newly renovated courtyard which he never did year to year. Fly would constantly have to remove these promised goals and began to view more as sabotage since the ideas presented never came to fruition.

The following month, a random federal inspector came into the art room after inspecting the science department labs, checking the building for ground water levels and ended up shutting down the Media Lab until further notice. It was easy enough for the several staff that used the Media Lab to use digital methods as that was up and coming technology, but Mr. Paul just could not flex. Weeks went by and Mr. Paul kept trying to sneak into his lesson plans that he was going to teach a communications unit in the Lab using the federally forbidden chemicals. Ms. Fly who was one to abide by regulations, especially directives given from a Federal Institution such as OSC, the Occupational Safety Commission, kept replying.

> Re: Federal Compliance
> Okay, sorry. In your lesson plans, was that a lab assignment because I thought we discussed in the winter no Media Lab use until the federal documentation is resolved. Use the digital component of the curriculum and students should be able to complete their final exam assignment in the Media Lab. Thank you.

Three and a half weeks later:

> Subject: Plans
> Hi, Fly,
> Here are my plans for the week. If it's okay, I was going to open the Media Lab next week for the first four days of Quarter 4.
> > Thanks, (for what?)
> > Paul

Ms. Fly emailed Coupon Suzy as she was running out of ways to approach Mr. Paul. The district director responded via email simply, "Tell him directly no—short word, less confusing…" And with that, Ms. Fly did so and attached another copy of the inspection claim pending closure to the research by OSC.

His continued attempts at noncompliance were perhaps inherently intentional if no one ever told him in his life a simple no.

With that among dozens and dozens of additional incidents and obstructions, Ms. Fly had to plea for help and sat down at her desk to construct a memorandum to Principal Don Voyage. The overarching theme and theory was that Ms. Fly believed that by not following simple directions and procedures on a constant daily basis, Mr. Paul continues to put obstacles into department-wide routines and programs that would otherwise run smoothly. She felt this to be a formal written complaint listing some negligent behaviors, poor performance, and inappropriate decision-making. Don had begun the school year with some eloquent words of wisdom and gave all the middle administrators zipped bags with the following sentiment, which Ms. Fly admired and tried to follow the wisdom:

> **Essentials for Being a Successful Supervisor**
> Contents:
> Lifesavers: to remind you of the many times others need your help and you need theirs
> Rubber band: a reminder to stay flexible
> Paper clip: to help hold it together
> Marble: to help you keep rolling (or in case you lose one)
> Sweet and sour candy: to help you accept and appreciate the differences
> Eraser: to remind you that every day, you can start over with a clean slate
> Cotton balls: for pep rallies
> Aspirins: for when you feel overwhelmed
> Stress ball: whenever needed!
> Good luck!

Ms. Fly looked at her list of questionable comments he has said over the years that she placed next to the zombie bag such as this kicker during a post-inspection meeting:

Ms. Fly: Why did you not have a medial summary in the lesson?

Mr. Paul: Mrs. Coupon Suzy said that a medial summary is just to let the kids know you're in the room.

"An excuse is the skin of a lie wrapped with a reason," Coach Ernie Hornung once said. Fly never heard so many ridiculous excuses not even from her Celeste Bag of Donuts like as to why she can't clean her room. Celeste was so stressed at school that gradually over many, many weeks, Fly noticed that she had progressively plucked out all of her eyelashes. Balancing home and work is a struggle for so many working moms, they have it pretty bad. When Fly told Coupon Suzy about it in general conversation, she was shocked at how unbelievable that could be. It's called trichotillomania, induced by stress and obsessive-compulsion. Teachers should know students are stressed and doing bad things to themselves all the time, how is this shocking? Fly tried to keep herself busy at work so as to start the healing after her dad's passing. Often times, this school year, Fly would see a rainbow on her way home at the end of the long bridge over the river and it brought warmth to her mind after the chaos at work. She had applied for a large grant and was awarded enough money to create an outdoor classroom for the students. The department was even interviewed for a brief cameo on the local news channel. A student being interviewed by the reporter smoothly stated that Ms. Fly just had an idea, and then the next day, she was like, "We got the grant!" and here it is as if the process took just a few minutes like a homework. Fly thought about how much work it was behind the scenes, but she never revealed to the students her effort. She thought of the quote from a calendar she had pinned to her office inspiration board with a picture of serenely stacked rocks in a Zen garden spoken by Lao Tzu, "A leader is best when people barely know he exists, when his work is done, his aim fulfilled, they will say: we did it ourselves." She took a marker and added an "s" in front of the he to make it "she."

This was a fun time where she, the teachers, and students could use their creativity to purchase anything from the home improvement store to make this happen. Ms. Fly had a large sum of money granted. Many people from around the school helped: custodians, teachers from all departments, art and special education students, families, members of the board of education as well as administrators not afraid to spend one beautiful Saturday working to transform a neglected zombie courtyard into a beautiful student-centered space for creativity and imagination. Mr. Paul in attempts to appear as a diligent helper actually sabotaged plans by showing his brute strength hauling the wood down to the wood shop without even knowing what they were intended to create. He made sure people saw him maneuvering the heavy twelve-foot wood pieces throughout the hallways to appear as a do-gooder. Quiet tension between Fly and Paul was hampered by his ability to instantly appear over-the-top helpful with his self-satisfied grin and then the worst; he stood next to Celeste in the group photo, and it was too late for Fly to move her without being noticed. She was mortified.

It was the end of the school year, and Mr. Paul scurried around the school to create a retirement gift for all the faculty to sign their Don Voyage message. So who was Paul to Don that one teacher of hundreds felt compelled to create such a wonderful and quite large gift that would give him great publicity and praise? Teachers are not even permitted to email the entire school unless they hold a title or leading a special organized event. Teachers do not usually associate with upper administration on such a personal level and it was almost awkward. Who did he think he was emailing the faculty looking like a hero with his "Hi, Everyone! Please stop by the library and feel free to sign the amazing gift I made for Don. Thanks! Paul." Naïve Ms. Fly felt duped and everything became totally clear that Don was just riding his three-year wave to the warm sandy shores of retirement, and just then, the wave crashed and crushed Little Fly like once when she was drowning at the beach, tumbling in the rumbling waves not knowing which way was up to the air above. She tried to scream underwater, but the only words that bubbled out of her mouth muffled for no one to hear were "You've been bamboozled."

In an episode of *Castle*, "Undead Again" (S4 E22) there was a zombie apocalypse, or so seemed to the naked eye, even Beckett's supersleuth trained eye. They realize it was performance art and several zombies tied to a homicide were pulled into the precinct for questioning. One of the zombies asked,

"Listen, will this take much longer? I have class in the morning." Castle, surprised, asked if he was a student in which the zombie replied, "No. I'm a teacher. Assistant Professor of Anthropology. I believe our fascination with zombies is a cultural phenomenon, an inner numbness of modern life."

So Paul crept in dozens upon dozens of repetitive actions, incidents, and increasingly disturbing behaviors which created a zombie-like toxic workplace. He was realizing he can control chronic issues he presented to Ms. Fly that would start to be invasive, irritating, meant to disturb and get under her skin, torment and see what he could get away with unbeknownst to others. He began to devise phase 2 of his revenge plan. She punched that zombie bag one last time as she headed out to the parking lot for a much needed summer break. She would need a thousand erasers to start each day over again with a clean slate. Bon Voyage, Don, and don't let the door slam you in the rump on the way out.

America the Beautiful—American Mayhem

Mass shootings and massacres are rampant in America. School violence every day is a real threat. They begin with people becoming numb to reality, a form of zombie that makes them prey on unsuspecting innocent victims. Accessibility to weapons and semi-automatic guns to young people is making it easy for these devices to get into the hands of mentally unstable individuals. Many are teenagers not mature and evolved enough to understand the consequences of their actions. Parents, teachers, administrators, friends, and family members all need to be aware of warning signs and report anything that is unusual immediately. Laws need to be implemented to ensure that all students and staff can feel like their school is a safe place to learn and teach. There is talk that politicians have wanted teachers to be armed with guns. Are you kidding? Art teachers only want to wave paintbrushes, not weapons. Teachers are not trained nor care to support death by gun. How would they be locked up safely from children? Could one imagine an unstable teacher holding a gun in their schoolbag? It is preposterous and dangerous for everyone in any school in any state in the country.

Raise awareness with school assemblies, prepare for self-protection with lockdown drills, and teachers should not be afraid to talk to the students when they are scared of unknown possible threats. Come up with plans of action for your class-room or duty for every period starting before school to after school and discuss with your classes, just as you would practice a fire drill and where the fire is and all possible escape routes. Discuss warning signs of unstable individuals, shooter's behav-iors, past incidents, character traits, the randomness or not, and effect on society. Teachers are scared too to go to school, their place of work, every day. But teachers know their students, past students, and fellow employees and need to speak up if they have concerns. Clear MO's can be devised if investigators go back to their schoolteachers to interview their behaviors and personalities in class. Every complaint brought forth to educa-tional administration and workplace management, no mat-ter how big or small, should be taken seriously. Until this part of American culture gets fixed, teachers and employees will con-tinue to look over their shoulders, around corners, lock class-room doors when possible versus the old Open Door Policy.

Discuss school violence in America: Rachel's Challenge, the first casualty at Columbine High School, Littleton, Colorado, April 20, 1999, 11:10 a.m., cafeteria.

The shooters were two students who planned the attack for a year.

The Five Challenges:

1. Look for the best in others.
2. Dream big.
3. Choose positive influences.
4. Speak with kindness.
5. Start your own chain reaction.

"I have this theory that if one person can go out of their way to show compassion, then it will start a chain reaction of the same. People will never know how far a little kindness can go" (Rachel Joy Scott).

Word Wall

"passive-aggressive" adjective pa•sive•e•gre•siv
   1. being marked by or displaying behavior character-ized by the expression of negative feelings, resent-ment, and aggression in an unassertive passive way
   2. denoting or pertaining to a personality type or behav-ior marked by the expression of negative emotions in passive, indirect ways, as through manipulation or noncooperation

---

FAST FACT

April 16, 2007, 7:15 a.m.
32 dead, plus 23-year-old male student shooter who killed self (student)
Virginia Tech, Blacksburg, Virginia

December 14, 2012, 9:40 a.m.
26 dead, plus 20-year-old male shooter who killed self after also killing his mom
Sandy Hook Elementary School, Newtown, Connecticut

February 14, 2018, 2:19 p.m.
17 dead, 19-year-old male to be sentenced (former student)
Stoneham Douglas High School, Parkland, Florida

May 24, 2022, 11:33 a.m.
21 dead, plus 18-year-old male killed by police (Uvalde High School student)
Robb Elementary School, Uvalde, Texas

July 4, 2022, 10:14 a.m.
7 dead, 22-year-old male apprehended (former Highland Park High School student)
Highland Park Fourth of July Parade, Highland Park, Illinois
School function for the Highland Park High School Marching Band

Does anyone notice a pattern here and if so, please send help!

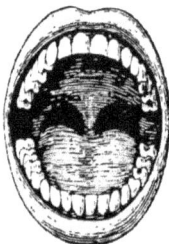

Notable Quotables

Where there is no vision, the people will perish.
—Proverbs 29:18

Lesson #2

This school year Fly finally learned the true meaning of Liar, Liar, Pants on Fire!

Gut Instinct

Act Out!

Journal Entry: Did anyone ever blatantly lie to you or have you ever lied that ended up hurting someone else? Do you know anyone who has lied and it created chaos because it was untruthful? Why do you think people feel the need to lie? Do you feel a white lie or a deceptive lie is okay? Why or why not? Would you ever apologize to the person you lied to and how would you do that? Listen to one of the many songs of different genres by various musicians over the decades dedicated to the concept of lying. Write an apology letter if you feel you might have hurt someone in the past on the following blank page. You can give it to them, tear it up, or burn it on the fire pit and just whisper, "Sorry."

Chapter 3
Jekyll and Hide and Seek

It's September again.

Hence it all came about that I concealed my pleasures; and when I reached years of reflection, and began to look around me, and take stock of my progress and position in the world, I stood already committed to a profound duplicity of life. Many a man would have even blazoned such irregularities as I was guilty of; but from the high views that I had set before me I regarded and hid them with an almost morbid sense of shame. It was thus rather the exacting nature of my aspirations...severed in me those provinces of good and ill which divide and compound man's dual nature.

—Robert Louis Stevenson
The Strange Case of Dr. Jekyll and Mr. Hyde

Cue the Music:
"Hot and Cold" by Katy Perry
"You're Somebody Else" by Flora Cash
"Come as You Are" by Nirvana

Tsunami

It is September and the entire month of August has felt like one long stressful, sleepless Sunday night. Initiate the eye twitching and other job stress-related oddities. People think that teachers have the good life, just hanging around for two months all summer long, and for many, that is probably true. Many teachers spend summer days taking college credits for promotion, subject area–related conferences for personal growth, workshops on infusing new technologies, and preparing for new courses they may be teaching in the fall. They might be reading curriculum at the beach, but it still gets done before school starts. Many need to take on summer jobs or add hours to their second side hustle jobs they have to maintain during the school year just to make ends meet, especially teachers who have families. The last few weeks of August were always the worst when boredom rises as the wallet gets thinner and the summer lump money runs dry. Then, the entire month of September feels like "Someone's got a case of the Mondays," from *Office Space*. It might as well be a zombie apocalypse as the Mayan calendar has impending doom, and the next few months will be riddled with hurricanes, tornadoes, heat waves, droughts, wildfires, and earthquakes across the United States. Total catastrophe will happen, dark skies, the earth explodes. Fly asked her family if they thought they should "bang out" of work on December 21 just in case? Fly's younger brother always used that term and did it a lot. "Banging out." She wasn't quite sure what it meant but assumed it was a last-minute decision and last-stitch effort to avoid impending doom at work. Would Fly really rather be at work struggling with Mr. Paul and all of his problems rather than being cozy at home with her family in case the earth's poles decided to shift and instantly squish all continents according to the Mayans or if the sun exploded and melted the planet?

Ms. Fly came up with a positive theme for the newly built courtyard, "Imagine" by John Lennon. She always felt at peace with those lyrics and wanted the courtyard to reflect this ideology. It only took about three weeks into September before the first incident of many to come would rear its ugly head. But

Ms. Fly decided to not waste too much time on Mr. Paul and took the advice of Mrs. Parabola and focus on more important departmental needs and the faculty that provided mutual and respectful collegiality and inspiration. Mrs. Parabola was always to the point during their twenty-minute lunch hours and suggested that Ms. Fly not waste her talent and precious time on him anymore if he was not going to do his part. This individual had messed up so badly for several years now in Fly's eyes; with curriculum, community, student safety, student's best interests, and let's not forget the federal regulations. To her, she had scratched a line in the sand, and ever so slowly, the line had been crossed, the swift winds blowing across the beach with each particle of sand filling in the line until it disappears. It had been enough years now to know better, well beyond the rookie mistake excuses, and she felt she had given him plenty of opportunity to do a better job so she turned her focus to people who appreciated being around her and getting her advice, help with their teaching and admired her leadership. Fly contemplated the phrase, "Those who can't do, teach." This was a repulsive statement to Fly as she actually enjoyed creating art when she did have spare time and valued the profession of teaching and enjoyed sharing her love of art and widgetry to each and every one of her students every day. Perhaps those who can't teach should just "do," as an observant student thought he just came out to "do" teaching. Do whatever, but please do it somewhere else.

Little Fly had always been terrified of tsunamis, and they often would appear, like in the movies, in her dreams when the workplace was in dire turmoil. Worse than depictions in the movies were the vast amount of recent tsunamis where people were just going about their day, working, eating, driving, walking, vacationing on the beach and the waters receded unexplainably, then rushed, swallowing everything and everyone in its path. The wave did not care what race, religion, social, or economic status you were or had. It relentlessly pushes forward over and over again until its thirst is quenched. Ever since that hot summer day, being plunged into the murky waters keeping her tight under the grip of the surface, tumbling as if in a washing machine, that she only went back into the ocean once.

And when she did decades later with her family, it happened again, so maybe some things cannot ever change. Did Fly not learn how to jump waves? Why did she not just dive through the enormous wave as her husband and child did, rather than attempt to jump over the gigantic growing wave that came to its true height and brute strength just as it glided toward her? She thought herself to be that ten-foot-tall Drum Major able to conquer water. It was like twelve feet tall as it lifted her feet off the ocean floor, elevating her body up, then dragging her alongside it to shore. To Fly, the wave did not look that large in the distance, but as it slowly crept toward her, its shadow towered above her, finally encapsulating her. The great wave won, and once again, pummeling her into the salty depths below. The hurricane season encroached which was as tumultuous as the manner in which Paul stormed his way to, through, and surrounding her spiraling out of control with one hundred mile per hour winds totally engulfing in his fury. There was no escape from the bands of wind slicing Fly on and on and what was worse about a hurricane is the predictability and knowledge it is coming ahead of time. The Mayan calendar predicted doom that year.

September began with Paul wanting superintendent approval for graduate level "Stress Management" courses and "Surviving and Embracing New Teacher Evaluation System" for salary increase. Knowing these were absurd requests, Ms. Fly, placing her energy elsewhere, simply forwarded to the main offices for someone else to deal with. As assumed, the requests were unfounded due to lack of substance and denied stating that "forty-five hours for salary advancement seems like a long time to talk about stress management." And one needs a course on surviving teacher evaluations? Denied. The rest of the fall was riddled with the same old nonsensical mistakes that wasted precious time to keep fixing: adding too many comments on report cards, not knowing where to get basic forms, not showing up for professional development courses even though they were for salary advancement, inability to properly fill out field trip forms, having No Good News items to add to the list that the other teachers had compiled which really was beginning to appear inequitable on how much of the department work the other teachers were doing in comparison.

Fly had to keep reporting No Good News to Coupon Suzy which was getting annoying. All of the "Good Stuff" rest on the shoulders of the other art teachers and Ms. Fly herself, as well as an unusual increase in workload that was brought on by the director and the district as the evaluation systems were changing. Was it mandatory to put all of this extra work upon the art supervisors constantly? Did the director feel the arts had to do way more work than the other departments so they would not get cut or they could be noticed in a "Look at me!" scenario? Look at how much work we do. Fly did not know the reasons for the ever increased workload, but either way, it is nice when teachers go above and beyond to create special activities and events that interested students can participate in outside of the classroom. Also outside of the classroom, after several more play dates out on the town with the girls, Coupon Suzy and her spouse stated oddly, "We decided to let you be our friends," and when Fly's husband heard that, they were both in agreement: thank you, but no thank you. From then on, the relationship amicably faded away and was kept strictly professional with meetings and exhibitions and for no particular reason except that Little Celeste was transforming into a more mature Celeste and was getting too old to do the little kid activities they once enjoyed together.

There was one noticeable change so far this school year in that there were finally others who were experiencing some of the items that Ms. Fly kept identifying to her supervisors; the same group of now senior Lost Boys were being rude and disrespectful to another female department head and that supervisor directly pinpointed their rude behavior to be the result of Mr. Paul's guidance. She gave specific information on how difficult it was to work on whatever project with Mr. Paul and that the boys he selected to help were unruly and mean. They were the Lost Boys. A parent called to say a situation was going on in Mr. Paul's classroom with their child, but that the teacher was unaware. And finally, Ms. Fly emailed yet another colleague for input on Mr. Paul's lesson for a new course because it just did not seem in alignment and to no avail, the colleague agreed that he himself taught a similar lesson for Freshman Foundation and said it was, "Probably from clip art and I think it is too rudimentary for a tenth grade course of potential XL Art-ers." While these instances helped solidify Ms. Fly's notions, it was not enough because entangled within the course of this "rudimentary" unit was also lateness, ignoring the district curriculum, the number of days required to complete units was very off target, the lessons did not help the sequence of learning from grade level to grade level, the teacher artwork examples were of poor quality, and there was no diversity in choice of artists presented as required by the district. For these reasons, isolated appeared insignificant but combined impacted the department, so Ms. Fly thought it necessary to cc: the New Principal Teddy. Just a few weeks prior at the turn of the New Year, Ms. Fly finally met officially with New Principal Teddy to inform him of the situation, as it would not have been decent to fill him in September upon taking over an entire new school. With that, he slowly absorbed all of the information she provided and things she had done to help, and he seemed to listen with an open mind. Ms. Fly thought there was finally hope and that changes could be made, so she was excited that maybe, just maybe someone intelligent could figure out a simple and effective solution to this problem.

There was one mediocre accomplishment and inspection after another year after year and Ms. Fly realized that Mr. Paul at this point may be beyond help and growth since he clearly did not take written and verbal suggestions seriously, in fact ignored or began now doing the opposite at times. Maybe, as suggested by Coupon Suzy, Ms. Fly did not have the "authority" to request such items from a "tenured" teacher, but nonetheless, it should be expected that teachers are doing their job to at least a certain degree of accuracy otherwise, what is the purpose of a supervisor? Fly and her husband would have vent sessions at home about their educational establishment workplaces, and they would often act out the scene from *South Park* where Cartman pulls over a man for driving forty miles per hour in a forty miles per hour speed zone. Dressed as a cop down to the aviator sunglasses reflecting the distant mountains, he yells at the innocent man to "Respect my authoritaih!" and beats

him repeatedly with the police stick. He does this in many episodes struggling with his inner ego and fighting hierarchy. "Hey,
you can't beat him up, that's not how it's done!" one exclaims.
Cartman replies, "But he is not listening to my authoritaih!" Fly
and her husband would mimic the line in commanding deep
drawls, "You will respect my authoritaih!" and laugh. They finally
left work vent sessions to ten minutes per person, a wise strategy
employed by a fellow professor in order to maintain a happy
marriage.

Mr. Paul must have been infuriated when Ms. Fly emailed
a memo about concerns and items and cc'd New Principal
Teddy. Mustering up the courage and feeling like Teddy was
receptive to conquering this dilemma, Fly sent it, believing that
one should be responsible for their actions and performance
and this was ultimately having negative impact on the students, faculty, and department as a whole making things more
difficult for others which was becoming increasingly noticeable
and unfair for the coworkers as some began voicing instances
and their concerns. She jotted everything down dated in her
lilac legal pad. Fly just simply wanted people to respect her
authoritaih!

Students came first in Ms. Fly's eye, their right to a sound
and fair education and right to learn and be taught with excellence and in a safe and inspiring environment. The right to all
be treated equally no matter their race, sex, identity, orientation, size, financial status, religion, etc. In reality, these student's
families were actually paying their teacher salaries via taxes so
owed it to them. Ms. Fly had gone to one of the most prestigious
art colleges in the United States, got her graduate degree in
education from an Ivy League University with a 4.0 and another
graduate degree in educational leadership, so why should
she start questioning her positions now? She had to stand her
ground. She sifted through her notes, and from exactly a year
ago, she found jotted down on the notepad that Mr. Paul was
supposed to be addressing things that were suggested during
the inspection process in order to improve instruction and
productivity. Of course, handwritten in the margins dated Fly
wrote, "Second semester- Don V. No help. Ignored issues." She
reviewed the contents that were for the teacher as well as for

her own reference. While these bulleted notes included professional terminology and pedagogical phrases, Ms. Fly's notes to herself included highlighted concerns, constant misinterpretation of information, evidence of not being self-sufficient, poor communication and comprehension skills, noncompliance with federal investigation, intentional concealment (information found out by others,) and then transformed into...insubordination. Not following directions on the first or second time. Fast forward to this school year, and nice Ms. Fly was starting to get fed up with how much time this was consuming of her daily life. So in a follow-up meeting regarding the cc'd memo she struggled to put her "nice teacher persona" aside and point blank with a serious demeanor asked, "What is going on?" Nervously, reacting to a new Fly approach, Mr. Paul stated that it was a result of the storm and rambled about some other irrelevant items, and she finally called his bluff by sternly responding, "This has been going on well before the storm." And with that, she ended the meeting, folded up her notepad, and walked out. She learned that strategy during her leadership courses. Meeting over, period, end of sentence.

Like a tsunami that gets very quiet and withdraws from the edge of the sandy beach, the water pulling away even very hard to see where it went, it crashes back to shore with unforgivable vengeance consuming everything in its path.

I Stepped from Plank to Plank

I stepped from plank to plank
So slow and cautiously;
The Stars about my head I felt
About my feet the Sea.

I knew not but the next
Would be my final inch-
This gave me that precarious gait
Some call experience.

—Emily Dickenson

The PTA Meeting

With the continued issues going on, whether the coworkers knew about it or not, he appeared now more as intentional "undermining" Ms. Fly than the initial rookie mistakes. His actions were morphing from one thing to another in a disguise no one could notice. Once an indifferent zombie-esque attitude was transforming into two distinct appearances much like the "self-portrait" duality image from last year. He would do things incorrectly but then literally look like the cat that ate the canary; with an over-the-top grin while intentionally being superhelpful to others in the department all at the same time. Simultaneously emerged hostility toward Fly while exhibiting "good guy" attitude to others. This must be the beginning of phase 2 of Paul's revenge plan, but Fly would not realize that for some time to come, and it crept up on her like that gigantic wave which appeared so small at the horizon. With practice, he could now swiftly transition from the sad puppy dog face dragging his feet from the parking lot, through the courtyard to the double door entrance, down the long glass-windowed hallway for everyone to see as if he were being the abused and apprehensive about going into work, then immediately turn with a swift scowl at Fly in perhaps 0.5 seconds, just a quick deviant sharp glance passing in the hallway. Sending chills through her body, Fly had to figure something out fast because she would not be able to survive much more of such intimidation tactics.

March Madness marked the start of "the silent treatment," ignoring, and not making eye contact on top of the fact there was no response to any conversation or questions in the past. Mr. Paul's buddy Don Voyage had gone bon voyage and he had to figure out how to manipulate the New Principal Teddy. One evening, Fly went home to pick up Little Celeste who was not quite yet mature Celeste and went back to attend a PTA meeting because a group of students were getting awards for a contest and she was too young to be left home alone. PTA back in Fly's grandparent's days had an entirely different meaning. They sat there awkwardly with all the Mommy Vals, the new principal, and Mr. Paul, yet at the same time, everyone was showing immense pride with the student's accomplishments.

After each student received their awards and certificates, Ms. Fly gathered up the students for a group photo for public relations as she did at all student achievement ceremonies. After successfully arranging the students with the New Principal Teddy and taking the picture, she and Celeste gathered their bags, and as they began exiting the school cafeteria, Little Celeste looked concerned and frightened and whispered into her mom's ear. Fly was concerned and bent over to hear what she had to say and stated, "Mom, Paul rolled his eyes and made a face at you as you were trying to get the group photo."

Fly's heart dropped and she began ushering Celeste out of there swiftly through the dark lit hallway devoid of student traffic; she tried to hold in the tears and anguish until they could get all the way down the hall to the other side of the school out to the darkly lit parking lot of that cold night to the safety of their car. His anger had become visible to someone else than Fly, which escalated and became increasingly more frightening. Celeste also had the super power to see the true Paul that he tried so hard to conceal from her. Fly had already informed the new principal, so she thought it relevant to let District Director Coupon Suzy know precisely what was going on in at first a handwritten letter from her lilac legal pad, then in a formal complaint. The letter was initially directed to Suzy as a work-friend and that for her own child to witness the aggression, well, he crossed the line. The follow-up was to have a formal paper trail of notification.

> Re: Employee Concern
>
> I am writing to you to formally express my concerns regarding department employee, Mr. Paul. As you are aware, Mr. Paul has had performance issues since he was hired; however, was granted tenure against my professional recommendation. Last month, I met with the principal and asked for an involuntary transfer of Mr. Paul for a multitude of reasons.
>
> Mr. Paul has proven to perform in an inconsistent, unreliable, and questionable manner. In addition, he continues to lack the ability to be

self-sufficient and has exhibited chronic insubordination, constant undermining and disrespectful behavior, and offensive and deliberate
unwelcomed actions, enough to create what I
feel is a stressful and unproductive, fruitless, ineffective work environment.

His characteristics as only I as his immediate
supervisor might experience and notice include
passive-aggressive tendencies, chronic lying
and excuses, indifference, deception, concealment and saboteur actions. Whether intentional or unintentional, this situation for me has
reached its limit. Numerous strategies to alleviate the strain and reduce personal conflict for
both parties have been implemented for years
with little, insincere, or short-lived success. It
does not help that past administrators turned a
blind eye to my concerns and complaints, if yet,
rewarded him for out of department and extracurricular activities.

Fly was one of the most truthful of people out there, which
also sometimes came to bite her in the butt. She recalls several
times when she was in high school where honesty was met with
adult conflict, but her parents always backed her up with facts,
whether it be a teacher or a priest in handwritten letters she
found alongside the *Taffy Sinclair* book:

Dear Mom and Dad,
This is to inform you that I did not complete my
homework assignment for Tuesday, May 19.
Fly

There were two hand-drawn lines for paren-
tal signatures.

Fly's parents responded:

> Dear Mr. Ford,
>   Our daughter is a very good student, who is on the honor roll, and she does her homework consistently. As per Fly, the children in third period social studies believed you were going to "go over" the questions on Wednesday, the twentieth with no mention of homework or of having to complete the questions on their own time.
>   We're sure there was a misunderstanding of the clarification of this assignment; therefore, we feel it is not necessary to sign this paper. Please feel free to call us if you wish to discuss this matter further.
>
> Sincerely,
(both Fly's parents signed the note
back but not the paper)

Fly also found this letter in the keepsake pile, clarifying her honesty:

> Dear Father Jerry,
>   Regarding the interview on Friday, February 1, I honestly must convey my feelings regarding our daughter, Fly, as a candidate for confirmation.
>   With your question to her about regular attendance at Mass, you tested her strengths. She could not bring herself to lie to you (as many of her Val friends boasted of doing). She does not lie to anyone, especially to herself. To me, this is reason enough for receiving the Sacrament of Confirmation. The in-depth feelings of responsibility for her own actions, which we earnestly tried to teach her, came shining through. We know that Fly will take her Confirmation Day at a deep level of commitment. Since she is true to herself, she'll be true to the Catholic Church,

as well as Christianity as a whole. The world is a better place because of God's reaching out to strengthen special children like Fly.

Sincerely,
Fly's mom

Fly was brutally honest in her letters to each administrator and supervisor she reached out to over these years. She supported her statements with evidence, just as she would have her art students support discussing a work of art with giving evidence and examples as to their rationales. When Fly begged for a viable win-win solution to be determined and acted upon, Coupon Suzy replied that this was an administrative issue, not a supervisory one, that there were many procedures that had to be in place for a transfer or "trade," the caliber of the trade and where to and from, and that it would be easier for Ms. Fly to ask for a transfer of herself, if she were a teacher, but no one gets to choose the school transferred to. She even suggested they themselves trade schools as an unusual possibility. As for the personal treatment of Fly, she recommended a meeting set up by the administration and union navigators, but if there was not enough solid examples, it could backfire, or as stated later in the spring, all of this information could make it look like Ms. Fly was the harasser! The Columbine students who went haywire felt they were bullied and then in turn targeted specific students discriminatorily. Fly did not have a violent bone in her body except punching boxing bags for exercise and stress relief. Fly sat contemplating the irony of the situation as there was a new law absolutely forbidding bullying and harassment of students in schools. The new law included mandatory documentation with official forms and prompt investigation with a swift resolution by designated neutral school building faculty. For example, for a student who may have been found to have concretely bullied another in a protected class, they could be suspended from school or other consequences. Ms. Fly's heart dropped as they celebrated "Bullying Awareness Week" in order to highlight and educate the school about the new legal changes and there Mr. Paul was, singing and dancing with an anti-bullying Swiftie song shakin' it off right along in the hallway in full view of the main office staff and assistant principals. As the song blasted through the hallways over the PA system, Fly cringed and retreated to her office in retaliation of such hypocrisy. There were flyers taped to the walls, "No Bullying Zone." Yeah right. She took a picture and put it in her binder.

Release the Kraken

Mr. Paul's formal inspections have not improved, and Ms. Fly dreaded conducting the next one the very same week as the PTA meeting. She always took extensive notes handwritten on her lilac legal pads for all of the teacher's inspections so that she can quote back to them their own words to be used as a learning device. She was highly trained in observational skills and lesson planning assessment by the university as well as the district and had observed repeatedly a dozen faculty, teachers, and fellow supervisors in the classroom for peer review. She even inspected Mrs. Parabola's classes and Foreign Language, proving one does not really need to know about Algebra or German in order to know what a great, solid, and inspirational lesson looks like. Inspectors look for planning, preparation, classroom environment, instruction and questioning, rapport with students, group activities, motivational strategies, and much more. Ms. Fly inspected a class completely in German, and while she could not say if the language part was accurate, the lesson components should be recognizable: Do Now Activity, taking attendance, demonstrations, motivation, topic question, interaction with students, higher questioning, sound discussion, planned activities, manipulatives, use of technology, medial summaries, assessing student outcomes, final summaries, just to name a few. So you can see, there's a lot that goes into teaching. Teaching is very complex but can be boxed into areas for assessment. The last inspection for Mr. Paul was not extremely terrible; however, the dialogue was basic in nature as in not really challenging student thinking. Yes or no questions were asked and it was unremarkable. Ms. Fly wondered how he interpreted the curriculum in that he was having all students create shared work yet they were creating individual portfolios which was confusing, and he called on boys twenty-one times and girls only four times, which has obvious levels and implications of bias, but unfortunately, she just let that one go, knowing she had to pick her battles. And there were equal amounts of boys and girls so it was not like there were only four girls in the class. She also began to let techniques like that go because the new law protected students who were gender neutral or identify in their own manner, so this should bring an end to the traditional issues and questions of male/female disparity in education, knowing there are more than two choices.

The next inspection was going to be planned and even had a teacher requested pre-observation conference, so Ms. Fly generally knew what this particular lesson was going to be all about. Whether Mr. Paul was nervous or just performing as normal, one would categorize this lesson as a total disaster soup to nuts, worse than the storm that destroyed everything earlier that year. At the end of the period, Ms. Fly ran to Mrs. Parabola for help and to exclaim she had just observed the worst lesson she had ever seen and did not know what to do, except write it verbatim as the notetaking and quotes stated. How could one keep having rookie mistakes? The lesson was about lettering and then Mr. Paul tried to show off by using a special computer camera technique, but to his surprise, the letters projected backward and reverse, and in turn, it completely confused the students. He was speechless and was taken aback at the mistake and scrambled to fix this key component of the lesson. The word *wolf* appeared as *flow* and could not be unseen by all. During the last observation, the bell rang, as usual, in the middle of his sentence or closing remarks and his words just faded away as he let the students just walk out on the conversation, not caring. It was almost embarrassing. But this inspection was not trivial like that and there was something direly wrong. He displayed an excessive amount of books as samples to illustrate the idea of lettering for the lesson, and it was overwhelming. She wrote it up and sent it along its new digital path for review.

A few days later, Ms. Fly lands in the emergency room physically ill, practically bleeding to death. She had symptoms coming on since the fall, but one doctor said she just had hemorrhoids which Fly was like, "What? That makes no sense. Why would I have that? I don't even know what those are." Over the winter, Fly took Celeste on a Val Scout trip to the city and that is when she first started having serious problems. Fly wanted to help broaden Celeste's horizons and start exposing her to possibilities the world can offer so she tried fencing, dance, music, water sports of all types. But Fly struggled that travel day and felt slightly ill for no apparent reason. Terrified to leave Little Celeste alone at the restaurant table in a big city full of danger and strangers, they both left their lunches and sat in the bathroom for an unusually long time. There were guacamoles everywhere. That was their secret duress word for stranger or weirdo. BOLO or be on the lookout. For instance, if they were in the checkout line at the grocery store and a strange man started unnecessary conversation or crept uncomfortably too close to their personal space in line behind them, Fly would calmly ask, "Oh, Celeste, did you want guacamole and chips for dinner?" Knowing that was not the dinner they had planned, Little Celeste would scan the surrounding area and spy the creep. When Celeste Bag of Donuts was little and just learning language, her favorite song was Green Day's "Boulevard of Broken Dreams," and true to herself being an eternal loner, she would head thrash and stomp her feet, marching around the living room in only a diaper, "I guacamone, I guaca" in place of "I walk alone, I walk a—" and the secret code "guacamole" was born.

But on this day, Fly did not know what was happening and it was not normal, and anytime blood is in the toilet bowl, one gets scared and confused. What was going on down there? They were in there for quite a while, but finally returned to the table to finish and settle the bill. She didn't think much of it, and in her busy working-Mom days, found a way to carve out some time to consult with a few doctors and specialists, and after several tests, finally one doctor sat Fly down in his office after an uncomfortable exam and flat-out stated, "You have acute ulcerative colitis."

Stunned, Fly simply asked, "I know what acute means but what the heck is ulcerative colitis? I never heard of it."

Her heart dropped and a wave of heat and fear came over her. She whipped out her phone to see if she could look it up quickly for an explanation. The other doctor said it was just hemorrhoids. Someone was wrong.

Fly's husband abruptly showed up at Celeste's school to pick her up. "Something's wrong with Mom," he said frantic and confused. They rushed to the hospital to meet up with her in the emergency room. Fly did not know the negative impact this unknown and upcoming chronic cycle of hospitalizations and the fear and trauma would illicit in her daughter Celeste and her husband for years to come. At the time, she was only concerned about herself and her health. The unknown of when a flare-up episode would occur and what could possibly trigger it was perplexing and not concrete. Queasy, butterflies in stomach, pain, urgency. The unknown about the debilitating disease was frustrating. There was no rhyme or reason; it did not discriminate who it attacked. It just was.

Fly immediately started on a regimen called Assacort and a biologic infusion in the hospital, and she was there for quite a few days. Who calls a medicine a name like that for a rear-end issue and Fly's husband even analyzed that the package art looked like the body part it was helping. Although they chuckled about the product name and design as analytical artists, how sad. Despite being sicker than a dog, she liked to say, she spent several days admitted to the hospital to help mend her back together. They tried a strong dose of Ramicadence, a multi-hour infusion, and as the wave of chemicals rushed into her body, she began to feel a sense of relief.

Returning to work, Fly met with the teacher in a delayed post-inspection meeting and that is where the stars did not align. Mr. Paul felt the lesson went well and as planned, which was the answer always to the first mandatory question posed. And after several years of this ongoing nonsense, Ms. Fly mustered up more courage than usual to flat-out firmly disagree and his perception was not what actually happened during this particular lesson. Maybe the medicine and intense amount of steroids helped give her super strength, but she was the higher educated one disputing the party college-educated teacher and perhaps she found comfort being heard and supported by the new principal. Each component of the observation model rubric was carefully reviewed and clarified, and suggestions and strategies were given to help improve instruction. So it was like explaining to an art student why exactly they got a D- on their painting project. You got that score because of planning and preparation, the way you created the composition, the painting techniques you used, the colors you chose to combine, your originality and creativity with regard to idea, effort, remaining on task and completing by the deadline. You follow the rubric and that how the evaluation device works.

What was next to come from the mouth of a person who said that there was no evacuation during the major natural disaster earlier in the school year was despicable. After being stuck in the storm and upon return back to school a week later, Ms. Fly was genuinely concerned and asked Mr. Paul, "What happened?"

He looked Ms. Fly directly in the eyes with that familiar deer in headlights look and stated, "They did not evacuate us until it was too late."

Absolutely stunned, she paused to think about how absurd the statement was because everyone was told to evacuate two whole days in advance and could only think to reply with, "Don't you watch the news? *Everyone* knew it was coming."

It was not like a sudden unexpected tornado or earthquake, relentless, making a destructive path along the way as it rips through the earth with unknown direction and path. It was a slow-moving and ravaging storm and everyone had the entire sunny and warm weekend off to prepare and batten down the hatches. Fly recalls because that was Celeste's birthday weekend, and they had to move it along in order to be preppers. And so with that, the ultimate blatant lie was told. Fake news, the ultimate oxymoron like jumbo shrimp. She sat there alone in her office, wondering, "Did he say that to everyone, and if so, how did they react? Did he only state this to me to disturb or gain sympathy that he was stuck in the storm or did he actually think the government did not let them know for safety they should evacuate?" It was truly perplexing and shocking, but Fly would not be able to prove what he said once again as it was done alone in the corner of the classroom, which seemed to be an increasing strategy he would employ.

Little did Mr. Paul know that Ms. Fly struggled with not only her health situation at the moment, but also writing the inspection report and confided in the New Principal Teddy for help and guidance as to how to proceed. She was given the thumbs-up supportive approval to write it as it was viewed and it even went back and forth several times via email for revision: "The discussed adjustments were made and summary reflects my notes verbatim. I'll have hard copies for you Monday morning. Thank you for your attention to this matter. It is greatly appreciated." Ms. Fly followed the well-known motto, "Honesty is the best policy." She visited one of her supervisor colleagues and in the classroom was a poster displayed containing some advice for students:

> THINK before you speak:
> Is it...**T**rue?
> Is it...**H**elpful?
> Is it...**I**mportant?
> Is it...**N**ecessary?
> Is it...**K**ind?

At this point, Ms. Fly had given Mr. Paul every opportunity to do a better job and improve not just with teacher tasks, but for the education of the children. Her job was to supervise, so if things were not being done accurately that would have to be documented or else the catch-22 double-edged sword was that *she* wasn't doing *her* job. And then there it was—a devastating response to the inspection report riddled with lie upon lie. Once again, Ms. Fly sat in her office at the computer regurgitating the shiny CD gifted to her and now reading an incredulous response. Why on earth would Ms. Fly make up something so outrageous like four students were eating snacks or lunch in class during the lesson, and it was completely denied as he wrote that no one was eating in the class. There was either food or no food, it was that simple. Fly was pretty sure she documented it throughout her notes in her notepad and returned to the evidence, the facts. He really thought he was hot stuff and this inspection shattered his reflection of self, like Narcissus in Greek mythology. The handsome young pageboy cannot find true love, so one day, he walks by a glassy pool of water and notices the most beautiful being he had ever seen. He stares into the dark abyss at his very own reflection, and when he leans in to kiss the water's edge, his lips create a wake of ripples in the water and his perfect reflection is obfuscated with the waves and he finally dies of thirst because he cannot help but attempt to only see himself as a perfect image, a perfect teacher.

And there were a few obvious slips of the tongue that the Young Yuppie-Mediocre Millennial Teacher Clique XL English teacher who Ms. Fly thought most likely wrote the letter, total plagiarism and slander on his behalf. The letter tormented Ms. Fly over and over again, and she was in disbelief with what she was reading. There were XL English level vocabulary words throughout the letter that even Fly had to look up what they meant, so it was clear this was a forgery. It was written like an XL English research paper far from the cryptic emails she was "abit" familiarized receiving from him. After several incredulous points Mr. Paul stated in his response that four students were not eating in the classroom, but then stated if they were, it was because he witnessed Ms. Fly accommodating her students with lunch during her class. This was a faulty statement because Ms. Fly did not teach during a lunch period and why would he be stalking or spying on her classes? She looked at the class schedules, and sure enough, this was an impossibility. He was probably mistaken when Ms. Fly let the LGBTQ, shy, and out-cast kids come sit in the classroom to eat lunch during her free period so they could have a safe zone. This was infuriating. He also stated that his flyers were not posted at a ridiculous height and behind the door where students could not view for that les-son, but the ones for that lesson were placed lower in admission the others were placed at the ceiling. Honestly, Fly went in and photographed the flyers as evidence, same as she had done with the mismatched organizer bins and incorrectly identified lesson samples and placed them in her binder as evidence. He also claimed the lettering he held up in order to show off his high-tech gimmick was not projected backward and reverse. It was a triple lie sandwich with a schmear of fibbing on top.

He went on and on in several paragraphs about how his reputation was being tarnished and how much he valued education and admired constructive feedback. The letter was so egregious and there it was, the finale, just as District Director Coupon Suzy predicted could happen: he felt that *he* was the one being unfairly targeted. He himself claimed to be the victim rather than the victimizer. Mr. Paul had morphed and transformed into the ultimate Mr. Passive-Aggressive Undermining Liar. He did not THINK clearly. He had proven to be not Truthful, nor Helpful, did not present much of Importance, it was all not Necessary, and he was really not Kind, at least to his direct supervisor.

Disgusted but trying to focus on her health, Ms. Fly was in the hidden back room of the Widgetry Lab the following week when out of nowhere, Mr. P.A.U.L. intentionally sought her out and tiptoed in like the Grinch about to steal Christmas stockings and ornaments, for no apparent reason and eerily said to her, "Oh, there you are. I forgot to wish you a *Happy Birthday!*" and abruptly receded like the precursor of the ultimate devastating tsunami wave. This was not the first time he sought Ms. Fly out at an inopportune time and in fact, with no area to escape either physically by a door or literally like during a lesson while teaching. But this time, she was trapped with nowhere for the unexpected and relentless crashing wave to go. This is the same person who recently refused to take the *Pay It Forward* gifts Ms. Fly's art students created to help those who suffered loss during the storm. It dawned on her he had become Chindi, a shape shifter causing illness and death. But a chindi of whom? He had taken her last breath as she could utter no more words.

Fly was familiar with shape shifting and transformation as she and her younger brother would play "Wonder Twin Powers Activate!" growing up. The brother-sister duo would transform into anything that they wanted to be to save the day. They fist pump and the explosion from their strong bond of their hands ensue in red blaring hues, "Form of an octopus! Form of an ice-unicycle!" With ridiculous transformation requests, they were off to fight the aliens! Fly would always pick something innocent like a rainbow that stretched across the entire sky and her brother would always pick something like laser beam flying moped. They watched movie classics like *The Clash of the Titans* where the monstrous Kraken got released and instead of conquering got defeated by turning into stone and crumbling into the sea with its true inner self being revealed. Duality is very complex. But like in *The Strange Case of Dr. Jekyll and Mr. Hyde*, someone could be one thing one minute and a monster the next.

Ms. Fly always understood that there are sometimes two sides to a story, perhaps three or more, even multi-faceted like a kaleidoscope. But she felt she was being punched in the stomach, sickened with vulgar and accusatory statements and delusions. It felt like the time in elementary school when she was targeted and *bam* got the wind knocked right out of her falling to the ground as that dodgeball squarely hit her in the gut. She could not breathe as she lay limp on the cold gym floor curled in the fetal position listening to the sound of squeaking sneakers just continuing to play around her. Was she writing her inspection as she candidly saw it, not holding anything back as she was drained from years of the abuse and neglect of duties? Was she possibly being a hard-ass boss finally and not everything was going to be painted as a cutesy-wootsey picture with bright rainbows and butterflies? Perhaps yes. Nevertheless, this letter drained the blood out of her mind, the ultimate insult to her intelligence and expertise in the field, not only of education, but administration, as well as the field of art. A slap in the face by a manipulative and spoiled, privileged jock. The audacity of this disingenuous attempt at covering up the reality with this capricious and arbitrary response which accomplished "abit" of what? It might as well have been dated April Fool's Day.

Fly went on like she just had a minor setback with this newfound diagnosis and, as her daughter was young, tried to brush it off, insisting she could do life as usual. She stated to her union navigator at this point, "Why doesn't he just punch me in the face and get it over with?" Two Krakens had been simultaneously released that spring semester. Fly showed her naiveté a second time and did not realize the ultimate threat had been bestowed upon her and that this disease, like Mr. P.A.U.L., would prove to become relentless. She went about her daily life and the miracle chemistry seemed to keep her mended together so she thought about it no further. And while she would not be able to walk the beach or kayak because she found that she always needed to be in close proximity of a bathroom, summer was upon her and she was ready to relax and forget the dreadful school year.

America the Beautiful—American Mayhem

There are many types of bullies all across America and they come in all shapes, sizes, and ages and can occur anywhere at any time. They are not all like the boy bully in *A Christmas Story* where one has to fear going to and from school or getting their tongue stuck to a frozen flagpole. There are blatant run-of-the-mill schoolyard bullies and then there are low-key manipulative secretive types that proclaim psychological warfare. Bullying can range from name-calling, to shoving, threatening, intimidation, cyberbullying, peer influence, spreading rumors, exclusion, damaging or stealing property, cell phone messages, and any comments related to race, sex, or any aspect that makes up one's unique identity. Bullying is a power imbalance defined as "any intentional, repeated aggressive behavior directed by a perpetrator against a target in the same age group." Bullying creates a multitude of mental health effects for those bullied. Bullying is not illegal in the workplace, but there are attempts to make it illegal for students to bully on school property. Students, not faculty and staff.

The six main types of bullying include: physical, verbal, relational, cyber, sexual, and prejudicial.

Baker's Dozen: Thirteen Reasons Why Not
(or ways to get away with bullying in school)

1. no regulations
2. no policies
3. no state laws
4. no repercussions
5. isolate and blame target
6. administration allows it
7. concealment
8. secretive sabotage
9. rage and revenge
10. undetectable deviance and defiance
11. complaints fall on deaf ears
12. cultural acceptance
13. privilege

Word Wall

"bully" verb bul•ly
1. seek to harm, intimidate, or coerce; to make timid or fearful, frighten, especially to compel or deter by or as if by threats
2. to cause someone to do something by means of force or coercion

synonyms: persecute, oppress, tyrannize, torment, browbeat, intimidate, cow, coerce, strong-arm, subjugate, domineer

FAST FACT

According to verywellmind.com, "A 2019 survey by the Centers for Disease Control and Prevention found that 19.5% of ninth through twelfth graders were bullied on school property in the 12 months prior to completing the survey."

Some states have put laws into effect that will help protect students from bullying on school property, in addition to creating "safe and supportive environments free from discrimination, taunting, harassment and bullying." This includes on school buses and during any school function. Oftentimes, there is clear teacher training and awareness, administrative certification and go-to assignments, specific building forms that can be completed describing the incident such as what happened? When? Where? Were there any witnesses? And administrators must legally follow up and resolve within a specific time frame.

Notable 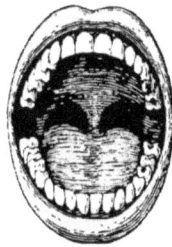 Quotables

People are like stained glass windows. They sparkle and shine when the sun is out, but when the darkness sets in, their true beauty is revealed only if there is light from within.
—Elizabeth Kubler-Ross, Psychiatrist

Lesson #3

This school year Fly learned that if it looks like a duck, walks like a duck, swims like a duck, and quacks like a duck, then it's probably a duck (unless everyone else thinks it's a beautiful swan.)

Aggravated Guts

Act Out!

Journal Entry: Do you feel like you have ever been bullied? Or has someone you care about been bullied? What happened that made you feel that way? Describe the bully and why you think they targeted you. Did you report it to anyone, or did anyone witness the bullying? What did others do to help you? Was there a form you could fill out, law that was in place, or clear procedure for consequences? Was the situation ever resolved and how? How did you stand up to your bully and by doing so, like in *The Against Taffy Sinclair Club*, did it backfire and make you look like the bully instead? Write your thoughts and experience on the next page.

Chapter 4

Cat and Mouse

It's September AGAIN.

A little mouse would run all around,
Searching for food that was on the ground.
A cat was always waiting there,
Because his food he would not share.
The mouse went running across the floor,
The cat had chased him right out the door.
The mouse was looking for a bite to eat,
And the cat was too quick on his feet.
He chased him as they knocked over chairs,
And even up and down the stairs.
As they ran up and down the halls,
The cat would smack into the walls.
The cat had chased him around the house,
But he could not catch the little mouse.
The mouse ran back into his little hole,
And the cat could not reach his goal.
The mouse was able to get away,
So the cat will try another day.

—"Cat and Mouse" by Jon M. Nelson

Cue the Music:
"Right 'Round" by Flo Rida
"Crazy Train" by Ozzy Osbourne
"It's Time" (I'm Never Going to Change) by Imagine Dragons

Irish Exit

Cat and mouse...cat and mouse. Cat and mouse is often expressed as cat-and-mouse game, an English-language idiom dating to 1675 that means "a contrived action involving constant pursuit, near captures, and repeated escapes." Fly grew up watching the well-known cartoon *Tom and Jerry*, mostly because it was one of three cartoons out of the total of twelve channels allowed to watch on Saturday mornings. The episodes were always the same: Jerry lives in Tom's house and tries to go about his business, but Tom would not have it, doing everything in his power to conquer the little rodent. Why didn't Jerry just find another house to live in? And who really was the instigator? Was both Tom and Jerry to blame for the chase?

Surprisingly, the first few weeks of the new school year went smoothly, except for the anxiety building up in Ms. Fly as to when things would begin to percolate. Like a pot of coffee, before the now instant J-cup world, you would hear the drip, drip, dripping; you smell the aroma getting more and more intense, inviting you in, yet it is not yet ready, and when the pot finally fills up, it is too scalding to drink, so wait or get burned. It was off and running only the third week of September. On Monday, Mr. Passive-Aggressive Undermining Liar wrote a very nice email to the entire school faculty, again, which was not permitted. There was his usual warm upbeat yet condescending greeting of "Good Morning Everyone," followed by a huge thank you to everyone for the gift card and helping with the disaster relief activities, and for simply asking how everything is going, and how the past nine months have been challenging, and how great his work family is, and how it means the world to him, and how everyone is so thoughtful, and how everyone is so kind through his "recovery." Recovery like he was a survivor like Fly's neighbor who actually has breast cancer? Women have babies in nine months for real and go back to work recovered in days and that natural disaster was nine months prior. And the fact he did not have the wherewithal or brains to move his car inland away from the predicted storm and his car floated away to where he did not know was his own damn fault. Fly's husband thought he was probably having a Storm Party, and it went unexpectedly south when the roof blew off and the flood waters rose and the power lines almost electrocuted them and so he had to make something up to cover up his poor decision-making and he got gift cards and sympathy and pats on the back from everyone else. He rejected Ms. Fly's student's *Pay It Forward* disaster relief gift bags but accepted money? There were certainly multiple stories going on here. And if he denied knowing to mandatory evacuate as he told Ms. Fly, he really should not be given funds, so it was just another clear example of being rewarded for ignorance.

But there it was: Ms. Fly knew it was inevitable, but when was it going to happen? Tuesday? Wednesday? By Friday of the very same week, Mr. P.A.U.L. had sent Ms. Fly an email and worse, copied it to the principal and both assistant principals. At first, Fly was mortified, and then she was really upset so much so she stormed up to the union navigator's office to discuss the atrocity. The day prior, Mr. P.A.U.L. had requested access to Ms. Fly's Super Widgets for his XL Art class, in which Ms. Fly had replied suggesting different ways in which he could acquire his own super widgets; after all, he constantly boasted about all of the widgets and such that he had accumulated with that special club Principal Don Voyage had given him as well as a grant he received to obtain many of his very own widgets in which he never once shared with the department even though he sent an over-the-top nicey-nice email to everyone that they could borrow them anytime and where they were located along with a list of a clear inventory of the numerous amount of widgets. But Ms. Fly recalled that last year he left broken widgets all over the room for her to deal with and did not even try to fix them or notify her. He just took crumpled scraps of paper and wrote "BROKEN" on the paper in large handwritten letters in marker, then rubber-banded the crumpled paper around the widgets as if in disguise, masked and concealed as to what the widget was, which was ultimately damaged by his hands because he did not teach his students how to handle the equipment with care. Ms. Fly even gave Mr. P.A.U.L. 40 percent more budget than the other teachers because he was teaching the XL class. So in essence, Ms. Fly was fed up and right or wrong, that was her response since she worked so hard getting grants to buy her few Super Widgets for her respectful students over the years. This was also done via emailing from the room next door, like the Wizard of Oz behind the curtain hiding his true self time-stamped when Ms. Fly was available next door to discuss. Sticking with the "Use small words" theory like a child asking for too many of your cookies, she simply said "no." She took very good care of them and treated them with respect as did her students. And what he would not even know is that Ms. Fly and Janeart were using the Super Widgets for all of their classes that particular week for very specific pre-planned lessons, so she thought, *Poor planning promotes poor performance.* Could he not have planned this way back in June or three weeks ago? In her mind though, Ms. Fly knew he was not really asking for her Super Widgets; there was something else he was seeking.

Like the scathing and blatant untruths riddled throughout the inspection response letter of last spring, Ms. Fly could not believe the audacity of this person, and it was really burning her like that scalding first sip you would have in the morning. She wanted to start the new school year with a fresh pot of coffee, yet already was choking on the coffee grounds spoiling what should be something smooth and enjoyable. The tone in this email was in a totally different voice than the disaster relief email that very same week. He claimed he was "confused" about Ms. Fly's response and that "he thought" this and that about her Super Widgets and commanded that he was entitled to acquire them. Fly wondered if this was kin to the cyberbullying that has been going on rampant in America recently on the rise and people did not know how to identify or rectify poor use of technology for communication. If hiding behind the computer and repeatedly over and over again relaying false information or obscured communication was some sort of cyberbullying, she did not know. But then, Ms. Fly gets called into the principal's office, and not knowing all of the widget history of the department, Principal Teddy insisted Ms. Fly give him the Super Widgets, not even share, just give them to him, and thus he conquered and acquired what he was seeking. Power, not widgets. So he had widgets upon widgets and Janeart, Johnart, Fly, and all the other teachers went without. And in a long letter, she wrote to the assistant principals in disagreement with Principal

Teddy, where she clearly identified that Mr. P.A.U.L.'s email was not about widgets at all whatsoever, but that not only was she both personally and professionally offended by the slanderous and plagiarized inspection response letter of last year, that this stint was another attack on her by essentially gaining permission to take her property, just as Little Angelica stole Little Celeste's heart necklace in plain sight.

The next week was even more painful for Ms. Fly. Not only was her ulcerative colitis wreaking havoc on her body physically, but being in school, at her place of work which she loved and where she thrived was now becoming more excruciating and unbearable. On Monday morning, Ms. Fly noticed peculiar behaviors from Mr. P.A.U.L., so decided to fight this clear intimidation tactic with a pen by documenting what she noticed in her lilac legal pad. She believed in that "the pen is mightier than the sword" saying and knew her documents will come in handy one day because it all was just so disturbing and wrong. She took a photo documenting that he stole her yellow plastic Dollar Hollar bin along with her Super Widgets without even an utter or word. Just silence.

Log Entry:

Mon: gave a copy of my sample widget agreement forms, he moved my super widgets to his cabinet and took my dollar store bin as well. Took a photo to document. No eye contact/ guilty/ sad

Tues: /Wed: excited/ probably thinks I got reprimanded by Teddy/ no eye contact

Thurs: made copies of new widget agreement and added his own past problems (safety, etc.) and only changed the name and font. Made copy for binder

Fri: hooked up computers, never TY about the widgets or computers/ sent email after school RE: all the work he did

Mon: Johnart's birthday/ very neutral, all chipped in for gift card/ very smiley

<u>Tues:</u> acts elated and giggly/ He cornered me in the storage closet and helped with putting heavy equipment up without being asked in front of Janeart!/ I thanked/ still no response or talk of the widgets. Mentioned that his favorite game to play was Mouse Trap when he saw the recycled games alongside Candy Land and Chutes and Ladders in the closet. Note: what does that symbolize?

So with that, he took the Super Widgets away from multiple classes and about a hundred students for his own selfish consumption, but of course, he could not see that past his own reflection of self. Ms. Fly continued to confide in her union navigators and met often to get advice and decipher what was going on.

To: Assistant Principals
Re: Employee Mr. Paul
This letter is to highlight items of concern that need serious and direct attention: The ongoing issues with this employee and to illustrate the repeated attempts to continue to undermine myself as a person, myself as an educator, and my position as a department supervisor. The latest example is the email correspondence only the third week of school. I feel this email is not about the Super Widgets whatsoever, but an attack on myself personally and professionally. My main concern is that this is one example of many that I perceive to be in the category of cyberbullying/ bullying/ harassment that encompass ongoing, repeated, questionable contact, and/or communication. It is clear that this email is an attempt to obfuscate the real underlying issues of poor teacher performance that has been documented in the classroom inspection reports, annual eval-

uations, and additional documentation, and possibly intended to intimidate or agitate me. While this is just one example of ongoing situations, please review the attached correspondence with regard to numerous incidents I consider, as a whole, borderline harassment. I am enclosing a very small sampling for review and assessment; my records of performance issues and employee actions/re-actions being with Mr. Paul's employment over the course of three principals. The persistent problems are progressing and escalating, and continue to hamper the goals and vision of the department and our service to the students and our school. These issues can no longer be ignored.

[paragraphs deciphering tactical behaviors with specific examples]

I feel I always support what is in the best interests of our students and appreciate genuine effort, hard work, and creative ideas the teachers in my department have. I feel that people should be respectful ("Treat others the way you would want to be treated"), responsible ("No excuses"), and reliable ("Actions speak louder than words") I view Mr. Paul's actions as deceitful, defiant, deviant, and destructive not only to myself but our department and school.

[Closing statement on how Ms. Fly's energies can serve the students more effectively in a positive learning environment and requesting a solution so that Mr. Paul can perhaps improve without him constantly having to defend himself or rationalize his behavior and actions, etc.]

I appreciate your time and energy in addressing this issue of accountability.

Their "hands were tied" they told her as Teddy was also their immediate supervisor. After all of that Ms. Fly started her Irish Exit strategy: to take off in order to avoid confrontation and situations that would knowingly arise at work. Bang out. Leave without notice before something goes bad! She recalled an episode of Lieutenant Joe Kenda which she watched religiously where he honestly stated, "I am deeply offended by men who treat women poorly." And Fly would one-up that sentiment and add also men who support men who treat women poorly. The women were trying to help, but there was nothing they thought they could do. If there was a law requiring a complaint form, it would legally have to be addressed and rectified, Fly thought.

Ms. Fly couldn't help but keep thinking of the famous Caravaggio painting again, *Narcissus*, from the Baroque era. The young man braces his arms, sleeves rolled up, overlooking a shallow pool. He is kneeled over, surrounded by darkness with only the dramatic chiaroscuro lighting illuminating his beautiful winged hair, sleek arms, and ruffled clothing. His eyes looking down, gazing at, and fixated on his own reflection so focused to ever see anything around him but his own self. He stares and stares into the pool of his dark distorted reflection, and unable to see beyond himself, he dies of his self-obsession.

A few weeks later during a meeting with Mr. P.A.U.L., Ms. Fly, as it was her job to do so, had to address some issues as fellow department members and students had started coming forward with complaints. This really bothered Ms. Fly, but she was feeling less crazy because other people were now also seeing warning signs. The new teacher Joanart stated that P.A.U.L. came creeping up behind her and scared her and that she was not usually a jumpy person. She appeared to be fearful. Another teacher Janeart was annoyed that he signed her up to chaperone a field trip without even asking her first and also he neglected to follow the rule that teachers are not permitted to do that because they have to pay a substitute and that he also took an artwork from the previous year that was created by one of her students and enlarged it for public display, and that the XL students were complaining to her about the poor quality of the artwork and bad rapport among the students in the class. Fly was not surprised as this was the same group of Lost Boys that had ganged up on her about the upside-down artwork. Some graduated, some were still present, and some spoke with hearsay. Just the fact and obsession that the artwork was upside-down reflected in its very essence the world in this workplace. It was all upside-down. All the teachers were frequently asked for important items they had students participating in and his response in this particular meeting was simply "I have no good news." And while the teachers started realizing the inequitable amount of work done, many chose to still remain friends with him, except Joanart who was clearly on edge.

Because of Mr. P.A.U.L.'s questionable performance in the classroom and claim of innocence, Administration thought it would be a good idea for both Ms. Fly and District Director Coupon Suzy to formally inspect him simultaneously to verify that the observation process was objective, fair, and neutral, and not subjective, as if Ms. Fly could be off target or making it up as suggested in his accusatory inspection response. So in theory, it could be said it was also to evaluate Ms. Fly's performance as a trained observer: a double-edged sword.

> Re: Untitled Message
> Hi, Teddy,
>
> I have not had a chance to speak with you, but when I met with Paul this week asking for clarification about his plans, specifically for the Fine Art classes, he had indicated to me that he was not using the district curriculum guide because he could not find it and that the unit I was asking about—he "just made it up." So add this to my pile, but I would like to compile a memo addressing this and additional ongoing issues before we meet with him. I can discuss with you next week. Suzy and I are doing the pre-observation meeting Wednesday for a lesson he will now be using from the curriculum guide as I gave him a hard copy. I am really at a loss. Thanks...I just wanted to give you a heads-up.
>
> Have a nice weekend!
>
> Fly

Coupon Suzy stated how awkward it must have been to have two supervisors in a tenured teacher's classroom, and with several years of teaching under his belt, he must have realized this was becoming serious that he needed four eyes looking to see what was going on. But as Ms. Fly expected, Mr. P.A.U.L. acted like a scared, sad little puppy dog and won the sympathy of Coupon Suzy albeit the notes compared from the post-inspection were almost spot-on in all inspection areas and rubrics. Although this was an unusual request and by no means ordinary protocol, the district director did her job, but then tried to step away from the situation and let it be known it was not her position to continue investigating these concerns, and that the curriculum portion was covered; at least for one forty-minute lesson out of a thousand lessons for that given school year. One thing was for sure, as state certified administrators, with proper training on all aspects of leadership and supervision, including classroom inspections and all kinds of meetings and reports, with second graduate degrees, Fly and Suzy's notes from their legal pads reflected almost identical verbatim. This was one thing P.A.U.L. would not know about administration; that there are classes, continuous training, and books and rubrics just on the observation process and that they are drilled over and over again with scenarios to create feedback and ratings no matter what the subject matter or topic. The district intentionally showed videos distributed by the inspection company on bad teaching so that supervisors could observe and discuss what teachers did or did not do and how that would be written up and reflected using scores of the rubric hyper-analyzed and explained in a 200-page book. There was only one item that Fly overlooked to P.A.U.L.'s advantage that the district director found. Erroneous information given to students that Fly did not even catch but was not surprising as she saw false information all the time. Fly could not recall what the error was, but it was something like calling black your favorite color, when in fact black is not a color at all but a neutral absorbing and absent of all light. Psychologically, black represents power and control, and is intimidating, unfriendly, and unapproachable. Teaching blatant false information to children here was not new and continued to be disconcerting for Ms. Fly and went against everything she believed in. He scored mediocre and unremarkable at best. Even Suzy was like, "Eh," with indifference. Her world was definitely not rocked as Mr. P.A.U.L. would like to think when he would start a lesson in his first year with "Let's rock and roll!" Fly's stomach would turn upside down and she would swallow her pride and kindly say, "Please don't say that ever again unless it's relevant." And at best, his long-forgotten wrath manifesto was only used a tool to squash Fly and no one else besides diabolical XL English teacher probably even knew about it. The wrath still affects Fly to this very day. The words. The lies. The slander.

Fly "pulled a Johnart" and took another sick day to avoid a Staff Development Day and rather than spend grueling time in workshops with Mr. P.A.U.L., she took her day off with Celeste and allowed her to play hooky from her own school atrocities. Johnart was about to retire, so he not only had to use up his sick days he could not cash out, he could care less about spending a day with his colleagues learning some useful / some useless information and chit-chatting over stale wraps. They had a wonderful day just shopping, having lunch, walking the beach, and feeling great that they could escape the confines of the toxic school environments. Celeste was now in middle school so no need to explain the torture at that crazy hormonal, cliquey seeking era. Her cell phone was stolen, she tried to deflect the Val wannabes, and got taunted by her unique dress style. Knowing this could not happen all of the time, they treasured every moment of that beautiful Irish Exit day. Upon return from her "sick" day, (cough, cough), Ms. Fly entered the art room, and as she was very sensitive to and observant of visual information, she noticed something out of the corner of her eye. Intrigued, she walked up to Mr. P.A.U.L.'s display board for the XL Art class and stared in disbelief.

She analyzed the images for a while but seemed like she was frozen in time. The very person who attempted to thwart Ms. Fly's brutal truth inspection report with big words he did not know the meaning struck once again with his bad teaching. Every corner she turned, Ms. Fly could not believe there could always be one more thing that perplexed her very being and stopped her in her tracks. Her jaw dropped. Mr. P.A.U.L. placed a photo he took of a male friend made up in black face as a teacher example for the students. His eyes piercing into that of the viewer, head slightly tipped downward, glaring up with an expression of evil pleasure. Lips clearly pale pink with whites of the eyes popping out from the dark. Next to this photograph were thumbnails of a portrait of a girl's eye flooded with light, fear in her eye as if hiding in a dark closet peeking out to track the predator as in horror films, remaining quiet, ever so quiet so the slasher does not hear the deep and rapid beating of her heart. Ms. Fly, ever the teacher, concocted a pop quiz for one of her Administrators AP Ave who seemed to actually see what was going on. Once, AP Ave asked Fly to figure out what her four-year-old child had painted for her as it was proudly framed in her office. It was a vertical line with two crudely painted bumps. Fly quickly stated, "It's clearly a hug," leaving Ave astonished at her artistic abilities to decipher imagery. Without stating specif-ically what was wrong, Ms. Fly immediately had the AP come in while Ms. Fly was teaching her class, and she meandered throughout the room to see if she noticed anything inappropri-ate that Fly had spied. Like a scavenger hunt and also a keen leader and administrator, she found it right away. She too was disturbed but nothing was ever done. Now clear racism can be tolerated on top of the very clear gender biases? So Ms. Fly, cringing, had to approach Mr. P.A.U.L. and asked him to remove it as she indicated to him that it was "culturally insen-sitive." He simply stated it was gold. Fly's husband, also a spe-cialist in the medium, analyzed the teacher's artwork. He said, "Well, it could be gold but it's definitely black face." Fly took a photograph of the display, in case she needed evidence of her statements and placed it in her binder.

Fly was watching the morning news discussing the great is it "black and blue" or "white and gold" dress debate. Was the photo of that dress in the showcase black and blue or white and gold? Ironically, the newscasters of the famous morning news channels were well: one fired for sexual harassment and the other not promoted because of race and gender, Fly pre-sumed. Everyone processes information differently and per-ceives same things in different ways. As Fly had a degree in wid-getry, she understood about optical illusions, lighting and color theory, light reflection, retinas, lenses, and the like. The fact that the dress photo was taken from a cell phone, overexposed, in poor lighting conditions and reflected in a glass showcase possibly made this a really bad photo. She researched on the computer and one source stated people with less developed brains have a difficulty seeing true colors and interpreted it as white and gold. Make no mistake, painting a white person's face all but the eyes and lips with an evil glare is something very specific. It was black face even if it were gold. So what then? He bubbles and boils inside, getting even more mad at Fly because she would not ignore racism in the school setting or anywhere for that matter. If she ignored it and said nothing, maybe things would not have gotten worse.

Over the next two months, in front of coworkers, Mr. P.A.U.L. became a very good actor. He would pretend to be "useful" and "helpful" in front of colleagues, but when no one was look-ing, he would glare at Ms. Fly and then look like the cat that ate the canary as if to find pleasure in upheaving her work world. She would look at him and even imagine seeing the one yellow feather sticking out of his grimace mouth. Like when he used his brute strength to volunteer putting the heavy equipment up but only when Janeart was in the room shocking Fly at the seem-ingly sincere gesture, as the cat swats at the mouse stunning it before the kill. It was obvious to Fly but not to Janeart. Fly's family had mice infest the house one time when they were con-structing a new home improvement center around the corner. Her cat would get them and bring them to her in the night, so much she was afraid she may wake up with a dead mouse on her neck so she pulled the covers way up passed her nose and the sleep eye mask covered the rest. As a teenager, she used to sleep that way to ward off any vampires in the night; the fear from her childhood watching all of those movies of being attacked when vulnerable. Blood sucked from your body leav-ing you pale and lifeless.

It was becoming the ultimate *Ferris Bueller's Day Off*. There is one scene where the principal calls the mom complaining that Ferris was absent "nine times" and accuses him of not really being sick, but as he stares at the computer, the reality dimin-ishes as the hacked computer alters reality. 9 absences...5, 4,

3, 2. The principal continuously tries to "catch" Ferris cutting school, and in the next home phone contact, the secretary, realizing it was not Ferris making a prank call, tries to look like she was helping the principal, but she was only getting in the way and was only actually creating more chaos. They appeared to be useful yet were destroying the situation and making it worse as they ran around the desk in circles getting nowhere. It was the day before Christmas vacation and holiday cheer was all around. Everyone exchanged little gifts, ate sweet treats, and spirits were lifted with Ugly Sweater contests.

> When all of a sudden, there arose such a clatter.
> Mr. P.A.U.L. intruded on Fly's class and she thought,
> > *What was the matter?*
> Away to her desk, he flew like a flash
> To trap her and tell her some made up trash.
> He would not oblige her presentations come
> > The new year
> As he planned to move his class and incite her
> > With fear.
> With meetings and memos and emails bestowed
> He invaded and trapped her to give her a load.
> Stunned by the news so lively and quick
> She knew that very moment, it must be a trick.
> She ran to AP Ave and exclaimed, "He changed
> > Course selection. I need help stat!"
> Shocked, she responded, "He can't do that!"

He did and add this to the collection. By sabotaging course selection, he himself put Joanart and Janeart's jobs on the line by not participating in getting classes filled for the next school year.

Invisibility

Fear from relentless behavior started setting in and his attempts of seeking power and control were becoming obvious to Fly but invisible to others. For instance, every year, there was the same art exhibition, the one where One Line Louie ruined it all with his ludicrous question. If you have to ask a question about a potential problem with no intervention what did he think was going to happen? He cared only about retirement three months later. How can Fly possibly explain that Mr. P.A.U.L. selected which years to take the smiley group photographs of students with their teachers and parents and intentionally omit Ms. Fly? But only when it served himself: the year he conquered tenure, the year the parent was a prominent Board of Education member, the year where he had to look good in front of others, but in a regular year, he intentionally did not photograph Ms. Fly with her students. She was invisible. Subtle but in existence. She looked over the photos year after year on those shiny CDs he would kindly give her, but she saw the pattern no one else would ever see, as it was preposterous. The pattern of what photos were taken and what was left out.

How can Fly explain about the emails and chronic mistakes and patterns that only Fly noticed and others would never fathom were happening in plain sight? Fly called around and found Labor Lawyer Luke she thought could help figure out what was happening and if it was illegal in the workplace. She decided she had to find someone neutral to get to the bottom of what was going on. To prepare, she organized her main points, her logs, and inquired with Administration if there was a Workplace Rights or Workplace Violence Policy, and there was no such thing in existence, the AP replied after researching. It was a snow day, so perfect timing to meet with the lawyer. She dragged her rollie cart through the plowed snow and scooted to find his office. She thought, *What the hell am I doing and how did I get to this point?* After precise explanation and sharing of documents, overall, he stated it was indeed a very tough and strange case, but it was not against the law to bully in the workplace. It was a lot of out-of-pocket money, but Fly needed answers because her gut told her something was wrong.

With that meeting over, Fly made it a priority to meet with the Superintendent of Personnel, only she did not want to disclose what was going on and just simply wanted to leave the situation. Fly tried another exit strategy just as Jerry could have found another home to live in to stop the relentless chase by

Tom. Realizing she will never win the game of cat and mouse, she requested to quit as an administrator and just go back to being a teacher so that she did not have to be "his boss." She thought it was because she was a she and not a he, as Mr. P.A.U.L. clearly followed directives given by Fly's male counterparts and fellow employees. She gave P.A.U.L. every opportunity to improve and do a good job; instead, he would get angry with denial and blame Fly for correcting him as was her job to do so. She was just trying to do her work requirements as it was written, and this she even brought to the attention of Lawyer Luke. She was supposed to ensure the safety of the students, that curriculum was appropriate, document positive achievements, disseminate information, and about two dozen more work-related duties and activities as listed by the board. A teacher was retiring, and she requested to take his position, and therefore, someone else could be in charge of the department and Mr. P.A.U.L. Soon-to-be Superintendent Sparkle Thief denied this request, blaming it on the budget and downsizing of departments which made no sense whatsoever. Had she come straight out and stated, "I am being bullied, you need to do this now or I am meeting with the board," maybe that would have seen change. But she was increasingly becoming invisible to those she complained to, not being seen nor heard, just shuffled along. If only she could use her invisibility powers more often on P.A.U.L., she may survive.

At the same time, Fly's mom was being harangued by her principal as she taught Middle School Health. Her favorite motto was, "The first wealth is health," by Ralph Waldo Emerson. She even created handmade bookmarks with an illustrated quote to give to people she believed it so much. She was a late bloomer and graduated from college the same year as Fly because she wanted the opportunity to raise her children rather than get an education at the time which she was not permitted to do after high school in the 1960s. Principal Byrd Vulture despised her because she was upper middle-aged, the fact that she did not teach necessarily for the pay check but for the love of teaching, and that her son in previous years was an absolute thorn in his side. Mr. Byrd Vulture would circle around the school waiting to corner her in the classroom doing something "wrong," catching them in the act of an eighth grade boy misbehaving or throwing a crumpled paper across the room to the trash can, then he would jump into the classroom and humiliate her without notice. Mr. Vulture would circle the hallway corner, sweep in storming up to her, and sternly command, "Do you see how Mrs. Parallel's students are all lined up like soldiers?" pointing his directional finger toward the students as if they were marching off to war. This continued until she could not take it anymore and found teaching inner city children who needed such a caring adult figure in their lives as many were new to the country. Believing in another saying that "only a person who risks is free," she faced this difficult job change with hope. She invented educational game boards of her own, brought them treats, made ditto packets for them as there were no textbooks, read special stories to them that all had good morals in the end, and made each child feel special in their own way. They treasured her.

The Unopened Boxes

Foiled, Ms. Fly sadly returned to her work and, every day, continued to have to correct Mr. P.A.U.L.'s chronic mistakes. How can a teacher not learn? Every day, there were issues with incorrect report card grades, erroneous lesson plans, student mix-ups, student complaints, wrong dates, bad art matting, nonstop incidents, and the like and it was truly perplexing to Fly. He would use the wrong tape like nonsticky repositionable tape on artwork mats, so it made it impossible for Fly to hang up the artwork. He made her job impossible to do. She took a photo to document next to the examples all the other teachers matted works to compare and contrast. He would do subtle things like pick up Janeart's dittos and deliver to her, but not Joanart's as he would leave them sitting there on the other side of the school intentionally. She was unaware that in the distant future she would be excessed. Maybe take course selection seriously next time. No classes, no jobs. Later on, Fly wondered if that one complaint by Joanart should have been taken more seriously. Joanart was young enough and super talented that she had no problem being snatched up by a really great school district. But Fly later wondered if he bullied her and hoped that was not the case. Had she known, however, what procedure or form to be filled out was in place to expedite an investigation into the claim? There was none.

Fly tried to focus her attention elsewhere, but it always came back to her putting on her to-do list to check his work. She was getting very drained by doing her work and doing his on top of being diagnosed with a serious illness. She made yet another meeting to try to assess and resolve the issue. Principal Teddy, even though in the past he agreed for Mr. P.A.U.L. to conquer her precious Super Widgets, finally indicated at this point that "He should be fired," so instructed Ms. Fly to start documenting everything and put it in his annual report so that it would be in his file. He said nothing before that counted, and they would have to start from scratch for anyone to do anything. Principal Teddy was to inform Mr. P.A.U.L. that he must acknowledge and respond to the directives of his supervisor. This sounded familiar and never yet had come to fruition, so Fly was skeptical. Additionally, Ms. Fly did not want to conduct his inspections for fear of continued retaliation and denial of evidence based facts. And yet, ironically, some Super Val Mom of an XL student put his name in for a PTA Award. What a slap in the face and Fly bet it made him feel so…competent because moms at home surely know what good teaching is. Assistant Principal Ave and Ms. Fly read that accolade and rolled their eyes at each other with glances of disbelief and fraudulency. Yea, they could see it in the school newspaper, "Black face teacher wins PTA recognition award!" This would not be the last time P.A.U.L. was rewarded for his bad behavior.

It was finally spring and the warm breeze through the art room was a welcomed wave of fresh air after being cooped up all winter. Ms. Fly was teaching when she noticed something out of sorts on his display board. "Thirteen Days Until the XL Exam!" She thought, *That's not right*. And looked at the calendar then asked a common student about the exam date. The student stated that Mr. P.A.U.L. changed the date. How can one teacher feel like they have the "authoritaih!" to keep self-changing administrative tasks and events? This was an international exam as well, so he tried to overturn a federal case, now an international one? And to hear this from an innocent student, how infuriating! In the meantime, the XL Exam Folders arrived, and all of the students and teachers had to scoot around a tower of boxes in the classroom and they needed to be locked in the school safe as they were part of this International XL Exam. In passing, Ms. Fly stopped Mr. P.A.U.L. and pointed to the tower of boxes, stating for him to open them to check for accurate inventory as XL teachers do every single year, then they can go to the safe. He looked dead into Ms. Fly's eyes, gave Ms. Fly affirmative multiple nods, and to boot a physical "Two Thumbs-Up!"

> Log Entries:
> 4/11: Joanart said she was scared of Paul and that he sneaks up on her
> 4/24: Student complaints/ at least four from one class and four from other
> 4/28: Student complaints of poor planning at the end of the XL Exam. Teacher was asked last week 4/20 when the boxes arrived to open them up and check the packing list and still has not done so (insubordination?)

Mr. P.A.U.L. had been asked repeatedly several times over the course of over a week to simply open the boxes and check the inventory so the exam was not compromised or if there was a problem, it could be addressed. She wrote a note, forwarded the email regarding the boxes from the XL coordinator, and verbalized in passing once again. Perplexed by the lack of action but necessity to do so, Ms. Fly orchestrated the following cold and to the point correspondence since the verbal requests were ineffective and the fact that this was an annual activity that usually XL teachers are excited for as if it were opening Christmas presents wrapped nicely in boxes:

> Re: XL Exam Portfolios
> cc: AP of Examinations
> As you know, the XL Exam Portfolios were delivered last week on Monday. As per our con-

versation, it is urgent that you carefully check the contents of the boxes containing the XL Exam materials. When will you be able to do this? In addition, if there are any changes in the administering of the AP Exam, please keep me informed.

Thank you.

Fly began de-personalizing her correspondence as he was no longer a Mr. Teacher to her, rather, transforming into a no-named employee of the district. That afternoon, while Ms. Fly was having a club meeting, Mr. P.A.U.L. stormed into the classroom armed with a sharp box cutter and proceeded to slice, slice, slice open the boxes. He refused to make eye contact and was red and sweating, angry faced and scowling at Fly. He began violently opening and slamming the boxes around after now *seven* requests do this basic task. The next day, he acted opposite as he replied in secret with a very long and ridiculous email stating that he was not aware he had to do this task and all the things he had been doing in the seven days, like giving extra help and so therefore he simply could not open the boxes. And of course, he copied the AP to cover his faults. It might have been easier to just open the stupid boxes herself and be done with the back and forth, but she was sick of doing her job and refused to also do his. Honestly, if he had a mental disorder like bipolar, Fly felt she could work with whatever the issue, but the inability to identify the problem was challenging. The violent act made her only think about his favorite show *Dexter*, and she had trepidation.

The XL Exam date came two days early without justification or communication. Fly was furious. After corresponding back and forth with the AP XL Administrator, there was no reason to move an international exam date, and as Mr. P.A.U.L. was unaware, the exam dates have been moved in the past but only because of conflicts with other exams on the master schedule and students not being able to take two XL Exams at the same time. And who was he to not inform his immediate supervisor or to collaborate with all involved and had to be made aware by an eleventh grader? Fly thought of all this as concealment and corruption at best. She put the pieces together with the following email:

> Re: Tomorrow
> Hi, Fly, (Don't "Hi, Fly" her as if nothing's going on)
> I popped into the art room today (Why are you seeking her out?) but I didn't see you. (Because she was probably hiding from you or in a meeting or using her invisibility powers) I just wanted to give you a head's up (is this what you feel is communicating better?) that I'm feeling pretty terrible today (Oh, so sorry. Not sorry), been fighting off something abit all week (Was it Fly's directions to open the tower of boxes?), and feel like it's catching up to me. (Your stupidity?) I think I am getting what you have. (Fly seriously doubts he has acute ulcerative colitis) I'm going to make some plans for tomorrow in case I don't make it in (Yes, please go away and stay home and away from Fly) and leave them on my desk at the end of the day. (Thanks, one thing you did right)
> Thanks, (Please do not give thanks)
> Full Name (As if Fly doesn't know who it is)

And with that, he gave himself a four-day weekend, not an Irish Exit at best, and sacrificed time the students could have used to complete the XL Exam. Fly bets he had to attend a wedding or had weekend getaway plans and thought, if so, he could have just mentioned a conflict and been honest which is one thing he struggled to be. Ironically, posted on the wall where the one-time black face images stood, was a self-typed handout on "Ethics, Integrity, and Plagiarism" which included ensuring images should be appropriate, use of manipulation, and things that would be unethical. He was becoming more unethical with each passing day, and as Fly's husband would call it, referring to the teaching profession, "conduct unbecoming."

The school year was wrapping up and June proved to be a real treat. First, P.A.U.L. refused to come to a department breakfast that Fly organized to thank all the faculty for their hard work and to simply sit and have some muffins, bagels, and coffee and talk about summer plans. He stood there, eight feet away in eyesight through the doorway just inside the next room chopping paper into bitty pieces using the guillotine-like massive paper cutter. Slice, chop, slice, chop, slice, chop as the 24-inch sharp metal blade sliced through the fragile pieces of paper. In Medieval Times, the guillotine would drop and at the sight of a beheading, the crowd would cheer and shout, "Huzzah!" as they did at the Renaissance Faire. Only the teachers gave side eyes and just thought it slightly odd and certainly had no clue what had transpired throughout the entire school year through Fly's eyes. One teacher naively and kindly asked if he would join and he grunted back and kept mutilating the paper, so she just shrugged it off and re-joined the breakfast party. Fly took this as a deliberate act of violence as he stood there in eyesight as he aggressively sliced.

Then, there was the bagel incident. This one sent shivers up her colleague's spine when she told it in the future. Ms. Fly had sent a friendly email to the teachers regarding some end of the year reminders, but also that she was going to have a bagel party with butter and cream cheese and the works for her classes the following day and to please stop by for breakfast as there will be extras. In passing of classes during the bagel party, Ms. Fly cordially asked Mr. P.A.U.L. as she did with all the teachers if he would like a bagel, and he scowled and angrily stated "No!" and scurried away. So whatever, firmly rejected just as he had refused to take the gift bag of positivity. The next morning, he copycatted and brought bagels to *his* classes. He sneaked into the art room in that Grinch-esque manner while Ms. Fly was teaching her class, again trapping her where she had nowhere to go, and being witnessed by all of the students, Mr. P.A.U.L. stated, "Here, Fly. I made this for you," and slowly handed her a pre-buttered bagel on a small paper plate. He "served her" a prepared bagel: sliced, buttered, and plated and gave it to her creepily. Like that box of chocolates he gave her for Christmas, she thought he may have poisoned it and tossed it in the trash.

Like she would even eat a buttered bagel from anyone no less from someone who bit their nails to the stubby quick. Like plucking eyelashes as Celeste had done, onychophagia is an obsessive-compulsive and anxiety disorder where one picks at or bites their nails and cuticles down to nothing. Fly was disgusted by this disorder and as for such a "germophobe" he would later categorize himself; it was the most germ-based problem one could have with all those saliva germs and hand germs all rolled up into one, and then touch the matted art and this bagel? He presented her this gift with his stubby fingernails. Later that day, Janeart came in and asked Fly if she was going to P.A.U.L.'s Big Party over the summer and Fly just responded, "What party? No." He was concealing more than misinformation. He was getting married and did not even disclose such basic information. More concealment. More resentment. Invisible and uninvited.

At this point, Fly had been dependent on infusions every eight weeks for the past year as well as massive steroid use, which made her appear with a slight moon face. She would enter through the emergency room and pass all of the sick people, travel through the dark winding hallways, and turn right doing the lonely walk of shame toward 2 North, the Cancer Ward. She knew what she had was pretty terrible, but she knew other people had worse ailments, so she happily greeted the nurses and made idle chit-chat. Many times, Fly's husband and Celeste would drop her off, made sure she was settled in and comfortable before they went on an adventure hiking or to the park, then went back to pick Fly up since she was slightly sedated and could not drive. Fly's husband called the favorite nurse Trish the Dish because she knew how to make the six or more hours in the chair feel like you were in good hands. After the high dose of anti-inflammatory drugs, Fly would drift off into sleepy land on these Sundays, happy to be resting and rejuvenating.

An entire day to quick fix the auto-immune disease. Fly's dad had a lot of problems as well; maybe it was hereditary, but all he could ever say was "Why couldn't I have just gotten tennis elbow?" Trish the Dish said to Fly, "I am so sorry you have to be here on Mother's Day!" but Fly replied that she was happy to be left alone and have some sedated peace and quiet and watch television of her choice for once. She was a working mom too, so they related, and it was what had to be done. Trish the Dish kept Fly in good hands and she was thankful for such kindness and caring. What a great Mother's Day. Unlimited *NCIS*, an egg salad sandwich, and some graham crackers. But Fly was blind to the escalating negative impact that would traumatize her caregivers, her family. Drop off—worry—pick up— will it work? Trish the Dish was one of the few Fly confided in about the triggers of her workplace issue. They had genuine workplace issue talks. Fly learned all about the nursing profession becoming more challenging as they had more job responsibilities, training sessions, safety protocols, more hours, and less nurses. It sounded just as familiar with teaching. They just keep putting more and more workload, with less time to do tasks and less help. It is not a great formula and leads to worker burnout no matter what the profession.

Fly found that the infusion nurses and nurse practitioners that her paths crossed with were the best, and there were so many to be thankful for and grateful for their services. Even all of the emergency room doctors and nurses she would never see again made a huge positive impact on her when she was at her weakest physical state. There was the nurse practitioner at the primary care physician, which Fly actually never even met her PCP in twenty years. There were a lot of older clients at that particular office as Fly's husband just picked it out of the insurance book, not knowing it was a cardiologist. She would perk up every time she saw Fly to get some fun new information about school, but she was also a shoulder to cry on. She would tell her own stories about how she loves songs like "Fancy" and wish she could be a little less stressed and a little wilder. Another helpful nurse was Kiki at Dr. Mendit's office. Coming out of anesthesia one day for a minor procedure, Fly cried frantically to her, asking if her awful disease was because she was being harassed in the workplace? She felt ashamed and defeated. She was spending tons of money on her talk therapist just to get through the week and the other good listener was her faithful hair dresser, Shearry Trendy.

Fly had been a hair model in the city, once strutting her stuff on an actual International Hair Show runway. She wore a huge old-fashioned wedding dress so large and heavy that they had to duct-tape it to her body. Fly loved getting her hair done because it is the first thing people see in an appearance, and it is like a sculpture. Shape, color, texture, style; it had all the elements of art right there as the best wearable art. Eyebrows too. Once a student asked Ms. Fly who did her eyebrows as they were "on point." Ms. Fly simply responded, "The '90s," and the class chuckled. After a few bad haircuts where the stylist did not listen to what Fly wanted for a haircut, she went back to the place she had gone to in high school and was put into the hands of Shearry Trendy. She listened and also shared stories of her personal life. One day, when Little Celeste needed to outgrow the baby haircutter, and Fly had destroyed her hair by cutting it herself as her whole head became one big set of bangs, transforming it into a reverse mullet, Shearry came to the rescue. Celeste and Fly only had Shearry cut their hair from then on, and she listened very carefully to what her customers were saying and how to achieve the goal they wanted. Sometimes, Fly would confide in her the stressors at work and keep her posted on actions she was taking, and of her ill health, but that mostly she needed a pick-me-up to look beautiful and Fly always either had a plan and photo of a haircut and color she wanted or Fly went in completely trusting Shearry and letting her utilize her creative license to do whatever she thought best. She always walked out looking fabulous either way.

At the same time, Fly tried to attend conferences and support groups for Crohn's disease and ulcerative colitis to educate herself and learn how to live with it. Why did they always serve so many foods and snacks that one with Crohn's or colitis cannot eat? She cried the first time she realized she could not even tolerate eggplant parmesan, which was one of her favorites. A low-residue diet they called it. Small bland meals no larger than her tiny fist, nothing fried, spicy, no vegetables, fruit, or anything disruptive to the gut system. She already ate pretty plain, but how much blander could it get? She thought about joining the fund-raising walks, but seriously, you have seen the commercials. These are diseases that make you uncontrollably have to go to the bathroom all the time with urgency so the last thing you want to do is be stuck somewhere walking a race for a cause desperately seeking a Porta-Potty. No thank you. Fly already had to take specific routes to work so that she could stop and use the restroom on the way. Every morning, she could not even make it to work without at least one pit stop. Breadnera always had the cleanest ones and music so was less mentally and physically painful and camouflaged any potential embarrassing noises that could not be controlled. And she went to one or two Crohn's and colitis support group meetings which she thought were awful. Acting like a fly on the wall, she was surrounded by a group of crotchety old women complainers discussing all the pain and torture of these disabling diseases. She decided to do her own thing, and she and her family participated in a few Glow Runs, which were way more fun and colorful. They were short course, so she tried to participate the best she could. Her husband and Celeste were all that she had left in the area, and they had become so patient with her runs to the bathrooms and dietary constraints.

It was Tuesday of the last week of classes and in passing of the periods, Mr. P.A.U.L. asked Ms. Fly if he could have a student clear off the folders on the computer desktops. Surprised at the seemingly kind gesture, Ms. Fly responded, "Thanks. That would be great. Just leave them plugged in though because the technicians are going to re-install software this summer since some of the programs are missing." Fly came in Wednesday morning, totally shocked at what she saw. She looked out of her office to the computer lab, and she went pale as the blood rushed from her head; a vampire might as well have drank her blood in the transfusion room. Was it all the medication? Was she hallucinating from the steroids, no roid rage as her husband would call it, or what could it be? No. P.A.U.L. had disassembled all of the computers, had unplugged all of the cords, mice, and mouse pads, and they were tightly wrapped in choked-off circles neatly under each screen placed perfectly on top of each keyboard all away around the room, each one identical. Infuriated at this, Ms. Fly arranged a meeting with Mr. P.A.U.L. on Thursday ten minutes before school and stated it would be brief but needed clarification on three items. She took a photo to document her accusations, just in case it was needed for evidence.

Weirder things were happening. First item, he had that bratty Lost Boy student who graduated return to visit and this was the main student who Fly felt Mr. P.A.U.L. encouraged to go out of their way to be rude to her and the other department supervisor. Mr. P.A.U.L. himself started acting mean and nasty toward Ms. Fly's students at random. Her students would return from a task of maybe asking to borrow a ruler and they would say, "Mr. P.A.U.L. was mean to us for no reason. We asked nicely." This upset her as the students were just kids and did nothing wrong to deserve such bad behavior from a teacher. Second item, students had complained to Ms. Fly that Mr. P.A.U.L. was giving them a participation grade for "cleaning" the art room. Ms. Fly simply asked, "Are you grading the XL students on cleaning the room as they had indicated?" He stated no, and Fly said he should clarify the confusion to the students. She also noticed that they peeled off her table labels and destroyed them in the process, but she let that one go. Third item, knowing the bell was going to ring shortly, Ms. Fly asked her final real question as the others were merely decoys, "Why did you unplug all of the computers?" He responded simply, "You said you were done with them," and Ms. Fly swiftly corrected him and restated her words verbatim, "I said just leave them plugged *in* because the technicians are going to re-install software this summer since some of the programs are missing." Saved by the bell. Administrative strategy at its finest.

Later that day, Ms. Fly witnessed Mr. P.A.U.L slamming the computers with a looks-could-kill face. To time stamp and document, she emailed the principal.

Hi, Teddy,

I just wanted to make you aware of a situation where on Friday, June 13, during period 8, Mr. Paul was exhibiting extreme scowling and facial expressions of anger and physical aggression which I feel was aimed toward myself with regard to completing a simple department task with computers. I followed up with him in a meeting this morning because this type of behavior has been noticed by and concerned many individuals throughout this school year. I know we meet tomorrow for my Annual—should we just discuss at that time or at a separate meeting? I wanted to give you a heads-up and time to think about it. I will email you a specific memo later today that I started in May, as well as bulleted items that I would like you to review for his annual report.

Fly could not let this go on, and although she was gaining wisdom and advice from colleagues and union navigators, she thought it to be her duty to address it herself. She met with him again so briefly, she did not even ask him to take a seat in her office where the once paper was crumpled and tossed into the trash. They stood there in that small space, and she directly approached him point blank and confronted him about why he did the exact opposite of what she had asked him to do. Actually, she did not even ask him in the first place...he volunteered ever so kindly to clean off the computer desktops, but when thanked and explained to leave them plugged in, that is when he did the opposite. Then she asked about his visible anger and aggression about slamming of the computers and keyboards vigorously on the tables since it was not the first time of such violent slamming of objects. The boxes, unopened for over a week towering over every single one of the 150-plus students who cowered by as they entered the classroom each day. He instantly began babbling in strange tongue, speaking in an incomprehensible gibberish language that Ms. Fly could not quite decipher like the stapler guy from *Office Space*, and then as if a suspect being questioned in a small uncomfortable room on *Cops*, he re-enacted with his hands in the air how he tightly wrapped the computer cords, and as he did so, to Fly it appeared as if to show strangulation with the cords as his red beady eyes mimicked the red sweaty dewy skin of his face. With his motions and explanations, she felt he was strangulating her with his large nubby nail-bitten hands tightly wrapped around her tiny neck over and over again repeatedly for each and every computer not standing a chance until she gasped to take a last breath of air before he killed her. He was motioning with his hands how he wrapped and tightened the cords each exactly the same in an obsessively compulsive pattern and placed them all the same neatly under each computer.

A wave of intense fear crashed over her body, consuming her from the top of her head, all the way, cascading through her feet where she thought once was grounded and stable. The heat surged as her armpits began sweating and her hands shaking uncontrollably. Fly never sweated, but she was experiencing a fight or flight situation. With his incoherence in an attempt to cover up or justify his actions and the vivid visual display of tightening thirty cords in a repetitive circular motion, he loomed dangerously close in her tiny office. Scared to death for her safety and assessing that this quickly became a volatile conversation, she hid the terror she felt and did her job by asking about what were some strategies he could use to improve his classroom management and rapport as he was also "very angry at the students," which was also not the first time. The students do not do anything to make teachers "angry," it is their lack of classroom management or regulations or expectations that permits students to do things they should not be doing. The once repeat rookie maker of mistakes was now becoming a repeat professional maker of mistakes. Flabbergasted, Ms. Fly ended the meeting with the principal-approved list of items that would be documented in his annual report. In Fly's mind and advised by multiple union navigators, she was never to meet with this employee ever again alone from that day forward.

Director Coupon Suzy became relentless with insisting that Fly needed to write curriculum after school and was angered that Fly could not because she felt extremely sick with the illness bubbling up inside her. Usually supervisors do write curriculum as they are the instructional experts in the field; however, it is not mandatory. Coupon Suzy was not getting the hint back and forth via email that Fly was not feeling well, had been in and out of the hospital, spending weekends in 2 North and then she started e-screaming nasty emails, stating, "You can't tell me that you can't write curriculum." Fly was forced to write the curriculum, but really needed rest, not exertion. She even had to do the school-wide class schedule in the hospital bed, as no one else could fulfill such duties.

Fly met Mrs. Parabola for lunch where she had a breakdown. Mr. P.A.U.L.'s actions just leveled up a notch. Mrs. Parabola said that several of her teachers asked why Mr. P.A.U.L.'s distorted Pop Art face was plastered all over the school, and Ms. Fly simply was speechless as she shook her head in disappointment. A seemingly funny senior prank to her was an embarrassment to the department. A student taped dozens of Pop Art decked-out dittos of Mr. P.A.U.L.'s yearbook photo all over the school, and in turn, students felt it would be funny to draw mustaches and private parts and curse words on the pictures. On top of the continued chronic and compulsive emails with erroneous information and poor performance, he was now increasingly exhibiting physical aggressions to illicit fear. People only saw the funny but confusing senior prank. She indicated that she did not deserve this kind of working environment where a teacher behaved this way simply because of being corrected on responsibilities. She took photos of the flyers. She documented the incident with her union navigator and also asked a department member, just to double-check her work, if Ms. Fly was being clear with information provided in meetings and memos and emails and other correspondence and Janeart replied with only affirmative response and praise at how great of a job Ms. Fly does for the department. Fly asked, "Are you sure I am clear with communication and fair with expectations and decent with my role as an educational administrator?" She was adamant in the affirmative. Fly was warned by her union to never be alone with Mr. P.A.U.L. in a meeting or anything in an isolated situation from that point further. That was the last time she ever spoke with him. Ms. Fly gave a binder of evidence to Principal Teddy to peruse over the summer. Fly's husband thought that if he ever did get fired, he would find her and kill her and she did not disagree. That summer, she was so terrified, Fly felt she had to look over her shoulder, even in her own driveway.

It was that time of year when the teachers submitted their achievements again. All the teachers submitted lists of all the wonderful art shows, contests, competitions, lessons, and innovations they implemented. Most of the art teachers listed well over twenty combined successful field trips, extracurricular activities, school beautification projects, and student awards.

Principal Teddy stated to "document *everything*," so she did and submitted her findings in a binder with a two-page synopsis of complaints echoing even deeper her reports and pleas in previous years to Principal Don Voyage. She omitted such things as the bagel incident as she thought about how ridiculous a gesture sounds on paper. A bagel? If it were filmed like it was in Fly's photographic memory, it could be documented as bizarre and insulting.

> To: Mr. Principal Teddy
> Dt: June 13
> Re: District Employee Mr. Paul
>   This memo is a report of several items from this school year you may already be aware of, as well as to request the following items be reviewed at the administrative level. Mr. Paul continues to disregard the district food chain ladder by neglecting to report to, consult, or communicate with myself as his immediate supervisor on decisions that impact and can be detrimental to the program. When consulted on departmental responsibilities, Mr. Paul's responses are most often not coherent or cognizant of the topic and often dishonest and inconsistent. Mr. Paul does not comply with basic information and instructions that I share with him to foster best practices and methods for educational, professional, and administrative responsibilities. Mr. Paul needs to recognize, acknowledge, and become more accountable for such continuous issues as exemplified below:
>   Students have been very vocal about their educational experiences this school year. As department supervisor, I have been the receiver and mediator of at least a dozen student complaints regarding the instruction of the XL course, the behavior of this teacher, and his lack of rapport with his students. Mr. Paul's

several instances this year of visible anger and aggression was questioned to which he replied in the affirmative and was unaware he was physically expressing his anger.

After giving me an affirmative two thumbs up upon delivery of the XL Portfolio boxes on April 20, Mr. Paul did not check the invoice or contents of the XL Portfolio shipment. The box on top stated "Open this box first: Invoice Enclosed." I informed him both verbally and via email that he was responsible to do so. (Attachment) In reference to Mr. Paul's claim there was insufficient time, it should be noted that there is a daily XL Prep Period in lieu of a duty for first time teaching XL courses. In addition, after the seventh cue, Mr. Paul avoided eye contact with myself and exhibited scowling and angry expressions that made me uncomfortable in my own classroom while working with my Club.

Mr. Paul was asked to select an XL senior to help design the senior graduation pamphlet as we do every year. Samples were given with specific directions. After three revisions, the font was still rendered unreadable, and Mr. Paul insisted it was correct. Mr. Paul who teaches units of instruction specifically on Typography for XL Art, Mixed Mass Media Arts, and Observation Art should be able to recognize this and also make connections to curriculum and instruction. Your very own secretary was the only one to continuously point out the fact that the graduation cover art was unreadable, and kept returning it for fixing, not me.

By not following basic directions the first time, misinterpreting, or ignoring, Mr. Paul's actions obstruct the full potential, progress, and effectiveness of this department. In closing, it is my assessment that this level of performance in such a small department on a daily basis over years makes a large enough impact to become counterproductive in the following areas: achievement of department goals and academic success, support of innovative ideas and vision, maintaining integrity, providing a productive and positive working environment for both students and faculty, aligning with curriculum and standards, and improving planning and instruction to serve the best interests of the students.

It was actually the principal's own secretary who kept returning the senior pamphlet design to Ms. Fly several times stating that the font was unreadable and too small. The secretary was not trained in art or design, she just knew what looked good to the basic onlooker. Each time Mr. P.A.U.L. denied the errors, but the secretary finally yelled, "Fix it!" as the deadline was that day and she was under duress. Mr. P.A.U.L. had four supply orders that were incorrect and attached with a note by Mr. P.A.U.L., "Off by two cents," so Ms. Fly simply handed it back with the words "Redo," not even underlined twice or anything. She really wanted to give him her two cents, and clearly, it was unclear to him what her advice was. She was just exhausted with the inept. Ms. Fly's emotions oscillated between being riddled with fear and flight and sick and tired of the ridiculousness and mad at the shear amount of her precious time that was being consumed by this ungrateful manipulative idiot savant saboteur. The other teachers would have mistakes on occasion throughout the year, but certainly not to this extent and there was one main difference. The other teachers would simply apologize and fix it without hesitation and make things right like normal people working together in a normal work environment. "Oh, so sorry, Fly, I did not see that...I will fix it and get it right back to you." No worries. Normal. Honest. Human. People make mistakes and there are people to keep everything in order and accurate for a multitude of reasons like to achieve "educational excellence." So when they all left for the summer, P.A.U.L. asked if he could email Ms. Fly the XL Exam scores over the summer, and after the black face insensitivity, the box incident, the date exam change, and the computer strangulation, Fly simply replied, "No thanks. I'll be on vacation."

America the Beautiful—American Mayhem

Fear of the disgruntled worker. Workplace violence and homicides have haunted the American workplace from ocean to ocean for decades. It is so common, just recently, Ms. Fly's school went on lockdown for an employee-related shooting at a pharmacy. Post offices, supermarkets, shipping stores, government sites and healthcare facilities. No place is off the list. According to the Federal Bureau of Investigation, 80 percent of active shooter situations occur in the workplace by current or past employees or an employee with a relationship with another employee. In 2015, News Anchor Vester Flannagan held a grudge because he was "not behaving in a professional manner" and he was often "corrected of his job performance" (20/20 on OWN, S5, E6). He was fired several times and even filed a discrimination lawsuit claiming he was fired because of his race, not work performance. Two years later, he walked up to two of his once coworkers and shot them during a live news interview. The cameraman had previously complained to human resources about him. Proper employee training, understanding warning signs, and practicing safety drills can help in a volatile and violent situation, but it will not prevent it from occurring.

Word Wall

"insubordinate" adjective in•sub•or•di•net
   1. disobedient to authority; defiance
synonyms: infringement, dereliction, insurrection, riot, revolt, mutiny, defiance, disregard, dissension, sabotage, non-compliance, nonobservance, indiscipline, noncooperation

FAST FACT

What does "going postal" mean? According to the Urban Dictionary, the term was "originally coined from a series of real-life shootings in the postal service. It now usually means someone is about to go nuts or off the deep end. It can also be trivial. Example: After finding her computer's wallpaper had been changed again, Jane went postal on her fellow workers."

Not-so-fun fact: 260,000 students miss school each day for fear of being bullied.

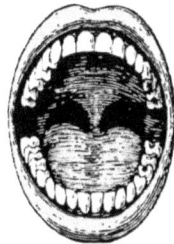

Notable Quotables

"Hang on to your hat. Hang on to your hope; and wind your clock for tomorrow is another day."
— E. B. White, *The Atlantic Journal*
June 19, 1833

Lesson #4

This school year, Fly learned that if looks could kill, she'd be dead.

Cruel Haikus

You can't take feedback
Instead of improving self
Take it out on me

Glare at, then ignore
Pretend I do not exist
A look that could kill

Sly as a red fox
You're a wolf in sheep's clothing
No one knows the truth

Work confuses me
Cross my i's and dot my t's
I will not comply

New laws for students
Teachers need support, not guns
A culture of hate

Why you so cray-cray
I'll never know the reasons
Your sick intentions

You have no good news
Fake news, info, and reports
The truth is out there

What reputation?
You're ruining my career
Who the hell are you?

You take on the chase
Try, Try You will not get me
Why don't you just quit

Gut Wrenching

Act Out!

Activity: What is your favorite board game? Why? How do you think your choice reflects some of your character traits and personality? What is the strategy of the game, and what is its significance to you and your friends or family? What is the challenging part of the game? What are the rules, and can you deviate from them? Go play the game and think about the interpretation and meaning of the goals and intentions. Play your least favorite game and figure out why it makes you feel uncomfortable. Make up a game you would like to invent. What would it be called, what does it look like, how do you play it, what are the rules, and how do you win or lose? You can sketch your idea on the next page.

PART 2
Wreckage

The artist sees what others only catch a glimpse of.

—Leonardo DaVinci

Chapter 5
Death by a Thousand Paper Cuts

It's September again, and August feels like one long Sunday night.

"Float like a butterfly, sting like a bee. The hands can't hit what the eyes can't see." Although Muhammad Ali could not swim, he convinced the photographer to take that famous photograph of him boxing under water.

Cue the Music:
"Hit Me with Your Best Shot" by Pat Benatar
"Numb" by Linkin Park
"Last Resort" (Cut My Life into Pieces) by Papa Roach
Bonus Track: "Sabotage" by Beastie Boys

Alien

September started out with a departmental lunch on professional development day. Fly was already dreading the onset of a new school year, let alone sitting in close quarters with that employee at the restaurant. Fly would have never suggested to eat out in a small booth together, but all of the departments were instructed to do so, so she held her breath and sucked it up. She enjoyed Janeart and Joanart, and finally Johnart was retired and long forgotten. They even joked about his Irish Exit, and he just left mid-year and was like, "Well, have a nice life." Totally indifferent to the thousands of young lives he taught art to and supposedly enlightened over decades of his career and livelihood. They sat and ordered basic stuff for lunch and there it was: Mr. P.A.U.L. stated creepily, "I *thought* about you over the summer when I was down at the Lake." Fly's heart sank, terrified with fear, and lost her appetite. It was kind of a *I Know What You Did Last Summer* moment. Why was he thinking about her when he clearly did not like her at all? He claimed there was a mini-marathon and thought her husband might have been participating in. Her guts were already unable to tolerate greasy foods and her diet was severely and sadly limited, so she offered up her fries to the group in which he replied with a goofy grin and happily took the food off her plate with an exclaimed, "Sure!" Disgusted at the blatant two-faced maneuver in front of the other teachers, she cringed and recoiled into the bench seat. The other teachers had not a clue what was really going on all this time, and it had taken a two-month hiatus only to be ramped up once again in an instant.

Fly researched her debilitating disease and found out there have been a lot of famous people that had lived with Crohn's and colitis. Fly read about the alien coming out of the chest during the dinner scene of the *Alien* film and that the scriptwriter of that famous terrifying movie suffered from Crohn's which inspired that horrifying scene. She could totally relate as that was a pretty decent visual depiction of how it physically manifests which is almost impossible to explain the pain of exploding guts to others, let alone it being such a taboo subject. Colitis girl…that is who Fly had become with a vicious endless cycle of unpredictable flare-ups and remissions like a roller coaster up and down not knowing when or what the next curve will bring. She had a sticker on her inspiration board affirming this: "Dear Crohn's and colitis, I get it. Every time I am doing well, you're gonna knock me down. But know this, every time, I will get back up." Those commercials were becoming increasing popular: the view from inside the bathroom stall at the concert or Porta-Potty at the baseball game where you can hear all of the fun things being missed out on. "Is today a great day for a flare-up?" says the commercial voice. No. There will never be a great day to feel like living hell, thank you. The pain could go from one to nine on the smiley face scale in a very short amount of time for no apparent reason, and one could still sometimes look great and other times look like they've been hit by a Mack truck. Fly's husband always knew how she felt on the inside by how she dressed on the outside. Crappy clothes? Feeling pretty okay, able to exercise, eat and maneuver through life and work. Dressed up to the nines? Feeling lousy, drained of all fluids, valuable lost time to excessive bathroom use, everything is a struggle with intense pain. Regardless, students, staff, and people at work had no clue what she was going through and she continued to do her job well and always with a genuine smile. Was it the food? Stress? Intestinal lining? Blood cells? Body rejecting itself? What were those things that triggered the height of the roller coaster? While it cannot be fully explained, the medical field thinks it is a combination of genetics, immune systems, and environmental factors. Did she get this because she was on that severe acne medication in her twenties, because she ate too many frozen meals, scraped her metal fork while scrambling eggs on her nonstick frying pan, or did a distant family member have it and was unaware? The worst part to Fly was the lack of knowledge about the disease, its relentless chronic nature, and ultimately, its unpredictability.

A teacher walks into a bathroom stall and is in and out within ten seconds. Another teacher walks into the bathroom stall adjacent and the running joke is, "You must be a teacher!" Teachers are notoriously fast at using the bathroom because there's only a few minutes in between classes, and no one can leave students unattended in the classroom which can be quite a distance away. Fly used to be the quick pee-er, but now things had changed for the worse. The situation was not only embarrassing, it was taboo as no one wants to talk about "bathroom" problems in the workplace. In that terrible teacher movie, the main character walks into the men's room and the other guy had to hold it in until she left, as he exclaimed, "Holy moly, I thought she would never leave," as his insides exploded. That was pretty spot on how it feels. Tons of students are also mortified to go to the bathroom in schools including her Little Celeste and many kids of parents she knew. Why feel so unsafe in school? Studies show that over 40 percent of students fear that harassment will happen in their school bathrooms. So no one knew and she had to keep the secret. One old wrinkly secretary one day, looking at the bloat even asked, "Are you pregnant?" Mortified, Fly just looked at her with disdain, but brushed it off with a joke, "No, I guess I should eat less vegetables," and scurried into the stall, hastily knowing full well she was unable to even tolerate vegetables at that point. She cried at no eggplant parmesan, no more house salads, no more steamed broccoli. Well, broccoli Fly thought she could actually live without.

Fly grew increasingly aware at how important teachers were in her daughter's life. If she did not like or trust a certain teacher, that was it; there would be no cooperation, no homework done, nothing to please the teacher or comply with requests. Celeste had a second grade teacher retiring and more interested in planning her daughter's wedding, and another XL Math teacher who belittled her because she was staring at the fish tank in front of the room instead of doing math problems. Infuriated that Celeste was always put in the "difficult" classes, Fly wrote a complaint letter to the principal and finally, she had a string of super-caring elementary schoolteachers. While academics were a struggle, Celeste often got accolades for leadership and humanitarian efforts, as she always tried to help. Fly found this letter she typed formally to the principal as Celeste could not take it anymore that the plastic grocery bags were decorating the tree tops at the school playground:

> September 4
> Dear Mr. Sienna,
>   I know it has been a long summer and was not sure if you notice that the back of the school-yard is littered and filled with glass. It was dangerous to play on the playground, and I almost stepped on broken glass, and there are plastic bags flying from the tree tops. I would not mind with helping to organize a group of students to help keep our environment clean and safe! And who knows if an animal or a person could get hurt. Thank you for reading this letter.
>
> From Celeste
Room 21
Mrs. Bleck
Fourth grade

She could have had a future in journalism, but that teacher gave too much work and treated the elective class so intensely she could not keep up with assignments. She could have had a future in writing music, but that favorite teacher retired after she started high school and was replaced with a less interesting and qualified teacher. He seemed similar to Mr. P.A.U.L. unfortunately, and Celeste knew he was not a good teacher, and she quit that class. Instead, she sat at home with her guitar lessons teacher strumming her first real tune she learned, the Beatles' "Blackbird": "Take these broken wings and learn to fly," as she learned to feel the music slowing and regaining speed and momentum. Administrators and hiring committees have a huge responsibility to hire, train, and retain high quality instructors who bring fun and joy to education for students. These future career possibilities were destroyed by specific teachers, and Fly wanted to stand up for the rights of her students. They did not have to seek careers in the arts, but they needed to be heard, supported, and respected as human beings worthy of a quality education.

But then, the law even took Ms. Fly's secret bathroom away, the one that was more private way over on the other side of the school in the dead hallway, and it had now become the safe zone for the one transgender student. She would often shelter the misunderstood students in the art room during her free periods. He was actually her student at the time and wanted to transition to female. While it was illegal to discuss with his parents, it was legalized to accommodate an all-gender bathroom. She researched more and wondered if her disease was covered by the Americans with Disabilities Act that was signed into law by President Bush Sr. in 1990. Upon discovery, the law should allow reasonable accommodations in the workplace such as a nearby or private bathroom, but Ms. Fly felt she had bigger fish to fry so she just had to make due with Breadnera on her drive in and trying to time running to the bathroom when she thought no one would be in there like during the Pledge of Allegiance or daily announcements. Fly mastered speed walking, and she walked so fast that even the grocery store automatic doors would not open fast enough for her speed, but on the other hand, sometimes she was in the bathroom so long that the automatic lights would shut off on her while she was in the stall, leaving her literally sitting in the dark.

But as Fly's secret restroom to use in peace without judgments now became the transgender bathroom, she thought they should just make a neutral bathroom for people who have issues "down there" and call it an "Everybody" bathroom. She kept researching, but there was not much information about how one gets this horrible diagnosis of ulcerative colitis, what the cures were or advice on living with it, and why now even she did not have proper access to a private bathroom. All Fly knew was that she was becoming a human pincushion and infusion fiend. Little do people know there have been presidents, famous actors, successful musicians, and athletes with these diseases and then there she was feeling like a Little Fly, a mere teacher, overlooked and misunderstood.

At the end of last school year with Mr. P.A.U.L.'s activity getting more visibly violent, Ms. Fly met with Principal Teddy to seek assistance with the new Personnel Superintendent soon-to-be Sparkle Thief in September. Even the Scheduling Administrator

Ave was assisting Ms. Fly by putting Mr. P.A.U.L. as far away from Fly as possible and playing around with the schedule so that there would not be run-ins. Hopefully, a few small changes could help decrease any potential conflict that could arise. The summer was over, and Ms. Fly returned to witness the complaint binder that she had given Principal Teddy in June was still sitting on top of the TV in the Principal's Office in the exact position where he placed it. The documents sat melting there in the sweltering heat, the plastic protection only to be warped and distorted by the hot summer sun. The significance to Fly was that he never touched it in the two months alone in the school sans thousands of teens and hundreds of teachers in the classrooms and halls. Ignored, untouched, unread. The whole summer had gone by and nothing. Upon meeting with Mr. Teddy, Ms. Fly stated she was going to use the "H-Word" officially and that she felt if the duress word was actually said aloud it was like something she experienced in the hospital recently. She had a severe allergic reaction to an infusion, and in a minute, a crash cart team appeared immediately out of nowhere, with a dozen professionals all with specific jobs to assess the situation, make life-saving decisions and ultimately and successfully handle any crisis situation in minutes. She swallowed the lump in her throat and boldly said aloud to him that she felt like she was being harassed. But there was no crash cart, no mad dash to save a life or assess and fix the problem. Just him staring back into her little all-knowing eyes.

Ms. Fly could not believe the email Mr. P.A.U.L. had sent the very first day of school. It actually read like a very sincere email, but with the history, Fly knew there was ulterior motive. His modus operandi was becoming more predictable with every new school year, but this was not the usual three weeks in. She was becoming a private eye, able to detect the next move he was going to make, or so she thought. He appeared to have a magical, albeit sinister way, of regurgitating the incidents from the past and bringing them up in a new way, perhaps to give him a fresh take, do-over, or redemption though she did not know for sure. This first email of many to come highlights his good deeds:

> Re: Cabinet
> Hi, Fly,
> I cleared out the cabinet in 234 today after school, I am going to keep the widgets locked up in the closet in 235 if you ever need them for Mixed Mass Media Arts for the second half of the year.
> Also, do you need me to set up/start up any of the computers in 234? I am not sure if they got to them this summer?
> I was able to talk to Miss Stiletto today about the ArtSmart Club and she said she was going to get back to me.
> Sorry for the email, I just thought it would be easier with no common time off this year. Thanks, see you tomorrow.
>
> Paul

Fly thought what nerve he had bringing up the widgets and like he is in charge or something and after persuading Principal Teddy to have Ms. Fly surrender her widgets to him in defeat. He found a way to conquer on command, probably using the sad puppy dog eye look or perhaps the sporty spice look behind closed doors. Not only did he use his usual fake friendly greeting as always, he was keen to mention he worked after school on his own time like he is some kind of saint. And did he seriously ask about helping with the computers after slamming them and their keyboards and then playing charades about the overly tightened strangulation cords? Maybe Fly was watching too many *Snapped*, *Dateline*, and *20/20* episodes, but it truly frightened her. She began looking over her shoulder more often in her driveway as she felt a dark shadow loomed over her as she gathered her bags and scurried to the front door to quickly lock behind her. Then he asks about a new club since he has already been removed from being in charge of not one or two but three prior clubs for a variety of reasons, not to mention the continuous double-dipping, and then states, "Sorry for the email blah, blah, blah," as he sits behind the cinder block wall next door typing away. Fly hated the phrase "blah, blah, blah" and its lack of importance. Also, AP Ave intentionally moved the schedule so the two coworkers did not have to share the same space or time off together. The next day, he commented on the annual report as they were not submitted before the summer, and he only replied to only two of the minor incidents and none of the other many incriminating insubordinations and dated materials that he blatantly ignored. Within the comments, he stated he went to the XL Coordinator, which he did, but no other immediate supervisors were notified that he changed the official XL Exam date, and that he was being so very helpful on his free and lunch periods helping the XL students that he was unable to open the Exam boxes and take inventory as Ms. Fly had requested verbally and written seven times for over a week.

By ignoring feedback for improvement, Ms. Fly interpreted this as an admission or lack of care blah, blah, blah of all the other offenses created last school year:

> Mr. Paul did not adhere to basic information, guidelines, protocol, and criteria discussed and reviewed in meetings regarding several important items, he was asked to clarify lesson plans repeatedly, emails from supervisor went unacknowledged repeatedly, suggestions to improve classroom management strategies for improved student behavior and classroom rapport, he must report to, consult, or commu-nicate with his immediate supervisor on deci-sions that impact the department program, he interfered with and did not comply with depart-mental goals regarding course selection pro-cess all discussed with faculty throughout the school year in faculty meetings and memoran-dums, he changed the date of the XL Exam set forth by the International Testing Center without the notification or consultation to department

146

chairpersons, and lost the paperwork consisting
of each student's XL login and password codes
compromising the security of the online portion
of the XL Exam.

Ms. Fly had been researching and reading up on best ways
to deal with a person like this. This was not textbook "difficult
employee" and not an issue of "troubled employee" or she
could only speculate, as that meant he had a problem with
drugs or alcohol, and there was a referral system in place for
that. It was not like Mr. P.A.U.L. was going to creep up to Ms.
Fly one day and say, "I'm sorry for all the confusion, but for abit
now, I've been addicted to anti-psychotic medication and I
like tequila a lot." It would be over if that was the case. Fly's
husband had a graduate student friend once that whenever
he drank tequila, he would strip down and run naked in the
streets of the city. It happens and everyone's doing it. She had
tried so many strategies that she had brainstormed with colleagues: ignore, coddle, keep enemies close, kill with kindness,
and none of these seemed to work. She re-read the leadership
checklists and books to find yet another path to succeed with
this employee. The narcissist thinks highly of themselves, and
they lash out when their ego is challenged. He wanted to be
praised, patted on the back, as the male administrators were
seen doing, the Boy's Club, and rewarded to boot, but there
was very little to reward in Fly's eyes. It was September, and
he once again had to be reminded to do basic annual items
like hand in the emergency snow day phone numbers and
other seemingly trivial but important items. Ms. Fly was annoyed
she had to put on her to-do list again to "Remind P.A.U.L...."
Fly decided that this school year, as she never did and never
will give him praise for bad behavior and poor performance
no matter how painful it would be. That is what he desperately
desired and he was not going to get a pat on the back for
behaving badly, not from Ms. Fly anyway no matter what. She
was standing her ground. If it was the student who painted the
ugliest painting she had ever seen in her entire life, she will just
keep walking by, not even saying "Nice try" or anything.

Sparkle Thief

Fly thought about the strange story she read about where there was a group of brothers being held captive by their father in a busy well-populated city and how, after years, one of the brothers mustered up enough courage to escape and seek help. The unusual part of the tale was that no one could believe something like that could happen right under their noses. Millions of people living in city dwellings, in an apartment building of hundreds of occupants, so close by, yet so far out of reach at all times. To pass the time, the brothers would act out movie scenes and entertain themselves. They were warned that there were bad people in the outside world and were not permitted to leave the safety of the small apartment. They developed a wolf pack–like mentality to acquire safety in numbers, but one courageous day, a lone wolf broke free and wandered to the city streets below. Not knowing what to do or who to turn to for help, he finally found a path to freedom. She thought about how things so outrageous could happen in total secrecy. Fly was trying to find her own path to escape the confines of her workplace.

Ms. Fly finally got another appointment with the personnel superintendent. At this point, not counting the thousand daily minuscule incompetencies, Ms. Fly came up with about five large issues she felt were egregious offenses on behalf of Mr. P.A.U.L. and prior Principal Don Voyage for neglecting and blatantly ignoring her complaints. Armed with a two-page document that cut to the point, Superintendent soon-to-be Sparkle Thief asked why this was not brought up the previous year, and Fly simply stated that it is too difficult to explain much less comprehend, and it would have been easier just to ask for a demotion, take the place of mid-year retiree Johnart, and not be boss to anyone except herself and her alien body. She let her know she should have just let her step down and take the retiring teacher's position. The superintendent read the memo and asked some inquisitive questions about the employee. The letter was plain and the request was clear and began as such:

Re: Employee

As the curriculum specialist, department leader, and an advocate for both students and the visual arts, I would like to seek your assistance with regard to an employee in my department. I am seeking guidance as well as your professional identification and assessment of concerns I have had over the last several years, and your expertise in deciphering appropriate actions and solutions based on the Board and District Policies and Procedures. For some time, I have been finding it increasingly more difficult to work with this employee, while implementing my leadership skills and administrative duties to the highest quality and caliber the district and myself would expect, as well as to maintain a safe, productive, and positive department for students and faculty. This employee has created an extremely uncomfortable and hostile working environment on a regular basis and is ongoing as you can see by the select attached items documented. While this employee is capable of exhibiting some good qualities and achievements, they are on an inconsistent basis and the below concerns far outweigh the contributions. I find this teacher's behavior to be unprofessional and offensive. The following are actions, performance, and behaviors that are of main concern, and that are observable, documented, and/or targeted toward myself as an immediate supervisor.

After she read the letter and asked some straightforward questions, she stated that this seemed like he was acting in a passive-aggressive manner and that it was deeply troubling. She would arrange to meet with Principal Teddy and they would discuss how to proceed. Fly thought about the elusive and notorious "rubber room" that was there somewhere in that Administrative Building. She had just read an article about the pros and cons of teacher tenure and one section discussed what Ms. Fly thought she could relate to, stating, "A district can bring charges at any time against a tenured teacher or assistant for insubordination, conduct unbecoming, inefficiency, incompetence, physical or mental disability, neglect of duty, failure to maintain certification or immoral character." The article stated that 25 percent of teachers exit the profession in the first five years, "many because of the rigorous requirements and challenging workload." Over the years, there were several teachers and supervisors that were rumored to have been removed from duty and allowed to collect a full paycheck, but they had to sit in the rubber room and staple curriculum papers all day. Some even joked that sounded like a sweet deal and what would one have to do to go there like it was a vacation resort. Or was the rubber room like the Holy Grail where it was something else, not a physical room made out of rubber where they put the teachers who had been bad? Ms. Fly thought this professionally published article hit the nail on the head and maybe they will remove him and her work world can be at peace once again. After all, people moved every year to different buildings for many reasons, so it seemed like an easy solution.

The list she reported to the administrators was clear, and Fly had composed several documents of disturbing behavior with years and notes of when the accounts had occurred. There were no less than 150 examples of observed and documented issues and complaints: visible anger and facial expressions (at least 12 times), dishonesty and concealment (at least 24 or more times), seeking out or avoidance in a not normal manner (ongoing, regular basis), compulsive emails (unlimited), body language or other odd behaviors (unlimited and ongoing examples), frightening comments/artifacts (unlimited examples), retaliation (unlimited examples of undermining via sabotage), complaints (students, teachers, local events). She explained how he went so far as to manipulate impressionable young male students to gang up on her, which any trained personnel in charge should know is a classic transference of power.

Here are some of the looks Ms. Fly categorized so far: the scowl, the ignore, the glare, the stare into the soul, the leer, the shark eyes dark and dead, the frown, the unappetizing, the sour, the bitter, the disgruntled, the seething, the sad puppy dog, the puppy dog head tilt when confused, the look to the upper left to seek an invisible answer, the rage, the silent scream, the better than thou, the rich elite, head held high snooty, the grump, the scorned, the privileged, the entitled, the blank, the blink-blink, the deer in headlights, the look the other way, the look at the floor, the no eye contact back to Fly, the two-faced (smile at others then sharp anger look at Fly.) Those were just a few, and one never knew when or where they would emerge.

Fly shared some of the disturbing documents where she told the superintendent that she used to *sparkle* and that she had lost her sparkle because of Mr. P.A.U.L. She, being a woman, should have known how important sparkle is to some people. As she perused through the documents listening intently to what Ms. Fly was reporting, she said sympathetically that she would get her sparkle back. She promised.

The Torture Logs

Ms. Fly felt like her job as a teaching supervisor was like a stuff sandwich, only she didn't say stuff. No one cared that these supervisors still taught one hundred students every day; they only saw the leadership role of what they needed to accomplish each given school year, which was a small percentage of her work day. They were monkeys in the middle between teacher and administrators getting it from both ends. Mr. P.A.U.L. and Ms. Fly were like the oil and vinegar dressing where every September 1, the separated parts get shaken up and perfectly mixed together, but only for such a short time and then separate back out, repelled by one another just as quickly as they mixed to a perfect taste. Not too tangy, not too greasy, but at the end of the day, the salad would be soggy and filled with separation.

Ms. Fly, more than ever, was determined to document every maneuver this person created so that if this was some sort of intentional incriminating series of acts she would have proof. In the summer, he emailed everyone in the entire district department about a great field trip idea, ironic because his field trips proved to be debacles; not to the point where he lost a student or left one behind at MacRonnie's, but signing up your work friends to chaperone without asking them first is pretty selfish and then scheduling that gracious school-wide volunteer activity for the same day ridiculous. He could never fill the buses either for some reason. Who would not want to go to an art museum? Why did he not realize teachers in the district were not supposed to email "everyone" because it would become pandemonium pretty quickly, especially when teachers "Replied All" to hundreds of staff. That became a running joke so be careful what button you press. So of course, he emailed everyone with his "Good Morning Everyone!" precursor followed by how he was researching additional art shows for "our students" and offered up one in particular (that the retired teacher Johnart did every year by the way) and that he made up a handout and he can "provide you with copies" (which he never did), and if anyone had any students who may want to participate, he would take care of entering the artwork by November. Well, this seems very nice but also a cry for "look at me!" obvious to Ms. Fly, so she and the other teachers just ignored this proclamation as this was retired Johnart's thing he used to do and P.A.U.L. indeed did not come up with an original idea on his own.

The October Agenda had clear and specific things that Ms. Fly had to disseminate to the group. Mr. P.A.U.L. must have only focused on the course presentations for enrollment, the one he shockingly tried to sabotage last year by having the audacity to tell Ms. Fly he booked the library so she could not do her presentations on classes the students could take the next year. This was the ultimate dog and pony show to fight for art classes to run as the competition from other departments rose every year. Does he not realize by not promoting the arts, he was shooting himself in the foot by potentially not having enough students in classes thus creating potential job loss? So he began emailing Fly repeatedly about his students being dropped from his classes and blamed specific people in the guidance department. Then, the AP asked if each of the art teachers could take a turn decorating the main hallway showcase with this year's school theme on celebrating how we each shine in our own unique way. This was part of the continuation of the anti-bullying campaign. It was Mr. P.A.U.L.'s turn and he had not changed it yet, so Fly approached him in the hallway so as to not be alone with him to discuss his ideas, but the teacher acted apprehensive and just stared blankly back at her with no response. Startled, Ms. Fly gave some suggestions and still with no response and only painful silence, she stated firmly, trying not to act annoyed, "It just has to be done!" And with that, he responded with several excuses as to why he could not partic- ipate. First, he ignores, then creates excuses. And to Fly, how flipping hard is it to decorate a showcase and why is he taking all the fun out of everything? With that, he simply placed a sign in the barren faded papered showcase: "Under Construction."

The next month came, and Fly knew she should have played sick on the staff development day by pulling a Johnart. The bus was going to leave from Ms. Fly's school parking lot very early in the morning to visit the art museum. She should have just taken the train in or done something to not be in the small confines of a bus with P.A.U.L., but she was too busy in and out of doctor's visits and tending to Celeste's sports games that it was not well thought out. She brought a book to read on the voyage. Celeste and Fly's husband got her a book about how to become a villain when she graduated with her Leadership Degree. An odd gift, she saw in her mind the two of them at the bookstore laughing about how Fly was too much like Mary Poppins and perfect and this ought to teach her a real lesson on trying to find her inner villainous evil side. Perfectionists have a specific way of dealing with the world. They are hyper-aware of their surroundings, they are creative, sometimes introverted, they know where everything is and how everything should be just so, they are attentive to details, they are sensitive, easily hurt, and sometimes can lead to debilitating anxiety or perhaps tragedy for some. So she brought this book that had been col- lecting dust on her shelf and read about how she too could become a villain if she followed the simple steps outlined in each chapter.

Director Coupon Suzy had previously sent an email to everyone with high importance, "P.S. If anyone gets to the school early, Ms. Fly will open room 234 for teachers to meet up or wait." Now, Ms. Fly is an early arriver always and could not believe it and it was obvious to her that Mr. P.A.U.L. intentionally beat her to it, parked in the lot, and actually raced her by running to get to the classroom before she could graciously letting all the other teachers into the room for them to wait. He even prancingly escorted several to the ladies' room and used the key to let them in chuckling and chit-chatting with them all the way down that long dark hallway. She remembered one episode of *Naked and Afraid* where the guy was so arrogant and self-assured he was going to make it. They always end up being crybabies and quitting because of a paper cut all the while having put down their female counterparts who end up surviving alone in the end, albeit naked and afraid but relieved they got rid of the male counterparts. They called it the "overconfidence effect" where someone shows such self-satisfaction at their biased performance which is proven to be less than they perceive. He would increasingly show elation during wrongdoing or inability to preform or help others. To Fly, he intentionally ignored the directives of the director's email notification, but to the others, he was being oh so helpful and polite. What a "nice guy," as Don Voyage expressed how others thought about him. Fly couldn't help but think how Don ruined her life and she shared her thoughts with Mrs. Parabola often at lunch while they tried to problem-solve their workplace situations. Unlike math, there were no real calculated answers rendered.

She sat alone in the back of the bus as the Young Yuppie-Mediocre Millennials Teacher Clique sat in the middle and the supervisors sat in the front. Coupon Suzy presented a look of confusion as to why Ms. Fly chose to sit by herself and read a book while all the others acted like schoolchildren on their way to an exciting field trip far away from the daily routine. Actually, if the disease was not in remission at the time, she would never be able to take the bus. The visit was fine, but Ms. Fly was happy the day was almost over and they were pulling up to the parking lot to de-board, when for the second time that day, Mr. P.A.U.L. waited for Fly to pass and stated sarcastically and creepily, "After you..." motioning his arm in the exiting direction. Had he never de-boarded a plane? It goes front to back, that is why Fly sat in the back to avoid contact and he deliberately waited patiently for her. There was no other way out. She told the principal and he stated that he was just being a gentleman, and she became increasingly infuriated that no one understood what was happening right in plain sight. She did not realize she was presenting signs of being bullied by wanting to isolate herself from everyone.

Ms. Fly never really knew when Principal Teddy met with Mr. P.A.U.L., but she did see the Superintendent soon-to-be Sparkle Thief come to the building which was unusual. But the principal was told to meet with Mr. P.A.U.L. and to tell him that Ms. Fly was his supervisor and that he was to do what she instructed. How is this information not understood? People go to work and people have bosses and people are supposed to do what the bosses tell you to do; otherwise, it would not be called work. She was sure they also discussed the latest ball game on the playing field and chuckled "abit" in secret code. This was seriously getting old.

The same week as the field trip, Ms. Fly sent another email about keeping doors open during instruction and to please see her if anyone needed assistance (who actually needs help propping a door open?), but she had to email it as per the cabinet meeting to all of the teachers knowing it was only relevant to Mr. P.A.U.L. Why did she have to ask so many times? It was the school policy and a safety issue and the principal told her to have her staff leave doors open at all times. At the time, it was called an Open Door policy, which today, the policy is the complete opposite for safety. November, December, February, and still, the door remained closed. Ms. Fly opened it once, and Mr. P.A.U.L. had important student information posted where you could not even see it as the taped memos were blocked because they were displayed behind the...guess what? Behind the door if it was actually ever open.

The entries in the Torture Log continued albeit brief as it was time-consuming and Fly had better things to do: inability to properly mat artwork for exhibition, impossible to display, steals handouts, adds aggressive amount of paper clips on photos of students in front of their artwork, conceals art-related student activities, places Post-Its over his own face and body in photographs—very creepy and bizarre, stated "Good stuff!" at post-observation meeting, but never implemented ideas, on and on.

The bleak cold days of February came and Fly looked forward to a few days at Casino Posh with her friend who was suffering from breast cancer. They decided they needed an "SOS!" or Save Our Selves moment. They found a common date; Fly was getting her Ramicadence infusion on Monday and Jade was getting chemo on Friday, so in between worked out perfectly. Both were taken aback when Jade's hair started falling out in clumps. After the initial fear, they apprehensively chuckled and decided to never complain about a bad hair day ever again. They had a lot in common as they were both in charge of departments, had daughters, and were both Drum Majors in high school, the ultimate in leadership by marching 150 students while swaying arms up high in the air conducting the cadence of parade music…all while marching backward facing them. At the Casino Posh, they discussed these were the cards they were dealt, so went down the hall and marched like Drum Majors in charge of the loud, dark, and smokey casino floor holding their heads high at the slot machines even as Jade's wig, Felicia, slid down and sat crooked on her forehead. She had named her wig Felicia, and it had acted like the uninvited guest showing up in the sparkly darkness of the casino. They played their favorite slot they liked to call "Cancer and Colitis and the City," and they were not as glamorous as the show's actresses but they did their best to shine. At the Club Posh that night, Jade was dancing solo like no one was watching, but they were. Two hunkamaniacs approached her and tried to get her to go to their room repeatedly. Jade was in her own world letting loose, and Fly started getting scared, so she broke out her superpowers and yelled at them, "Leave her alone! I'm a teacher!" They always had fun, and then reality reared its ugly head as they drove back to their homes awaiting.

Ms. Fly's log book turned into a visual diary. Rather than continue to write about all of these incidents, she had been taking photos, so she printed the photos and emails and placed them chronologically in a binder. New year, new binder. Her handwritten words became an emotional documentary. Notes she wrote in the margins: I tried so many approaches: "Hey P.A.U.L., why don't you...?" suggested by past Principal Don Voyage. "Just ignore him," said Mrs. Parabola. "It could backlash on you," warned the Director Coupon Suzy. "Maybe if he got married, he'd grow up," surmised the Union Navigator. *Why was there a constant struggle? Why did this happen?* She scribbled her thoughts in the margins: Afraid of the backlash. Two colleagues warned about. Try to ignore. Almost mocking of the profession. To come to work and deal with this every day is unbearable. Ongoing. Fight or flight. Physical reactions. Hysterical crying. Scared. I want to just do the job I love. Shine goodness on school and opposite toward me. Deviant. Defiant. Anger. Restraining order? Look into that. Workplace violence fear. Could he find my home? Am I in danger? How far will he go?

Ms. Fly returned to a meeting with Principal Teddy and was made aware that he only just met with Mr. P.A.U.L. three whole months later. He had to get "approval" by his union to meet with the principal about his actions and behavior. And then after finally meeting with the superintendent again, Principal Teddy stormed into her room and commanded Ms. Fly. to stop documenting and that she would not want to get on Sparkle Thief's "bad side." Teddy turned the tables on her abruptly. He said, "You heard what she said, you are to stop documenting *now*." Sounds of her mothball-riddled grandmother thundered through her brain. In the beginning of the school year, Fly had full support and was even told they were going to start an official file on P.A.U.L.'s actions with documents, but alas, several months went by and all of a sudden, Superintendent Sparkle Thief kept Fly's sparkles all to herself, the ultimate villain. Fly didn't even get to come up with her own villainous name or super power, but in a moment, Sparkle Thief did just that, contrary to any policies or promises. Principal Teddy needed to get tenured, so rather than rock the boat, they both ganged up on Ms. Fly, insisting that she was the one who needed to stop, stop documenting. Fly wanted to get two of her fabulous female friends and pull an ultimate *9 to 5* on Teddy, perhaps flatten his tires, tie him to his desk, and make him read every word in that melted binder out loud while turning the heat on high, force him to eat that moldy oversized school cafeteria food with expired milk and watch him sweat for a change. One can daydream.

In the second meeting, the superintendent downplayed the accusations by saying, "When he refuses to eat cake, bring him an apple," and to simply play his game. Fly hates games. She also compared Fly's situation to that of a custodian who kept taking extended weekends and insinuated that that was more concrete to prove unlike Fly's situation. How dare she compare this to a three-day weekend. So like a student being commanded to do something they did not want to do, she stopped at the store on the way home and bought a huge pack of ballpoint pens like the quantity you buy at Small Mart, opened the pack, and decided to write until every last pen was emptied of ink. That was an art project Celeste had to do: "Empty the pen." And she wrote and wrote to and from work every day and during her long stints in the bathroom, which she began calling her office, recording every last detail against the wishes of the Man-command.

Fly could tell once again when Mr. P.A.U.L. was spoken to, as it was the same with the last principal. P.A.U.L. would avoid contact for about a month or two, and then all of a sudden, bombard with multiple items while teaching when he thinks he is starting to be under the radar. He rushed twice to bring Janeart's Sub Plans to her rooms when she was out sick, beating Ms. Fly to the door once again to let the students in as if doing a good deed. It was not Mr. P.A.U.L.'s job to do so and he didn't for others and Fly thought unless he was sincerely communicating that he was willing and able to assist, please don't. It was becoming clearer to Ms. Fly this was a power-play tactic and a constant struggle; to take the power and authority away from Ms. Fly and put it directly in the hands of Mr. P.A.U.L. to look so sincerely helpful in front of administration and other teachers from other departments and to beat Ms. Fly to the door and kindly open the door for the patiently awaiting students. It was not about a closed door or sub plans or course selection or a showcase or artwork or field trip or widgets, but about a thousand ways to attempt to conquer and to strip away Fly's power and authority, undermining her over and over again like a thousand paper cuts. Not one stands out as being the most painful, but at the end of each day, she was sliced to bits.

Disturbed by the charades between Mr. P.A.U.L. and now Principal Teddy Table Turner, Fly met with her own union representative. who at first was shocked by the documents and exclaimed, "Well, obviously, someone is lying!" with regard to the previous year's ludicrous inspection response letter. Obviously, there were either four students eating or there were not. There was food or there was not food, large or small, Styrofoam lunch tray or bag of chips or granola bar. And Mr. P.A.U.L.'s reputation? Who did he think read these inspections? The entire school had no stake hold in his claims. These were confidential documents. And it was not like he was Teacher of the Year or anything, like Johnart, and had to regain trust and truth.

Fly was promised her sparkle back, but like an Indian giver, they took it back and kept it. Fly inquired again about a workplace violence policy with still no luck. Fly's husband's workplace had a clear policy, procedures, and consequences. Fly read her husband's workplace Policies and Procedures on Harassment, and it seemed fairly clear on who does what and how in these situations. There were contact people, forms to complete, and a timeline in which any incidents should be reviewed and rectified. It was a document agreed upon by all levels of the educational institution: twenty pages right there in black and white so everyone had the expectations of workplace behavior and code of conduct just the same as students had. There were even two employees at his work where they had to change their schedules so that their paths would never cross in the classrooms or office, much like Ms. Fly's AP was trying to move rooms for Mr. P.A.U.L., so he could be placed as far away physically as possible. Why was it so difficult to address and come up with a feasible solution for everyone? The entire spring was sucked up by meeting after meeting with the union navigators higher up than the building level that she had been consulting with now for five years. This was getting out of control that no one knew what to do and how to address a situation.

Box-O-Torture. It's late spring. Time to wrap up the school year once again. Fly was exhausted by being told by Mr. P.A.U.L.

via email "I have no good news," over and over again. Really? Who does not have one thing in an entire month that is nothing good to report? This was intentional sabotage and was so absurd Fly and her husband would make a running joke about it at home, especially when watching the local or national news, they would groan, "Ugh, there is no good news!" and then chuckle about how cruel and awful American society was as they reacted to the stories of how horribly people treat one another and that was all that was reported. Schools were a mere microcosm of all this stuff going on in America. Only she didn't say stuff.

Families of people being tormented at work get the brunt of the pain, whereas they do not directly get beaten to death with the attacks, they are the quiet listeners, the encouragers of strength, and problem-solvers. Celeste and Fly's husband got a double whammy between this work situation and her physical ailments, both taboo and terrible, and for standing by her side unconditionally every day, she is eternally grateful for them. Fly did not know, though, the lasting negative emotional impact the fierce storm of colitis and chaos at work would have on her family in the future. People like P.A.U.L. should know how they negatively impact families and not just their targets. Fly also still could not come to celebrate her birthday every year since that dreadful spring break, but Celeste would still bake her a cake and plead for her mom to please not sing because she was so tone deaf that Little Celeste would exclaim, "Mom, even your lip synching hurts my ears." Each birthday, she faced with a cringe, but with every year, too, the pain became less and less severe.

All teachers were given clear instruction on final exams in a meeting, an email, and a memo. So for all the different learning styles, verbal, visual, and tactile. All teachers were corrected on minor details such as spacing or typos and agreeably complied, made changes without a fuss, and re-submitted with no-problem apologies and completed correctly and promptly without issue. Not Mr. P.A.U.L. He had an outrageous amount of errors too numerous to count this school year. The new XL art teacher was requested to open the XL boxes the same as Mr. P.A.U.L. the previous year and clear differences stood out:

Janeart complied immediately without problems and, in fact, found an error in the inventory that needed to be addressed immediately. She also asked about the XL Exam date and if it should be changed, only if there was a conflict. This year, Ms. Fly was not met with a sharp box cutter slicing open of packages and slamming them all over in her room in order to illicit fear and anxiety. There was a clear pattern that all of the other teachers responded to daily duties and tasks in a normal fashion, and Mr. P.A.U.L. did not by comparison. Knowing he was also the topic of contractual discussion as he saw Superintendent Sparkle Thief and union presidents go into meetings with Fly and Teddy, he disguised his deviant behavior with emails that appeared superficially kind and sincere. Fly did not take the bait, rather, seeing right through him she battled back with words:

> Memo: "It is imperative that you comply with all written and verbal directions given with regard to assessment duties with the preparation of final exams to ensure cohesiveness and accuracy. Please note the following and address the situation immediately...With regard to the semester final exam you submitted for review, changes were neglected to be made. We discussed at length the recommendation and ideas to improve the unit of instruction. I am not certain why the recommendations were not implemented to improve instruction for our department students. Please ask for assistance as necessary to prevent such issues." (Meeting Notes)

Fly is in the hospital again and texts Diamond Heart Vana a photo of her French toast and omelet breakfast, and she replies, "This is what a mom has to do to get a decent breakfast in bed? Lay there in agonizing pain while practically hemorrhaging." She did not have a choice when flare-ups would get the best of her, consuming her being she once was. It was becoming clear to Fly that her body was unable to tolerate the work stresses and the painful flare-ups had been now noticeably in direct correlation with Mr. P.A.U.L.'s work shenanigans and aggressive attacks. On a Post-It in the log, she wrote to herself: There cannot be this much confusion surrounding one teacher. She opened the mail and the billed amount for each infusion was about $17,000, and she thought about how many cars she could have purchased with that amount of money. What was this miracle drug and why did it cost so much? Fly was grateful for good insurance and felt bad for those women in the meetings that did not have insurance and just dealt with the pain, agony, and chronic rushes to the bathroom.

There was another meeting with several levels of authority in the principal's office as well as an individual who was supposed to watch Fly's back no matter what even if she had a reputation of not really fighting for the rights of fellow supervisors. Year after year, they got stepped all over with contractual issues and negotiations never really getting anywhere positive. The workload was inching up, piling the responsibilities higher and higher on the supervisors and they had a hard time fighting back. They even took a pay cut one year to save jobs even though there were none really in jeopardy. It was all a ruse to open up the contract and get rid of higher paid employees. It became clear to Fly that Mr. P.A.U.L. was using insubordination and all of these other tactics as a tool for harassment and intimidation, creating a toxic working environment Ms. Fly once loved so much before he came to the department. Then once again, Principal Teddy Table Turner stormed at her from across the big table and yelled firmly, "This has to stop!" He was clearly visibly angry with his face sweating and boiling with red fire. Fly thought, *Yes, this has to stop!* He was angry that Ms. Fly told him a few months ago that she was not going to stop documenting so that she could protect herself; for what she did not know but no one can stop someone from writing thoughts and happenings on paper and she had all of those pens. And then he threw a Mantrum and demanded, "He is not going *anywhere*." Ms. Fly's union representative just sat there dumb as a stump and the neutral AP side-eyed and said nothing and Fly left torn down, not only by P.A.U.L., but by Sparkle Thief and Teddy and her supposed supporter. Her union was supposed to support her, but instead, it was like calling a company with an urgent matter and the computer voice answers and Fly's yelling, "Representative! Representative! Representative!" until after a ten-minute excruciating wait she gets disconnected. The neutral AP found Fly in the hallway later that week and whispered closely in her ear, "I am very sorry about all this. It's a man's world." Her eyes widened with dark sadness. Where have people's moral calculators gone? There were laws for Fly's students, but not for her or other teachers—the hypocrisy!

She walked out of that meeting toward her once secret bathroom to escape. When she walked by the main lobby showcase once decorated with a flimsy "Under Construction" sign, was now fully decorated highlighting the physical education department with all of the balls and cleats and bold shimmering signage. Fly thought she might hemorrhage to death right there. The dodgeball once again hit her square in the guts, knocking out all her wind as she fell to the lobby floor was right there in the showcase. Mr. P.A.U.L. graciously made a sparkly showcase for another department, ignoring the assistant principal's anti-bullying awareness display he was supposed to do in his turn. She guessed he was not aware or blatantly disagreed with the anti-bullying campaign.

Fly had collected a thousand pieces of paper that school year with intentions to seek justice and simply divide once and for all the oil and vinegar. Each piece of printed paper sliced her delicate fingertips as she weeded through the pages in her binders as she vividly recalled each instance with disgust and fear. Each piece of paper cutting just as her insides were every moment, cutting her organ apart, the delicate lining of her colon simultaneously being shredded with no immunity in sight. The times resonated over and over in her head the abundance of daily attacks, sometimes multiple in one day in a variety of strategic methods: When he gave her artwork taped with drafting tape so as to disintegrate in her arms as she tried to display setting up to look like her fault. Or giving her work poorly mounted so as to get destroyed in transit reflecting on her not him. Repeatedly keeping the classroom door shut. Placing flyers on top of Fly's Club flyers or on the other hand, placing aggressively hand-cut arrows pointing to an activity Ms. Fly typed on a flyer, responding, "I have no good news" all of the time and then submitting announcements of prestigious events which were merely showcases, glorifying and exaggerated achievements in his mind. Posting all around signage that says "Art makes you smart" as if to justify his poor teaching and stupidity. Art only makes you smart if you are guided by excellence in education, critical thinking skills, and technique. Reluctant to produce art invitations he was requested to do by the director, he made a point to present them to Ms. Fly in front of coworkers, as he did with the pre-buttered bagel in class, serving as if giving a gift to her with arms reached out, "Hot off the presses!" Chronic emails that go on and on, clarifying basic information. Constant projects he was going to do for the students and never did year after year. The final exams once again intentionally being completely incorrect and displaying anger and rage upon having been requested yet again to fix it. And then, after weeks of hiding, dodging, and eluding Ms. Fly, he runs into her room at 7:29 a.m. to bombard once again with a plethora of paperwork and items at an intentionally inopportune time to prevent her from getting her class motivated and lesson started at 7:30. To refuse or tell him to come back later would make her look like the insensitive one, so she wrote and wrote in her logbook anyway—she knew what was happening. One might see all this and think he was just merely incompetent, but Fly knew better. He tried diligently to do good and look good in front of others in the building, so it appeared to her as a mirage; an optical illusion that you may believe you see but, in reality, isn't there at all. The wavy water line appears in the distance in the desert never to be obtained or reached at the horizon as it keeps moving forward as do you. You can keep walking down that long dark school hallway becoming trapped in a maze like an M. C. Escher tessellation.

The bridge lay dead ahead. She crossed over this bridge twice a day as it gave her sunrise and sunsets and a span of thoughts to hold on tight during tumultuous windy days. Humiliated and tormented by her colleagues and bosses that were supposed to help, she drove home, blasting Icona Pop's "I Love It" enraged zany tune in her mind as she thinks about killing herself instantly at high rate of speed. "I crashed my car into the bridge, I watched, I let it burn. I threw your stuff into a bag and pushed it down the stairs. I crashed my car into the bridge, I don't care!" Fly was petrified of dying in a car crash by a random distracted reckless human being at the wheel, and it was the one unnatural fear she had as her aunt died instantly in a car crash a long time ago. A mom with young children in the back seat sped into an intersection and the woman was blinded for a split second by solar glare that early morning. As her boyfriend made a left hand turn toward her children's high school, the woman side-swiped them and she died instantly, not knowing even what hit her. The last picture of her Fly had was a black and white photograph at her wedding the year before, dancing joyously in a circle, holding hands with loved ones.

Fly always listened to music since her dad passed away, and it gave her hope that others who created the lyrics have been down similar paths, even if the lyrics were about romance or other personal themes, the main cadence resonated within her much as "Jar of Hearts" resonated with her father at the end. She didn't even care about her precious Celeste or anyone else at that point and only that she could not survive one more day living in that toxic working environment. She had already died 999 times throughout her entire life and could not bear one more cut. Actually, she thought her cute, sleepy, indoor cats had the life and were lucky even if just with nine lives. Fly was so sick that she and her husband would speak in British accents playing out a scene from *Monty Python and the Holy Grail*. He would state, "Bring out your dead!" as he pretended to push a cart of people who met their demise from the black plague, and Fly would respond with a British accent after pretending to be unwillfully tossed into the cart, "I'm not dead!" as a man tries to get his payment.

"He says he's not dead," states a passerby. He responded, "You will be soon!"

Fly responds, "I'm getting better! I feel fine. I think I'll go for a walk. I feel happy!"

He gets smashed in the head and thrown onto the cart of dead people. Fly's husband always reminded her that they were to grow old together and sip mint juleps on the porch together as they watched the sun set at the close of each day.

Fly didn't know what a mint julep was and never had one, but she thought she would wait until the time was right to try it when her thirst needed quenching on a hot summer day in retirement.

It had become utterly unbearable, and no one except her husband and a few close friends knew, believed, and understood the pain from the secret psychological torture bestowed upon her at the hands of the Institution of Man every day and perpetuated by people in charge who wanted to just play his game or did not know what to do procedurally nor seemed to care or prioritize. And superficially it appeared as she was warned: that because she had to chronically fix Mr. P.A.U.L.'s errors, she looked like the difficult one, not him. What if Teddy just made a different decision and made it right, right then and there? All she was asking for was a simple solution to a complex problem: Keep It Simple Silly.

When no one believed what she was saying or at least they dismissed the claims completely and becoming overwhelmed in shock and in hysterics at this last resort and cry for help, Fly had serious thoughts and desire of gunning it along the stretch of parkway to work and then upon smooth arrival at the bridge going full force at 100 miles per hour, aiming for the space between the spans of heightened road she had observed each time she approached, and finally with a swerve to the left, she drove until she plunged into the river below. Unable to escape, she sinks down and down into the depths of the dark flowing water never to surface. Drowning as they hold her head under water, unable to speak or tell her story. Tumbling in the riptide-like current in the shallow waters and sharp rocks she had once felt like near drowning as a child along the same nearby beach. Not knowing which way was up or down as she spun in somersaults brushing against the harsh rock and sand churning into opaque pieces of ground glass. Which way should she go so she doesn't drown?

A young woman lay on her back floating in a shallow stream, her lifeless body floats by with her hands open in surrender. Her eyes staring up sadly at the sky, mouth slightly open as if to mutter quietly for help, but she has given up; in her face, she cannot take the pain any longer and appears not amused. Her dress flows, encapsulating her body and weighs her down just under the water. The landscape surrounding her is equally as important to the figure as it engulfs her on all sides, surrounds her with the ironic beauty of the colorful foliage on the perimeters of the water's edge. The weeping willows drape from above as if a cascade of never-ending tears. Driven out of her mind, the figure was innocently picking flowers in the forest as she falls into the stream and drowns all the while singing. There is a delicate balance of splendor and insignificance. This is one of Fly's favorite artworks, a Pre-Raphaelite oil painting *Ophelia* by artist John Everett Millais.

She had asked to resign, to quit her position, and downsize. She applied for several jobs in other districts, but she now had too much experience and even seeking a teaching job they all told her she was too administratory and having too much administrative knowledge and leadership degrees was overkill for a mere teacher position. Fly even admitted she was willing to take a pay cut, commute the other direction, teach any art class offered. Fight or flight, hit and run. The fight-or-flight response affects the brain and body, creating physical characteristics such as sudden fear and chaos, sweating, shaking, hyperventilating, dizziness, fainting, seeing black spots, and like the world is spinning around you in a vertigo-like fashion. No policy on bullying or harassment in the district for staff, no method to form a complaint and create sound resolution; that was all she was asking for.

Fly tried to survive that last month of school with P.A.U.L.'s totally blatant deviant manipulations from chronic emailing outside the art room next door, seeking then hiding from Fly, Grinchesque–like sneaking around, ignoring and refusal of eye contact, incompetent final exams, taking misinformation and wrong advice from a male special education teacher over Ms. Fly's instructions completely undermining her over and over in ways that were near invisible to others, displaying a sign that stated "Clutch Like P.A.U.L." She had to look up the meaning of clutch even as it was yet another sports term she was not familiar with. Why couldn't he "hit it out of the ballpark!" as Don described about Janeart? And she was a "home run." Ball analogies Fly could live without. Fly guessed if you wrote the affirmations in big letters and posted them on your bulletin board it must be true. But Mr. P.A.U.L. never "clutched" for anything for the department nor his students, so perhaps, he did for the field she did not know. There certainly were a lot of balls in that show case. The art room was not the football field by the way. Art students do not need to "Hydrate! Hydrate!" with their recycled water bottles while coloring and designing their artwork. P.A.U.L. continued to be chronically insubordinate and submit completely erroneous documents regarding all aspects of teaching, and/or blatantly doing the exact opposite of what is required for job duties. He crept in that one final day and scooched his papers in Ms. Fly's direction, snarkily remarking, "Here's for my *multiple* courses" with an attitude. Why did he constantly get mad at her for his work requirements, she may never truly comprehend. The papers sliced Fly over and over, and she knew she would either need a lot of bandages to mend the wounds or figure out a way to not get cut up and shredded by his papers being off by two cents.

With this repeated for years and years, Fly felt chronically bullied, No, the "H-Word" harassed at the hands of another. She thought of her transgender student and how she tried to help and shelter him, soon-to-be her, even giving up her secret bathroom for his comfort, and why no one did that in return for Fly. She even cried to Director Coupon Suzy one spring afternoon, trying to explain what he was doing to her and that she was being bullied. Suzy just dismissed it, claiming that she herself was being bullied by the Tres Brujas in her department and that it is what it is, justifying the atrocities. It just seemed that everyone was very dismissive of Fly's claims, didn't want to get involved, and just looked the other way in order to gain tenure or simply left due to retirement. She even recently overheard two postal worker employees discussing among themselves as she mailed a package that "Management isn't listening and the union is no help." This seems to be going on rampant. Sick of hearing about it during work venting sessions, the only one who truly believed what was going on every single day was Fly's husband, her best friend and confidant, as the saying goes. He would always say, "I got you," even before she could end her question or statement and say, "Let's go for a walk." For everything else, it was a cruel world. How could she make a change,

Fly thought, as she gripped the steering wheel extra tightly that one day driving over that bridge. Changing her mind and staying the course.

So thinking about Celeste and how she herself was chronically bullied in school needed to make a change even if the teachers and others didn't listen or do anything. Fly mustered up the energy even with her debilitating ulcerative colitis, and instead, Fly got her laundry baskets of paperwork in order and called the State Administrator's Society for help. She got pumped up by Scandal's "The Warrior" and would blast it, even posting the picture on her inspiration board of the legendary '80s lead singer dressed in war paint and scratched and torn up on her shoulder pad by a monster in the opening scene of the video reminding her that she will prevail. "If you survive! The Warrior." The photo in her petite presence, blurred, ferocious, torn up. Her husband was always the cheerleader for the last few years, but he was also getting sick and tired of hearing about it compounded with her physical ailments. It had taken a lot out of her family to deal with her illness and workplace issue, and it was all too much to endure. Like the brave brother who led the wolf pack to safety and escape, Fly knew what she had to do, so that one day, she woke up, stepped outside as that wolf pack brother had, and desperately sought out for someone to listen and help. She got an appointment, and with a six-hour drive ahead, she stepped on the pedal and drove to the State Capitol to meet with the state legal representatives from her union. She thought the meeting with Superintendent Sparkle Thief was opening Pandora's Box, but little did she know. Even the director knew that meeting was going to lead to nowhere, so she called Ms. Fly with her very own claim that she herself was being harassed by the Tres Brujas in her department, that perhaps they could switch offices. She acted like being harassed in the workplace was no big deal like everyone just gets harassed in the workplace. Well, that would have been a great idea over a year ago when that final straw was brought to the director's attention after that dreadful PTA meeting. But now, it had gone too far. She just wanted to scream at the top of her lungs, "Citizen's arrest! Citizen's arrest!" as did Tom Hank's character in *The 'Burbs* and have someone held accountable for their actions.

Fly entered the hotel in the State Capitol City, but was placed in a room far from the front desk in a separate building, and a man followed her up the stairs as she dragged her cart of files and evidence. Rather than enter the room and have him snag her and drag her inside, she did an abrupt 180-degree about-face, pretending she forgot something in the car and left. Why do women have to fear men like this? If anything needs to stop, it is this disgusting ailment of society. She went to the front desk stating that room was unacceptable, and she needed to be closer to the front door for safety and she was relocated. The next day, Fly nervously dragged her abundance of notes and files into the legal department for advice, and the attorney stated, "I have people come here all the time, and if they do not have a claim, I turn them away immediately." After thoroughly looking through the binder Teddy simply ignored, the lawyer stated, "You have a case here. Who are all of the players?" Fly drove back for the last day of school, which was basically a barbeque, and she saw a note on Mr. P.A.U.L.'s dry-erase board that said "Good News." Curious that there was something written next to the "Good News" note, Ms. Fly quietly and curiously walked up to that side of the office to get a closer look when she read, "It's summer vacation!"

America the Beautiful—American Mayhem

Suicide is a serious problem in American culture from all walks of life. Students chronically bullied in schools where the problem is not addressed and ceases, are more likely to have suicidal thoughts. Anyone can be an unsuspecting victim. After the three-digit 988 Suicide and Crisis Lifeline was launched in 2020, 96,000 calls were received in the first week. In 2021, the lifeline handled over 2.5 million calls. Kate Spade designed so many beautiful bags, accessories, and even shiny gold pencil pouches. It was a sad, dark, and deeply disturbing day when Kate Spade, the beloved designer and entrepreneur, took her life. "She always had such a great ray of light about her. She was so jovial," stated a fashion journalist in a CNN interview. Suicide rates in America from 1999 to 2014 from ages 10 to 74 had increased according to a study by the Centers for Disease Control and Prevention. "For white women, the suicide rate increased by 60% during that period." Women need support to get through their struggles in life. The famous designer was known to coin the quote, "Leave a little sparkle everywhere you go."

The ABC's of Bullying

A   is for Arrogant Audacity

B   is for Brutal Biased Bully with Body Language Behind Back

C   is for Cowardly Corruption Concealment Compulsion Conspiracy Cat that Ate the Canary Looks

D   is for Deliberate Deviant Defiant Discriminating Danger *Duress

E   is for Entitled and Exclusionary Egomaniac

F   is for Fraudulent and Failed System

G   is for Gutless Grudge

H   is for Heaps of Hostile Hatred and Harassment* *The H-Word

I   is for Intimidation Isolation Incompetence Indifference Ignore

J   is for Jekyll and Hyde

K   is for Kindness Deprived

L   is for Low Self-Esteem Compulsive Liar

M   is for Manipulative Man with chronic Microaggressions

N   is for Noncompliant Narcissist

O   is for Oppression of Others

P   is for Power-seeking Passive-Aggressive for Psychotic Pleasure

Q   is for Questionable Pattern of Behavior Quest for Torment

R   is for Relentless Revenge

S   is for Senseless Stalking Saboteur

T   is for Targeted Two-Faced Threatening Terrorist

U   is for Under the Radar Underminer and Underachiever

V   is for Victimizing with Violent Vengeance Vampire Vulture

W   is for Wolf in Sheep's Clothing

X   is for X-Colleague Wannabe

Y   is for Yell at the top of your lungs for help

Z   is for Zombie Like a punching bag no matter how hard you hit it always comes back at you full force

Word Wall

"harassment" noun huh•ras•muhnt
1. the act or an instance of harassing, or disturbing, pestering, or troubling repeatedly; persecution, to annoy persistently
2. to create an unpleasant or hostile situation for especially by uninvited and unwelcomed verbal or physical conduct

synonyms: persecution, harrying, pestering, badgering, intimidation, bother, annoyance, aggravation, irritation, pressure, force, coercion

FAST FACT

According to the Crohn's and Colitis Foundation of America (CCFA), there has been a rise in inflammatory bowel disease. Approximately 1.6 million currently have IBD and about 70,000 new cases are reported each year. There may be as many as 80,000 children in America with IBD.

Notable 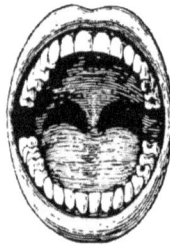 Quotables

Today is a good day to fight. Today is a good day to die.
—Crazy Horse, Oglala Tribe, *Native American Wisdom*

Lesson #5

This school year Fly learned the true meaning of "I see" said the blind man.

RELIABLE CASSETTE MECHANISM
NORMAL BIAS 120uS EQ

B FAITH NO MORE "The ...G" [...]

maxell XLII

MASTER
MASTER

POSITION
IEC TYPE II • HIGH (CrO₂)

Toxic Workplace Playlist #3

"DEEP CUTS"

A DATE FIGHT   N R   ○YES ○NO

B DATE FIGHT BACK   N R   ○YES ○NO

Side A (FIGHT)	Side B (FIGHT BACK)
Sabotage - Beastie Boys	Numb - Linkin Park
Stitches - Shawn Mendes	Hit Me With Your Best Shot
Push - Matchbox Twenty	Down in a Hole - Alice in Chains
Smooth Criminal - Alien Ant Farm	Chandelier - Sia
We Don't Talk Anymore - Charlie Puth	Last Resort (Cut My Life Into Pieces) - Papa Roach
Cut You Up - Peter Murphey	Sugar We're Goin Down - Fall Out Boy
...Baby One More Time (Hit Me) Britney Spears	Jumper - Third Eye Blind
Criminal - Fiona Apple	Because of You - Kelly Clarkson
Heathens - Twenty One Pilots	Whats Up? - 4 Non Blondes
Kryptonite - Three Doors Down	Cold Water - MK + JB
Uninvited - Alanis Morissette	Shout - Tears for Fears
Misery - Maroon 5	Call It What You Want - Taylor Swift
Torn - Natalie Imbruglia	
Bad Blood - Taylor Swift	Policy of Truth - Depeche Mode
Do You Sleep? Lisa Loeb	What It's Like - Everlast
Everyday is a Winding Road - Sheryl Crow	How You Remind Me - Nickleback
★ It's Time - Imagine Dragons	Message in a Bottle - The Police
	White Flag - Dido
Brain Stew/Jaded - Green Day	The Climb - Miley Cirus
	I Love It - Icona Pop

Gut Response

Act Out!

Journal Entry: What is something toxic in your life now or in the past? List the things that made it feel toxic to you and/or others also in that environment. How did you respond to it? What are some paper cuts that you have received figuratively and how did all the little things combine to create one larger painful wound? The parts equal the whole. Have you suffered from physical or emotional pain brought on by others, and if so, how do you manage through it? Write your experience and thoughts on the next page. You can share with a friend, crumple it up, send it through the paper shredder, and let it go.

Chapter 6
Dear P.A.U.L., Et Al.

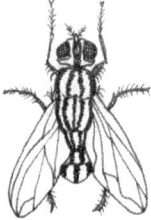

Cold November Rain.

"You need something, Agent DiNozzo?" Jenny asks.

"No, just checking in with our fearless leader," Tony replies.

"Got it!" Mike announces.

"What did I tell you, Tony?" Jenny demands.

"Not to call you our fearless leader," Tony admits.

"And?" Jenny prompts.

"To take the day off," Tony mumbles.

Later...

Tony tells McGee to calm down and not get his panties in a twist before stating that they just spoke to Jenny who told them that she's fine and that she needed a little alone time.

Ziva then interjects with the thought that they're worried that Jenny might be under duress.

When McGee asks if Jenny used the duress word, Tony reacts with triumph while Ziva grudgingly admits that Jenny didn't. McGee then states that Jenny's probably fine.

Tony thanks McGee for his advice, stating, "The great McOz has spoken."

Later...

"There's a reason sleeping dogs are left to lie, Jethro," Ducky mumbles.

The Next Episode: Jenny is dead.

As it cuts back to the present, Vance remarks that Jenny put up one hell of a fight.

"Not good enough," Gibbs grimly replies.

Vance tells him that Jenny was outnumbered five to one.

> Was the "duress" word used?
> —McGee in *NCIS*, "Judgement Day" Part 1

Cue the Music:
"Mr. Know It All" by Kelly Clarkson
"Timber" by Kesha and Pitbull
"Jumper" by Third Eye Blind
Bonus Track: "What's Up?" by 4 Non-Blondes

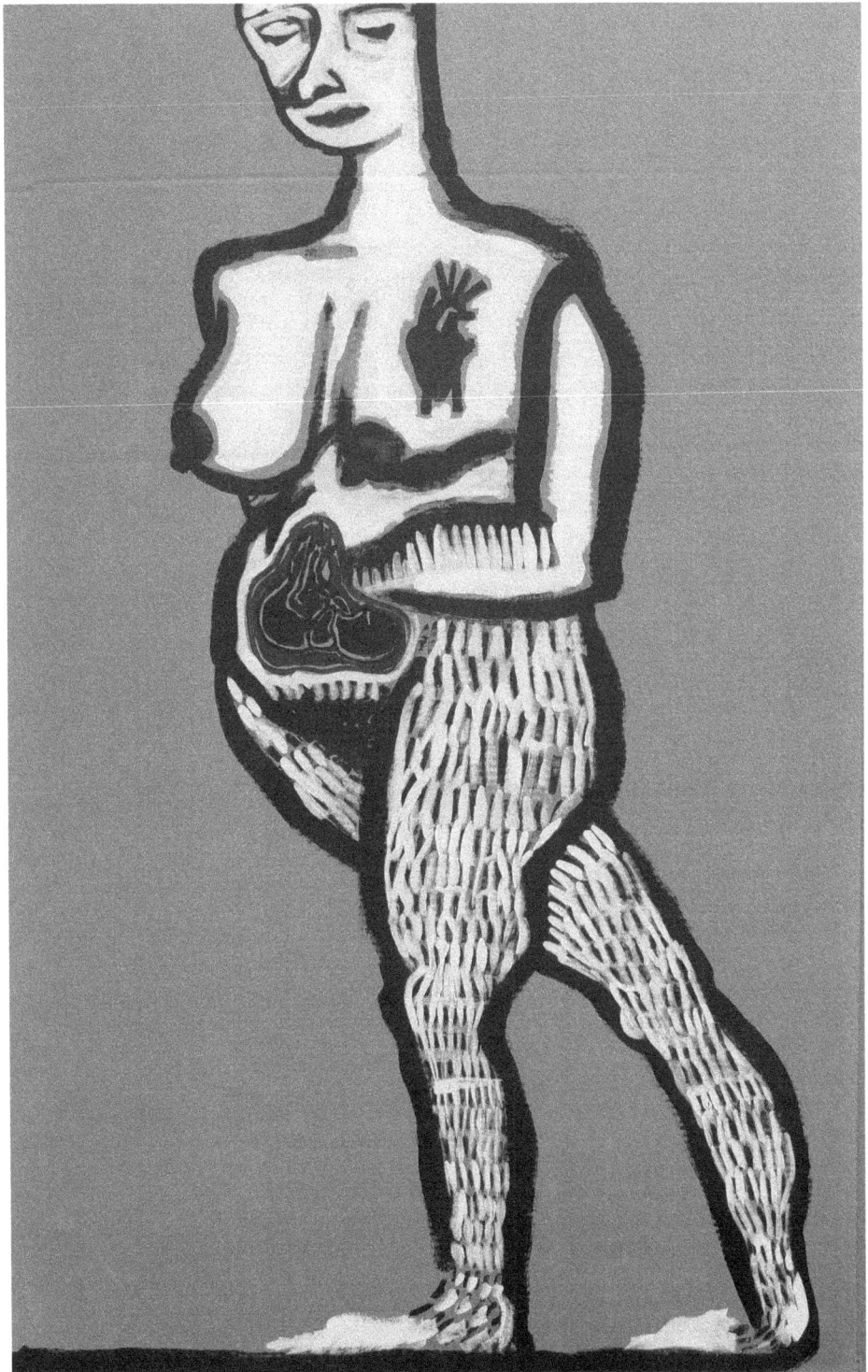

ZANA K. ELIN

In the Air Tonight

The summer months were a season that Fly tried to enjoy, but her guts did not permit her to do the things she wanted and loved to do on those long hot days. Basic summer fun things people take advantage of: walking the beach, biking, dancing, yoga, or kayaking. All of these became impossible tasks. She had to be careful where she voyaged to and had to be mindful of available bathrooms with quick distances as issues could arise at any time without notice. Anyone with Crohn's or colitis or any irritable bowel disorder would know the challenges during flare-ups and how grateful they are to the patient family members who sit and wait seemingly forever while they are in the bathroom. Fly's husband was running in a mini-marathon and, about ten minutes in, turned around and walked away with a bad ominous feeling. Celeste and Fly said it was all right and they had fun at the event anyway with all the music and festivities. In fact, Fly got even more sick than the usual acute colitis when just then, she got the call from Dr. Mendit that he figured out the problem and she was diagnosed with *Clostridioides difficile*. Fly once again had to ask, "What the heck is that?" and the response was pretty clear that it was something bad on top of bad, and she must have picked it up in the hospital since she was there being infused or admitted to the emergency room all the time. She could barely fathom that things could get worse and she asked herself, "What did I do to deserve this?" She was disgusted, and immediately, her family had to quarantine from her as they began bleaching everything every day floor to ceiling. It was already bad enough, but Fly wondered how they would get through this next phase, and she felt terrible guilt of potentially endangering her family now since it was contagious. They had to renovate to get an additional isolation bathroom stat. There went another tens of thousands of dollars for a renovation project.

Fly looked back at photo album pictures of her younger self as she shared them with once Little Celeste becoming the celestial teenager and said, "Dear photo, did you ever know future Fly would face such challenges and wreckage?"

181

With sincere and factual review of occurrences, a letter was drafted to Superintendent Head Honcho that hot and sticky summer. Fly did not know what the school year was going to bring, but she knew a certified letter had been sent. Fly's legal paperwork was now piling on top of Mr. P.A.U.L.'s papers, but she was beginning to feel that it was no longer the fault of this employee and whatever his deal was, but it was the fault of the district for not doing anything about it, constantly ignoring complaints, and not having clear policies or regulations. Nevertheless, the paperwork on Mr. P.A.U.L. could not fit into a normal-sized binder, so now the documentation graduated to a three-inch binder. It was a clear case of this employee's actions being swept under the carpet with a really big broom or shop vac. Those suckers pick anything up from the dusty to the slimy and waterlogged sludge of the earth. Fly would have just liked to know why this sinister behavior was going on and no one else she was aware of was repelled by the perpetrator. Perhaps he thought himself a perfectionist, only he was not; maybe he tried to find vengeful ways to get back at Fly for constantly correcting his mistakes, or perhaps he simply did not want to take commands from a woman. Why did he act this way, targeting her, she will never know for certain. A quest for an explanation was in order.

She heard nothing from the district the entire summer, but upon returning to school, she learned that Superintendent Sparkle Thief retired and that was that; a clear explanation as to why she did not want to pursue her complaint. She retired, never returning her sparkle! Fly was so angry her sparkle was stolen, but she tried everything in her power to get it back. The letter was one fairly long paragraph from the State Administrators Society's legal department asking for assistance in the matter Ms. Fly was continually bringing up to eight superiors, five union navigators, over the course of five years with no less than twenty-five complaints both in written and verbal format. She was in agreement with what the lawyer had extrapolated and synthesized from her mounds of paperwork. After thorough review of the evidence presented in June, the letter further expressed that this teacher she supervises has consistently been insubordinate by not following directives and has created an environment that Ms. Fly perceives as being hostile and one of fear and intimidation. The lawyer was astounded at the clarity presented in June, and surely, this would fix the problem by moving him to another location; as that happened all the time throughout the district, it should not be a big deal. The letter also stated that the district was in violation of policies requiring an investigation into claims involving harassment.

The legal process was an interesting but scary learning experience for Fly. During that first week of school, the attorneys prepped her for her presentation to the district, but they stressed Fly needed to be very angry at them for which she was having a difficult time with practicing anger and blame. She believed people should fight for their inherent rights as human beings and any injustices addressed, but in a civil and constructive manner. There are solutions to all problems if they are just worked through reasonably. The summer vacation instantly felt like a thousand years away as she faced impending unknown. She had formed complaints with Ultra Scent Works, Sack of Donuts, and Yummy Cooky Farm to improve conditions and service not to be a complainer. But products spilling and destroying her hardwood floors, managers making fun of Celeste's friend for stuttering, and allergic reactions to ingredients not properly labeled need to be reported. Celeste was going through the drive-thru one day to get iced coffees with her friend and the impatient person with the headset taking the order yelled at them to come on already and place the order, then mimicked stuttering speech as if they were playing a prank on the drive-thru employee. Furious, when they drove around the corner, they pulled over and Celeste Bag of Donuts got her gangster on and called the establishment and asked to speak to the manager. She came home crying at the blatant disregard for his stuttering disability as well as her complaint, but even more mocked it verbally over the speaker. The man who answered the phone for the complaint was the manager himself. Listening intently to their story, Fly became furious and called the 800 number to make a claim and give details of the incident. She had been waited on by that person a few times, so Fly knew what she was saying. He had "an edge" to him just as P.A.U.L.

did as one colleague acknowledged. That manager was gone within a week. That is called accountability.

Upon request, the now new Super DaNile asked Ms. Fly for information pertaining to the investigation the district was conducting. She looked at the once principal from another school and wondered how he got the position of leading personnel having no experience whatsoever. He was a shmoozy boozy principal; that's it. Maybe he climbed the food chain ladder from teacher to supervisor to assistant principal to principal to head of personnel? Human resource specialists are usually specifically trained to work with people, the employees, hiring and overseeing human relations. A whole different degree of specialty, but same certification for Educational Administration. Fly had the certification to be superintendent head honcho if she wanted to be, but that by no means she would be qualified. So there he was climbing the food chain ladder and newly in charge, once seen patting Mr. P.A.U.L. on the back as they chuckled carelessly during that art event. She could not believe this was now not only the third superintendent she had to reboot matters with, it was also three principals in that she had to deal with this employee. And that is all he was to her now, an employee because he was their hire, not hers.

That very same day Mr. P.A.U.L.'s absurdities erupted once again, initiating phase 3 of P.A.U.L.'s plan. It was September after all, and she had gone a whole two months without nonsense of any kind, not even from middle school Celeste. Fly could even tolerate Celeste's tween nonsense over this of a grown man. Ms. Fly provided four pages of documented information and a brief timeline of events, same that she gave to Sparkle Thief, stating that she feared that the pattern would be starting up again as it was the beginning of the school year and that his actions are not normal based on other faculty behaviors and that she constantly feels threatened and intimidated, fears future harassment, and was concerned for her well-being, safety, and health. There were the same categories as provided in writing previously to all other supervisors: visible anger, facial expressions, physical aggression, dishonesty, concealment, seeking out, avoidance, compulsive emails, odd body language, frightening comments, retaliation, undermining via sabotage, fear, and complaints from others. There was the same list of no less than 150 examples. For instance, displaying a black face artwork was listed, and while that specifically is not harassment, she felt it was the fact that he retaliated in manipulative ways because she rightfully had to call him out on this inappropriate display afterward. This type of action went on every day.

Fly thought she was being overly thorough, even gave them a copy of that shiny CD, and with her statements, she indicated she could furnish documentation upon request. She did not know when Mr. P.A.U.L. was going to be notified but definitely was not right away as the nonsense just poured in oblivious to Fly's trek to the state capital. His MO was if he had been notified, he would cower and hide in avoidance, presumably with the puppy act, dragging his feet into the school ever so slowly, hoping fellow teachers would see his sadness and then upon a stroke of confidence pounce.

Log Entries:

September 2: In response to his first email of the year asking if he had to print and sign the annual report or just finalize it. Replied, "The procedure is the same as years prior: simply finalize. Thank you." He could have just as easily asked a coworker while eating a bite of his sandwich but no.

September 3: Emailed an incorrect period and place to provide Extra Help in which I firmly replied, "As discussed in our department meeting, the schedule was posted in the office. There is a class in that room at that time. Please find another time or location. Thank you."

September 4: Asked if the new teacher could observe his class in which I stated, "No. That is against the teacher's contract." It seemed he was constantly trying to pin something on me; catch me in a fly trap; if said "yes," the union navigators would be all over me. Also, did he think he was a "master teacher" or something like when I inspected that awful lesson or when he thought he was so great and shouted to the kids, "Let's rock and roll!" What was he now a music teacher? Teachers in other teachers' room was a no-no. His request is only acceptable for college students doing observation hours or student-teaching. Thought Mr. Paul is probably trying to get the new teacher as an ally as had already discussed with Sparkle Thief this type of situation where Mr. Paul is trying to get others in cahoots to gang up on me.

September 5: Talking with another department supervisor in the hallway and Paul was ten feet away staring at me, swaying his head left and right as if trying to see something; just standing there for a very long time that the colleague even thought it to be unusual. Wondering what the imperative issue was, we broke off the conversation and he asked if he could share his lesson plans with the new teacher. This was getting fairly annoying as he was definitely not the Teacher of the Year; in fact, Janeart was so deserving of this elusive high honor ironically at the very same time. How can one have such polar opposites in one department I will never know. Not convinced the new guy should be taking advice from Mr. Paul, and why is he being so adamant and fixated about the new guy?

September 6: In response to emailed department items, Mr. Paul replied to all with his over-the-top nice greeting, "Good Morning Everyone! I know it is hard for all of us to sync up so I thought an email would be easier. I made a substitute lessons drawer in the back bottom right drawer to the right of the computer for everyone's plans. Have a great weekend!" So infuriated as I had already organized a clearly labeled drawer since there were so many new members of the department that year and this

information was clearly already covered in the
back to school department meeting and also in
the agenda. Who does he think he is?

The next week, Ms. Fly met with her assigned Attorney Labor
Lawyer Lackadaisical, union representative, and the Boy's Club
Administration to once again review the materials for which she
deemed holistically as harassment since she felt it was no longer
pesky bullying as he was clearly not complying for yet another
year and has leveled up again. Don't get her wrong, everyone
liked leveling up in like at the slot machines, but not here. There
was a clear pattern of behavior, and Fly was informed she met
all of the criteria as a "protected class" individual, as well as
having a history of solid work performance and a clear record
of complaints. The key was that she left a very long paper trail
and did not keep all the shenanigans over the years a secret.

The following week, just two weeks of teaching his courses,
Mr. P.A.U.L. ran to his union navigators to have the Schoolwide
Class Schedule Masterpiece changed, giving up the main specialty class of computer arts he was originally hired to teach. It
was within contract regulations to have that many preps. Even
though he was given his schedule of courses in June with those
snide remarks as he submitted his documents, it must have taken
a toll on him to teach so many classes in just the first two weeks
of school. So perhaps that is why he was recruiting the new guy
with the scam to have him take over the specialty class without
letting Ms. Fly know. This took some nerve and several administrators could not even believe the audacity. Furious, Ms. Fly
wrote an email to her union representative, "Unfortunately, as
I feared, the issues continue with regard to both the teacher
and administration. The latest situation dramatically highlights
the continued attempts to usurp my position as a supervisor
on many levels." Then she gave a timeline of events ending
the accounts of the event with, "Principal Teddy Table Turner
'informed me' that 'they' were all ok with the decision and were
going to switch the Schoolwide Class Schedule Masterpiece to
accommodate Mr. P.A.U.L.'s request effective today ("they"
referring to Principal Teddy Table Turner, Mr. P.A.U.L., Mr. Pee.,
Mr. Bee, and Mr. Jay." Does anyone…anyone see a pattern

here? Even the assistant principals disagreed with Teddy, and clearly, this is five men bypassing three female supervisors to cater to this one male teacher with no authorization and resulting with the new guy from another department teaching a brand-new class unplanned two weeks into the school year and potentially unqualified.

Ms. Fly ensured that her union representative was aware of the additional situations: "Mr. P.A.U.L. actually 'sought me out' specifically at an inopportune time to request permission for him to help the new teacher with his courses." Excuse you, you just gave up your class and now you want to help the new guy teach it? His emails and behavior were so unsettling that she documented and called the state attorneys from the parking lot on her twenty-minute lunch hour. She wrote, "He continues to usurp my authority and, in fact, just smiles and walks by knowing this has occurred...For two teacher union men to change the Schoolwide Class Schedule Masterpiece and assess this new teacher's teaching qualifications and act upon is completely negligent." The union representative called and stated, "He can't do that!" Well, it was actually the social studies teacher and Spanish teacher who did. Did they all not see now this is exactly the behavior and clear breaking of contractual regulations that she had been talking about all this time? Now the new guy was in charge of a $30,000 brand-new state-of-the-art computer lab with no experience. She cringed at what could happen to the curriculum and upkeep.

And after about another week or two of daily aggressions, there it was: the deliberate standing with his back to Ms. Fly at the door in the hallway while greeting his students as they entered his classroom with that crazy over-the-top crocodile smile so that people could witness. She knew then they finally met with him. Fly thought had he been approached with news flash of the legal situation he may never had pulled the ultimate toxic quest to conquer and use his persuasive powers to manipulate all of those men at the bottom of the food chain to alter the Schoolwide Class Schedule Masterpiece not only to make him have less courses, but also to complicate the new guy's workload. There he stood facing away from Ms. Fly as not done in a while, frantically and feverishly waving his two hands at the students as they pass by like an excited child on a parade float, then rubbing them together like a mad scientist. The Jekyll and Hyde he once displayed was back with his world domination in check. Refusing to make eye contact, she knew he knew she knew. His observed and experienced behaviors did not match the tones of the chronic emails. Seeking praise but avoiding eye contact, contradictory visual and physical demeanor. Fly didn't even care about his current incompetencies as she was trying to get the past ones understood by administration. She couldn't just keep "adding to the list" over and over at the onset of the supposed investigation, or else the story would never end. Weren't over 150 examples enough, she thought?

It was Fly's Bewitching Week where everything hits all at once for Fly and her anxiety is at its height for the whole school year. From the end of October through election day was one treacherous, evil week. Then Ms. Fly had to call all the parents of "problem" students which she dreaded. She remembered an episode of *Fresh Prince of Bel-Air*, called "The Mother of All Battles," where the daughter, about Celeste's age, was being bullied by a girl at school and the parents met up to discuss the situation or rather, misunderstanding. After snootily refusing hors d'oeuvres and beverages from the gracious hostess, the parents of the Bully Girl insist it is the other couple's daughter who has the problem and the Dr. Father medically mansplains that their "daughter suffers from displaced aggression syndrome... where a child acts out repressed hostility of an unhappy home life." Ironically, the Dr. Father is a child psychiatrist and thinks he and his wife who asked if they were using too many big words, to boot, know it all. Turns out the Bully Girl's parents were the epitome of bullies and the scene swiftly ends with a "Yo Mamma" joke and a punch to the Dr. Father's face. Ms. Fly would dread picking up that school office phone to call the parents because, more often than not, they behaved exactly the way their child did or vice versa. The apple doesn't fall far.

Fly wondered what type of childhood Mr. P.A.U.L. must have had that he acted out the way in which he did. She only knew he was from an elite neighborhood in the city perimeter much farther away from the urban hustle. She thinks about the art teacher poster where there are cartoons of a series of paintbrushes, and this time of year marked the second picture. The first cartoon is of a brand spanking new paintbrush ready to be used by art students for the first time. Perfect freshly cut hair, new shoes, and first day outfit crisp and coiffed ready to take on the next ten months. The second image is about where she was at the time. Slightly used, paint colors hardened on the handle, yet still slightly pointed at the tip when rinsed. The third image is a paintbrush on the backside of the school year looking haggard and highly utilized by hundreds of art students but now hastily washed and getting destroyed by the acrylic paints that become permanently dried on destroying those once flawless bristles. The handle is chipped and chewed on, they are becoming neglected and beaten down and some-one placed the brush upside down in the cup so the bristles are also permanently bent to the left and paint colors accu-mulate. The last image represents the end of the school year. The brush is damaged beyond repair, tattered, scarred, and mangled and ready for a vacation, and new paintbrushes will need to be ordered for September as they are no longer func-tional. The teachers in the building looked the same. Exhausted, decimated, and disheveled looking, ready for the school year to end, only to need the entire summer to recuperate. But Ms. Fly was leveled up with all of the additional and unnecessary dread and fear, anxiety and upset that came with all of Mr. P.A.U.L.'s miserable mishegoss.

Cue up the amazing tune "In the Air Tonight" by Phil Collins. Fly saw a concert on her brother's birthday in the city in the mid-'80s. The urban legend from her own recollection goes something like this; although this could be like the game of telephone and totally altered beyond recognition in the end. Phil witnesses someone drowning in a pond or river one night, maybe a different body of water she was not certain, perhaps at the hand of another or the victim was yelling to a person nearby for help and Phil was witnessing all of this, but either did not know how to swim or actually could not reach him for some reason. He was too far out in the water. The person that could have saved the life of this person drowning just ignored him and let him drown. He was either forcing him to drown or being a bystander just watching it all unfold, but either way, he died. Fly's dad said there's only two things you had to do on the earth: pay taxes and die. Disgusted at this despicable act of indifference for human life, Phil, in anger and frustration, wrote this song which is of course, a masterpiece. He later found this person, sent him tickets, and invited him to one of his concerts, and when Phil began singing the song "In the Air Tonight," the stage crew shined a spotlight on the man in order to confess the terrible act he had done. Fly is drawn to this magical song because there were very few people who came to her rescue as she screams continuously while drowning. The excuses: you can't swim, it's too dark and murky, the waves are too high, there's a riptide, there's a shark in the water, we need a bigger boat, you have no power, it's a man's world, there's nothing we can do, etcetera, etcetera, etcetera, and blah, blah, blah. Very sorry underlined twice. Fly was screaming at the top of her lungs, but she swore they all must have ear buds in.

The phrase that speaks loudly is, "So you can wipe off that grin, I know where you've been, it's all been a pack of lies," speaks volumes of truth. And as any *X-Files* fan knows, "The truth is out there." "The Tunguska Episode": Scully continuously discusses the "lawlessness of men prevents her from doing her job." And that is in the FBI not some dark and shady public school. The secrets. The politics. She goes to fight the circle of men. To defend herself. To right the wrong. The song blasts in her head over and over again, Scandals' "The Warrior," thinking she will prevail. "Yes I am the Warrior! Victory is mine!"

The music in her head transitions to "I can feel it coming in the air tonight," a more somber gut reaction. The official music video starts off with an out of focus blurry Phil, severely unrecognizable, unimportant, obliterated, and underlit with stark black and white contrast. Gritty and grainy black and white filming. On the left, his figure is reflected in a mirror that gets shattered and crumbles to the floor silently in slow motion. He sits alone in a dark room, as Fly has felt, only confiding in her family and closest friends, therapist, nurses, well, and her amazing all-ears hairdresser, about the horrors that were to come. Looking like a mask, his face undulates bigger then smaller within his mind thinking deeply about what he has witnessed. He tries to open doors to freedom but to his un-success.

Fast forward to over thirty years after this amazing concert: in an interview on a late show, Phil Collins reveals the song was indeed not about a drowning, but the feelings of watching someone drown and not helping them based on a divorce he was going through. It was speculated that a man was sneaking around behind his back or that another man was caught with his wife and that the person that had the spotlight shined brightly during the song was the perpetrator. Art at its finest brilliance!

Cold November Rain

Fly was seriously having second thoughts about switching districts so that she could make more money to raise a baby. It was crystal clear that she made a devastatingly wrong decision when Celeste was little. Fly even thought back to that first teaching job when she got recruited from her Ivy League school to the inner city schools halfway across the country. For the opening day ceremonies, the teachers all loaded onto school buses, drove through what appeared to be cement house dwellings in a sparse gray and beige flat landscape in the sweltering humid heat, where the lead motivational speaker raised her arms high in the air, proclaiming to someone up above, "Lord Jesus, please give us the strength and power to teach these children and get through the school year!" with a gospel like chorus to the sky. Fly sat there astonished by the cultural differences and thought the administrator might just break out her dance floor moves to "The Neutron Dance" like from the hit '80s movies and then they would start running after the criminals putting bananas in tailpipes. She should have known. While trail blazing for a new job, this current district called her before she even got home that day like she was a hot commodity, while other districts were so snobby, Fly asked for them to take her off the candidate lists. She took the wrong fork in the road and at that, a hard left flinging her into a barren field of despair.

Fly felt like this work situation was engulfing her life, unable to focus on her medical condition. Two of Fly's doctors who were friendly colleagues joked among themselves. If Fly came dragging herself into the doctor's office, crawling on the floor in disguised agonizing pain, she must be close to dying and really be in trouble so get her help stat. She consumed her after-school life with nonstop medical appointments and Celeste's games on the ball field. It was only eight weeks into the school year. One specialist in rheumatology, disturbed with what Fly told her about her workplace issue formed a letter to the attorney. Why this person completely believed Fly, unlike all of these other people over years, was beyond comprehension and she appreciated the doctor. Maybe she had struggled herself at some point in her career or had read extensive medical research papers and studies on rheumatology and effects of work stress on the human body, but she knew what Fly was trying to tell her. This doctor understood the correlation of stress-induced workplaces, as did her attorney as it was called "physical manifestations."

> Dt: November 13
> Re: Workplace harassment/ hostile work environment claim
>   We have been following Ms. Fly for the past few months. As you may know, she has a diagnosis of ulcerative colitis and had been well controlled until recently. She presented to our rheumatology practice with new complaints of acute leukocytoclastic vasculitis and entero-pathic polyartropacy. As a result, she has struggled with maintaining her normal activities. She has been treated effectively with steroids, but this is only a temporizing measure. Ultimately, treatment of this autoimmune condition will require a combination of disease modifying agents and a balanced lifestyle. She has been under tremendous stress these past few months, and it is very likely that the stress considerably contributed to the reactivation of her autoimmune condition—the ulcerative colitis and the related complications noted above. It is critical for her to manage her work/life balance with proper diet, rest, and activity. Additional stress-

ors contribute to activation of the immune system which can make ulcerative colitis difficult to control.

Clearly by "stress," she meant "unnecessary harassment" at work since she was very happy in her home life. Time was of the essence as Fly liked to say, and she had hoped this medical letter would make a difference in the legal situation. Then Fly met with her gastroenterologist specialist, Dr. Mendit, who was trying to help control the excruciating and disgusting C-Diff situation. She was so mad at the medical system for picking up whatever this was in the hospital or the emergency room, the one place that should be fixing you up. This solidified her loathing of hospitals as they look sanitized but are not necessarily. The smell of disinfectant and bleach with the cold darkness of the dimly lit rooms and halls. It's the invisible that is the scary part of all this dislike of hospitals. She sat across from Dr. Mendit at his office desk one cool autumn afternoon where they discussed several strategies. To her disappointment, the Ramicadence was no longer working and collided with back to school stress so that was no good news and she would have to switch to Humirror. Little did she know she would have to stab herself in the quads with painful needles to do so. They make the commercials looks so inviting, and they conceal the reality of treatment. Not only was she being stabbed in the back at work, she literally had to stab herself knowing it was coming. To prepare, she set the materials up on her home office desk, sat upright in the wooden chair for stability, cried for a minute, then puffed three deep breaths as if to begin a fist fight, and screamed a guttural yell as the needle pierced her skin and had to hold it there for the allotted amount of time. Then she could breathe. She needed the privacy, but when done, Fly's husband would quickly come from around the corner to see if she was all right. She did not know which was more painful, the momentary piercing shot in the leg, the work situation, or that her family had to live all this with her.

Typing at his computer Dr. Mendit said there was a treatment she could try for the C-Diff. She had already been in and out of the hospital, and every time now, since the summer, the nurses would yell, "C-Diff...rule out!" They would put a contam-ination sign equivalent to a skull and cross bones like a scene from *Contagion* on her ER curtain, and once an old lady who was walking to a station near Fly ran in horror, exclaiming to her old man husband to "Get away...get away, oh Lord!" Like Fly had the plague. Another time, they had to move her to the psych ward because she had to be separated from everyone, and nurses had to put on full yellow plastic garb and double gloves just to enter the room looking like Dustin Hoffman in *Outbreak*. No one else was allowed. Always trying to look at the positive side, Fly thought alone in the room that at least she did not have to have a roommate and she could have some quiet time and watch whatever shows she wanted to on the TV. Working moms always put themselves last, so she quickly did any work for school, then she tried to make the sour into sweet at some iota of a level. But the screams of insane patients echoed throughout the wing from the psych ward hallway were messing with her own mental stability.

He said, "There's a treatment that is called a fecal trans-plant," and that seemed innocent enough, as the courteous Fly nodded in agreement, hanging on to his every word of intelli-gent well-read advice as she jotted it down in her notepad. So Dr. Mendit continued to explain when the words coming out of his mouth slowed and she zoomed in on exactly what he was explaining with the process and how it happens and what the outcomes are as well as his scholarly research of percen-tile effectiveness. Her reaction was stone-cold, and after she picked her jaw up off the floor, she reacted as if it was even more preposterous than almost anything P.A.U.L. had said to her all these years. Absolutely ludicrous! Except Dr. Mendit, knowing he loved reading research papers and always kept up on recent studies in the field, was one of the smartest and best doctors in the area, so terrified, she knew he knew his stuff, only she wasn't thinking "stuff" in her mind. Fly was actually happy that for the first time ever, she was older than one of her doc-tors, so she knew they were together for the long haul since the ulcerative colitis would be unfortunately a lifelong event, and he had been her doctor for a few years already. It's not like anyone ever woke up one morning and was like, "Hey, I don't have colitis anymore, what a miracle!" He stated that Fly could swallow pills with stuff that was healthy and compatible, perhaps her husband could be a willing donator. Only he didn't say stuff, he said fecal matter. *Hmmm, what exactly is he saying?* Fly thought still intently listening to the process. Wasn't she eating enough stuff from people already? He meant literally, though, not figuratively and her jaw dropped to the floor in shock again as he clinically explained like it was no big deal to eat someone else's stuff. She sat there staring straight into his eyes, wondering if it was an early April Fool's joke or if she was on *Candid Camera* because it sounded absolutely absurd.

Fly went home, and thankfully, Fly's husband was so funny that he stated that was one of the best things he's ever heard and he would be honored if she could eat his stuff. He was so amused and intrigued by the concept and was eventually disappointed that this discussion ended and never came to fruition. She memorized all of the colon phrases in tow and even Celeste got her a key chain in the shape of a colon that said in bubble thought, "Colon, you move me." Let's get the bottom of this. I'm a pain in the rear. You can't make this stuff up. It will all come out in the end...she hoped. "Is there a Butz here? Seymour Butz? I wanna Seymour Butz!" as Bart Simpson prank calls Moe. Fly's husband always wondered how someone would have the passion to go into the business of gastrointestinal as a specialty, and he always asked, "Family history?"

Returning to work one morning, Ms. Fly received an email from Mr. P.A.U.L., communicating to her that Principal Teddy Table Turner was allowing him, no, giving him special permission to be absent so that he could travel to one of the other schools and photograph their final season game. Livid, Fly immediately knew this was clearly rewarding bad behavior or a clear foreshadowing sign that her claims were being dismissed. He waltzed down the hall and out the building with her once Super Widget in hand.

It was 7:00 a.m. on Election Day. Although the air was cool and crisp outside, Fly was unusually hot and sweaty in the dimly lit room. In fact, she felt as wet as the river below the bridge. The amber leaves gracefully fell off the trees one by one no longer able to hold on to the place where they have grown evergreen and happy to sit in the sunshine and rain over the past several months. She and her mom stopped by a park on the way to being admitted to snap some photos at full pregnancy, in fact, a week overdue. It seemed calmingly warm toned and naturally beautiful compared to the washed-out and artificially fluorescent sterility of the maternity ward. There was a changing of the guard at the nurse's station as she anxiously awaited for the arrival of the doctor to initiate the induction process. Fly lay on her side quietly in a calm fear that the inevitable was about to happen. By the end of the day, her baby would surely be born. She should have come out a week ago, but she must have been comfy or lazy or just going to be one of those late for everything kind of people like Elizabeth Taylor. Late even to her own funeral.

It was 7:10, and then 7:15, but who was counting? The shift change seemed to go on forever. Fly had been up most of the night in the dark hospital room. Finally at 7:20 a.m., sipping his cup of coffee, the doctor came in to check things out. In the distance, she saw a nurse preparing the long needle to break her water. The doctor examined to investigate the progression from the dilating tablet inserted the previous afternoon and removed at 4:00 a.m. He stopped to inspect the yards of fetal heart monitor tape that had been accumulating to the right of the head of the bed. Back and forth. His head was increasing in pace as he evaluated the long tape he stretched from arm to arm. A slight hustle had begun in the room and several nurses arrived.

"Your water has already been ruptured," he said "and I need for you to listen very carefully. See these blips in the heart rate? The cord has come out ahead of the baby and her oxygen has been cut off, she needs to be born immediately. In a moment there will be a lot of people around you doing things."

"C-section: stat!" deeply echoed through the air with a rush of immediacy.

At once, there must have been a dozen people surrounding Fly, each doing a different pre-determined task from simple shaving hair to oxygen and tubes and IVs. She looked with terror toward her husband silhouetted by the window and told him to call her dad at work immediately. Before she could tell him to also call her mother, she was flipped over onto her knees with a nurse on her back shoving the baby's head in being wheeled down the corridor a hundred miles per hour toward the operating room as the nurses were yelling for everyone to get out of the way. Now more than ever in her life, Fly was truly alone and was so scared, she began to hyperventilate. Is the baby all right? When and how did the water break? How did no one realize it? What went wrong? She didn't learn about this possibility! She felt sick. By the time the anesthesiologist told her to turn her head because of nausea, the room faded to black.

Fly woke up several hours later in the recovery room, feeling totally paralyzed, confused and with double vision. She could barely remember what happened or how she actually got there or where she was for that matter. This was not the way it was supposed to happen. No one ever went over any of these procedures in the countless prenatal classes she and her husband attended or were in no soon-to-be Mommy books that were read. After she realized where she was and that she had an emergency C-section, her first question was if the baby was all right.

One can never overpack. Luckily, Fly decided to throw in the Polaroid camera at the last minute, and it proved to be a necessity over the course of the next day as it was the first vision and impression she was able to see of her baby girl. She had to squint one eye to see the photograph clearly. Although born blue baby with low scores, she had regained her color, she was loaded with dark hair and looked like a mini Elvis Eskimo with a green paddle taped on her hand for the IV antibiotics. She nestled safely in the Infant ICU. That photo was worth a thousand words. An unbelievable serendipitous chance meeting occurred that day. The nurse on duty happened to be the mother of one of Ms. Fly's art students and she claimed he loved her class. Knowing after days she still had not seen her child, she said, "Hang on, let me see what I can do." A while later, the nurse came rolling a cart in with Fly's Little Celeste all bundled up in a cloth. She cried and held her for the first time, smuggled in and ever appreciative of the working moms and the moms of her students who reciprocated kindness from time to time. By the time Mama Fly left the hospital with her little baby Celeste, all of the autumn leaves had fallen to the ground and the cold November rain whipped at their faces as they tried to get her into the infant seat.

If they were not already in the hospital or if it was not in modern times, the outcome could have been tragic. This haunts Fly to this day, as the maternal mortality rate in America is at an all-time high for a first-world country. And wasn't it bad enough that at four and a half months pregnant, they thought the baby's spine was outside her body, and then there was placenta previa—whatever that was. The worst was the follow-up appointment with the doctor's colleague. Fly and her husband both attended and asked point blank what had happened; how could that happen as Fly was there for so long in their care? They asked, "What happened?" in an accusatory tone. They were in disbelief at what had occurred on that cold November morning. While they were thinking this doctor almost killed them both from negligence, his associate simply stated, "Oh *no*. He *saved* your lives."

The Inquisition

'Twas the day before Christmas
And all through the District
Six months later
The letter made her Sickish.
Page by page all through the house
Not a truth be told
Not even an ounce.

It was the day before Christmas break, and Ms. Fly was presented with the findings of the district's own corrupt investigation. Everyone involved was interviewed by the untrained Super DaNile and district advocating District Lawyer Codswallop. She was disgusted, quivering and shaking with disbelief at the insulting "results" that were, in their assessment, not quite terrible enough from their perspective to be deemed as a legal definition of harassment and that Mr. P.A.U.L. really liked working with his colleagues and he was unaware of any of the items discussed, even though Fly had photographs and printed emails and evidence to the contrary, and he kept stating the importance of his "reputation" for whatever that means in the education world. It's not like teachers are walking around the dank, dark, fluorescent-lit, cinder-block, mustard-colored school hallways trying to be the Fonz or anything, "Aaayyy!"

She went painstakingly through "their" results with notes and highlighters. First to bat, they misspelled her name, a probable intentional calculation in case it went to litigation. They stated they had gone through all of the documents Ms. Fly provided, but if that were the case, the following dirty dozen pages should have read differently. Over and over, they attempted to make Ms. Fly's claims "difficult to corroborate," even though she gave them clear copies of emails, memos, letters, photographs, and lists of items requested, even a copy of that shiny CD.

Mr. P.A.U.L. denied or did not remember one allegation even though others who were interviewed did recall events. He interestingly enough did remember meeting with Mr. Table Turner as well as Mr. Voyage, but never any meetings with Ms. Fly. Fly thought this this ultimate blow; to kick someone when they were already down. But like Rocky Balboa in fiction or Muhammad Ali in nonfiction, bloody, swollen, and limping from blow after blow, she got back up, however, was not educated on the grand Boy's Club scheme. That no district or employer is going to incriminate themselves in an investigation that they themselves conducted. Then it would be like Lawyer Codswallop stating, "Oops, we are guilty and so sorry, here is compensation for pain and suffering." She was blind to the fact if they found Mr. P.A.U.L. guilty, it would reflect that they were guilty for harboring the employee and negligent for ignoring Ms. Fly's repeated pleas for help year after year.

They not only trivialized some of the items presented, they hand-selected the most seemingly petty items she discussed like the odd French fry incident when taken alone and out of context must appear ridiculous on Fly's part to even care about such a thing. In his defense, he stated that he was a germophobe and would never do that. The nature of being an artist and art educator is that you basically touch *everything* so that made no sense. They kept writing that each complaint item was difficult to validate or corroborate. Wasn't she screaming at the top of her lungs for help now for years? What would it have to take for someone to really listen and understand and believe in her cries for help? And P.A.U.L. not only denied giving her the smoking video CD, he never remembered it and that in his opinion would not be appropriate for the class and he would have had the students do a more appropriate topic for school like recycling. He claimed he did not lie to Ms. Fly and that in itself was a lie. She even gave them a hard copy of the physical CD and others remembered about it because it was egregious and insensitive. "So sorry" underlined twice. Judge Judy once said in a court case, "If you have the truth *here* (and she swings her hand back and forth in front of her forehead), you don't trip yourself up." He was unaware he was chronically undermining her authority as a female professional supervisor. Mr. P.A.U.L. lied or did not recall not one complaint that Ms. Fly presented to the district throughout the entire questioning. But there would be no way one person could make up such accusations if not one instance of those 150 instances given in a categorized list of offenses. The findings were full of insults and deliberate indifferences toward the serious nature of the accusations.

That was it? They were just going to allow this person to have poor performance and retaliate against his supervisor over and over again to the point she felt harassed for being a woman in charge? They did not walk in her shoes and know the things he had done year after year. This was in direct opposition to Fly's three lawyers' interpretation of the claims. She immediately met with the local attorney Labor Lawyer Lackadaisical representing her, and he basically surmised that, while this was a terrible situation, there was no smoking gun and that Mr. P.A.U.L. would literally have to run Fly over in the school parking lot with his car for something to happen. She was merely asking for a transfer of him away from her, so she could resume her normal teaching life and administrative duties and enjoy her career and livelihood once again.

And there it was—the official "definition" of harassment. And in the closure, it was mansplained: District Lawyer Codswallop talked about protected classes which Fly under-

stood and that "Harassment becomes unlawful where enduring the offensive conduct becomes a condition of continued
employment or the conduct is severe or pervasive enough to
create a work environment that a reasonable person would
consider intimidating, hostile, or abusive." So from Fly's perspective she thought herself to be a "reasonable" person, just ask
any of the other people she supervised and observed, ask her
Teacher of the Year, assess all of her success and accolades,
and listen to the pattern of behavior that was listed. The et al.'s
created a line of defense to deflect the threat they saw in the
sparkle-less Fly. She was utterly dumbfounded. They broke the
law and they won.

> On the Twelve Days of Christmas the district
> gave begrudgingly:
> > **12** Pages of Lies
> > **11** Trivializations
> > **10** Underminings
> > **9** Dancing Deceptions
> > **8** Petty Slights
> > **7** Bad Behaviors
> > **6** More months of P.A.U.L.
> > **5** Men in Charge…
> > **4** Master Manipulations
> > **3** Non-Self-Incriminations
> > **2** Hostile Environments
> > And **1** Big Inquisition

Fly was so stressed out about everything, she sulked the
whole cold winter. She now had to switch to a new infusion drug
because the pen needle was not working. She was crying every
morning driving on her way to work the rest of the school year,
sometimes paralyzed, almost unable to get out of the car in
the parking lot at work, and one day she got a speeding ticket
on her way in. Her mind was in another place and triggered by
emotions, she did not even know how she got to that speed
zone that morning. She cried to the cop that there were men
peeing in her backyard from a home construction renovation
and that she was being harassed in the workplace and that

she had a medical issue and with being pulled over, the water faucet poured from her eyes in full force; crying in hysterics, she could not take it all any longer, and the police officer was the first to come up to her and she unleashed. She had to fund a renovation so that she could have a second bathroom so her family could be safe and she could have privacy. Fly wished she had that Crohn's and Colitis Emergency Bathroom Card and just said she had to find a bathroom immediately. She knew she was not supposed to be the fastest in the zone, only the fastest if being chased by a wild animal, but she was blanked out from stress and agony. Seeing she was distraught, even the police officer said he felt bad for her, so reduced the actual speed she was going in the speed zone so that she would get in less trouble. Fly was not sure until later, but she knew she was busted by the fuzz going well over the "50 mph" in a 30 speed zone and thought she was lucky to not be arrested and hauled to jail. Or might jail be like the hospital that would offer up some quiet time for reflection and three square meals she was not sure, but it sounded kind of tempting.

Fly had a warrant out for her arrest once in college. But it was before cell phones, so a letter came in the mail to her parents and she was witnessed hitting a car and running or as Fly's husband likes to interpret the event as "taking out an entire city block with her Chevy Caprice Classic tanker." In honor of P.A.U.L., she would say that there was "nothing further from the truth." She lightly clipped a car turning right onto a ridiculously tight old fashioned one-way road with her ridiculously large box car she got handed down from Mothball Gram, pulled over, assessed there was no damage, left a note on the car, and drove away, thinking nothing more of it. Well, she did the walk of shame to the inner city precinct, claiming to be turning herself in arms reached out ready to be cuffed and stuffed. But it was all a misunderstanding and sorted out. So after this police event, she was scared and angry, shaken with adrenaline, Ms. Fly got to school late that day and in passing while still teary eyed, blurted out the story briefly to one or maybe two of the teachers getting ready for the day that she told the police officer that she was being harassed at work.

The next day, Fly was asked to go to the Principal's Office. Mortified, Ms. Fly went into Principal Teddy Table Turner's Office with her union navigator and given a warning that Teddy was nervous but didn't think anything was "going to happen." For what? Because she said the "H-Word?" After all the ignoring, is there no such thing as freedom of speech? And why did the teachers she was talking to just assume the statement in the police story was projected at Mr. P.A.U.L., maybe she meant overall by everyone, so what did he or she know and from who's point of view? Fly in fact thought she was being harassed by *all* of the members of the elite Boy's Club for some time now starting with long gone Don Voyage. Look at the wake from his ripples he started from tossing that paper into the trash. But now they want to silence her on top of denouncing her claims? It made Fly physically ill. She consulted with the lawyer who said that she could indeed have a lawsuit or litigation in his opinion, but would she want her daughter to go to college or not because it would cost tens of thousands of dollars for her in legal fees with a 50/50 chance in the end. The state would no longer pay for the attorney moving forward with litigation. She already just dropped 60 G for an additional bathroom and renovation for her issues to protect her family. And it was noted, the nail in the coffin, that school districts have unlimited insurance funds to fight claims such as these, so Fly was the underdog at this point. Fly wished to be run over in the parking lot, so it could all be over.

Fly was conscious and well aware that the acute ulcerative colitis could kill her one day perhaps only in mind and spirit and that was clear when Celeste told her that she heard that Glenn Frey from the Eagles died from UC as well as rheumatology and other ailments. To try to maintain some normalcy, Ms. Fly went to a conference in the city with the other supervisors where Director Coupon Suzy could absolutely not comprehend why Fly could not carpool with the rest of them and was resentful, possibly from the bus incident or the lack of wanting to be allowed to be friends in the past. She was fixated that Fly would have to spend her own money to purchase a round-trip train ticket and not be cheapskate like the rest all commuting together by car.

Fly remembered the time when they were on a previous conference and employees were permitted $10 for breakfast and the receipts paid in cash could be reimbursed upon completion of the event or professional development. Well, Fly decided she was allotted the $10, so she purchased three buttered bagels for her and two other participants as she would simply be reimbursed. Had it been Principal Teddy Table Turner getting a ten dollar Big Boy Breakfast with all the food groups and syrup and coffee and eggs and pancakes and toast at You Hop, he would not have been questioned. But the finance secretary kept calling Ms. Fly in her office about why she purchased three buttered bagels at $3 each under the allotted price and was inquisitional as to whether she ate all three of them. What if she did eat all three bagels? How dare they even bother especially with her medical condition covered by the Americans with Disabilities Act which never really was at her fingertips. It was not like she was buying a dozen donuts for breakfast, and it was none of their business if Fly actually ate all three buttered bagels. Maybe she wanted all three bagels because they had stopped providing breakfast at the opening day ceremonies. If Fly was obese, would they ask the very same absurd question as there are plenty of people who eat a lot for breakfast. Maybe they could be taking a day off from Pound Pounders. Maybe that was all she could physically eat and that was actually her breakfast, lunch, and dinner being away from home and routine at a conference and all she could eat was white bread. How dare they after everything she had been through be relentless with the phone call to justify if she had indeed eaten all three buttered bagels. But no, it was all of the auditors, as it was being noted that employees of districts were scamming their way to obtain thousands upon thousands of dollars for personal use at the district's expense. There was even a recent movie made about that, how about those people? Three bagels.

So how could Fly describe in a professional manner that basically, she has to run to the bathroom nonstop all the time and being stuck on the highway for an hour and a half minimum to two hours in a car in bumper to bumper traffic with no rest stops accessible was just not acceptable. Anyone with

Crohn's or ulcerative colitis knows you might have an abrupt, instantaneous, and unforeseen urge to run to the bathroom at any moment, thus sitting in a car with colleagues was not an option unless they wanted a potential stuff show followed by the Hazmat team. A five-alarm poop possibility could happen anywhere, anytime. If the phrase "Time is of the essence" meant anything here was another interpretation. Ms. Fly was beginning to have problems even making it through her 45-minute classes at that point and she was being pumped with infusions and pills, puffed with moon face and filled with chemicals. She would have five minutes between classes to run far away to the faculty ladies' room the very same Mr. P.A.U.L. so courteously and casually walked the female teachers to that PD Day, hope the stalls were empty, pray no one could hear her mess, use all of her accoutrements, including wipes and creams and witch hazel and tissues and gauze, run back to the classroom, and teach another lesson as if nothing ever happened and she had all the time in the world. One day, Fly and her husband were doing a quick check out at the grocery store and the cashier asked in an itty-bitty baby voice as she scanned the baby butt ointment, "Awww, who's the Desigoopy for, pooor baby?" Fly shot her a stern look dead in the eye, "Me." To which she was shocked, eyes widened in disbelief, and had no reply. So Fly took the train against popular demand, so that she could have the necessary privacy to use the bathroom train car. They totally did not understand. They just bragged about going to several donut shops here and there along the way and also felt offended when Fly did not order food at lunchtime.

Torture Log Diary
Dear Paul et al.,

Boy, you players, you really had me duped that you were actually going to help me, but instead set me up with abominations. You et al's., all are as personal as a flu shot, nay, as personal as a colonoscopy. You requested all of my complaints, constantly acted as if you were going to help simply rectify the situation, and then tried to trivialize the seriousness and severity of this case by focusing on the French fries and Post-Its and not the hundreds of incidents repeated over and over. This was an inquisition, not an investigation as all you men sat stoically at the Round Table surrounding me with your manliness. Just look at all the players at your Round Table and see that I am the only woman. Hear me roar. Why might you dare incriminate yourself and even state there was wrongdoing? Well, that would make you accountable and negligent for never ever addressing the escalating situation until now. All I can see is the ridiculous Spanish Inquisition scene in Mel Brook's *The History of the World Part 1* movie where they start dancing and singing "The Inquisition, oh, the Inquisition!" like it were a carnival. You now too have targeted me as you believe every seemingly innocent lying word and denial that comes out of that employee's mouth. He clearly contradicted himself and compulsively lied, which is not terribly shocking since this is what I am trying to tell you is one source of the problem. Where is the accountability? I am not even asking for an apology just a regular ol' transfer, which is in your power to do so and common and permissible. And if it is work performance issues, then why is there no policy or repercussions for that aspect of the situation? If you are not doing your job...you're fired! Why should I have to justify myself, be crucified by you and your literal Round Table of men? Look around the table—all men—and me, Little Fly, you feel you can shoo me away as if a bother to you and your stiffly starched suits. I am a reasonable person and to state the legal definition and defining guidelines as what a "reasonable" person perceives as a work environment that is intimidating, hostile, or offensive. And *then*, you even reward Paul with special privileges, chummy conversations, and you, Paul, knowing you are in hot water go overboard being Teacher's Pet to the PTA Mom getting Teacher Awards and such abominations continue right under their noses. Why do I have to decide between litigation and suing for equality and social justice for decent human rights or my daughter's college education expenses? Should I say, "Hey, Celeste, are you sure you wanted to go to college in a few years because I got this thing…" Or the other, wishing you would just simply run me over with your dumb car in the school parking lot. So you are to take away my daughter's continuing education in order for me to afford suing you and hoping that when the coin is flipped the 50/50, lands in my favor? Your exhibition of deliberate indifference, turning the other cheek, blaming the victim, and silencing my thoughts is incriminating. Utterly disgusting. Cowards.

You got no guts.

Sincerely,
No, Really Not,
Ms. Fly

America the Beautiful—American Mayhem

Every ten minutes, a mother dies in America due to pregnancy complications. American mothers and babies are dying at alarming rates during pregnancy, childbirth, and postpartum.

Maternal deaths are a clear signal of discrimination against women due to lack of appropriate health care. Clear discrimination against pregnant women in America can be witnessed by the recent heinous overturning of *Roe v. Wade* teleporting women's rights over their own bodies, choices, and decisions back fifty years. Among eleven developed countries, America has the highest maternal mortality rate. We are gambling with women's lives.

Word Wall

"discrimination" noun de•skrime•nash•en
1. the unjust or prejudicial treatment of different categories of people or things, especially on the grounds of race, age, or sex, discriminating categorically rather than individually
2. the quality or power of finely distinguishing
synonyms: prejudice, bias, bigotry, intolerance, narrow-mindedness, unfairness, inequity, favoritism

FAST FACT

A "hostile" work environment is defined as "unwelcomed or offensive behavior in the workplace, which cause one or more employees to feel uncomfortable, scared, or intimidated in their place of employment," according to legal dictionary. Recommended steps you should take:

1. Ask them to stop or ask a supervisor to tell them to stop.
2. Keep a log of incidents, keep all notes and copies of offenses.
3. If they do not stop, have supervisor tell them to stop again with evidence.
4. If harassment begins, report to supervisor again.
5. After following the chain of command and policies, it continues and your employer does nothing, file a com-

plaint with the EEOC, the Equal Employment Opportunity Commission.

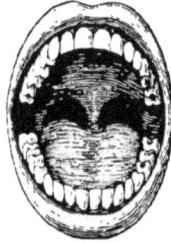

Notable Quotables

When you're accustomed to privilege,
equality feels like oppression.
—Clay Shirky tweet
12:13 p.m., July 22, 2016

I did not lie. I participated in a full campaign of misinformation.
—Mulder, *X-Files* S1E6

All disease begins in the gut.
—Hippocrates

Lesson #6

This school year, Fly learned that silence can be deafening.

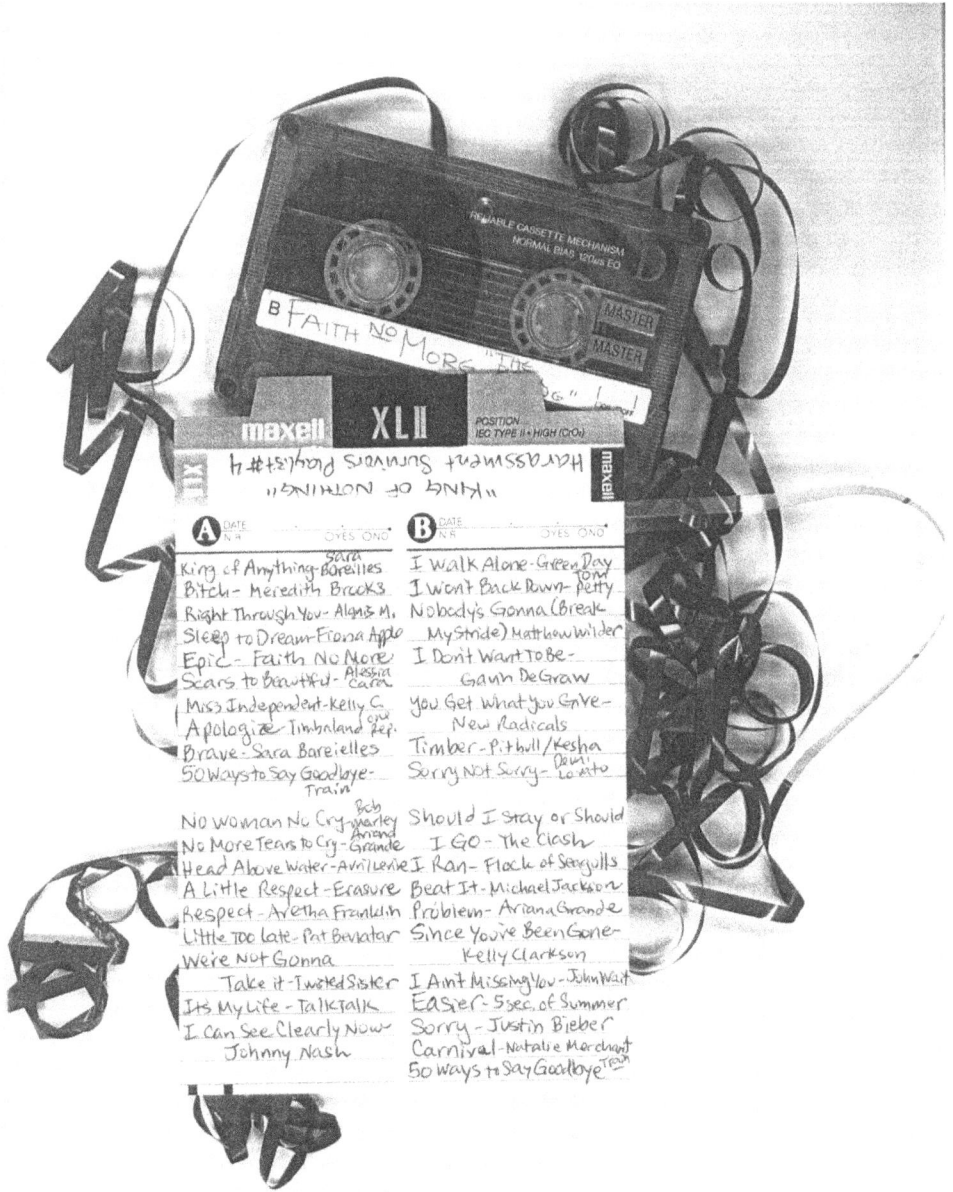

Spill Your Guts

Act Out!

Activity: Take the next page, spill your guts, and write a letter to someone or something that has hurt you in the past. Take those thoughts and tell them really how you feel. Let it all out. Maybe you have an unwarranted traffic ticket, unpaid bill, untimely tax letter, damning bagel receipt, or something that you would like to go away. When done, make it into a paper airplane and fly it away right into that fire pit. It's okay to cry or scream or feel anger or hurt and then let it go.

Chapter 7
Would You Rather...?

Wake me up whenever September ends.

Worn Out

Thy strong arms are around me, love,
My head is on thy breast;
Though words of comfort come from thee,
My soul is not at rest.

For I am but a startled thing,
Nor can I ever be
Aught save a bird whose broken wing
Must fly away from thee.

I cannot give to thee the love
I gave so long ago,
The love that turned and struck me down
Amid the blinding snow.

I can but give a sinking heart
And weary eyes of pain,
A faded mouth that cannot smile
And may not laugh again.

Yet keep thine arms around me, love,
Until I drop to sleep;
Then leave me-saying no good-bye,
Lest I might fall and weep.

—Elizabeth Siddal

Cue the Music:
"Bad Blood" by Taylor Swift
"Cut You Up" by Peter Murphy
"Stitches" by Shawn Mendes
Bonus Track: "In the End" by Linkin Park

Take a Bow

"Just beat it, beat it, beat it, beat it. No one wants to be defeated," blares in Michael Jackson's video of "Beat It." Does it not matter whose wrong or whose right? "They'll kick you, then they beat you, then they'll tell you it's fair." The video starts off with six men lined up in a diagonal line boldly lit by pools of light. It is a full three minutes until the rival gangs all meet up in a smoky dark garage to face off in a duel. The leaders of the separate sides are bound with twine at the wrists as they dance with pocket knives moving toward and away from each other, weapons coming close to the bodies in attempt to cut the other up. This is how Fly felt about the current situation. M. J. is all alone in the beginning of the music video until the next part where he in his token red leather jacket and travels to the duel and breaks up the white man in the black outfit and the black man in the white outfit separating them as they then all get along together dancing in waves of movement. Fly was perplexed as to why it was so terribly difficult for everyone to just get along and work together on this situation.

It was September and Fly was disgusted at the district from the epic failure the last week of June last school year. She sat in the hot, dark auditorium as if she were about to watch Celeste's super long Windy Ensemble where she might be lulled to sleep by the six-minute concerto arrangements or a really bad high school theatrical performance. Super Head Honcho stood up there on the stage welcoming back all of the teachers stating that they were all "one big family." What a crock. If that were true, Fly would have immediately filed for divorce in June, but she was stuck in this job. In fact, it seemed it could be easier to get out of a marriage than this coworkership. He stood there saying, "Art is a reflection of civilization," undermining everything Fly was set out to do for her career. How dare he talk about art like he knew anything about it. Then a Board of Education member stood up there telling all of the hundreds of teachers that if there were problems brewing, they should be resolved before things boil over. Was he referring to Fly's case or was there more stuff going on in the district that she was unaware of? This board member was the dad of one of Fly's students, and she contemplated going directly to him with her complaints. But she didn't think he would believe her as he only witnessed the "Nice Guy" persona Mr. P.A.U.L. projected.

The very last day of school two months ago, they had the nerve to hold a meeting to try to iron out the problems as they had mentioned could be the next step in their quasi-investigation inquisition. Fly went via Labor Lawyer Lackadaisical for that next maneuver, in hopes they would see the light. One last chance to tell her story. After the district blatantly ignored her lawyers all spring as if to not be in receipt of Fly's lawyer's emails, they finally organized the event for both sides to meet together but separately and hear their stories. Only they thought they were stories of she said-he said. No, this was more she explains, he covers up. They were back at the Round Table. It would have been nice to hear what the words Mr. P.A.U.L. said to the mediator because after he heard Fly's complaints alongside her union representative and lawyer, Mr. Mediocre Mediator simply asked, "Ms. Fly, if you could change Mr. P.A.U.L.'s behavior and that if Mr. P.A.U.L. started listening to you and following your directions in September would that be okay?"

The lawyer, Fly, and her representative all looked at each other perplexed, thinking alike at how absurd a theory. If he hadn't listened to Ms. Fly at that point repeatedly year after year, what really made these people think he will suddenly change and finally do what he was expected to do in September? Also, why would it even be a consideration that it was Fly's job to "change *his* behavior?" She looked around the room, and it was clear that maybe all of these men need an attitude adjustment. He fixated that Ms. Fly kept calling Mr. P.A.U.L. "This Employee," and that is what she meant; that he was their employee, and therefore, they should be responsible for his behavior.

They all sat around and came back with an assessment that it was 50/50 that both sides were equally understandable, but while one of them stated that they would like to see some way to fix the problem, there was ultimately no conclusion or ability to resolve the problem even though in the beginning of the meeting, they wanted to find a resolution. "Impasse." Dead end. Fly was livid at that point, as if her claim of harassment from an entire year ago was falling on deaf ears. Like she was making all of this up and it was not important to them whatsoever. Not even the most elaborate hoax or con artist could possibly make up all of these accusations; the absurd behaviors and chronic actions toward her by this one mere individual. Fly was stunned as to this raffle-like mentality, and after a few key phrases by Super DaNile, Fly's attorney stated directly to her under his breath, "They are going to try to *fire* you. Complete a Notice of Claim immediately, have it notarized, and bring it to my office right away." Fly was scared to death. What the heck did she do to deserve this type of backlash, and what lies did this employee use behind that door to cover up from the claims and evidence presented? Why do people in charge not believe people that come forward with injustices and why is it so difficult for the Round Table of highly educated educators to come up with a simple solution? Kids take tests all the time, and there are always answers. Why did they believe him over Fly, his ridiculous claims of innocence and denial? If a student had made the same claims about being bullied in school, it was now a law that the teachers or administrators must file a written report within twenty-four hours and take immediate action and create a resolution, and then the perpetrator student would get suspended from school or other appropriate response. So Fly knowing all of these procedures for students in schools could not figure this one out. What a performance. Take a bow and you get a standing ovation for playing the part, pull back those red velvet curtains, and the winner is...P.A.U.L.! Fly had to live with the fact that good people lose, and sometimes, the bad guys do win.

If it was not clear before, it was very clear now that they were all in cahoots with discriminatory actions and retaliation on top of all of the behaviors Fly had experienced at the hands of their employee. Is this what happens when you speak up for basic human rights? Fighting for social justice? The summer was filled with legal eagle maneuvers: a voyage to the Equal Employment Opportunity Commission to file a federal charge, getting papers notarized, and then the district kept insisting through the lawyers back and forth that Fly go to a hearing, which was erroneously for injury not discrimination so they used that as an excuse and fake leverage to do absolutely nothing more to rectify the problem insisting she go to the hearing or else they do not intend to "do anything" unless she sued. At that point, the State Administrative Society would no longer fund Fly's fight for justice, so she had to think about where she might get tens of thousands of dollars and then have her daughter not be able to go to college. Celeste and Fly's husband were ever the rocks that kept her grounded during these tumultuous times. The model in the *Ophelia* painting, Elizabeth Siddal, was also a poet. She wrote the poem "Worn Out" that spoke to Fly and to the overworked moms that were just simply worn out and broken down by the system and the Institution of Man. Her smile was broken and her sparkle extinguished. The summer was riddled with pain and misery and destruction that could have been mended by using intelligence and knowledge to bring the power of change and break the cycle for the next school year. Instead, she was riddled with tolerance of systematic gender discrimination, bullying, harassment, intimidation, and retaliation of women in the workplace.

It was September 6, and chills ran up and down her spine as Fly walked to the parking lot to get a bag she forgot to bring into school from her car. She froze right there momentarily on the hot pavement, hand resting on her door handle as she gazed up to see the face-off. This employee's car was intentionally backed into a parking space directly facing Fly's car as in a clear duel. It was as if the cars were bulls ready for charging and then the red flag waves through the air. Fight! It was an obvious visual form of aggression to Fly, and she took a photo just in case and she could picture the enraged look on his face as he made the conscious decision to find her car, drive all the way around the lot to pass closer spots, and purposely select this space and then back in locking eyes on Fly's car all the while. Fly had now been so traumatized by this employee that every time she saw anything that car color, even a paper clip, she started shaking and sweating with the fight-or-flight anxiety or some form of PTSD. It was real raw emotion. Thoughts of intense fear would riddle her body, beading with sweat, racing heartbeat, shaking hands, hyperventilating with fast-paced reflex of a traumatic experience.

Celeste had the exact same reaction after she broke up with Dirt Bag Dude and what he did to her exactly still remains a mystery to Fly and her husband but haunts Celeste every day. She even jumps out of her seat when she hears the city "Petersburgh" announced, conjuring up the unknown mistreatment bestowed upon her leaving her traumatized by Peter.

Principal Teddy Table Turner would have stated that it is simply where he parked, or she's overthinking it, or whatever lame excuse such as the bus incident. "After you…" motioning Fly on. No, she did not think that was a gentlemanly gesture but one of power: he commanding her to go ahead. Fly wished she was better at quick responses. Maybe this was her Achilles' heel or kryptonite, the inability to speak up at a moment's notice, which made no sense since she could do that just fine in the classroom. She wishes she would have just said, "Thank you, but no thank you. You go. I'll wait." But she didn't. Crystal clear to Fly, he exhibited seemingly nice manners in front of the others on the bus while stabbing her in the back elsewhere, but he claimed this never happened and they just believed him that it didn't. He may have just as well said they were never on a bus or at an art museum, or they got there by a UFO, and they would simply believe him. She had contacted her union representatives to see what the district was going to do to rectify the situation and the response from her own colleague was "They're not doing anything unless you bring your lawyer and sue, which seems like you are being charged a lot of money." Thanks for the support. She wanted to scream through the phone for a real representative while frantically pushing the zero button. So there she was in school, her place of work, for another entire school year with him and with no action, repercussions, or paperwork in his file or attempts at a solution were ever discussed. They just did nothing, and it was September again. Fly came by the phrase and thought it to be true as she reflected on her life, "Discrimination can happen against any one person by another, but oppression includes an element of power and works on a larger scale."

When Fly was Little Fly, she would rummage through her parent's albums and play them on her record/8-track/cassette player. She wished she had kept that as a time capsule of technological history. Little Fly's mom would blast and sing along to "I Am Woman" and other powerful songs of the time as she cleaned the house, wearing her favorite bandana head-scarves and curlers. Little Fly would play a particular album over and over again. The cover art had this fierce and feisty strong woman with great hair and fashion lying in a dark background. "One of these days these boots are gonna walk all over you… boom, boom, boom, boom, boom, boom, boom…" She put her autumn boots on and in the rain as she boarded the train, that song popped into her head, figuring she was finally going to get to use those boots to walk all over the Boy's Club.

She took yet another sick day to try to fight to the death if need be; this unnecessary war that was forced upon her and it could have ended six months ago, twelve months ago, several years ago if just one of those educated administrators came up with one solution to the problem. Fly did that all the time in the classroom. The students would be given a design challenge, and they would all come up with a variety of ways to solve the problem in a visual manner. Perhaps just a simple transfer as requested may have been a sound solution. Fly's husband thought for sure there was a feeling of nepotism or a connec-tion to that employee somehow, because why would they put the district in a potential spotlight or in the news? He was a lia-bility on so many levels. She packed up as many binders of evi-dence as she could carry on her back in her backpack: emails, log entries, photographs, notes, memos, and she selected the most important and blatant examples to make her point that she has been harassed, discriminated against, and now add retaliation to the bucket. In the cold early autumn rain and with Notice of Claim in hand, she took the journey by train to the Equal Employment Opportunity Commission Office in the city. She showed ID at the main desk; they gave her an ID sticker and told her where to go. Upon entering the EEOC, there were empty seats around and she walked up to the main window. After she explained that she needed to speak with someone regarding her email correspondence and that she had not heard from anyone since the summer, she would like to follow up on the status of the possible charge. The worker stated, "You can't just come in here!" Drenched from the pouring rain, she pleaded that no one was responding and that she had traveled all this way to get an answer.

He felt sympathy for her distress and said, "Hold on. Let me look. Please wait a minute." She sat by herself, clutching her soaked backpack of evidence as if to protect it for if it got lost or ruined from the rain, how might she ever prove the unbelievable atrocities that have happened to her? A woman entered frantic, speaking Spanish, explaining feverishly about whatever her situation was about. She sat across from Fly stewing and wondered what happened to her and if anyone believed her. About twenty minutes later, the worker excitedly comes out from the back room and exuberantly shouts, "I got it! I got it! Here it is! There *is* a charge!" On a tiny torn piece of copy paper, he wrote the Charge of Discrimination number down and hands it to Fly. With that magic golden ticket, he allowed her to see the specialist that had been working on her case since the mediocre mediation debacle and Notice of Claim. It's official: a permanent federal charge against the district that can never go away with Mr. P.A.U.L.'s name on it in black and white. This representative hit the nail on the head with her wording and how she to the point interpreted the plethora of items.

Interpreted, written, and typed by the hand of the EEOC administrator, it stated that Fly was a female employee at this establishment and that she believes she has been discriminated against on the basis of her sex when she was harassed by her subordinate, this employee, who has been consistently insubordinate and fails to follow basic instructions regarding teaching. It stated that Fly has to constantly correct him and request for him to complete tasks. When he is approached about his deficiencies, noncompliance, and inadequacies regarding his performance or incompetence, he handles the situation in a passive-aggressive manner, undermining Fly's position as a leader and dismissing her expertise. He is unstable and unpredictable and inconsistent with his work, and she feels threatened and he intimidates her. Then the charge stated a few recent instances within the allowed time frame: this employee bypassed the food chain ladder and requested unqualified male teachers to change his preps and that he aggressively handed his course syllabi prior to that instance. Fly finally was relieved that a five-second aggressive interaction with this employee that could not be seen by anyone as she was alone in the class-room when it happened was recorded right there on paper. The EEOC administrator also stated that the male administration rewards male teachers and then circled back to the original State Administrators Society legal department letter indicating that Ms. Fly had previously submitted no less than twenty-five written and verbal complaints to her supervisors, all of which have been ignored. Based on this, it concluded, she believes she has been discriminated and retaliated against in violation of the Title VII of the Civil Rights Act of 1964 and other federal, state, and local anti-discrimination statutes.

Fly felt validated for once and taken seriously, no less at the federal level, and for that, she was humbled and grateful.

Bad Blood

About a week later, Fly was struggling to make it through the school day without having to run to the bathroom in between every period. She spent her Sundays organizing all of her med-ications for the week up to ten or twelve pills a day. She sorted them out like playing a mancala board game: *clink-clink-clink-clink-clink-clink-clink*. Repeat. She had also started yet another infusion medication Eternityo, administered in the Cancer Ward since everything else only worked for a short time. Luckily, she met a very nice special education teacher whose niece and many of his family members also had ulcerative colitis, so he understood what she was feeling and, unlike the supervisors and colleagues, comprehended the physical ailments of the disease and gave his cell phone number to her so that he could cover her class anytime for a few minutes. He said they had to fight her district so that she was allowed to bring her cell phone to the bathroom in case of emergency as she was only ten. Fly was very thankful at this gracious offer. He, like most people in the building, also had absolutely no clue about the employee situation. Then her ability to teach one or two periods was get-ting worse, and then one day, there was so much blood, more than she had seen before. On the surface, Fly looked just fine to most onlookers, masking the truths about her physical body and her mental turmoil of having both the relentless disease and the hostile workplace, but bubbling below was a volcano about to erupt. Alarmed, she called Dr. Mendit and she told him she thought she might be on the verge of hemorrhaging, and by the time she finished teaching her classes for the day, she drove herself to the emergency room and told the doctor she thought she might need blood, but he did not think so. Even Teddy Table Turner asked what she was doing there and that she needed to leave, but she waited to teach all of her students that day. She adored her students and they made her laugh. One quirky student came up to her and said, "You look like the type of person who might have a cat hair roller," and sure enough, she ran over to her desk drawer and pulled one out for him to use. Later that day, Dr. Mendit drew a diagram on a folded-up scrap of copy paper of a procedure he thought Fly may have to have since now none of the medications nor infusions seemed to be working. They remove the damaged part of the colon and create a J-shape and Fly looked at him with the same expression as the fecal transplant idea, the look that his ideas were ludicrous. He was trying his best at sketching to impress the art teacher, and he said it was like creating a sculpture out of your small intestines.

One thing that the EEOC representative omitted was the correlation of workplace hostilities with ending up in the hospital, the physical manifestation. She thought it was an important connection that the hospital discharge paper dates directly correlated with the workplace hostilities. She never went to the hospital during those restful summer months as she was relaxed and happy at her home life even if she could not kayak anymore, she could sun-tan in her back yard relaxed and safe and with the two best people she loved most in the whole wide world. This school year, she had to work awkwardly alongside that employee now knowing the claims against him, and that at some point, he was under the microscope, but somehow no one seemed to care and nothing happened. He even had an air of snootiness to him, as he pranced up and down those dank hallways sniffing in the air like a dog looking for a scent, as if smelling the air of Fly's defeat. Admitted to a single ER room again, Fly was poked and prodded every hour until at 3:00 a.m., a nurse came in with a bag of blood stating, "Please sign here, you are going to need a blood transfusion."

Fly sat up quickly and questioned, "Now?" The room was almost pitch black and filled with cold, stale air.

He simply stated affirmative. She called her husband immediately and was scared. Her mom had a blood transfusion in the '90s and that was when there was the HIV in the blood crisis so she was not sure what to think, but she did have a premonition that she was losing too much blood.

Fly knew her body pretty well and was usually proactive with her health. At this point in her life, she was the Anesthesia Queen, having had so many procedures: multiple cysts that had to emergency be removed since college, the emergency C-section, and now this. She thought she read in the C-section report that they removed all her organs and then put them back in, so she tried not to think about it too much, even though she could feel everything moving around inside her for a while. They did some more testing and scans, and it was grim. Again, she could barely fathom that things could get worse, and after fighting so hard for workplace human rights, what did she ever do to deserve this? A surgeon she did not know came in the next day, stating matter-of-factly that Fly needed to have her colon removed, and between the triple threat of family history of colon cancer, the permanent disgusting C-Diff situation and the acute UC, there was nothing else that could be done. Shocked and alone in that dark cold hospital bed, she sat there, reflecting on what to do. He nonchalantly asked her, "How's tomorrow?" as if she were making a casual mani-pedi appointment. Fly told him no and that she was busy. She didn't even know him and he wanted her colon, no questions asked.

She called her mom and was able to get a specialist for a second opinion instead since this was not a minor surgery; it was an entire organ and quite a large one. Elvis's colon weighed at least thirty pounds from an enlarged colon among other ailments when he passed and died alone in the bathroom. Fly didn't want to die alone in the bathroom. Fly wanted nothing of it; it's not like taking off a strange freckle. She asked Dr. Mendit if they could just make a 3D Print and replace it to lighten the heaviness of the situation. He stood there by the edge of the hospital bed, clicking his pen in cadence as he further explained the procedure. Knowing Fly for a while, he knew she was thinking she was having nothing to do with that idea, so his job was to persuade Fly she had to get this body part removed. Fly's husband was there and said, "You should have just eaten my stuff!" She went to go see the other surgeon, and the nurse spent three hours getting her medical history as she kept taking deep breathes and sighs as in, "There's more?" The surgeon reported in a grave manner as the tears streamed down her cheeks that her entire colon needed to be removed because she had "no quality of life left." You got that right. She and her husband walked to the parking lot below where Fly lost it in hysterical emotion of terrible loss. She booked the surgery for after her anniversary in case she died but before Thanksgiving in case she lived. And with that along with yet another speeding ticket on her way back from pre-surgical testing, the EEOC charge vanished into the distance and any potential litigation was thrown out the hospital window.

All the while, the same shenanigans were going on at school, but Fly was so sick and in both physical and mental excruciating pain with feeling defeated that she paid no attention. That employee now ignored Fly at every cost and boxed paperwork to her in the main office to avoid crossing her path. He submitted his paperwork on how many parent conferences he had. He did the math on the parent–teacher night form he boxed to Ms. Fly and added up how many meetings he held, how many were no shows, how many were conference calls and added them up and divided and got 200 percent. It will never change. If he wanted to continue to be incompetent and blame Ms. Fly for not accepting 200 percent as a valid percentage of parent conferences held, then fine; he would have to have hundreds of meetings instead of the 125 student meetings on his rosters and logic says it is physically impossible for one fine evening even if every parent showed up twice, it would still only be maximum 100 percent, which will never happen in the public school system. Even if the district directions given to faculty were incorrect, 200 percent would not be reasonable, according to Mrs. Parabola. Fly took another sick day to play hooky again with her daughter rather than spend the day in the teacher sessions on the dreaded Professional D-Day. And with that, Ms. Fly was 200 percent out of there!

Fly thought about some choices as she looked at the novice sketch Dr. Mendit drew on the hospital scrap paper. Would she rather continue to be harassed and discriminated against in the workplace or get her colon removed? She thought that three surgeries, the removal of a major organ, an ostomy bag, and being opened up and sewn back together several times would be far less painful than dealing with the double harassment and toxic work environment. Without hesitation, she went for the colon removal. She knew about the game "Would You Rather...?" and the choices were never good ones, but you pick the less bad scenario. That must be the point of this ridiculous game of choice.

She woke up from the anesthesia strapped to a bed after the first surgery. This situation had made her so physically ill, and there she was lying on a gurney surrounded by nurses and curtains under a fluorescent light with beeping going on next to her. That was it—she decided she needed to get out of that work situation immediately upon her return, which would not be for five to six months. Ever the teacher, she asked the surgeon if her colon could be donated to his medical students to study, but he said no, and with that, she never did know where her colon went. The week earlier, Fly had to speak with an ostomy nurse, but she did not really comprehend the actual scope and magnitude of what was about to happen. She walked around with a black "X" in permanent marker on her right belly, wondering what exactly the X marks the spot was all about. She had to realize in order to live that she would have to undergo this life-changing event where she could never be an Indian giver and could never get her body part back.

Look what had become of her body. A mutilated Frankenbody cut vertical from sternum to beyond where her C-section was. She was hideous but could deal with ugliness. What was worse was the trauma and stress it had been on her family, but the two of them hid it so well. Fly kept affirming to Celeste, "Don't worry, Sweetie Pie. Everything's going to be all right." Maybe they were just words or lyrics from a Bob Marley hit, and she actually did not know if everything was going to be all right, but she had to affirm it aloud to make it a reality. What else was she going to do? Lay there in the ugly hospital room crying and feeling sorry for herself? Not Fly. Not now. Not later. Several times that school year, she was poked with needles, hooked up to tubes, injected with fluids and blood and infusion chemicals, she was bruised, stabbed, shot, swollen, scarred, and disfigured, yet she still kept getting up to put her kickboxing gloves on. Fight!

In recovery, she saw a movie alone on a Tuesday matinee with all of the retired people in the theater as she nursed her health back together. She never had before gone to the movies alone, so decided to embrace the fact she had to take all of her sick days and the much appreciated additional sick pool days they gave her. The particular movie she went to scared her to death. Would you rather survive a plane crash or be eaten by a pack of wolves? Or she guessed that poor guy got both. Would she rather send her daughter to college than spend the money suing the district? Would you rather be lucky or good? Would you rather lose weight without trying, have your child sleep through the night, or hit all the green lights? Would you rather chew ground glass for a year or redo a high-profile double murder trial? The prosecutor went with the ground glass. Fly thought about how much her colon was worth and wished she had brought the district to justice in a court of law. Like Erin Brockovich said, "I want you to think real hard about what your spine is worth. Or what you would expect someone to pay you for your uterus. Then you take out your calculator and multiply that number by 100. Anything less than that is a waste of our time." She had dreams of suing for a million dollars per school year, no three million dollars for all of the pain and suffering of Fly, Celeste, and her husband, and multiply that by 100 for losing a major body part. Or maybe she could have gone for the 200 percent. She had spent so much money, she would have also liked to be reimbursed for her weekly mental health therapy sessions to get through the harassment, medical expenses, labor lawyer fees, productivity time wasted on documenting or dealing with this employee, days taken to survive the workplace and so on. She was sickened almost to death and felt not as a victim but rather, victimized. Week after week, she sat on that rough but fluffy couch, clenching the throw pillow as if to shield her body from harm, tears rolling down her face as she tells her story of physical pain and unnecessary work torture.

She was scared and disgusted, but unlike the work situation, this had a finite ending in sight corresponding with the end of the school year. Ms. Fly would never teach in this condition, even though many people can go back to work, but usually only if they had desk jobs, not active running around teaching. The place where stuff now dribbled out, not where it normally would, was disgusting, and Celeste, thinking it looked like an alien, they called it Allen. Allen would gurgle and hiss, and they would say, "Shut up, Allen, you're so annoying!" Fly knew she could never stand in front of a room of teenagers with a gurgling abdomen as Allen would surely have gotten detention on the first day of school. She noticed the original X mark was sliced and scarred, so she guessed the surgeon decided to place Allen about an inch and a half below where they originally thought. Then she developed a sense of "phantom colon" she liked to call it, and it made Celeste and her husband laugh in hysterics. They would say, "There's no such thing as phantom colon!" Fly, ever the optimist, she always said, "You can't know what it feels like!" Her colon was missing and felt like it should have still been there. Fly's husband called her the bionic woman and thought of the body parts transformation to be spectacular. Any time Fly got down in the dumps, he picked her up, exclaiming, "You're bionic!"

Fly treated her sick-out time as if it were summer vacation as she was taking her well-earned sick days anyway: walking, reading, going to the movies, keeping the house clean, driving Celeste to and from school and activities. Fly was proud and remembered one day when Little Celeste Bag of Donuts was in second grade, and she had to pick her up because she got hurt at school as she was always walking into things like flag poles, especially on her birthday, and had to sit in the principal's office after school as she missed the bus. Fly never picked her up as she worked far away and her husband was usually around more than she. She walked into the school's main office stating that she needed to pick up Celeste and one of the secretaries yelled, "Who are you?"

Taken aback, Fly responded, "I'm her *mother*."

Was she so wrapped up in work that she was not even known to the know-it-all secretaries? She was making up for those lost moments that year. Fly was never one to "take it easy," but she did for these six months to ensure she remained healthy and strong.

Once, she went to the library for an Ostomy Support Group Meeting and she was not sure what it was going to all be about. It was so specific she was shocked that it was something that existed, but when she went there, she was an uncomfortable participant. "Hi. My name is Fly and I had acute ulcerative colitis, so living with this bag." Some were quick to dismiss her because she had a reversal surgery in her future. One was obese, one in a wheelchair immobilized, others were from all walks of life, but they all had unwanted hot sacs of stuff on them. Another time, one of Celeste's Totally Val frenemy helicopter moms offered to walk with her one day, but Fly knew she only offered as a gesture of fake kindness as she did with coordinating every bake sale, fund-raiser, car pool, and team party. Caring Karen always seemed to care and offered the gesture, so one random day, Fly was getting a little bored at home, so she devised a test to Karen and she accepted it. After they walked the neighborhood, Fly knew it was a ruse as she had become a Master of Detecting Deceit and knew it was only to appear superhelpful in front of all the other Val Moms. She just wanted a little sincerity. She walked alone after that day.

She also took the time for a one-on-one meeting with one of her state senators to tell her story about the need of legislation and regulations about this type of situation, and she gave him a letter stating her concerns and that this is happening in public schools in his county. He was shocked, as Fly sat there trying to be brave and hold back the tears as she gave her seven-minute version of the devastating events over the past seven years. He finally said point blank, "Do you want me to call the Superintendent Head Honcho and let them know we are watching them?" Fly kindly declined, as she needed to get resolution and not create more problems as they might interpret that as a threat. She was happy to become proactive and seek information so that this does not happen to other people in their workplace. She was directed to the Healthy Workplace Bill that had not passed through the very State Capital she had once fled to, but unfortunately, appeared to be no longer in negotiation, dismantled or at the least, no one replied to her emails and contact to become a member and activist.

She stands there stoic, emotionless, staring at the onlookers, the hunters. Pierced with arrows bleeding and shot by whom lanced into her torso, she looked dead into their eyes knowing what has happened and what fate lies ahead. Fly reflects on a self-portrait painting by Frida Kahlo entitled *The Wounded Deer* made in 1946 after the artist experienced a surgery to improve the debilitating pain in her back caused by a bus accident in her early years in Mexico, which left her impaled in the pelvis with a metal handrail, on top of having polio which gave her a limp. The accident left her with lifelong physical pain and mental anguish and suffering that she would try to overcome by creating her art. This painting depicts a deer in the woods with nine arrows piercing the body, blood dripping down. The head reveals the likeness of Frida herself. A branch lay broken in the grass in the foreground. Dead trees fade off down the path toward the distance where the sky is dark and stormy with lightening. In the corner of the painting, she writes "carma," referencing her destiny or fate; that which she cannot control or change. Fly kept effortlessly waiting for karma to hit those who had betrayed her and maybe it had, maybe it had not or is yet to be bestowed upon the people who caused all of this wreckage.

Gag Order

Shut up, Coletta! You're ruining my interview, Fly's internal monologue proclaimed. Fly thought about a phrase, "What if they gave a war and nobody came?" She realized they were done with the war on their side by simply walking away, not caring, so she had no choice but to walk away herself as well. Despite multiple interviews in districts elsewhere where she was "overqualified" and "too expensive," she realized she had to leave. One hiring principal even so roughly demanded, "Let's address the elephant in the room." Fly felt like she was the invisible elephant in the *X-Files* "Fearful Symmetry," where an elusive escaped elephant stampedes around town without being noticed, then dies in the street as Scully sadly states, "She ran herself into exhaustion." This episode was most likely based on a Joel Sternfeld photograph, *Exhausted Renegade Elephant, Woodland, Washington, 1979*. While embarrassed that she thought the elephant was Coletta acting up, he merely wanted to know her salary and said it was too much. Fly never heard a teacher say, "Hey, I am just making so much money at this teaching gig! Right on! I'm set for life!"

She also researched going on disability, but there was no way the income would even have been close to what she was making in order to keep her home with the new renovation. She was stumped again and had to figure out a solution. She had the Labor Lawyer Lackadaisical which she now had to pay $485 per hour out of her own purse, draft a transfer request on legal letterhead to a different building which was not only the next closest, but one she thought might be more conducive to actually being able to teach in a nontoxic peaceful working environment.

She felt defeated when she read the legal letter in black and white:

> It is with great reluctance, but a realization that the only way to resolve this seven-year escalation of harassment from Mr. Paul that Ms. Fly has decided to utilize her rights under Article VII, Section FU, page 13 of the contract, to wit, Involuntary Building Transfers.

It clearly explained the situation for which they were intentionally blind to:

> As you know, Ms. Fly has been on a medical leave and will be returning in June to serve out the rest of the year as supervisor. Ms. Fly's health

is of paramount concern to her, so effective September, she will be stepping down as super-visor and resume her position as a teacher in the art department at X-High School under the caveat that her seniority date remain intact.

The lawyer then concluded:

Because of what Ms. Fly has endured for the past seven years and the deleterious effect it has had on her health, she is compelled to take this course of action. In this way, it is hoped that a humane and peaceful work environment, free from the hostilities of the past seven years and free from retaliation or reprisal shall be the result.

It was delivered by the contractual deadline during the stark cold days of winter. She longed for the days before this employee entered her life where previous schools and districts in her career led her to be prosperous, productive, positive, and happy.

For Fly's second surgery, the J-Pouch was constructed out of her own body material of the small intestine. The ostomy was also reconstructed, and she and Celeste called this one Coletta, French/Greek meaning "People for Victory." By the third surgery, Allen and Coletta would peacefully live happily ever after together forever inside Fly's torso. She opened the mail, and the billed amounts for the surgeries were stagger-ing. She could have bought a really nice house for the cost of these procedures. In between the second and third surgeries, Fly's mom asked if she would go to the Grand Lake with her as she was supposed to go with Fly's dad for their fiftieth wed-ding anniversary. She was scared to fly there but did so, as her ostomy bag filled with air with the altitude, and they laughed. They had a wonderful week eating out and sight-seeing with the gorgeous snowcapped mountains and large reflective lakes, boutique shops, and cheesy casinos. The night before they were to leave, they went to the fancy restaurant where her parents intended on having a special celebratory dinner. But Fly physically could not eat for some reason and she felt bad. Just as once, she could not even bear a smile even if she tried; she could not swallow one more bite of that expensive dinner. She tried but with each fork-full, she almost could not get it down her throat. She thought not much about it and they had a splendid time.

It was about four in the morning, and Fly was savagely vomiting in the bathroom. Gagging beyond comprehension. Was it something she ate or was it what she thought it was? She feared the worst: that there was a blockage in Coletta and the food had nowhere to go to escape the body. Poor Coletta. Fly would never look at tomato mozzarella caprese the same ever again. After speaking with her surgeon on the other side of the country, Fly's mom rushed her to the nearest emergency room and was admitted as she held a bag to her face. It was unstoppable and relentless. The hospital and staff were so charming and sincerely nice Fly kept calling it a hotel instead of a hospital. They gave her a gift of a sheer lavender bag with a gray carved rock inside that said, "Inspire." She was deeply touched at the kind and unexpected gesture. They medicated her, took an enormous amount of tests, and then a specialist came in and poked Coletta and successfully released the blockage. They said that if she had gotten on the flight that morning, she probably would have died on the plane, and that this most likely happened because of the high altitude they resided and were not used to.

The head ER doctor was hippy like and sported colorful clogs with socks and a seemingly hand-knitted sweater. She had the clinical and educational assessment as to what happened, but that she was more worried about her lipase and amylase levels from the bloodwork. Fly said she felt fine, had no symptoms, but the doctor was extremely alarmed and insistent that her levels were through the roof and Fly and her mom became worried. Not only that, Fly felt so terrible for wrecking the end of their wonderful vacation and how much money it would cost to stay longer and change flights and add more hotel nights. The doctor called Fly's husband to explain the situation since Fly was sedated, and he didn't know anything but understood she needed to see a specialist immediately upon returning home.

She returned to not only having to be administered an endoscopy for a possible pancreatic problem, but at the same time, the district administered to her a Stipulation of Agreement, only Ms. Fly was not in agreement at all; it was a three-page gag order. And the obvious parallel of work and medical shined once again. "Gag once, shame on you. Gag twice, shame on me."

She was last resort willing to quit being a supervisor, move to another building, negating all of the money and time she spent earning multiple graduate degrees and doctoral credits and using her leadership skills and they cornered her that the following were terms she agreed to not under fraud, duress, or influence. Fly had already used the duress word a very long time ago.

> Section 1 discussed her resignation, transfer to a school she did not request, and that it only indicated for only one numeric school year, the following school year, leaving it open for them to fire her.
>
> Section 2 did discuss Fly's agreement of retaining her teaching seniority and tenure status.
>
> Section 3 was a full page pretty much stating that this would be placed in her file and that no one will "disclose anything whatsoever concerning the facts underlying the terms of this agreement." And that no one "attorneys, directors, officers, administrators, agents, related entities, employees, independent contractors, assigns, heirs, successors, predecessors, or any other representatives" to disclose the details of this settlement to any person. Settlement? They forgot any possible zombies, aliens, and krakens Oh my! This included "no release of information to any member of the print, television, radio, internet or other media now existing or which

may be invented in the future." Something that did not even exist yet? Pure science fiction! For one, Fly did not ask for a settlement, but simply a transfer and does this not sound incriminating? A settlement would have included Erin Brockovich's monetary wish list for all of her pain and suffering. And what the heck are they even talking about? No one believed anything she said and now they are covering up their rears? Clearly, they got the EEOC charge.

Section 4 highlighted in bold the district ten times and stated that Ms. Fly never would she ever never file any "action, complaint, proceeding, charge, grievance, arbitration, nor commence any proceedings, administrative or judicial, against the district in a court of law." No way Mr. Head Honcho.

Section 5 acknowledged that Ms. Fly has had the opportunity to discuss this stipulation under no duress and gives up "all of her constitutional rights." Were they serious? Like did they think she would be like, "Sure, this sounds great! Who needs constitutional rights anyways?" And duress, duress, duress! Did they forget she had over three college degrees with 4.0s from leading educational institutions in America? Fly was an educator. Maybe they should have given this to Mr. P.A.U.L. He would have no clue what they were saying and he would say, "Good stuff! Do you have a pen?"

Sections 6, 7, and 8 were filled with the droning blah, blah, blah, yadda, yadda, yadda. Fly did not agree to any of this nonsense except Section 2 and she thought they were even further discriminating against her with clear retaliation as such.

Fly was immediately insulted again and infuriated. The nerve of this school system. She was just trying to quit again, and no one was just letting it happen. She was trapped again. She had the union legal team go back and forth, stating that they were unfairly targeting Ms. Fly, and they should treat her exactly as they have treated other supervisors who have stepped down in the past. In the meantime, Fly was more concerned about the potential pancreatitis which was another mystery disease, but this one sounded much more serious than a full colectomy if that was even possible. She had to prepare herself to face that employee for one last week before summer vacation, and she dreaded every disgusting moment of a thought that entered her psyche. Like injecting her legs with the needles in the past, she would take three deep puffs of air, endure the pain, and then let out a scream to release the torment.

She lay there on the gurney ready for the endoscopy. She couldn't quite figure out how they got a camera down there but trusted the specialist she was sent to. All hail the Anesthesia Queen once again and the test was completed, but her blood-work numbers were still alarmingly high. Fly and her husband went to the doctor's examination room to hear the results. He cut to the chase, and both Fly and her husband sat there motionless in shock, hearing that it looks like pancreatic cancer, but if it was, he could probably cut it out as it was near the tip. Fly's tears streamed uncontrollably down her face as she was told she could not have the third surgery of the reversal pro-cedure to finalize the colectomy and J-Pouch procedure. She spent all this time just to possibly die from pancreatic cancer? She was not having any of it. She was bionic, wasn't she? How can this be after all of this time and work and dedication to her body parts that yet, another lay in jeopardy. She exclaimed, "No! I have to go to work next week and deal with issues there!" She begged and pleaded for this not to be worse as she had to face that toxic environment just one last time…now with a bag. She and her husband could not fathom things could get worse.

She returned, and teachers were confused as to why Ms. Fly flew into the school but for a moment and then was leaving, but clearly, the rumors had spread like wildfire throughout the hallways. She was packing up her things as the district finally solved the problem of such a heinous gag order and created a normal transfer document as it should have been done in the first place. Trying not to hurt herself from the surgeries, she packed up her boxes and had the custodians ship them to the new school, but not the school the legal team requested, one of the other schools where District Director Coupon Suzy resided and ruled. Fly got a gut feeling that this was not going to be the greatest of ideas, or perhaps it could be great, but she had no choice if she wanted to get away stat! Anything would be better than sticking around there with toxic Mr. P.A.U.L. and two-faced Table Turner. She would miss Mrs. Parabola and her constant words of wisdom and her rock-solid mathematical responses rather than the artsy multitude of possibilities. She would also miss some of the custodians, security guards, and secretaries. On the way out the door as he brought the last cart of her boxes to her car, one kind custodian said, "Don't worry, Fly. You'll make new friends." And she felt that he knew the reality somehow.

Fly had only received highest inspection and assessment scores for her performance as a teacher her entire career, and also when she was a supervisor. Ms. Fly pulled up her annual report and there it was: *ineffective*, the lowest score you can get. She refused to sign and part of her guts quivered, wanting to sue them so badly for constantly retaliating against her: Man. Dictate. Life. Feeling like a cave woman being dragged by the hair by the cave men, she catches herself being just happy that they so kindly recoiled the gag order and were allowing her permission to, with no other choice because the Boy's Club could not come up with a solution, quit her leadership position, be demoted, make less money, lose a decade of expertise, trash her second master's degree and PhD credits, and move cowardly to another school. She emailed Principal Teddy Table Turner so that the ineffective issue was time-stamped and documented that they intentionally tried to lower her evaluation scores and to please change them to reflect her scores from the fall before she went out on sick leave.

> Dear Paul et al.,
> There seems to be quite the confusion among school staff, teachers, administrators, custodians, and secretaries up and down the

building hallways regarding my recent crafted and planned departure. Everyone seems to think I am leaving because of my health, but it is mere smoke and mirrors, a guise, a ruse to cover up the reality of how I have been treated and tormented. You all did absolutely nothing, but let me go back to work in September at the toxic school, and look how sick I got. And Paul, since you have decided not to engage with me or even look at me for that matter in over two years, I doubt you and the others realize the impact your indifference for humanity, the lack of human rights and destructive behaviors have made on my life both professionally and personally. What's even worse than the torment experienced is the ignoring of the truths, the complicit and hypocritical acts and the absolute lack of acknowledgment of the complaints presented for seven years. All decent-natured human beings deserve to be able to leave the safety of their homes, the care of their children, and enter a place of employment, their school, and in doing so maintain a fair and productive quality of life free from fear. They should be able to go to work anywhere, the grocery store, bank, bakery, donut shop, movie theater, night club, and know that they will not be harmed to any extent even harassed to death, by a fellow employee. Just as students should be able to go to school and feel safe. And who is to really decide who is or who is not a "reasonable person that would consider a workplace intimidating, hostile, or abusive?" I have been telling everyone in my path for years that this is how I feel, look at the pictures and emails and notes in chronological order in binders dated year by year—only to be dismissed, undercut, ignored, and worse, grossly exacerbated by those whom

I have complained to in essence, highlighting extreme negligence and lack of accountability.

I went into Administration from teaching to help make a difference and positive impact on a greater number of students than just in the classroom, yet the last several years have been a lesson in fight or flight, strategies for survival and true test of my skills as the middle-person administrator sandwiched between the teachers and the main office Administration. It is downright disgusting that the experiences I have endured are due to wrong and hurtful choices of poor quality workplace colleagues and bad bosses. When the workplace becomes no longer the place where you can't wait to go and teach the children something new and exciting every day in a subject matter that you are so dearly passionate about, but rather becomes a place of fear, daily terror, and chronic torment at the hands of one man, then a group of men, and yet supported by the others in the Boys Club, one must decide to lead their own way out. Lesson learned.

I have come to the conclusion that it has been far less painful to have my entire colon removed than to have endured all of these years of combined workplace hostility, hypocrisy, and harassment. I now hold the gun that starts the marathon, and I will decide when the race and if the race starts, only in hopes do I make it to the finish line.

Sincerely not yours,
Ms. Fly

America the Beautiful—American Mayhem

Word of the year? "Complicit." Enough said.

Word Wall

"complicit" adjective kem•pli•set
1. involved with others in an illegal activity or wrongdoing, having or showing complicity
synonyms: collusion, involvement, collaboration, connivance, abetment, conspiracy

FAST FACT

According to Census.gov, "On July 26, 1990, President George H. W. Bush signed into law the Americans with Disabilities Act, which prohibits discrimination against people with disabilities in employment, transportation, public accommodations, commercial facilities, telecommunications, and state and local government services." People with inflammatory bowel diseases such as Crohn's and ulcerative colitis are covered under the ADA even in remission, since one cannot assess based on just looking at the person with IBD.

Notable Quotables

There is just so much hurt, disappointment, and oppression one can take…The line between reason and madness grows thinner.

—Rosa Parks

Lesson #7

This school year, Fly learned she would rather have her guts removed than continue existing in a toxic work environment.

You Got No Guts

Act Out!

Supplies: Scissors
Activity: On the following page, use scissors to cut vertically along the lines. Take what you need. Take one for a friend and pass it on.

Peace

Strength

Time

Love

Acceptance

Healing

Fun

Courage

Patience

Hope

Truth

Happiness

Freedom

Creativity

Passion

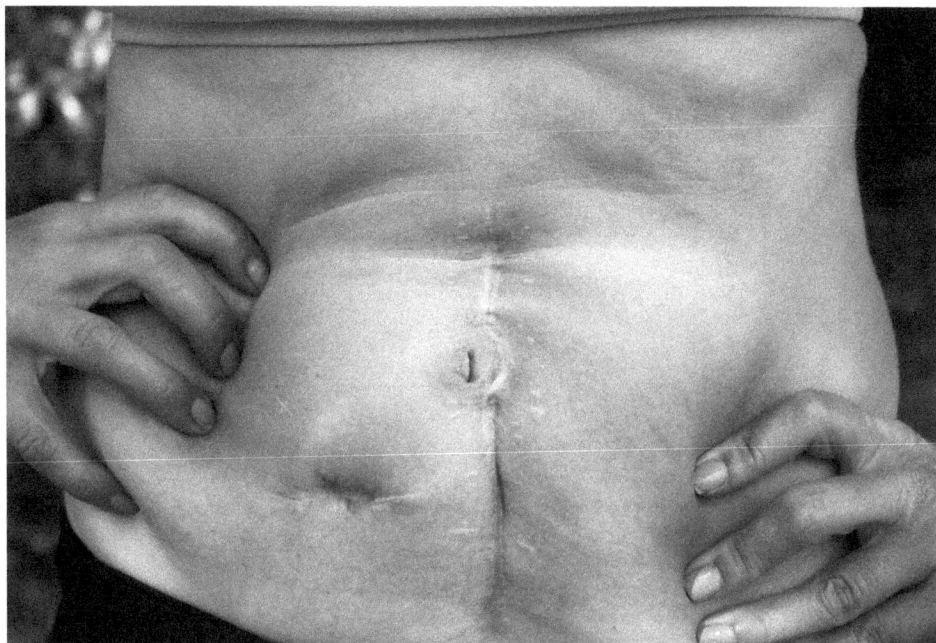

PART 3
Wretched

A man paints with his brains and not with his hands.

—Michelangelo

Chapter 8
Retaliation Nation

Remember September?

Scully's One-Minute Monologue Introduction:

Time passes in moments. Moments which rushing pass define the path of a life just as surely as they lead towards its end. How rarely do we stop to examine that path? To see the reasons why all things happen. To consider whether the path we take in life is of our own making or simply one we drift into with eyes closed. But what if we could stop? Pause to take stock of each precious moment before it passes. Might we then see the endless forks in the road that have shaped a life? And seeing those choices choose another path?

—*X-Files* ("All Things" S7E17)

Cue the Music:
"Uninvited" by Alanis Morissette
"Little Miss Can't Be Wrong" by Spin Doctors
"Big Girls Don't Cry" by Fergie
Bonus Track: "I Ran (So Far Away)" by Flock of Seagulls

Work Like the Snow

Round 1: Fly was driving on her way into the new school when she was startled by a white SUV on her right that was driving aggressively and honking at the poor person in front of her cautiously driving and stopped at a red light. Lo and behold, it was the XL English teacher who wrote that false statement with those big fancy words for Mr. P.A.U.L., and she was acting like a thirty-something crazy workaholic mom talking to someone on the speaker phone, beeping at the car in front of her, her horn blaring as if screaming aloud, then abruptly making a fast sharp turn to the right and sped away. Maybe her XL hair was slicked and pulled back too tight that it was pinching her ability to think clearly. As Fly was driving in, she wondered what the new school year would encompass and be like as she had new classes she was going to teach and was not familiar with the school environment as the district was very large and diverse between the multitude of buildings. She was worried about a conflict of interest in that Coupon Suzy was the recipient of several complaints about Mr. P.A.U.L. in the past, but was hopeful that maybe she can turn the page and start a new chapter in her career.

She thought about the brown bunny that Celeste accidentally ran over as she swerved around a corner in their neighborhood and how badly she had felt for taking this little innocent life. The rabbit as a spirit animal is timid and creative, hyper vigilant and steps through fear. She could not avoid the innocent creature as she drove to go watch the sunrise last week for she would have hit the oncoming car on that sharp S-shape blind curve. "You are valued, dear bunny. Did you plan to see the very same sunrise that I went to go see? Rising ever so slowly upon the moving river, glistening in the mirrored currents?" she reflected in her poetic journaling as she felt remorse and sadness at the incident.

Celeste wondered if it was the very same soft brown speckled bunny that had been eating the grass in their yard as of recent in the last days of summer vacation. A few days later, Fly's husband was in the driveway and stated that he thought the hawk that was looming around the back yard had eaten the back yard bunny, or so he thought because he found just a few scraps of light brown bunny hair and bone at the top of the driveway. The circle of life was in full swing. The hawk is a bird of prey and represents guardianship and cleansing, victory and healing, and is a messenger. Just a few days later, Fly was in her kitchen and was happily stunned when she looked out the back door and saw the brown bunny on the back step looking at her. They just stared at each other for the longest time. She took a photo and sent it to Celeste and her husband and wrote, "It's back!" She did not know who was the fateful prey of the victorious hawk the other day, but she knew her back yard bunny returned. And in one fell swoop like mystical, magical objects that disappear and reappear, she felt the bunny came back to perhaps give her a warning to step through impending unknown waters of fear and despair.

Ms. Fly went to her new school that last week just after the pancreatic testing and met with Coupon Suzy. When the custodian said without question or hesitation that she would make new friends, she felt relief and trusted what he said and wanted to believe in his genuine and sincere advice although she would be missed. She was super hesitant and had foreshadowing in her dreams that were dark and mysterious. Nevertheless, Fly went over to look at the new rooms she would be teaching in and look at the computer lab. She was really taken aback when she learned the computers only had 4.0 dongle bytes capacity and that was at least five or six years outdated. How could she teach under such circumstances? Was not Director Coupon Suzy the head supervisor of the district to update technology? This was not a good start. Fly was walked down the long hallway by Coupon Suzy like a puppy on a leash, and the vibe was dark and negative. She snarled blatantly at Ms. Fly and had a snooty look plastered on her face as if she just ate a sour lemon or curdled milk, or worse, both together at the same time, yet not uttering a word as if she will only do the bare minimum of what she was told to do in transitioning Ms. Fly to the new location. Fly just tried to hold her head high, being the ever optimist, and gave Coupon Suzy an artsy notepad as a gift with a little note thanking her for letting her join the department. Fly had the custodians move over her twenty years of carts, manipulatives, and Dollar Hollar bargain organizers to the new closet, but Coupon Suzy kept stating that there was not a lot of room. If she said it once throughout September, she said it fifteen times to make it clear to Fly that there was no room. No room for her stuff. No room for her. To Fly, it appeared the other teachers had plenty of room, so she was not sure why she had to keep repeating it to Fly. Suzy appeared peeved that she had to move her own supplies to make room for Ms. Fly. Fly's husband would hear this and mockingly state in a deep theatrical voice, "There is no room at the inn," like when Jesus was born in the manger.

Fly had come to the theory last year that if you can't beat them, join them so they could keep their $6.50 an hour stipend to deal with all of the P.A.U.L. nonsense. Over the summer, she luckily dodged the cancer bullet and the levels just simply vanished without a trace nor explanation. She was able to drive to visit family; although Fly did not feel terrific, she was happy to just be alive and able to take Celeste to see her grandmother and relatives and to visit colleges. They were all sitting around the living room when double, double, boil, and trouble, Fly's stomach hurt so bad, she could not even enjoy the conversation. Fly apologized and ran to the bathroom several times and, upon returning, said that she was sorry and did not know why she felt so terrible. Her aunt looked at her joking and exclaimed, stating matter-of-factly, "It's because you got no guts!" Not completely understanding the extreme nature of a colectomy, they all just laughed and carried on the festivities.

> Journal entry:
> It is September.
> I am trying to start over with a fresh start, but have been met with the great un-welcome. In June, I was met in the new school with contempt and disgust. This is not a great start. I was hastily shown around with a smirky disgusted look on Coupon Suzy's face and was told there was little space for my stuff. Okay, I am going from an office and running a large program providing art education to hundreds of students every

year to being *demoted* to the worst courses and a specialty one I am not trained to teach, so I have to take yet another college course to learn the technology. It's like I am the unwanted stepchild. Why? We were once friends.

The first week of school was daunting. Fly was placed in multiple rooms with multiple new classes to teach, and she was running each period from room to room calculating to be over three miles of walking per day in this new school according to her physical fitness app on her phone. She kept thinking, *I'm not retired Victoria. Why did I get the retired teacher's exact schedule? This is not what I was hired to teach. Why didn't the schedule get looked at more carefully?* She used her 50 percent coupon at the Crafty Store to purchase a rolling cart to help alleviate her homelessness. She migrated from place to place seemingly with no home base in which to rest and, along the way, invisible to so many students and staff that she surmised there was something strange in the water in this new school. The summer months had passed and they were back, and Fly was trying to find her niche; however, with constant snide remarks and comments by Coupon Suzy, she could not avoid feeling that she herself was now one of the Tres Brujas, and she trembled in fear like that little bunny before becoming prey. Suzy came shuffling Fly's way and snarkily and sternly commented, "I got a ticket for distracted driving because of your notepad."

Well, welcome back to you too, Fly thought. She also spoke about Fly's daughter like she had no idea who she was and that their girls had never gone to the parks and roller coaster rides together in the past. "Your daughter is sick from school?" *Yes, and you very well know her name is Celeste*, Fly thought. The kids had play dates together multiple times, and they even visited each other's homes at one point. But there was a clear sense of cutting any personal relations for whatever reason will never be known. So of course, Fly kept it inside that Celeste had a meltdown the day before, if she really cared. Or how about a "how are you feeling after all your surgeries?"

And at the same time, the new boss insisted Fly keep secret some items Suzy had once uttered "confidentially," mostly because she called her teachers the Tres Brujas and, additionally, was disgusted by their flip flops and hairiness. She pointed out where in the minifridge Fly could put her lunch because everyone had their own spot, and Fly was only allowed to take the spot of retired Victoria, stripping away any individuality and identity. Fly could actually not reach this spot, and she was not going to start climbing the filing cabinet to retrieve her small yogurt there was no room for. She would eventually stop bringing lunch. She was not permitted to have scented lotion for personal use and was scolded after putting on some luscious Ultra Scent Works hand cream, she was not to have any cleaning products except with natural ingredients however that was not going to be provided by the district, and she was allotted one skinny ass drawer per room for her 150 students' artwork and supplies.

It was only September and Suzy would storm up to Fly, point to her car where she parked having gotten to school early to prepare for class, and state matter-of-factly with a side of snark, "Those parking spots are for the supervisors," intentionally rubbing it in Fly's face that she was no longer a supervisor. Fly did not see any signs indicating this "rule" nor was she informed of anything in an administrative email or memo, so was not sure about breaking this elusive unwritten rule. She was quick to insinuate that Fly stole the parking space of her supervisor friend who arrived late daily, and while she realized there were actually no assigned spaces, Fly decided to park elsewhere. Another made-up rule was that Ms. Fly could only leave class copies of boring articles for students to read and answer questions when the Tres Brujas were absent. This seemed ludicrous to Ms. Fly as she would never have her teachers leave such specific sub plans, but being frail with her health, she did it anyway only to be told she made too many copies at the end of the school year. But she was assigned to three classrooms spread across the building so had to make multiple class sets of these so-called magazine article sub plans for each location.

And she was to never, never ever to leave coloring sheets. Fly thought that was odd because in the other schools, she found students always enjoyed those and art-related word searches when any of the teachers were absent like they were a special treat and kept them occupied while there was a substitute. It also had become so popular those adult coloring books for calming and relaxing oneself so what was the big deal? Coupon Suzy even gave coloring books to all the art supervisors one year as holiday gifts, so there was a solid inconsistency going on. Fly made the fatal error of leaving a small stack of coloring sheets in a folder when she was unexpectedly absent when her car died. They were put there if students finished their work early, but Mz. Coupon Suzy who was becoming Bansheeesque did not read that part of the substitute plans and held them in the air when Fly returned, shaking them with a stern look of reprimand and disappointment.

She proceeded to scold her like a middle school boy, as she had overheard her do to one of her students. Fly would never speak to a child in the manner in which Mz. Suzy did and differences were starting to mount. Fly was concerned about the mixed messages and not sure what was happening. Fly was feeling a tone of treatment as if she were a first year teacher, a teacher who was doing wrong or worse…that she had never been nor acknowledged that she was a supervisor and equal for the past dozen years. All autonomy was stripped away down to the course syllabi in which Mz. Suzy insisted as a "rule" that no iPutzes were allowed in the classroom. Fly had updated this and put her own rules omitting the iPutzes because unless you were a Mothball Gram, no one even had an iPutz; it was almost as outdated as cassette tapes and flip phones. But Mz. Suzy was correct and that was the way it was going to be. Everyone's syllabi were the same created by Coupon Suzy only, and worse, using Times New Roman 12 point font only. Fly knew the other schools did not function this way and was shocked at the strict self-inflicted regulations. Deep in her thoughts wondering what the situation was, she could not help think if she was being punished for everything that happened to bring Fly to her building. She even went home one day and discussed with her husband that she thought perhaps someone like Super DaNile, Head Honcho, or any of the Boy's Club for that matter had whispered in her ear, "Give her hell!" Suzy had done a complete aboutface, a 180-degree turnaround, and Fly could not understand why. She would still meet with Mrs. Parabola for lunch, and they would try to understand the behavior. Mrs. Parabola would questioningly state, "You'd think she would *want* someone who knows what to do, when to do it and how to do it rather than train a new person." Fly guessed that she wanted the opposite, a young inexperienced crony to train in the manner in which she wanted a person to be.

Fly was almost too busy with the new college class and new school and new preps that she did not have time to dwell so much on what her problem was. Fly got home on the third day of school when she had to quick change and then go take a crash course in Dongleshop until 10:00 p.m. on Tuesday nights until Christmas to learn how to use Dongleshop so that she could teach Dongleshop in the outdated lab, which she had never taught before because retired Victoria taught Dongleshop. And actually, the lesser tenured teacher should have been the one with the crappy schedule, but it was not seen that way, only who had less time in the building. Even the split teachers who had less seniority should have been moved to the full time at one location over a new hire, but no one took action or spoke up. Ironically, this was the exact specialty class that Mr. P.A.U.L. had surrendered to the new guy stranger because it was too hard for him to teach so many classes. Maybe they should have just transferred him here as originally requested, and it would have worked out better for everyone. Fly was quickly changing and could not find her cat until she found her lying motionless half hiding under the basement couch dead. Fly just kept going, and with everyone back to school, her husband had to hastily wrap the cat up and stuck her in the refrigerator until the weekend. That's September. Zero to 100 in 0.5 seconds. She dare not tell Suzy as to avoid another snarl and eyeball roll and she could just hear any rant: Ewww, cats are disgusting creatures, they're super smelly, they lick their own butts, and they want so much attention.

Fly kept thinking about that line from *Planes, Trains, and Automobiles,* when Del Griffith is trying to hail a cab at the airport, and it is stolen insensitively by a scumbag. He looks up directly at the man after every torturous experience he had been through traveling and says, "What is your problem, you insensitive jerk?" Only he didn't say jerk. Mz. Suzy clearly lacked any iota of empathy after everything Fly had been through physically, mentally, and discriminatorily. Fly was disgusted, unwelcomed, and had a bad case of invisible disability.

Fly tried to hide the pain and thought of some nice displays she could create in this new place with her albeit minimal space, but she knew how to be tiny and mighty, so she painted a beautiful growing tree mural on bulletin board paper in one of the three art rooms she would be teaching in after one of the Tres Brujas said Fly could have the smaller side wall and counter space. Fly put up fresh bulletin board paper and decorated the tree with sparkly Dollar Hollar owl cutouts as a spirit animal to signify wisdom, intuition or the ability to see what others do not see, and a symbolic announcement of a life transition or change and so she tried to embrace that. She finished the beautiful tree mural which she wanted to add art vocabulary to throughout the year, and she added a color wheel and some positive inspirational art quotes. One free period not too many days later, Mz. Suzy and Una Bruja came in to hook up some computers, and as they appeared to be having their own private conversation by not greeting Ms. Fly, she just did not interrupt them. But a few minutes later, Ms. Fly just stood there in disbelief as they looked around the room as to where to place the large monitors in this fairly large room, and after much discussion among themselves, *plop!* Right there in front of Ms. Fly's new bulletin board display. They continued to place several large-screen computers blocking her entire work area for her students. She had already set up community supplies in her bins in that exact location. Fly thought she must have left her invisibility shield on. It was as if they did not even know she was there nor recognize that they already gave her that itty-bitty space and then took it back immediately without hesitation. More Indian giving thievery. Fly realized she was treading on treacherous mean girl territory here in contrast to the last work situation.

June was far away behind her as September rolled on. Every June year after year was like a pressure cooker ready to explode then in an instant on the last day of school, dissipates. Ms. Fly had a gut feeling of impending doom in June, but she was increasingly becoming more weary of the situation with every unfolding day and felt dread crash over her body like a third wave of the great tsunami. She was just recovering from the second wave of men gagging and drowning her, sucking her in the undertow by holding her legs down beneath the dark depths so that she could never reach the surface even as she tried to stretch those strong arms as high as possible as when conducting the band, but instead, they all went off tune in disarray and she fell to the bottom of the sea.

Even after the first wave of Mr. P.A.U.L. ignoring like *In the Air Tonight*, hoping simply she would drown and he would get away with it which clearly he did. Waiting. Waiting for that spotlight, she patiently did. He stood there constantly watching Fly drown, smiled, and walked away proudly. Wasn't the tsunami first wave enough? Why did it have to unexpectedly keep coming back and back again leaving devastation in its path? The tide had withdrawn once again over the summer, only to demolish her and everything in the raging wave's path once again. The conspiracy was rearing its ugly head in so many unfathomable ways every day.

The fall went on just the same but with chronic unexpected disturbances. The "students acted like they had no souls," as some prior teachers had inquisitively assessed, and Ms. Fly wondered how and why that could be. Another fellow teacher in a different department stated that moving to this building, as she had a few years prior, was like hazing and Fly wondered why that had to be. What did Fly need to prove and why did she have to be punished after everything that had happened? Initiation. Perplexed, she continued to try and tackle student behavior which she had never had a problem with since her early teaching days in the dangerous inner city, the battlefield days. What was the toxicity coming from? The main office turnover? The disgruntled teachers? She only felt the low morale and the churning of the witches' brew growing hotter and hotter until one day, it will surely boil over. Some of the middle school boys were the worst she had ever seen in her career. One snapped her hand-crafted hall pass in half, the one that Celeste had made for her for the new classrooms. The very same student brazenly stood behind Ms. Fly during a group demonstration, mocking her maneuvers from behind. Babyish and biased, she could not tolerate all these behaviors and tried to get administration to help but they did nothing. Other boys thought it to be funny to make comments like, "That's what *she* said." Har, har. Fly didn't think they knew what they were talking about and how inappropriate it was perceived. Everyone in the new school kept calling her Fia, which was so impersonalized that even after several emails for the secretaries to correct, every document still said Fia so everyone just kept calling her Fia. This was not the way her old school was and she was realizing this was a completely new beast. To this day, Fly's husband likes to shout that one out mocking her entire work experience, "That's what *she* said. Huzzah!" And they laughed for but a moment or else they would cry.

Fly and her husband got engaged over a game of darts. Whoever won got one thing, whatever they wanted. Fly was really good at darts and even played one time with members of the Blue Öyster Cult at a bar during a family reunion. She did not even know anything about the "(Don't Fear) The Reaper" song, but her brother did. Fly won and asked him to marry her with a 25-cent ring from the grocery store gumball machine. Fly asked what her soon-to-be spouse wanted if he had won at darts and he simply replied, "I just wanted a Big Mac." A few months later was Fly's first year of teaching, and she got called into the principal's office and was mansplained what the Pay for Performance Program was and sternly told it was not good that she was taking a Friday off. The school had high absence from teacher burnout, and she had to beg to take one day off for her wedding. And then worse, her soon-to-be in-laws told them they were not coming to the wedding for whatever reason no one ever knew. Fly's husband's parents adopted him then threw him away like a piece of trash over and over again throughout his life, but now, after years of emotional manipulations and deviant behaviors, the cord had been permanently severed or so they thought. Fly thought that was why they got along so well was because her husband shared a similar upbringing to her own father: brought into this world, treated poorly and unfairly, then thrown away like a piece of crumpled paper all the while suffering emotional trauma. Fly's soon-to-be-mother-in-law on the phone the last time they ever spoke just two weeks before the blessed wedding day, asked in a One

Line Louie tone, "Do you know he's adopted?" Like that had anything to do with anything about marrying him in the next week. His "real" sister, the one born to his mother after many still births or miscarriages Fly did not know for sure, called his entire side of the family to tell them that their wedding was canceled, and they were uninvited. Fly kept getting the RSVP cards with nasty notes on them. She never even met these people. Mortified, Fly was compelled to handwrite a letter to each and every family and friend on her fiancé's guest list to clarify the situation that their wedding was not canceled and they were re-invited if they would like to attend. There was only about one table of family members that did in support of Fly's husband. His mother tried to blame him for something, and it was so insignificant, no one even knew what had happened except they were out to destroy his special day, their special day.

Fly was devastated and disappointed in the behavior and never understood the audacity of blackballing. Did it make someone feel so empowered they can ultimately control the other? To exclude and ostracize? To be banished like an evil witch as Suzy intended for her Tres Brujas? Who has the right to "cancel" someone else's wedding behind their backs? It was not like they were even paying a penny for it; Fly's parents were, as they refused to pay for anything initially anyway. Fly's dad was so infuriated, he landed in the hospital, unable to breathe clearly only to break out without permission with air tank in tow because he was not going to miss the special day. Fly could just see him maybe ripping out his IV saying, "Get my suit! I'm outta here, you freaking kiddin' me?"

Fly came home from work and Celeste was suicidal to the max. Fly was in shock and did not know what to do. Eight weeks in, Fly took her first sick day; only for once, she was not the sick one. A few weeks into school and Celeste became irate one day when she came home from school. She was in complete inconsolable hysterics, crying, screaming guttural cries up to the ceiling as if possessed by the Devil. Like the girls in *The Crucible*, she was not making any sense and was in a dizzying downward spiral. Fly frantically tried to gather information and find out what was happening, tried to hold her and console her, but there was trauma in her wide, wet, glazed-over eyes. She kept screaming she was going to kill herself and that she could not live with herself. The screams and cries of anger, fear, loathing, and torture went on for hours. As a teacher of teenagers, Fly knew a lot about the mental health of her students, but she certainly did not want to come home to find Celeste having been pushed over the edge by whatever even occurred it was real and now. That was happening too much every day especially with now everyone having phones in their pockets, not the iPutzes Suzy insisted were still popular and could potentially disrupt a class from learning. She had watched a show on a teen who was bullied literally to death, and with all of the technology addictions intertwined with teenage emotions and hormones, she took it seriously.

Also in sympathetic hysterics but trying to remain calm, Fly picked up the phone, sat on her bed, and fearfully called the 800 suicide hotline number, not knowing if they would send the police or what could happen. They talked her through the immediacy of the situation, and it seemed she was in a less dangerous situation since she was with her mom. With that, she took off work the next day to stay with Celeste and find out what happened once she calmed down. She knew what it felt like to be pushed to the limit, to be standing on the edge of the water wanting to drown or drive at high speed to crash because you feel so broken and out of control. Bullied, tormented, ashamed, and mortified, she would help Celeste get through whatever obstacle it was. Tortured at school repeatedly throughout her education experience, she hated school forever. Period. End of sentence.

Ms. Fly tried to have her students celebrate World Kindness Day, which only made Mz. Coupon Suzy angrier, and Fly could not quite figure out why. Ironically, Ms. Fly was instructed to have her new students participate in the Peaceful World Poster Contests. Fly had placed several flyers around the classroom with the quote, "Believe There Is Good in the World," with the "Be the Good" highlighted in bright blue. All of this positivity could not even combat the aggression, ridiculous demands, and seemingly detached behaviors that was increasing with every school day. Fly consulted on the side with two of the Tres Brujas and informed them that they did not have to contractually do everything that was insisted, and they stated that it was just easier that way than to deal with the wrath if they did not comply with the ridiculous demands. After that, Fly was fed up with the three months of handing all of the lengthy lesson plans, quizzes, rubrics, presentations, and examples that she obliged Suzy with to try to make things easier on everyone but made everything worse. Mz. Coupon Suzy created inconsistent written feedback on every week's plans in her illegible scribbly handwriting, which was not allowed or normal for this district, so what was her deal? Her plan book was already three inches thick, and it was only November. And also, the Tres Brujas were all tenured, so these requests were not allowed. Fly knew that it was not permissible to write on teacher's plans and to require all of these items be submitted weekly, so one Monday morning, although the Dos Brujas decided they would continue to comply with noncontractual requests, Ms. Fly abruptly stopped and instead handed in a flimsy but artsy two-pocket folder with one slip of paper inside containing all of the required information. Well, Mz. Coupon Suzy Banshee could be heard for miles with her silent scream and her fury was unleashed, echoing up and down the hallways. The sparring began, only Fly did not want to spar nor had the strength and was trying to focus on maintaining her health after all she had been through. Fly was in her right after consulting with her new union navigators, but there would be no turning back. When Mz. Banshee approached Ms. Fly about the flimsy folder, Fly replied that she verified with her union navigators that was all she needed to submit and Mz. Banshee replied with a curled-up snarl, "Well, good for you!" and stormed away. Fly realized she had reached purgatory and had to find a way out as soon as humanly possible. Mrs. Parabola did the math and figured that a Type A personality plus a Type A personality equated to an F-Minus…less than zero.

Fly recognized that the basic fundamental philosophies that she held true from her higher education, about her educational processes, what she believed in as per art education and personal being were not in alignment with anyone in this new building, especially Mz. Coupon Suzy Banshee. Fly reached out to Lawyer Lackadaisical who had been working her case over the previous two years, but as she had stepped down from administration, he could no longer represent her and dropped her like a hot potato. He would not even release her file to her to bring to new representation. And Fly thought it odd out of the numerous members of the district-wide department, how can it be explained that Mr. P.A.U.L. was the very first person listed in the group emails from the District Director Coupon Suzy? It was not alphabetical, it was not listed by school, it was not by seniority, it was not by area of expertise, it was not by height or weight, so every time the district email popped up…whoomp, there he was!

> Suppose we did our work
> like the snow, quietly, quietly.
> leaving nothing out.

> —"Like Snow"
> by Wendell Berry
> from his collection *Leavings*
> (Counterpoint, 2009)

The Brunch Club

She sits there staring off into the distance with the ring finger of her right hand gently perched on the corner of her mouth, sulking, devoid of rings, gems, and sparkle. She is weathered and forlorn, looking at only the hopelessness that surrounds her in all directions from the north, south, east, and west. She cannot help the deeply drawn wrinkles that drape her forehead and cheeks. She appears dirty and exhausted. There is nothing on this earth that could bring a smile to this face at the present moment. Death and despair lay all around in the barren landscape. It is filled with dirt and dust, and the air is filled with stagnant and quiet stillness. Burrowed in her arms hiding from harm and danger are her three children slightly concealed by her figure. They are gently nestled on her torso ever so closely for strength and safety as they rest under cover of a half tent opened to the elements. Their backs are to the camera concealing their identities of innocence or shyness or sleepiness.

The child on the left appears to be holding their head down in shame, the child on the right rests their head on her shoulder with fist clenched, and the littlest in the middle lies fast asleep in her arms completely unaware of what was going on in America at that time and place, completely innocent. The black and white photograph devoid of color is called *The Migrant Mother* by Dorothea Lange, 1936 taken during the Great Depression to document the migratory farm workers after the dust bowl's destructive path. She wonders if that small potato will be enough to sustain her family for the day and she appears to be thinking about what to do, staring with a brooding gaze. One of her children later in life revealed that the mother was ashamed of this very famous photograph because she felt helpless rather than hopeful.

Blackfoot Prayer to the Four Directions

To the West:
Over there are the mountains. May you
see them as long as you live, for from them
you receive sweet pine for incense.
To the North:
Strength will come from the North.
May you look for many years upon
the Star that never moves.
To the East:
Old age will come from below, from
where comes the light of the Sun.
To the South:
May warm winds of the South
bring you nourishment.

Fly felt like the mother in this image, as she tried to figure out what to do. Her uncle read the "Blackfoot Prayer" at their wedding, and she liked that it gave her a sense of direction. Fly thought about her precious and precarious daughter, Celeste, and the pending doom they each faced with each new sunrise, each new school day; both Celeste and Fly simultaneously tormented by others at school. The balance of family and work, while always challenging for working moms, was becoming increasingly more difficult. Bigger kids, bigger problems. All across America, schools were increasingly becoming unsafe zones rather than safe zones. Fly read Celeste's Rinstagram account where she posted a picture with a quote, "Girls just want to have FUndamental Human Rights."

Amidst this, there was constant practicing of lockdown drills because of increasing amounts of active shooter situations across America. This added anxiety for both students and teachers, security and custodians, administrators and secretaries alike. The relentless number of drills and lockdowns in case of an active school shooter scenario was terrifying. Could you imagine someone like unhinged Mr. P.A.U.L. carrying a firearm? Fly was sure he would have used it on her not against an active shooter, who by the way could be one of your very own students or a total stranger. You start to look at your students through a different lens and from different points of view. Fly had one student that year that was having hallucinations and thought he was God and showed guns and violence in his artwork, so she knew he was a candidate for potentially unleashing terror and reported it to the school psychiatrist.

Fly remembers how close the art supervisors were in the past and how these relationships were turned upside down with the crashing and tumbling of the gigantic terrifying waves on a windy day at the rough water's edge. The teachers in this new workplace did not want to associate with Ms. Fly because she was a former supervisor, and the supervisors from most of the disciplines did not want to associate with Ms. Fly because she was now a lowly teacher. One of the art supervisors thought it to be funny to compare each of the supervisors to characters in *The Breakfast Club*: "a brain, an athlete, a basket case, a princess, and a criminal." Fly wasn't sure if she should be amused or disgusted by the stereotypes and her being casted as Molly Ringwald. She had even been called "Art Angel" by Mz. Suzy as Ms. Fly always came to the rescue when an important document was misplaced or something needed to be remembered from a past agenda or meeting, so not sure what has happened since now she was being treated like the "Art Devil." Maybe because once she stated if their kids didn't have prom dates in the future, they could go together and was disappointed there was now no back-up plan? No matter how hard Fly thought, she could not come up with why she was treated like she was in that Saturday detention. Like the letter left for the principal overseeing detention in the movie, "We think you're crazy to make us write an essay telling you who we think we are. You see us as you want to see us." It is the job of educators to embrace all students regardless of stereotypes and try to figure out who they want to be, their own unique identities. Friends come in and out of their lives as they figure out who they want to be surrounded by, but sometimes that is nobody. Coupon Suzy was seeing Fly as she wanted to see her not as she was. She was acting like the basket case teen in the movie, not as an adult in charge. The thought passed through Fly's mind, "We're not in high school!" and paused with a chuckle, "Well, actually we are," as "Smells Like Teen Spirit" thrashed though her head. And as for breakfast, well, actually, Fly preferred to have brunch, more versatile.

Fly reflected on that poignant teenage movie set in a Middle America High School and remembered the scene where the custodian found Vice-Principal Vern snooping around the teacher files in the dingy basement looking for some dirt on someone. "I have been teaching for twenty-two years, and each year these kids get more and more arrogant."

And Vern is corrected by Carl the custodian, "Oh, come on, the kids haven't changed. You have." Then he surmises the truth. "You took a teaching position because you though it would be fun, right? You though you could have your summer vacations off. And then you found out it was actually work."

Vern shakes his head in disagreement and says, "These kids turned on me."

Turns out the custodian was the smartest one in the room in that scene.

Adolescent development is a challenge to all teenagers and has remained consistent over decades, the only changes being technology such as the cursed cellular devices and ear buds, but there has always been music, cars, fashion, hair, drugs, gangs, dancing, dates, French fries, cologne, cosmetics, and cliques. The major challenges adolescents face are biological with physical changes, and social and psychological challenges. They want friends, to fit in, mold their identities, and to be understood. Fly watches the movie and thinks that maybe Mr. P.A.U.L. just thought teaching would be easy and have summers off. Someone must have told him, "Hey, why don't you be an art teacher, that looks easy!" and he would stare with those blank eyes slowly absorbing the concept. The last scene of the movie comes with the lyrics, "Don't You Forget About Me." Actually, please do.

Mz. Coupon Suzy Banshee had a way to illicit fear and intimidation and the other Brujas had been there long enough to learn how to deflect or avoid her. The part-time Bruja was Suzy's favorite, allowing her to not leave articles for sub plans, allowing her to post lame Do Now's on the dry-erase board, which were not activities, but just taking out their supplies. Fly was clear about this teacher's pet and the preferential treatment and made her experience even more inequitable. Of course, the part-time Bruja loved this school, in which Fly stood there perplexed as to why. She could breeze in and out without repercussion or consequence, duties, or faculty meetings.

It was clear she showed at least two work personas she was aware of now: one from before when she was an equal supervisor and this new demented version of power monger. But it was quite obvious to Fly that Suzy must have felt threatened by her presence or jealous rage, but she could never see clearly through the murky churning waters what exactly it was. For the first time in Ms. Fly's teaching career, she thought she just might follow that rule she never had until that point: don't smile in class until after Christmas. One day out of nowhere, Mz. Suzy cryptically requested to meet with Fly, never stating why or what it was pertaining, leaving the air of mystery, sparking anxiety, and resulting in a million knots in her stomach all school day. "We need to talk later," like the chain restaurant manager in *Office Space*. What is the problem? *Not enough flair?* She had a ridiculous amount of expectations and unwritten rules that Fly came to surmise she would just make up, place it in her reports, and reprimanding toned emails for whatever domineering reason to make her feel in control or in power. For the first time ever in her life, Fly did absolutely everything wrong.

Even when there were good things happening or things done correctly, she was still wrong. She didn't even put her yogurt in the right place in the fridge. *No iPutzes, no* ear buds, *no* two students, *no* stacking chairs, *no* displays, *no* coloring sheets, *no* signs, *no* treats, *no* cupcakes, *no* cookies, *no* parking, *no* ownership of sub plans, *no* lotion, *no* cleaning supplies, *no* touching stuff, *no* moving stuff, *no* sharing, *no* that artist, *no* that project, *no* widgetry, *no* clubs, *no* requested field trips, *no* consulting your union, *no* bins here, *no* shelf use, *no* lunch there, *no, no, no*. And yes, she commanded things that were not contractual over and over again, and being now a former supervisor, Fly knew this and Mz. Coupon Suzy Banshee insisted anyway, then held it against Fly when she was corrected. She would scribble her chicken scratch handwriting all over lesson plans, but return them at the end of the week after the lessons were taught, so what was the point? The others meekly just did it as they knew the wrath dare they stand up to her totalitarian rulership. The Witches' Brew was getting hotter and hotter, scalding the lip that dare taste it.

And there it was, the dreaded post-inspection meeting. Fly's game may have been a little off from her medical year and condition, and trying to acclimate to a new environment with no room, but the ratings were off just as much. The first meeting, Suzy berated her about at least a dozen items she must have had a list on that wretched police ticket notepad. After time, Fly would note that Suzy would never give an inch for any response. She sternly reprimanded her for not doing things she was not required to do, and when Fly stood her ground insisting she did not have to do it, infuriated Suzy even more. Once, she sent a two-paragraph email because while Ms. Fly was assisting a student individually by the teacher desk at the end of the class, some students started "stacking chairs" onto the desks, and once just one goes up, it is like a domino effect of sound and teenage reaction. Like trained rats with the bells every forty-five minutes, the teachers and students in schools just "do." "Move to the next period, go to locker, go to cafeteria, go to gym, go to library, go to homeroom, etc." Mz. Banshee was lingering outside the art room for no reason, perhaps to spy on and "catch" Ms. Fly doing something she felt was wrong in her eyes, circling overhead like Mr. Byrd Vulture. When those students left the room, Suzy stormed in pretending to wash her hands at the sink, and one would have thought someone died as she angrily yelled at Fly, "Totally unacceptable!" and walked out before Fly could even respond. That would become Suzy's MO she would find. Yell and storm away. Had she given Fly a second to respond, she could have discussed the simple accident because the student with cerebral palsy and his aide had a five-minute pass and stacked his chair accidentally starting the chain reaction.

Fly thought about that song to *The Breakfast Club*, "As you walk on by, will you call my name when you walk away?" You could hear her banshee screams resonate throughout those dark dank school hallways again, as she slowly tries to bring impending death to Fly squashing her like an unwanted bug. Fly reflected on how those chairs got stacked a minute before the bell and how outrageous it was! The educational system must be going to hell if kids are stacking chairs early so that they can get the heck out of school.

The classroom is a microcosm of the school at large and the poor behavior of these students was clearly reflected in the faculty and support staff. Teachers know well the makeup of any given class. Some years, the combinations of students in class are better and some are worse depending on the slide in numbers and statistics. This year, Fly felt that everyone was angry in the building though from teachers to administrators, from secretaries to nurses, and from security to custodians. It was like 55 percent disgruntled, 20 percent indifferent, 15 percent beaten down, and 10 percent unsure/conflicted, to which Fly was part of that percentage. Demographics are key, but there will always be and are more diverse than depicted in *The Breakfast Club*: the bully, the class clown, the teacher's pet, the shy, the obnoxious, the blabber mouth, the hyper, the preppy, the jocks, the trendy Vals, the studious, the goofy or funny, the socialite, the emo, the scary, the introvert, the mayor, and the always-appreciated helpers. There are so many students with a wide range of disabilities, diseases, allergies, sensitivities. There are LGBTQ+, trans students, students of different races, from other countries and continents, students who do not speak

English, have different religious backgrounds, mixed races and mixed religions, adopted, transient and homeless students, unclean students, and students being abused or neglected, living in poverty. There are ever more students with special needs, emotional trauma, and language barriers. Students have different economic and social backgrounds, and everyone carries their own baggage. Teachers have to teach them all at whatever level on an individual basis. Fly's suitcase was fairly large, but she knew each and every one of her students had their own suitcase of baggage at their side as well.

On the carousel of life, students come in different sizes, shapes, textures, colors, and patterns, but one things she knew: they were all on the same path of growth hopefully moving forward not in a circle, or worse, backward. Ms. Fly would keep the special notes or emails from current students, past students, and parents appreciating how she treated their child and made them feel special and experience a fun part of their school day. But here, something was not adding up as Mrs. Parabola stated at a dinner meeting. One day, Mz. Banshee stormed up to Ms. Fly and asked her as if giving a student a test, "What's wrong with this display?" Fly thought, first, she used this strategy with Mr. P.A.U.L. so not sure what she needed. She thought, *Oh crap, did I post the artwork on the wrong cabinet, used too much tape or paper or ink…What could it be?* After stating she did not know Mz. Banshee snootily stated, "This is not a direct reflection of the diversity of our students." The display board hosted a variety of portraits and artwork printed from the Dongleshop class. Fly was quick to respond, "It is exactly a direct reflection of the diversity of my students because this was a homework assignment. I did not select these Donglebyte images to express themselves. They did." Another point for Fly as she baffled and stumped Mz. Banshee, leaving her to storm out wailing and shrieking down the hallway, echoing and resonating for only the two to hear.

So after stressing about the mystery meeting all day, Fly kept writing in her notepad everything that Mz. Banshee was saying as she began journal entries once again that September at the onset in case she decided to seek litigation. Coupon Suzy Banshee had no clue what legal lines she was constantly crossing as this was clear retaliation against a person who had filed a federal charge with the EEOC. How could she be so blind? Fly kept writing Mz. Banshee's words verbatim in her lilac legal pad, making no eye contact. She commanded Fly to put the pen down, and Fly locked her eyes on her notepad and firmly replied, "No."

"Put the pen down!"

"No." Fly ignored Mz. Banshee and just kept writing in case she needed to bring these notes to a lawyer unbeknownst to Mz. Banshee. How naïve. Maybe she should have gotten a lawyer right then and there and said boldly that she was going to sue, but she did not. And she refused to use that dumb gender stereotyped pink pen she handed out to everyone in the office singing, "Happy Pink Pen Day!" Fly didn't even think that was a thing, but she may as well hand her a pink power drill, race car, or doll. She was fine with her own gender-neutral colored pen thank you very much.

There was zero percent empathy or leadership on the part of Mz. Banshee, and with several months of abuse and hypocritical behaviors, Fly had enough and was not going to be "sat down and talked to" like that. "Who do you think you are? Running around leaving scars?" played in her head. It was the first time Fly had ever a poor score in instruction, and she was livid. She was an Instructional Specialist with only the highest scores to prove it for her entire career. She had perfect scores by multiple observers throughout her years in this district and all of the other districts she had worked throughout her career. Mz. Banshee gave her a 50 in Instruction. 50! That's out of 100 percent, not even 200 percent! The next day after being intimidated, retaliated against, and reprimanded like a child, Fly mustered up enough strength to only show her newly found resting bitch face who just wanted to smile as did the *Migrant Mother*, but she could not gather up the strength. She had been beaten to death. Fly hated that term, "resting bitch face," but could figure out no other way to get her unamused point across. It was at least better than Mz. Banshee's elitist angry sour puss face. Fly felt like she was in that club against Taffy Sinclair. Worse, at the end of the day, Fly went to get her book bag from the room where Mz. Banshee was having her club meeting. She apologetically walked up to Fly as she was trying to leave and said, "Are we good? I love you." Red light! Fly's eyes widened out from their brokenness but said absolutely nothing back as Mz. Banshee forced a hug on Ms. Fly. Fly stood there stiff and stoic, but so angry no words came out. She bit her tongue. Wondering what the heck that was about and extremely uncomfortable at the unwelcomed advancement, Fly grabbed her bag and stormed out the door. You don't just "hug it out" after months and months of reprimands. Total violation of personal body space, especially with all of the surgeries and scars Fly bared beneath inside her torso, invisible to others.

But Mz. Banshee wanted to see only what she wanted to see and with ratings so low she had never had, Ms. Fly had to write the first of many inspection response letters in case she needed them for court. Fly even thought that Mz. Banshee strategically picked the unannounced inspection, knowing full well that a majority of the children had been receiving their Holy Sacrament of Confirmation, which created an unlevel plane of absenteeism from the get-go. Mz. Banshee also negatively commented that there was an all boys' table even though it had to be clarified that with twenty boys and seven girls in the class, one student whom Mz. Banshee did not even bother to gain knowledge was nonbinary, it would be physically impossible, even alphabetically to not have at least one all boy table. Mrs. Parabola could not believe the written comments as she herself had inspected Ms. Fly's lessons every year so could not understand what was her beef. The report read recommendation after recommendation, "Ms. Fly should do this, Ms. Fly should do that." Mrs. Parabola supported Fly's gut intuition to use her knowledge and expertise to refute everything she stated that was untrue or sought out to be retaliatory. Her annual report was no better when Mz. Banshee pointed angrily three times that the form still said "Supervisor," not "Teacher" and clearly that annoyed her. Maybe go talk to Mr. Super DaNile to iron that out and how did she think Ms. Fly actually felt having to quit her job and live the past ten months unwelcomed? Fly learned why the Dos Brujas kept quiet.

March On

Fly was so shocked at Mz. Banshee's rantings that she met with the second principal of the year, the Now New Principal to discuss the matters as she had already met with her new union navigators many times repeatedly over the previous months about the audacity of Mz. Banshee. They just stated Fly got the worst supervisor in the building, as if she should join the social studies department. They were also very wary of Fly because she was a once administrator so they held their guard up. Mr. Now New Principal had no clue what Fly was trying to say and again in the vicious cycle, as a new nontenured principal he was certainly not going to rock the boat, same as Don and Teddy. So instead, wanting Celeste to have funds to go to college, she researched ways to seek justice and she had heard on the news about Gender Equity Legal Defense Funds that were set aside for sexual harassment in the workplace, and although this was not a case that was sexual in nature, it was certainly continued discrimination and inequity, based on her gender and she was feeling violated so she filled out the intake form anyway to see what opportunities might unfold.

Hello, Fly,

Below is a copy of the questions on our intake form. If you could respond to them, I will input your information on our end. Thank you so much!

1. Name
   a. First Name: Fly
      March 14
      To: Legal Defense for Times Up
      Personal Statement:
      - I am not a rich celebrity, famous actress, or rock star except in the eyes of my daughter and students. I am an artist, mother, and public schoolteacher. I have more than two master's degrees of education, one from X University. It is my hope

that my story, whether through litigation, legislation, Healthy Workplace Bill, Advocacy, or a (work in progress) written Womanifesto Activist Essay (*Would You Rather...Have Your Colon Removed or Be Harassed in the Workplace?*) can "Be the Change I Wish to See in the World" (M. Gandhi). A woman in 20X today in a leadership position for their livelihood and career should not have to endure years of ongoing harassment, quit their job, be demoted, and relocated in order to escape a work environment riddled with hostility, intimidation, and fear, as well as offensive, inappropriate, and unprofessional behaviors embodied by the "It's a Man's World" culture (literal quote from my former female assistant principal). Worse, immediately upon the first legal formal complaint backed by lawyers (July 20X) after years of no less than twenty-five verbal and written complaints to administration and supervisors (20X-X) the barrage of district employer retaliation began. Despite most of my claims and statements being backed by a dozen binders of chronologically documented evidence, the district continues to refuse to incriminate themselves by admitting the harassment was taking place and, in fact, encouraged the behaviors to continue by inaction and even rewarding the teacher, empowering him even more.

- My daughter who has been negatively affected by this experience since she was seven always says, "Everyone is human, but few are humane." Is this the lesson that a now teenage girl is taught by our current society? I believe all humans have the right to work in a safe, professional, and productive environment with dignity, respect, and constructive problem solving. Women should have the right to be a supervisor of male faculty without being subjected to repeated behaviors that are passive-aggressive and appear to reflect the notion, "I'm not going to take orders from a woman" by exhibiting chronic and deliberate insubordination. In fact, the X State's Dignity for All Students Law (DASL, 20X) inspired me to also speak up at the onset of the harassment, taunting, and bullying. I hear all the time from fellow teachers, "Where's the DASL for teachers?" particularly in the current climate of school violence. The children are watching! It is disgraceful that this large school district just outside a metropolitan City does not have a policy whatsoever regarding harassment in the workplace for employees. According to current policy, a teacher would have to have a substance abuse problem to be removed (or have a "smoking gun like run me over in the parking lot") in order for there to be disciplinary actions. Changes need to be implemented and clear policies created statewide, regionally, and locally for reporting and addressing workplace harassment. We do not tolerate this type of behavior for our students, so why is it acceptable for their teachers?

- I have endured a tremendous amount of pain and suffering. This workplace experience has affected me physically (to the point of hospitalization directly correlating with workplace hostility from X to present), emotionally (to the point I had to seek talk therapy to survive the workplace torment), and financially (money spent on legal and documenting fees, time documenting to protect myself, sick days taken to avoid harassment, loss of productivity and wages, etc.) over the course of years. When I had my colon removed in November 20X from autoimmune conditions exacerbated by work-related stress created by this teacher and administrators, and when my union would no longer pay for my legal representation upon potential litigation in April 20X, citing it would cost me more than a teacher can afford or use what little of my daughter's college fund I had, I knew something has got to give. After years of attempts to find other employment and being told I was too far on the teacher scale, in order to begin to overcome this adversity, I had no other choice, but to quit being an administrator in order to take an available demoted position in another building, where retaliatory behavior appears to continue.

(There is a two-page timeline of events written here.)

<u>Summary:</u>

- Unlike many women who have come forward on the red carpet in this current national climate we live in, I have spoken up since the very beginning and documented since the very first time I felt the official H word in April 20X with a specific incident targeted toward myself. According to Lawyer X, I have met all of the criteria for legal action regarding workplace harassment and gender discrimination. I am entitled to have acknowledgment instead of ignoring and complacency, and reimbursement for the pain and suffering I have endured at their hands. There has been no recognition, apology, reprimand, repercussions whatsoever— not even a letter in this man's personnel file. I now have the health, the stamina, the documentation, and the determination to do what is right; I simply do not have tens and tens of thousands of dollars to move forward and make an example of this school district (that apparently has unlimited supply of money in legal insurance) so that it does not continue to happen in the workplace. I have to see this teacher and the entire administration tomorrow at an art gallery reception for students and endure their smug self-satisfied conquering glares and hypocritical beings once again. Where is the humanity? Time's up!

Fly got several phone calls immediately, but there was nothing much that could be done as the regional attorneys who consulted with Fly could only do pro bono cases that were for more minority/poorer women, but she was happy to have her story heard by women fighting for workplace rights and equality. She felt it was in a sexual nature in that they were all men all ganging up on her because she was a woman, and she felt psychologically violated. That Now New Principal got "let go" and she would have to start her story from scratch yet once again. The vicious cycle of nontenured, tenured, retiring administrators who won't do anything to raise red flags was getting very old to say the least. She reflected on finding that *The Against Taffy Sinclair Club* book and forced herself to relive it and read this elementary school grade reader. This school year, was this just a case of who can work to get the bigger boobs first? She would go to her kickboxing bag at her amazing kickboxing gym as "Sweet but Psycho" blasted from the speakers. She sings along, "Yeah, people say, 'Run don't walk away.' 'Cause she's sweet but a psycho. A little bit psycho.' Oh." She let it all out puffing words in a deep cadence, "FU-FU-FU-FU" as she practiced her punches jab-cross-hook-hook, jab-cross-hook-hook, punching the bag in the gut as hard as she could with uppercut-uppercut. She would swing her right leg around in a roundhouse finale and kicked her bag in the big ol' rump.

America the Beautiful—American Mayhem

The Time's Up movement is a nonprofit organization of celebrities that began on January 1, 2018. The main focus is to raise awareness and funds to help support victims of harassment in the workplace and raise awareness about the need for gender equality in the workplace. The Time's Up letter states, "Systematic gender inequality and power imbalance fosters an environment that is ripe for abuse and harassment against women." The Me Too movement began in 2006 and helps identify sex crime allegations and supports victims of sexual violence, harassment, assault, and sexual bullying to share their stories.

Word Wall

"retaliation" verb ri•ta•le•at
    1.   to return like for like, especially to get revenge
    2.   to repay in kind
synonyms: avenge, redress, requite, revenge, venge, castigate, fix, get, penalize, punish, scourge, correct, discipline

FAST FACT

Retaliation and the law: According to the EEOC, "Laws prohibit punishing job applicants or employees for asserting their rights to be free from employment discrimination including harassment. For example, it is unlawful to retaliate against applicants or employees for filing an EEOC charge, complaint, investigation or lawsuit, communicating with a supervisor about discrimination including harassment, answering questions during an investigation, refusing to follow orders that would result in discrimination, resisting sexual advances, requesting accommodation of a disability or religious practice, asking about salary information.

"It could be retaliation if the employer: reprimands, give lower performance evaluations, transfer to less desirable position, engage in verbal or physical abuse, threaten to make reports to authorities, increases scrutiny, spread false rumors, treat family members negatively, make the person's work more difficult."

Notable Quotables

I've learned that people will forget what you said, people will forget what you did, but people will never forget how you made them feel.

—Maya Angelou

Lesson #8

This school year, Fly learned the high cost of simply wanting human rights and a peaceful work environment.

Hate Your Guts

Act Out!

Mama always said there was an awful lot you can tell about a person by their shoes. Where they're going, where they've been. I've worn lots of shoes.

—Forrest Gump

Journal Entry: Think about someone you know and envision you are literally walking in their shoes for an entire day, twenty-four hours. Describe every aspect of the shoes—new or old, color, texture, type, size, and purpose. Where do these shoes take you throughout the day, and what do you experience through the other person's lens? After experiencing a day in their shoes, how could you show more empathy, what would you do to help that person big or small? Where did these shoes come from or go to as they walked "A Day in the Life?" Write about it on the next page and share stories with a friend or family member.

Chapter 9
Mzzz. Falayyya

Can't deal with September Again.

Madeline Albright once said, "There's a special place
in hell for women who don't help other women."

—Madeleine Albright

Goodness
Grace
Decency
Freedom

—Joe Biden on Madeleine Albright

Cue the Music:
"Walking on Broken Glass" by Annie Lenox
"Cry" by Ashnikko featuring Grimes
"Bitch" by Meredith Brooks

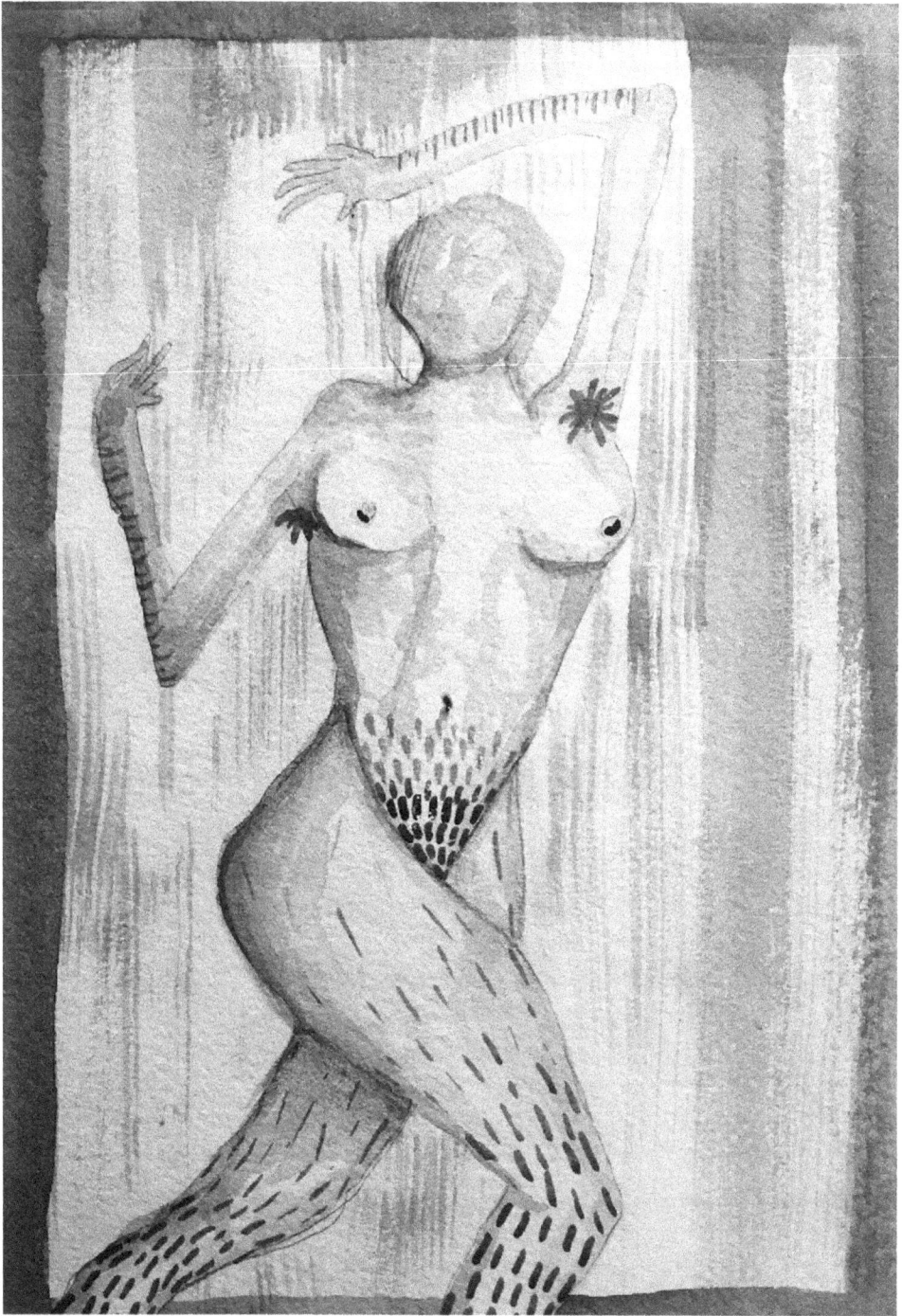

101 Shards of Glass

Round 2: Fly drives slowly going South on the two-lane ocean view road as the waves to her right crash close to the dunes on the side of the road. There is no beach, only a thin barrier between the vast ocean and the path forward. She is on her way back to work for the new school year, and her stomach fills with warmth and quivers of dread as she grips the steering wheel with white-knuckled intentions. There will be no students in session today, only the faculty. She slowly glances to the right at her 2 o'clock and sees a long shadowy figure not too far off shore and, as she squints her eyes to make it out, recognizes it as a large shark swimming out to the vast open waters. As the waves crash on her right, she returns her gaze to the road ahead which is rapidly disappearing into the distance slowly as the horizon becomes engulfed in the same muted overcast gray tone as the sky. The sky and earth become one diffused ripple of movement. The light of the sky reflects on the water which is now coming at her from ahead in a shallow wave of several inches in a glided roll toward her car. She attempts to thwart the oncoming tsunami wave by swerving the car to do a 180-degree complete about-face. As she quickly turns the wheel left to achieve her plan, she is pummeled by a rogue wave at her 9 o'clock, and everything fades to a wall of cold gray water. Instantly drowned, she drifts off to sea in the direction of the shark. Fly wakes up in a pool of sweat and exhaustion with this meeting of certain watery demise and then pushed under by hands, unable to breathe air or swim.

"Okay, class, raise your hand if you like to be bullied?" She looks around, slowly glancing over the people in the room. No one? "Bueller? Bueller? Bueller? Bueller?" And she sighs at the silence. Fly was always drawn to one particular vibrant painting *The Brooding Woman* or *Te Faaturuma* by Paul Gauguin. She felt exactly like the woman sitting in the foreground, and she even had a postcard of it framed on her desk at the previous school so that when she had to think and absorb information or make a decision, she would look at it and feel it would be all right to take her time to contemplate whatever dilemma came her way. Brooding is of "showing deep unhappiness of thought" as to why she is forced to think about things put upon her rather than just exist and be: going to work, doing the work, returning from work. The cycle, pleasurable if allowed. Nursing the feelings in her mind, she just sits there on the floor, bathed in the light of pale orange glow, head resting on her left hand, as it is so intensely heavy with thought she cannot even hold it up anymore. The phrase, "It's not the work, but the people you work with," is becoming highlighted with every passing day. She is trapped in this empty room, as the other figure in the distance is free on the outside perimeter.

Fly sits in an empty room alone brooding, but rather than have the feel of a warm tropical and colorful Tahitian day, she feels as if she were in that black and white photograph *The Migrant Mother* and she sits on the floor which is as cold and hard as a sheet of metal, not warm peach-colored like in the Gauguin painting. And Fly's walls are not cool greens and shades of lavender but walls of two-inch thick glass, and when she thinks and thinks and thinks some more under the pressure, they implode inward onto Fly and millions of shards of glass shoot at her from all directions. She sings "Walking on Broken Glass" in her head, as she relates to the words, but not necessarily the upbeat tune that if you were a child or could not understand the lyrics, you would think it was a happy-go-lucky upbeat song to sway to. She switches songs to "Cry," which Celeste introduced her to one day in the car and Fly said, "You know what, Celeste, that's exactly how I feel at work. I like this song. It speaks to me." They turn up the volume and scream along, "Bitch, are you tryna make me cry? Are you tryna make me lose it? You win some and lose some. This could get gruesome." In her vision, Fly is curled up in fetal position in the middle of the glass room, and the windows again implode on her with more force as the intensity of the music is heightened, and she not only walks on the glass, she rolls in it, then makes a glass snow angel, feeling no pain. A long time ago, Fly had been sliced by a piece of stained glass as she tried to score, then snap the colorful magenta glass into her desired shape to fill whatever puzzle piece of the stained glass window she was making. That stained glass was so sharp she had to rush to the emergency room as the wound was not going to heal anytime soon. Stitches mend and leave scars. Later that week, while working on her stained glass window, her apartment building was on fire. She was in it. No alarms sounded, no warning, just billowing smoke. She was not sure which experience that year was more terrifying, the slice of the glass or being stuck inside with fire. But she chalked it up that at least statistically, she would probably never be in a house fire again, so check that one off the list.

Fly cleans up Celeste's room one day snoopily and stumbles across a diary page:

> Tuesday 3:53 p.m.
> Okay, it's been hectic. I almost got killed a couple of times. I almost fell on a glass table and I almost got crushed by a garage door. I also got my finger crushed by a bouncy ball and cut my eye on a bag. 4:30 p.m. Nail salon!

Seeing Celeste in so much pain from schoolyard bullies at every turn of the hallway brought Fly to tears and was more painful than the issues she had surrounding her J-Pouch, which left her with never-ending bathroom issues and so bland and boring low-residue diet, but it was at least a little better than before. Maybe time will tell. But the pain endured from Fly's new boss became increasingly intolerable and cuts at every angle occurred when she least expected it. She felt like she was cut and burned on fire. How could Mz. Banshee cut someone down so badly after what happened and even she, the recipient of several complaints herself, about Mr. P.A.U.L.? She did everything in her power to continue to keep Fly's sparkle extinguished. It was the first day of school, and the only thing weighing on her mind was, "How can I get out of here?" People will remember how others make them feel. Teachers should be inherently inviting, warm, uplifting, challenging, and inspiring, not the other way around.

101 SHARDS OF GLASS

STICHES	SNARL	NASTY	GLARE
BLOCK	MEAN	DEMEANING	UNFRIEND
UNINVITE	INCONSISTENT	UNWELCOMED	DIVISIVE
INEQUITABLE	SABOTAGE	RESENTFUL	FAKE
FAÇADE	CONQUER	STERN	STONE-FACED
TOTALITARIANISM	SCATHING	UNAMUSED	ABRASIVE
SHAMEFUL	SNEAKY	UNDERMINING	TWISTED
PERSNICKETY	INVADE	UNTRUTHFUL	INSULTING
EAVESDROP	BLOCK	SNOOTY	UNKIND
HYPOCRITICAL	CRUEL	AGENDA	CRUSHED
MANIPULATIVE	INSOLENT	CLAUSTROPHOBIC	DROWNING
AGITATED	PEEVED	BELITTLING	EMPTY
ENRAGED	CRINGE	CONFUSED	UNCLEAR
CORNERED	VICIOUS	ISOLATION	UNFAIR
UNBALANCED	CONSPIRACY	UNIMPRESSIVE	GRUDGE
STANDOFFISH	UNPREDICTABLE	EXTINGUISH	SEETHING
DEMORALIZING	COMMANDING	DEMANDING	IRRATIONAL
DISCRIMINATORY	DISTASTEFUL	ESCALATING	INSISTENT
REVENGE	JEALOUSY	RESTRICTIVE	ENVY
UNWARRANTED	UNREASONABLE	PIGEONHOLED	WRETCHED
PUSHED	DEMOTED	REPRIMANDING	SCREAM
DEMOLISHED	EXHAUSTED	INSIGNIFICANT	FUTILE
DISTORTIONS	UNTRUSTWORTHY	SEEKING	PAIN
IGNORE	TENSION	NOTHINGNESS	INVISIBLE
RETALIATORY			

It was September again and it was off and running! It started with Mz. Banshee insisting "No iPutzes" again be a rule on the Tres Brujas' course syllabi, and Ms. Fly knew better than to combat, just as the Dos Brujas had warned. She gave the wrong date for students to buy their sketchbooks in school so they did not have their money, and she acted nonchalant like she did not care to the detriment of the student's best interests. Fly was weary; it was an intentional maneuver. Mz. Banshee was turning out to be a "Do as I say not as I do" type of beast. She was 200 percent correct all the time, and Fly was 200 percent incorrect all the time, and it was becoming pretty apparent and aggravating.

She had to get out of there as it was apparent nothing was going to change. The Brujas fearfully stated that it was just easier to go along with commands than deal with the repercussions of saying something. Fly found this to be true that Mz. Banshee was very confrontational and very difficult to speak with. She could see why the others remained silent, but Fly was determined to do the right thing as there was the signed agreement that she should be in a "peaceful working environment." Fly was determined to make some changes; maybe they could add a form in the contract that would intervene with issues such as this. If there were procedures in place, Fly would not be in this predicament or the last.

Mz. Banshee tried everything in her power to make Ms. Fly's work world difficult. Not only did she have yet another new course she had not taught before, she was put in all of the art rooms again ensuring she had as little permanent space to be as possible. Fly didn't mind getting her exercise in during the school day, but it was clearly inequitable as all of the other teachers had a home base classroom with less courses to teach than she did. She became "deskless." And there was a third principal this year, but this turned out to be Good News. Assistant Principal Ave from the previous school who knew all about the issues with Mr. P.A.U.L. finally got promoted and was transferred to this building, even though the year before, she was beat out by a random man. Another cover-up from the district. Fly met casually with new Principal Ave to congratulate her. Fly brought a house-warming gift as a token of appreciation. Although Fly made it clear to Ave that it was not going so well at this new school and that she did not know why she was being treated the way that she was, they also talked about how she wanted to decorate her new principal's office.

The new Principal Ave texted Fly, asking if she could have some of her Dongleshop students artwork for her new bare wall as she was trying to decorate her new and well deserved space and always admired Fly's students' artwork. She had finally made it to the top from teacher to supervisor to AP, now Principal in charge of an entire building. Having had a long history, Fly happily obliged at the request and was excited to help. A few weeks later, Mz. Banshee was in a meeting near the new Principal's office when she saw Ms. Fly's display of artwork and went ballistic, and unbeknownst to Fly, it was going to be the end all of her life at this new school, her ultimate demise. Shrieking echoed up and down the hallways. Fly and the new Principal Ave could not figure out why she would display such hatred toward a beautiful display of artwork created by teenagers. The pattern brewed that Mz. Banshee would begrudge any student achievement Ms. Fly presented.

The Fly Story

Fly became Fly in the '90s as a nickname she acquired from one of her husband's friends because he thought she was so fly like the Fly Girls such as J-Lo who made it to success on *In Living Color* and Fly looked like she was a character right out of *The Matrix*. To be fly is to be cool, good, and fun, and Fly strived to maintain those qualities, but instead felt like the kind of fly no one likes: a fly eating rotting trash, buzzing around smelly garbage, and people constantly shooing her away, trying to smack her down. She cannot find the light to escape the space and remained trapped in the dark.

Fly was teaching a lesson one day and a yellow jacket entered the classroom. At first, Ms. Fly does not notice, but the kids do. As she teaches and is mid-sentence, students begin to move oddly in their seats, maneuvering around the classroom and some unexpectedly get out of their seats dodging and bobbing their heads as Muhammad Ali would do in the boxing ring. More get up and they are gliding and moving in opposing directions. Little peeps and soft screams arise from the audience and suddenly with Ms. Fly's performance being interrupted asks what was happening. The students proclaimed, "A bee!" Kids start standing on chairs and ducking under desks as they are being attacked by this little yellow jacket buzzing in and out around their bodies. In a split second, Ms. Fly runs to the light switches, turns them off, speed-walks to the other side of the room, opens up one window, and the bee swiftly escapes exiting out the window. The students stood there amazed and cheered, "Huzzah!" There was applause and relief, and the lesson resumed as if nothing ever happened. The students loved that trick and were happily amused she knew how to free a bug.

Principal Ave must have known she was walking into a building with poor morale, so tried from day one to create some incentives to raise school spirit. She gave out sparkly jewels to each teacher. Fly put hers in her ID holder to feel a glimpse that she was getting a little of her sparkle back. There were a variety of activities and committees to make sure everyone was treated like a jewel and seen as individuals, but together, they can create a treasure chest that was bountiful and plenty. She gave an article for faculty to read, and all Ms. Fly heard in cafeteria duty by a coworker surrounded by all of those buzzing disgusting flies was "We have all this work to do, and now we have to read an article too? Geez!" The article was called "The Fly Story," and they were not quite sure why they were assigned to read it. Fly's friend, Mrs. Parabola, knew this teacher. Another one who does the bare minimum like the required "fifteen pieces of flair" as in *Office Space*, yet still gets tenured and a job for life. He just teaches the five classes and leaves at the bell. Fly really wanted to show her thirty-seven pieces flair, and express herself by flipping off her bad boss if only in her mind.

"The Fly Story" by Price Pritchett goes like this:

> There's a small fly burning out the last of its short life's energies in a futile attempt to fly through the glass of a windowpane. The whining wings tell the poignant story of the fly's strategy—try harder. But it's not working. The frenzied effort offers no hope for survival. Ironically, the struggle is part of the trap. It is impossible for the fly to try hard enough to succeed at breaking through the glass. Nevertheless, this little insect

has staked its life on reaching its goal—through raw effort and determination.

Across the room, ten steps away, the door is open.

Ten seconds of flying time and this small creature could reach the outside world it seeks. With only a fraction of the effort now being wasted, it could be free of this self-imposed trap. The breakthrough possibility is there. It would be so easy.

She just needed to have just one person open the glass window for her so she could escape. But instead, Mz. Banshee ran into her classroom one day and projected her voice at her that Ms. Fly had let two students push the art cart to the next location, not one as told to do so. She seethed with her cringy face, "I thought we were clear!" and rapidly did an about-face, 180-degree spin, turned off the room lights, walked out, and slammed the door behind her. She actually turned the lights off with Fly in the room and slammed the door shut on her. She had never experienced blatant rage like this in the workplace in her entire life. Fly was mortified, but at the same time, secretly thinking, *Don't let the door hit you in your big ol' rump on the way out.* What kind of leader uses this demeaning tone with the people they supervise? Like the stacked chairs, one would have thought a student chopped off their finger in the paper cutter because they were horsing around because of bad classroom discipline and using something they were not taught properly, respectfully, and safely how to use. It was very unprofessional, yet there were no witnesses. Perplexed again by this seemingly trivial item, Fly now knew for sure that they had very opposite philosophies on everything art education and related to teaching teenagers. Fly truly believed her philosophy was better for adolescents and progressive as she was lucky to have attended a top notch teacher school in America. Fly believed the buddy system was a better choice and a chance for students to socialize with a special task, but Mz. Banshee only saw it as a negative thing and sought to isolate people and seek ultimate power and control.

One day, Ms. Fly left her in-school suspension duty a minute early to go socialize with the wheelchair-bound student before class in the hallway as he had a five-minute pass and was always just waiting there with the aide. This student reminded her of Fly's older brother because they both loved Led Zeppelin so much. He also had cerebral palsy and thought she would say a quick hello to the student before class; he would like to talk about "Stairway to Heaven" and was amazed that Fly's brother had over fifty Led Zeppelin t-shirts, and it brought a smile to his face even if for a moment. So Ms. Fly stood there waiting for the bell to ring chit-chatting to the student who was happy to see her, and then out of nowhere, Mz. Banshee stormed her way down the long hallway toward Ms. Fly. Fly could see her yards away coming at her in the periphery out of the corner of her eye, and she tried to stay fixated on the student in hopes of Banshee avoidance. But she slowed down, slowly slurring her chosen words creating anticipation of impending doom for Fly. Firmly and ominously stated with her slippery tongue in front of him and his personal aide, "Mzzz. Falayyya...you are not to leave your duty...you are to provide hallway supervision," and just kept walking as she buzzed on by. She was saying her name in a disgustingly demeaning manner. Fly was beginning to see her requests as absurd and attacking. First, there were no students in ISS that day; second, she demanded Brujas in between bells to get to the next classroom location, set up the computer and screen, watch the student behavior inside the classroom, stand outside the classroom to not only supervise the hallways, but also to greet every student as they entered. Physically impossible to meet her demands. And Fly did not even have time to go to the bathroom for that matter! Fly knew this statement was absurd so emailed to clarify with administration about the duty in which Mz. Banshee had no authoritaih! over. It was just another attack and grasp at self-empowerment.

She had totalitarian control over everything. Autonomy eradication. Maybe she was watching too much of the highly contagious fake news to lead her to this negative cult-like leadership attitude. She booked field trips for everyone and gave nobody any individuality to create their own experiences for their classes. She even booked Mzzz. Fly's field trip during the week she was supposed to be giving mid-year final exams. Fly thought she overheard something on the phone that Mr. P.A.U.L.'s class viewed inappropriate art and there was a complaint, but she would not be surprised about that. Mz. Banshee would lock up supplies Mzzz. Fly would need for her students to mat, frame, and exhibit their artwork and would day after day conveniently forget to give the materials for her to do her job to the point that Fly's husband took the supplies from his school and gave it to her so she could prepare the artwork by the deadlines. Fly even told Una Bruja point blank, "She will not give me the matting tools I have been asking her for two weeks and the show is tomorrow!" They looked at her in disbelief, but this is exactly how bullies get away with murder. "Why won't she give them to you?" she asked. And they could find no explanation. This is where Mzzz. Fly began to feel even more targeted than the other Brujas. Similar to Mr. P.A.U.L. in the past, Mz. Banshee would withhold important information pertaining to Mzzz. Fly being able to fulfill her work duties and obligations. This was not her first rodeo. Fly asked a second time, a second year in a row for display boards, and excuses after excuses were rendered as to why she was not fulfilling her sincere requests, so students can display their artwork on an otherwise cold cement cinder block walls.

The Brujas did not have any fellow woman's back despite the fact that years prior, Suzy flaunted that "Working women need to look out for one another, unlike those stay-at-home moms." This was another 180-degree turnaround, so left Fly stumped. She looked at her school ID photo that was taken in September the year before. Her husband stated, "Wow. You look great in this photo! When was this taken?" Smooth, tan skin from the long relaxing summer and a smile as if excited for back to school in a new place with a fresh start. It was taken the week before moving to the new school, and Fly was just happy to be alive and away from all those heinous men. What happened? She felt naïve and looked at this photo resting with the magenta jewel upon it and that back to school smile that had become broken once again.

Mzzz. Fly tried to rub her jewel to get it to shine, but it still was dull by the daily darkness that surrounded her, she stood there like a sculpture being slowly chipped away becoming a hollow shell, then being diminished to a pile of rubble, arms torn off, and nakedly sheathed like the Venus de Milo. Such the ever-increasing hypocrite, for Teen Art Appreciation Month, Mz. Banshee distributed coloring sheets to the whole school! The worst was when Fly asked Mz. Banshee if she could leave school five whole minutes early so that she could beat the busses so that she can get to her out-of-state weekend trip and she was replied with, "Well, no, not really...there are cameras everywhere so no." Some teachers sneak out on the daily early. Fly was asking for one time to get on the road. In her twenty-something years of teaching, Fly never heard anyone say no to a five-minute early leave request when she was not even teaching the last period. Teachers sometimes have to leave a few minutes early for doctor appointments, pick up their kids, etc., and it is usually all right if you gave your supervisor a heads-up. Fly felt so degraded and disgusted at the continued negatory response, she ignored her and did it anyway. She felt like the criminal climbing through the ceiling in *The Breakfast Club* in order to escape being caught. She grabbed her bags, walked up to the second floor, speed-walked to the other side of the school, walked back down to the first floor via the hidden staircase, and left out the back door undetected and hopped into her husband's car, hoping not to be seen. "Go, go, go!" she quietly commanded as if she robbed a bank in an organized heist. Fly would have let any teacher leave early, even Mr. P.A.U.L. Disgusting!

She got a flyer in the mail that her local senator was holding another one-on-one meeting session at her local library and jumped on the opportunity to express her concerns in more depth. She composed yet another plea about her story and presented it, hoping that maybe there are policies that can create change if school personnel are not going to make a difference.

April 11

Re: Legislation for Peaceful Workplaces/Anti-Bullying for All Employees: Proposal of Fly's Law

Dear Senator,

I am writing to you to express my concerns about the issue of hostile workplaces and environments that I have personally experienced. Bullying in the workplace is not illegal and proving harassment and/or gender discrimination is nearly impossible and disadvantageous with regard to time consumption, legal time restraints, finances, and other legal hardships. I am proposing that there be state legislation to address and protect all employees from instances such as but not limited to: bullying, hostility, intimidation, passive-aggression, violent acts, retaliation, adverse actions, threats, and hypocritical, deviant, or manipulative behavior that are chronic enough to cause disruption of one's ability to complete their job requirements in a humane and peaceful manner.

Let's take a look at "petty slights," a term used by the EEOC to describe unwanted actions that are not illegal. How many petty slights officially constitutes harassment according to the EEOC? What types of petty slights does one need to endure in the workplace in order for it to become illegal? I have a list of hundreds of examples I have personally experienced and heard about in a variety of workplaces and they can be mentally and physically damaging over time.

Employees should be able to go to their place of work without fear and anxiety that something will happen due to the negative action or unpredictable behavior by another employee or person in their environment. Negative and subversive behaviors undermines one's human spirit, work ethic, livelihood, and potential. While my firsthand experience is in the public school system, I have witnessed this at the Sack of Donuts Shop, the Dollar Hollar, and other establishments. Unacceptable negative behaviors can occur between any staff in any rank including secretaries, custodians, teachers, administrators, managers, security guards, etc., regardless of being designated to a "protected class" based on race, age, gender, sexual orientation, disabilities, religion, etc. All employees regardless of their human makeup should have the right to work in a safe, humane, peaceful, positive, equitable, and of course, professional work environment free from hostility and retaliation. Often times, the "schoolyard bully" is not picking on someone of a different human trait, but because they feel, they have to have power and control over a particular person for a particular reason.

The state recently passed DASL for students; Dignity for All Students Law in which public schools are responsible for creating a "safe and supportive environment free from discrimination, intimidation, taunting, harassment, and bullying on school property." There are systems in place for reporting such instances to trained faculty in each building. How then can school districts be so hypocritical in that this very behavior that we would not tolerate for our students can occur among any staff member in the building? DASL requires schools to support "civility, citizenship, and character" which expands on the original aspects of "tolerance, respect, and dignity." Frequently, fellow educators agree with the concept of "DASL for Teachers." Why cannot there be a Dignity for All Employees Law (DAEL) or I would like to call Fly's Law that parallels the DASL for students act? Employers need to be accountable for their employees and be able to address the situation in a concise and systematic manner without further humiliation, fear, or retaliation for the individual filing the complaint.

Walking through the grocery aisle last week, I overheard a woman talking to another that she "had to leave her job because her boss was too difficult." At another workplace at a local college, it is not uncommon to witness ill behaviors that lead to toxic environments to the point that professors have to alter schedules in order to avoid confrontation. Another made a verbal threat to a committee member to sign their promotion packet in order to intimidate and belittle for self-serving purposes. That committee member quit, and there are no regulations to report such inappropriate instances. I am not sure if there is one person I know that has not had an issue of being a target of someone's negative behaviors once in a while; my one brother at Small Mart, my other brother working at the Train Terminal, but chronic unnecessary negative and unsubstantiated, relentless, or targeted abuse should not be tolerated and there should be a system in place such as the one for DASL situations and incidents available for all employees.

I live in this county and have worked in this and currently that county. I have driven to the state capital with all of my documentation of harassment and discrimination and will go there again to help make a change in our current state of workplace conditions. Because litigation was unobtainable for several reasons and filing a complaint with both the EEOC and Times Up with no results, my toxic workplace led to severe health issues and hospitalizations, affected my daughter (mostly due to ongoing gender bias) and family, I had to legally request to transfer myself to a different building away from the person targeting me, in which lead to a gag order, loss of my position in educational leadership, no longer use of my second graduate degree or certifications, was demoted overall as indicated in this passage written by my legal representation, and continue to experience retaliatory behavior on occasion in the new building.

"Damages sustained by Ms. Fly as a result of the respondents' continued and unrelenting harassment, discrimination, retaliation, and adverse action toward Ms. Fly, including, but not limited to ignoring years of complaints of harassment and physical threats and intimidation by Mr. Paul against Ms. Fly, the failure to provide a safe work environment free from threats and intimidation, failure, and refusal to support Ms. Fly as supervisor against the actions by Mr. Paul against her, treating Ms. Fly in a disparate and discriminatory manner from her fellow employees and coworkers based on her age and gender and in creating a hostile work environment for Ms. Fly. These actions all stem from Mr. Paul and potentially others, seeking to force Ms. Fly to leave the district. The respondent's inaction has resulted in an unrelenting terror campaign against Ms. Fly based on her age and gender and in retaliation for her complaining that discriminatory and harassing actions are being taken against her.

After Ms. Fly brought Mr. Paul and others' improper, harassing, and discriminatory actions and treatment to the superintendent's attention, the campaign of terror has continued unabated and no assistance has been given by the Administration to stop these improper, harassing and discriminatory actions. These actions have been taken against Ms. Fly in retaliation for her complaints of gender and age harassment, discrimination and retaliation and for pain and suffering endured as a result of the aforementioned actions. The respondents and all other persons involved in the actions against Ms. Fly violated federal and state laws including, but not limited to State Human Rights Law, Title VIII, the ADEAS and 43 U.S.C. B.§§ 1983, 1985, 1986."

I hope to be able to help in some way to make changes in this State regarding legislation that addresses all forms and aspects of bullying and hostility in the workplace and to ensure all persons are able to complete their job requirements in a humane and peaceful manner. Thank you for your attention to this important matter. It is unfortunately a reflection of our current culture and society, but that does not make it acceptable or appropriate.

Thank you for your time.

Sincerely,

Ms. Fly

Help Wanted

It was apparent Mz. Banshee loathed the teaching style of Mzzz. Fly. The university she attended focused on progressive philosophies and approaches to educating art to children in schools K-12, not cookie cutter art whatsoever. It was like Mzzz. Fly's students were having too much fun learning deep aesthetic and artistic concepts. Close reading of artworks unlike Mr. P.A.U.L.'s "closed reading." She infused a combination of art concepts and techniques, various media, interesting artists, highlights from art history, discussing and reacting to art, the required vocabulary, as well as assessments large and small to name a few. Most important to Fly, art education allows students of any age to explore ideas, concepts, and experiences and to use materials to create visual and personal expressions. Sometimes, they are their hopes and dreams, their fears and interests, ideas, and innovations. Sometimes, a student would be sitting there seemingly "staring off into space." Fly always knew they needed time to think of possible ideas for whatever visual design challenge they were given. Mz. Banshee would probably have written it up as students not being on task. Artists need to think, look, analyze, absorb, reflect. It takes time to conceptualize ideas into visual building blocks of line, shape, color, and textures. It takes time and deep thought to use creativity to create original works in context of a given day and age. Art is indeed a reflection of civilization.

Similar to never learning about emergency prolapsed cords in prenatal books, Fly wondered why her higher education never once even an iota mentioned schoolyard bullying, school violence, guns in schools, mass shootings, and warning signs. Surely, it is a part of school life, and for certain, they should have learned about it even if as a cautionary tale. She never thought people in schools could be so brutal and that her career and passion could ever become so tainted and spoiled.

Teacher inspections became more of an under the microscope scrutinizing subjective surveillance. Fly just wanted to bust through the glass even though she knew it would mean her demise. Why would Mz. Banshee purposefully exhibit internalized oppression toward her once colleague and display such biases against working woman moms she once supported? Was she exhibiting self-hatred and siding with the Boy's Club? Was this second generation discrimination and bias against her own? Why did Mz. Banshee focus on dead white male artists, but insisting she was a teacher of cultural diversity? Was she blind? She would insist that Fly could not teach tidbits about certain artists because she taught those in her classes. This philosophy made no sense and one can learn about many artists and sometimes repeat artist for a variety of classes. Needing to know what was going on, Fly began researching a little and found out that one can be biased against their very own group and that was what was happening here. Status-blind it was called. Even Mrs. Parabola stated, "What is she one of the boys?"

Never had she ever had such critical analysis of her lessons than by Mz. Banshee, but just as under the magnifying lens in the classroom, she was shunned and blatantly ignored in the office right in front of the other Brujas which was not the first shunning Fly ever had. She would have conversations directed solely at Dos Brujas in Mzzz. Fly's presence and never give an inch to invite Fly into the conversation even if they were just talking about house plants. It was increasingly uncomfortable. Fly decided she would go sit in the library on her free period where at least the librarians liked her company and art displays.

Mzzz. Fly received an Official Certificate of Achievement for being a School Jewel. She created a huge artwork display in the school library commemorating students who had tragically perished in an accidental car collision. One could almost not hold the tears in about the tragic event, yet Mzzz. Fly's students were strong and were proud to create works of art in their memory. Mz. Banshee just snarled, and one could see she may be trying to brew up something in a bitter jealous revenge. Another time, Principal Ave asked Mzzz. Fly and another teacher to present a professional development workshop on a new technology application as she had seen her use it in the classroom and thought it was terrific. This was just another accomplishment that Mz. Banshee seethed at.

Fly had taken Celeste to a Woman's March and tens of thousands of people showed up. Celeste was ever so increasingly aware of the inequality of women and became increasingly the same disgusted. Women around the entire world were rebelling against the discriminatory POTUS in power. All of these tens of thousands of marchers fighting for basic human rights. Just look at who was in charge of the nation, so why couldn't this happen in a measly small school district? It was happening right out there for everyone to see and no one could do anything about it. One thing is for sure the hatred brewing pushed a divide in the country and people needed and excuse to pour even more hatred out toward others and had the American "right" and liberty to intimidate and humiliate. The so-called leader of the nation was the ultimate bully and it became an acceptable norm of America. So Celeste marched screaming and shouting, holding her hand-crafted poster, "She Inhales Dirt and Exhales Flowers" all the while waving a tampon high in the air expressing her profound nature of what can only be experienced as a woman. Tampons.

Fly did meet with Principal Ave and firmly stated that she needed to get out of that school before she lost another body part. Fly still had all of the issues that come with a J-Pouch bionic body part, but her work life was so stressful, she barely had time to take care of herself and Celeste. One day, Fly had to drive herself to the emergency room. She had gone to the walk in clinic with a sharp pain in her right side just under her rib cage. Since it was close to where Allen and Coletta used to live, she took it seriously and the doctor thought it could be her gallbladder. Do you need that body part? What is it? The young man took Fly in the wheelchair zipping past the hard core back door part of the ER, the part where the car accident and gunshot victims go. There was screaming and blood everywhere. Could he not have brought her another way to get to the sonogram room? The doctor looked and he looked as he scanned her wretched torso, but he was perplexed. "Well, it's not your gallbladder," he explained. "Your gallbladder is not where it should be. It's way down here." After Fly explained she had her colon removed, it was good to know her body parts were not where they were supposed to be for future reference.

Then, her car blew up and died. Fly was so stressed out and disgusted by this new school that she bought herself a magenta sports car. She would rev it up, put the top down as she pulled out of the parking lot, and speed home to get to the safety of her family singing "Fast Car" by Tracy Chapman: "Any place is better...Is it fast enough so we can fly away?...Leave tonight or live and die this way." Mz. Banshee inspected Mzzz. Fly's class on the very last period of the very last day supervisors were permitted to inspect teachers which was quite obvious to Fly and an ultimate blow. This was the third time her teacher inspection ratings were not in alignment with the twenty-something years of prior teacher inspections she had along her educational career all over the country.

Mz. Banshee's comments and opinions were at times absurd and nitpicky. She obsessed that Fly used the color term "magenta" rather than use the correct vocabulary word "red-violet" and insisted that Mzzz. Fly use the term "red-violet," even though it appeared that Mz. Banshee missed the point that the motivation question of the inspected lesson was:

"What is your favorite color and why? How does your favorite color make you feel?" *Mzzz.* Fly's favorite color was not fuchsia, pomegranate, wine, mulberry, and certainly not "red-violet." Fly's favorite color is magenta and sorry that was not on the terminology list for middle school art curriculum. So Fly had no choice to write once again an inspection response letter in rebuttal. Inspection after inspection, Mz. Banshee would find things to write about even if they had nothing to do with the inspected lesson. Fly bet if Mr. P.A.U.L had heard this was going on, he would writhe in evil pleasure. Once, she even mentioned that *Mzzz.* Fly brought in cupcakes which, according to Mz. Banshee's personal "rules" was not allowed and Fly was like, "Huh?" Mz. Banshee had herself brought in cookies from the art show for her very own students and even offered them to *Mzzz.* Fly's students the previous week. More egregious was that the observed lesson was not even for that class nor in that room, so what the hell was she talking about? All of the other Brujas fed snacks to their classes or clubs that very same month, so why the targeting? She changed her rationale for "no snacks" over and over, as if maybe she herself were afraid of the calories and sugar and sweetness and goodness. Fly just wanted to pull out of the closet that sparkly birthday cupcake shirt from her fortieth birthday and wear it one day and see if that was also objectionable. And Fly brought cupcakes to her advanced students because it was her birthday if she really wanted to know. Fly consulted Principal Ave who indicated Mz. Banshee was incorrect, and in the response letter, *Mzzz.* Fly stated she would be obtaining the Board of Education Policy on food in the classroom for clarification even though this had nothing to do with the lesson. Worse, Mz. Banshee, after displaying such disgust over cupcakes, had her very own art students do paintings of guess what? Cupcakes!

These response letters must have just made Mz. Banshee scream even louder as one could hear the echoes and feel the vibrations from the pitch and length crescendo up and down the hallways like in the painting *The Scream* by Edvard Munch. Fly knew she had to stand up to this behavior, as she was confident in her educational experience and lessons and what the actual "rules" were not these ridiculous made-up ones. She was not about to be judged and defined on one minute of kids stacking chairs early because one student with disabilities stacked his early.

Emails are turning out to be terrible communication tools or maybe it should be stated, "User beware! Your messages may be mistaken easily." And never "Reply all!" There was no mistake with the email that Mz. Coupon Suzy Banshee sent the last week of the school year.

> Sat. 6:37 a.m. June 21
> To: Ms. Fly, Mr. Chai, Mrs. Latte, Mr. Brew, Ms. Frappuccino, Mr. Mocha, Ms. Acai
> Re: Please forward to teachers with Administration Credentials
> With so many of our department now achieving Certification, I would be proud to write a recommendation letter.
> Job Title: Director of Fine Arts and Multi-Media
> Moonbucks District
> Start Date: July 1
> Application Deadline: June 23
> Thank you,
> Mrs. Coupon Suzy Banshee
> Director of Fine and Visual Arts
> Supervisor of Fine and Visual Arts

She actually sent an advertisement to Mzzz. Fly for a job in another district! So unprofessional. "Professionalism is knowing how to do it, when to do it and doing it." Okay, that saying is not from educational leadership book, but from the contents of a fortune cookie Fly got that summer at the Chinese takeout. She placed that fortune next to the half-heart necklace and "inspire" rock in her inspiration jar.

Then finally, it was the end of school and there was the annual report meeting planned, and once again, strategically scheduled on the very last day of school in the sweltering heat blatantly implied, "You're not important, but I have to do this, so it will be last minute as if an afterthought like your inspections." Inopportune timing. Fly had presented Mz. Banshee with a page of at least two dozen extracurricular events that she had her students participate in that year. She was berated. Rather than praise that Mzzz. Fly's students had great achievements, in the meeting, Fly was caught off guard once again when she provided several ridiculous and false, nay fraudulent, accusations of things Mzzz. Fly did or did not do. But Fly, trying to maintain her flyness, held her head high and came back by questioning Mz. Banshee to explain the exact circumstances of each and every one of the accusations. Who, what, where, when, and why? Which student are you referring to? Which guidance counselor pertaining to what issue can you explain? But when confronted, Mz. Banshee never replied with any answers to clarify her accusations and just moved on to the next bulleted item. She could not mention any specific details. Just tell her what student and what issue? Then, she insisted that Mzzz. Fly did not inform her about one art event that took place way back in November stating, "You did not tell me you did that art show at the bookstore." Fly thought for a split second that could be the case, but Fly was very thorough and knew Mz. Banshee was full of it, so she went back to her emails with only an hour left in the school year and found the one where she had indeed informed her about this extracurricular event that she volunteered to do on her own time on a busy holiday week evening. Fly forwarded it to Mz. Banshee when she got home because her accusation was in the documented meeting that goes into her personnel file. Fly stated, "I just wanted to make you aware that because it was stated in my annual report meeting to the contrary, that I had indeed informed you of the art exhibition in November. See the attached email for reference. Have a nice summer."

Fly immediately called the original Labor Lawyer Luke and paid the $500 cash to meet for one hour. She wanted to make sure she was not crazy and that she wanted a professional opinion on what she was facing once again. He surmised all of these behaviors and actions to be incriminating and retaliatory. He stated that the emailed advertisement for a job in another district was "very telling and obvious" for Fly to go away. Shoo and leave out the open window. He ended the conversation with the question, "So what do we do about bullies?" And they discussed that it is not against the law. The previous lawyer stated that it would be easier to sue a district if you could prove "retaliation" rather than "harassment" and circled right back around to the "smoking gun" of being run over in the school parking lot by the bully. No, P.A.U.L. and Suzy must have been in cahoots this entire time with his name first on the district email list for all to see. She was in a whirlpool spinning round and round, not a path moving forward.

With this information, she immediately went into school over the summer to plea with Principal Ave begging to be trans-ferred, and as she actually saw the parts that make the whole, agreed to see how things went in the fall and then take action by the holiday break. She carefully listened. All Fly wanted was a little empathy. An apology, accountability, amending the law and policies so that this could not happen to anyone else in the workplace would be nice, but she felt may never hap-pen. The continuous vicious cycle of falling through the cracks with endless tenures and retirements was a well stirred-up turn-over soup. Maybe even some acknowledgment that Fly had been through so many surgeries and pain and survived. She would go to the gynecologist's office, and for the second year now, they ask the routine questions, "Last colonoscopy?" Fly's response would stop the nurses in their tracks, "No. I don't have a colon." Stumped, they would discuss and laugh it off. Fly's mom who would complain of her chronic foot pain would say, "Oh, my feet hurt." And Fly would simply reply, "I don't have a colon." Good point. And she meant it. On top of all of that, she was sick and tired of not only herself but people she loved get-ting bullied and pushed around by other people for whatever reason they had. If the bully gets ISS, so too should faculty.

Fly decided to have some fun and applied for a side hustle which proved to be amazing! She worked just a few days a week over the summer at a wine and paint night. What could be more fun than working with artsy people in their twenties and teaching tipsy adults how to paint while pretending to be a Britney Spears style entertainer/art instructor on stage with a microphone head-piece and sparkly hat. She was happy at work for once in a long time, and this side hustle proved that work can indeed be fun and productive and caring. As she wrapped up one warm summer evening class teaching a large group of adults a sunset dream life painting, a man and his partner pulled Fly aside and stated with a huge sincere smile, "Oh, Fly, you are changing the world one painting at a time! Thank you!"

America the Beautiful—American Mayhem

Hey, everybody. Did you hear the fake news? Women are angry and marching in the streets all over America and the world! People with souls and seeking human rights marched in several Annual Women's Marches in protest of the then president's administration. It inspired women to vote and run for political office, and their agenda prepared to "combat violence against women, reproductive rights, and racial and economic fairness." Resist! There is much legislation to be approved in order to protect women's rights, not take them away.

Word Wall

"oppression" noun o•pre•shen
1. unjust or cruel exercise of authority or power
2. a sense of being weighed down in body or mind
synonyms: dejection, depression, desolation, despondence, forlornness, gloom, heartsick, melancholy, unhappiness

FAST FACT

What is internalized oppression? In social justice, internalized oppression is a concept in which a member or group of an oppressed or perceived inferior group comes to live the stereo-types put on by the perceived superior group. They often use the methods of the superior group against their own kind. The self-hatred of an individual in a marginalized group can lead that person to use tactics against their own gender, race, sexual orientation, and religion.

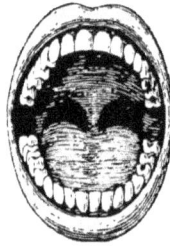

Notable Quotables

There is nothing worse than a sharp image of a fuzzy concept.
—Ansel Adams

We need a little dark in order to show light.
—Bob Ross

Fairy Godboss: A woman with a voice is
by definition a strong woman.
—Melinda Gates's Button from Women's March

Lesson #9

This school year, Fly learned the true meaning of "there is a special place in hell for women who don't help other women."

More Cruel Haikus

I know what you did
Kindness will conquer hatred
In the Air Tonight

"Do as I say to
Not as I do," Cut-Throat Bitch
You're not welcome here

Rules I make for you
Does not apply to others
I'm holding a grudge

Bombard then ignore
A pattern I've seen before
Kick me when I'm down

Criticize to death
You are no good in my eyes
I'll tell you who's Boss

Nothing is perfect
In your eyes workplace failure
Looks and words that burn

Hot bitter revenge
What I say is the end all
Futile God complex

Try to hunt me down
Linger and touch unwanted
Unclear behavior

Abuse out of sight
Behind the dark closed curtains
You think no one knows

316

Trauma all over
Reprimand, then Hug It Out
Inappropriate!

Workplace violence
Rampant in society
Why is this legal?

You don't know the pain
Bullying cuts deep inside
Internal torture

Working Moms hold strong
The great challenges we face
Equality now

To sue or not to
That is the question for peace
Justice will be served

"Cut-Throat Colleagues I"
Bullies as leaders
Perpetuates the strong hate
That divides us all

"Cut-Throat Colleagues II"
Bullies as leaders
A dark workplace created
I will delete you

Trust Your Guts

Act Out!

Journal Entry: What does it mean to be a woman in American society yesterday, today, and tomorrow? Have you ever participated in an organized march? If so, where, why and how? What was the American atrocity you were fighting for? Who supported your efforts and marched with you? Did the march have any effect or outcomes that were different than in the past? What are some other ways you can try to make changes through legislation and policy? Write your ideas on the next page and share your story with friends, family, or a political leader.

Chapter 10
Blind Spots

It's a cruel September again.

Good Thoughts.
Good Words.
Good Deeds.

—Freddy Mercury

Cue the Music:
"Fighter" by Christina Aguilera
"The Way" by Fastball
"Never Going Back Again" by Fleetwood Mac

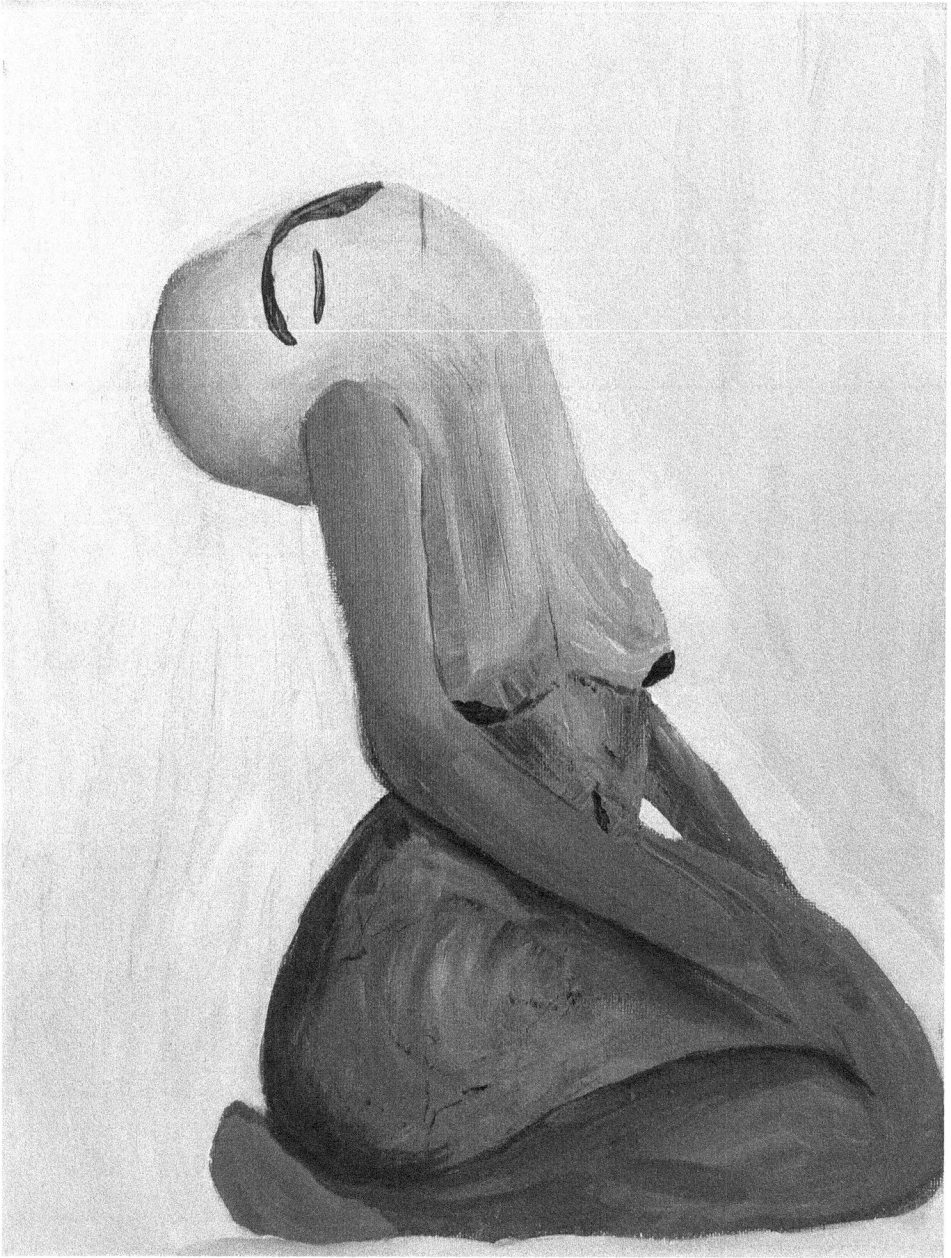

The Red Truck Story

She wakes up facing a beige wall with diffused lighting. Head tilted with her left cheek on a paper pillow, as her eyes slowly open from a deep sleep. A cold metal railing like a baby's crib keeps her from falling to the cold floor. She has to think and remember where she is. Was she rising from a drunken Friday night? Did she pass out from anemia or blood loss? A strange plaid-patterned curtain. Was it the '70s? As she becomes more alert, she realized she was hooked up to an IV, had air in her nostrils, a heart monitor and blood pressure tightly wrapped around her arm. The recovery room. Like an escape room she cannot move. Frozen from weaning anesthesia. She had become a human pin cushion and didn't even flinch at sharp objects anymore. It was her annual summer J-Pouch check and all was well.

Round 3: The top of her fiery hair and eyes peek out from the top of the computer's edge, she lingers with her gaze, and Fly can see it in the reflection of her computer screen as she viewed the online professional development video slide show. Fly cringed and grasped the edge of her desk as Mz. Banshee slowly walked around her desk in an awkward scooching maneuver as the space was tight, weaving in and around pieces of furniture and that stupid mini fridge she could not reach and she crept in Fly's direction. Fly was attempting to watch the mandatory video on sexual harassment in the workplace, and she was on the slide about retaliation and its definition. Banshee just sat her big ol' rump on the edge of the desk chit-chatting for no good reason, and she was not getting the hint that Fly was trying to get work done. What did she need? There was a test at the end, so she had to pay attention! So just before the bell rang, she pretended she was going to be late to class, and in an accelerated motion, Fly had a vision that Mz. Banshee piercingly screamed at her, "Get out!" And as she abruptly stood up, collected her schoolbag, and dashed out of the office, Fly bumped squarely into Mr. P.A.U.L. with his wide eyes and books and papers flew all over the hallway. As Fly tried waking herself up from the daydream, she envisioned the men in the administration building had transferred Mr. P.A.U.L.

to the very same building. With PTSD surging through her veins, she trembled, hands quivering, and beads of sweat ran down her temples.

Fly wondered why the haranguing continued. She was in the office the following day looking at Suzy's photos on her cork-board inspiration board, and Fly saw a photo of their girls having fun at the regional art show years earlier when they were in elementary school. Fly had asked now a third year in a row for a corkboard for her Dongleshop students and wondered why it was so difficult to obtain a simple corkboard. She wondered why Suzy chose such select words that day: "Your daughter..." pretending to not remember Fly's daughter's name and wondered why that photo was still there. She was deep in thought, contemplating what happened when all of a sudden, like a floating apparition, a banshee-type figure glided in and saw her staring at the wall and Fly was caught off guard with this unexpected ghost. There was no excuse, just dead silence. "Can I help you?" the apparition ominously asked in a whisper, and Fly poked around at her boss' desk and just said that she was looking for inter-office envelopes which were on the bookshelf.

Between P.A.U.L., the Boy's Club, and Suzy, she was having increased nightmares and sleep interference. She contemplated the past which was pretty terrible, the present which was unconscionable, and wondered what the future might hold. Even if she did get transferred, it would be another entire school year of hell, 180 days longer than she wished. She felt trapped waiting on a timeline that was out of her control. It comes down to the unfortunate fact that bullying is not illegal anywhere! Did she have a case for retaliation because of the Federal Harassment Charge—that is actually illegal, and Mz. Coupon Suzy Banshee seemed to be blind to why Mzzz. Fly would never put her pen down or stop documenting the absurdities that only got stranger and more daring. Sometimes, it seemed all a bunch of nonsensical mishegoss as she and the lawyer chuckled and tried to make light of a serious situation. It still doesn't justify the relentless nasty attitude toward her. Just look at the national leader. No Good News! Leaders should have certain qualities and characteristics such as empathy, gratitude, and integrity. Innovation, optimism, trust, collaboration and more.

Regardless, Fly made it clear that she needed to get out whatever the situation was before she lost her mind.

Fly started her vision quest. She was adamant that she was going to escape out the window, find a solution, grow from the experience, and let her journey be known. The vision quest had to speak to her, though, like spirit animals, they select the person. The person does not choose their spirit animal and the vision quest had to work itself out in its own in due time. While time was of the essence in her book, she also could simultaneously practice patience, so she did, knowing if she could just make it to the holidays; change will happen. Regardless of having the strange dreams, Fly would start yet another year with high hopes and positivity driving into work with her magenta hot-rod top-down singing, "Ain't nothing going to break my stride. Nobody gonna slow me down. Oh no. I got to keep on moving." Fly laughed to herself remembering when her grandfather would talk about Green Dog, the old musty green station wagon her grandparents would drive around all over America, road tripping without a care in the world, making it to all fifty states. "Brand new in '72!" he would proudly exclaim, looking at the huge old piece of boxy metal just as big as the once beloved Caprice Classic.

At the back to school faculty meeting, Principal Ave even spoke in code that the theme of the year would be "Kaleidoscope," and as such, everyone has a different perspective or viewpoint. In her opening, motivational speech, the principal gave an example in front of everyone that Fly might have one viewpoint, as she pointed to Fly directly, while Suzy has another viewpoint, as she pointed to Suzy directly, and they can both be correct. Different angles and perspectives of the same thing, but that everyone had to work together in a constructive and peaceful manner. Fly, while taken aback since she had just met over the summer with Ave about wanting to be transferred, heard it loud and clear, and if Suzy heard it as well, it would surely trigger her in the wrong direction. The principal was simply trying to get people to work better together not against one another. All of last year's many-colored jewels could together make this amazing kaleidoscope, if allowed.

As the autumn days got colder and more tense with a chill in the air and further away from the warm relaxing summer days, so too did Mz. Banshee's relentless heartless actions. First, over the summer, Mz. Banshee added war paint to her email photo icon, which was probably taken from that "What painting do you look like?" selfie app, which placed people's likeness into white men's artworks. Her email icon self-portrait was splashed with war paint covering her face. War paint. Everything means something, and that is taught in art class every day. She had become an evil warlord and took on the role of male world dominator right out of *Braveheart*. Fly pulled up this email and her hands quivered as Mr. P.A.U.L.'s name was still first, even though there were new teachers. September started with an unbelievable and insensitive request for Mzzz. Fly and the few XL Art teachers in the district meet in a "Collegial Circle" to discuss the XL Art Program. Fly's heart sank and became nauseous.

Was she nuts thinking Mzzz. Fly was going to sit in a small enclosed room with Mr. P.A.U.L. to discuss the curriculum and great assignments and assessment for XL Art? Last year, the same thing was supposed to happen at a professional development and Fly just left the building and decided to get her nails done instead. Was it not humiliating enough she had to resign and move, but to sit in a small group and brainstorm ideas with him and share her trade high score secrets? No way, not touching ground on that one. He couldn't even open the boxes, so what made anyone think she was going to have an intelligent conversation about curriculum? He probably didn't even know what curriculum was, let alone pedagogy. How ridiculous a request that she would not back down from and what kind of blinders did she have on that could have her not "see" what a bad idea that might be. Mz. Banshee sought out Mzzz. Fly one last final time in the cafeteria duty to request her presence and appeared confused when Mzzz. Fly said, "No. I am not available."

Later in the year, Mz. Banshee would intentionally set up Fly to display her student's artwork at an art show and placed her directly next to Mr. P.A.U.L. just one inch away to intentionally attempt to continue the intimidation tactics. She continued with the painfully obvious microaggressions when trying to be politically correct, only actually coming out opposite. She made several insensitive references to bathroom breaks and issues, but not in the sincere manner like that teacher at her old school. She denied a special field trip for the XL Art students. Fly was furious she could not give these special art students an opportunity to be the Regional Best, which was actually the name of the prestigious art event. The year before, Celeste was selected from her school to be a Regional Best, and it was such a wonderful opportunity and experience.

Mz. Banshee came to do an announced inspection in the fall on the XL Art class and still was not satisfied with Mzzz. Fly's performance, which was the same as to how she had performed for the same course in the past. Even before the inspection, Mz. Banshee made it clear, as her rule, she did not normally observe XL art classes. This was not normal as any class is fair game for an inspection. Why? Because maybe she wanted to catch some eighth grade boys acting up so she can write up classroom management issues like Mr. Byrd Vulture?

That very day, she began an onslaught of lingering in through the doorway and walking into Fly's room for no reason other than to spy and intimidate. Ten times not allowed to be there invading her space. Mz. Banshee tried to appear to be completing tasks like getting a supply out of her closet or asking Fly questions that could have waited for a free period. Upon switching classes, Mz. Banshee would linger and not leave the art room well after the bell had rung, and these behaviors went on at least a dozen times in one month, which makes it almost every day for the month of November. Fly consulted with her union navigator, and once again, they stated Mz. Banshee was out of line, but not sure what can be done. Fly tried to meet with her head union president many times, but he too denied her requests to meet over and over. She thought it may be because he was colleagues or friends with Mr. P.A.U.L. and so surmised she could not even go to the person who should be helping her not ignoring her. Fly continued to consult with and get advice from her longtime friend and colleague Mrs. Parabola as they now had to meet for late lunch. She suggested without hesitation to continue to write response letters to make clear counter statements because she was retaliating for whatever reason. Little did Mz. Banshee know she was submitting these statements, so if in a court of law, it would be the only way the treatment of Fly could be documented in black and white and placed in her permanent personnel file for review and scrutiny.

She kept other items in her lilac legal pad to record unusual situations like when Coupon Suzy Banshee entered the class-room with a roll of tape, making chit-chat for what Fly did not know. They were told to tape the floors to indicate where students should stand if there was an active shooter in the building. Fly again pretended like she was being interrupted of doing some important work stuff, but Mz. Banshee did not get the unspoken hint again, so they just worked with taping the floor. Chit-chatting away with Fly trying to ignore, Banshee stared at Fly's hand, advanced, and touched the blue ring on her pointer finger and asked, "Is that new? You don't usually wear a ring on that finger." Fly just cringed as to why she would make such an intense observation and just said it was Celeste's and she got it as a gift for her sweet sixteen. She did not need to know she wore it to think about Celeste throughout the day as a good luck charm for her safety. The workplace was getting out of control and even famous newscasters, famous people, actors, talk show hosts were all being accused of hostile work environments and discrimination and bullying and biases and harassment and me too.

Infuriated, Mzzz. Fly could not even wait until the holidays and went to Principal Ave and told her she was sending a letter to Super DaNile January 2 by the contractual deadline to be transferred because the previous request and signed agree-ment with the district was unresolved and had not come to fruition in this new school. It could not be more simply stated that in the signed agreement, "It is hoped that a humane and peaceful working environment, free from the hostilities of the past seven years and free from retaliation or reprisal shall be the result." It seemed like a simple request and that was all Fly was asking for. She should not even have to ask for it twice, as it should just exist on its own: "a humane and peaceful work-ing environment." Fly thought about the scene when the teens were reviewing the new code of conduct in *Pleasantville*. Be pleasant, courteous, but now only permissible paint colors can be used, and she indicated they were black, white, and gray, which are not colors at all. No magenta, no violet, no chartreus, no turquoise, no salmon permitted. Fly thought that Super DaNile was never qualified for that position of human resources as he had been a principal and possibly just a teacher prior. Fly heard nothing in return. Dead silence day after day. January, February, March. She kept busy focusing on what was important and she was educating herself with a university course on diversity, which included topics on cultural competence, gender bias, understanding racism, American with Disabilities Act, confronting implicit bias and microaggressions.

But she knew that Principal Ave put Mz. Banshee in her place after Fly gave her a lengthy complaint letter documenting dates and times of all the walk-ins. Mz. Banshee one morning stormed into school at the bell, and she refused to make eye contact with Fly and behaved exactly as Mr. P.A.U.L. would have. She was glad her invisibility powers were still working. She thought, *Thank god, please do not look at me or I may turn to stone.* The last time she stormed into the building like that she exclaimed, "Didn't you get my email? The Wi-Fi is down!"

Fly stared blankly, blinking, wanting to say, "How the heck can I get your email if the Wi-Fi is down?"

The students were screaming, "I can't learn! There's no Wi-Fi."

Mzzz. Fly cordially gave them sketch paper and some markers.

Around the holidays, Fly was selected to teach a painting of an antique red pickup truck with a green Christmas tree in the back at the wine and paint night, which she still did on the weekends for a fun side hustle. It was interesting and she tried to find fun facts to share with the drinking and painting adults, but found no solid information or symbolism or history about the red truck and why people loved the image so much, but it was clearly a thing. Christmas music was in the air and people were having fun singing and painting away. A few weeks later, it was an extremely cold winter morning in the New Year, and Fly approached the bridge driving to work, the very one she had many a time wanted to gun it into the river and just end all the torment she suffered from work. The sun was not yet visible but slowly making its approach toward the horizon into the dark still sky. The water was like glass with thin sheets of iced-over water reflecting the salmon sunrise from the east, glistening like a smooth mosaic with the cold turquoise ripples below. Then, red tail lights emerged upon the crest of the bridge as an abrupt stop with less than a mile left on the span of this elevated passageway. Fly sat there and sat there and sat there. No one on the bridge really knew what was happening, but the cars loading up the space creeping inches from each other having to split and hug the railing to allow emergency vehicles to pass made it clear something happened over the crest. There was nowhere to go. Everyone was trapped on the span above the dark icy waters. There was no pull-off, no turning around, no exit or way out. She tried not to think about the crumbling of American infrastructure or the Mothman tragedy. A fire truck blazed on the opposite side of the bridge getting to the supposed scene somewhere up ahead, going the wrong way on the span. That was an unusual sight, so Fly knew something was direly wrong. It seemed like hours passed and Fly will have to dread another call to Banshee that she was trapped with nowhere to go and would be late. Fly hated being late, but she already called Banshee and the attendance lady to have her first classes covered. Suzy sounded perturbed while the attendance lady was sympathetic that she had nowhere to go and it was out of her control.

Fly sat there endlessly, and she looked down and at least had her drive-thru breakfast sandwich and coffee. She was thankful for the surgeries had helped her to gain the power of control over her guts that was her new digestive system, and it really worked. She sat there watching the sun rise and the quality of light changed with every minute that passed. Her thoughts wandered and the fact that she was so close but yet too far to a presumed car accident to see details made her think. She looked at the time stamp on the sandwich bag, and it stated, 6:38 a.m., and the accident was now being reported at 6:41 a.m. and it was a cold 28 degrees. When she pulled out of the Sack of Donuts Shop Drive-thru, a slow red clunky truck was moving down the same path to the bridge at a sluggishly creeping speed, blocking her from moving at her own speedy hot rod car pace. She was not thrilled about this clunky red truck but just sighed and slowed down in the darkness of predawn. She tried to be patient when the red truck made a left at the light where she also turned, and then another left turn as she did for about a mile or two. She sighed and realized she will have to be patient until she could pass him on the bridge, but just then, the red pickup truck turned yet another slow creeping left. The red truck saved Fly's life by adding a those few short minutes to her commute.

A helicopter landed at the base of the bridge and, later, lifted off. One can only assume the worst. As the sun rose and the sky ever so slowly and gradually became lighter shades of salmon, all of a sudden, a small rainbow burst appeared, and at that point, she knew someone ahead had passed away. The serene landscape of teal, lavender, coral, and orange glow was sublime and magnificent instantly destroyed by either a thin sheet of ice or a distracted reckless human being with this untimely death. On the bridge, she always saw these rainbow bursts but on her way home, and she always knew it was her dad looking after her at the end of the day. He was speaking to Fly through all the colors in order to say, "It will be okay. I am okay now. I am thinking of you. Be safe on your journeys."

It was Fly's turn to pass the wreckage, and she felt sick to her stomach as three cars were a mangled mess of metal, crumpled against the guardrail of the bridge span with glass sparkling everywhere. One started to be towed away as the fatal car rest embraced in the median. She burst into tears as she slowly resumed highway speed and almost had to pull over to compose herself. Three people didn't make it to work that ice-cold day. Someone didn't make it home that day. That's all Fly could think over and over, and when she pulled into the school parking lot, much time had passed from the start of the school day. She tried to pull herself together to "check in" with Mz. Coupon Suzy Banshee. She walked the long quiet empty corridor, which was the full length of the school as classes were in session and it felt like an eternity. Slowly opening the office door there, Mz. Banshee was sitting at her desk peering over the computer and Fly burst into tears. Fly really tried so hard not to but raw emotion consumed her body to the bone. Not like Banshee was the consoling type, but she acted like she didn't have time for it and was indifferent. Fly could not take one more thing. Fly was mortified that she was hysterically crying in front of Suzy, so Fly quickly brushed it off by stone-cold saying, "Somebody didn't make it." The reality was that Fly was happy to have been just seconds behind this accident and that she did make it alive after everything she had been through. But why she was really hysterical was because she actually did make it to work. This work. The "somebody" that didn't make it was Fly. She was dead inside, broken down, chipped away at for a decade, as her body cascaded down to the ground into a pile of dust.

The very next day, the same clunky slow red truck appeared again, and Fly took a photo of it. She shared it with her XL Art class, and in the background, the telephone poles appeared as religious crucifixes in the distance and she got chills up her spine. What were the odds of seeing that red truck two days in a row? Was Fly meant to die fighting or live to fight? She thought back to the famous photograph of Muhammad Ali and his famous Rumble in the Jungle fight in Zaire where after rounds and rounds of quick jabs and crosses, over and over again repeatedly, being beaten down over and over again, Fly knew she had to wait for Mz. Banshee to become exhausted from tormenting and then seize the opportunity when it presented itself to take her down with a side blow. That's what Ali would do. He took it, took it, took it, then strike! Fly and Celeste had taken a road trip to the Muhammad Ali Museum because she liked some of his characteristics, inspirational quotes, and that he was a fighter, not only in the ring, but for human and social equality, power for change, and hope for a better future.

The winter was long and cold, and every turn, Mzzz. Fly continued to suffer from bad boss behavior. The union navigator stopped Fly in the hallway and stated in a surprised manner, "You have an ally!" referring to the principal, like this was World War II that was being strategically played. Fly could not understand why the district would want a potential lawsuit or did they think they could just squash Little Fly like an insignificant insect? A few weeks later, Fly walked into the faculty lounge and the very same union navigator was having lunch with Mz. Banshee. Caught, she murmured a meek "hi" as she must have instantly realized how it must have looked to Fly. Fly thought she might be in an episode of *X-Files* as the tables had turned once again, and "trust no one" popped into her mind. She apologized later that week stating how it must have looked, but that she was simply eating lunch and would never discuss anything confidential. Mz. Banshee never did acknowledge that Fly ever even walked through the room; she completely and intentionally ignored her. Just in one door and out the next with not a greeting or "I see you." Fly forgot she left her invisibility powers on or else she was in one of Mz. Banshee's many blind spots.

Fly had an art series once about being in the periphery and had fully understood the concept as did Suzanne Vega—the outskirts, the fringes, the edges what one does not see in their frontal line of vision, "left of center." Same as the students she inspired to capture moments of importance: As you peer through the glistening glass of the car window, droplets of water illuminated from the traffic light and street lamps behind, shine in a pattern of red and amber hues. Some of the droplets are dripping so elegantly down the glass in a delicately dancing waterfall. The cold storm makes it hard to see the rough surface of the concrete road in the distance toward the destination. Barely can you see your reflection nor anything in the rearview mirror. A moment of quiet introspection and delight and then *click*, the shutter releases and an image is born. Fly tried to hold back the waterfall of tears each morning as she struggled with this never-ending nightmare.

Mz. Banshee continued to try to alienate Mzzz. Fly from others in department meetings where the Brujas thought it funny to inquire if they burned down the classroom could they go to the rubber room? No one wanted to be there. They sat talking about childhood girly dolls over pertinent agenda items wasting Fly's time and then Mz. Banshee pulls out candy cigarettes from her desk drawer, and she and Una Bruja pretended to be smoking at the office desk. Fly thought they should be beyond paper dolls and that they should not be stereotyping, but she just kept quiet. Mz. Banshee then cringed and pursed her lips and puckered her eyes when one of the teachers excitedly told Fly to share the good news about Celeste. Mz. Banshee squinched her eyes as if she swallowed curdled milk upon hearing that "her daughter" received a huge scholarship for college, but the Dos Brujas were excited. Day by day, she encroached on what little space Fly had. Mz. Banshee put a flyer over Fly's classroom door flyer just as Mr. P.A.U.L. had done as if there was not enough door space for all messages to students. For the P.S. I Love You Suicide Prevention Day, the department was blatantly the only department who did not participate and the office doors were the only ones in the entire building not decorated to raise awareness and say, "You matter." Fly decided to decorate her own door, but wondered why no one else saw this blatant act or did just no one care at all? Was it just a job? It was almost as if she was saying, please commit harm to yourself by inaction. Was she not supposed to be the leader? Then *lead* damn it.

March Madness

When I look upward, I see the sky serene and happy; and when I look on the earth, I see all my children wandering in the utmost misery and distress.

—Mashipinashiwish Ojibwa
(on an epidemic of smallpox, 1760s)

Like a mosaic filled with blocks of squares in solid colors, she could not see the full picture until she stepped back from the artwork. Take any pointillism artwork, and up close, it appears to be nothing but multi-colored dots. Standing in the art museum, if you slowly take one step back at a time, you will begin to see the picture and what all of these thousands of dots combine to be an image of. Fly came into the office on March 5, and there was a tower of boxes behind her desk chair so high that she could not move her seat to pull up to the workspace. Mz. Banshee put about three square feet of boxes in Fly's way. The next day, there were even more boxes, but now stacked all over the top of her already small desk so that she could not even eat her lunch there, so she just looked at the Una Bruja with her clean and tidy workspace and left. Like she wanted Banshee sitting at her desk arranged behind her, peering at and breathing down her neck anyway. She was literally boxed in. She took a picture or two for evidence. She could not believe the audacity and sent a text with photos to her husband in disbelief. Fly felt she was able to capture what the elusive bullying looked like in many of her photographs.

"Inconceivable!" It was like the guy who just wanted to hold on to his stapler in *Office Space*, but they kept moving and moving him farther away from everyone, moving his stuff, or making it impossible to work. When Mz. Banshee did make a comment, it was a snide remark like, "I opened up one of the drawers in the art room and then I saw the magenta paper and was like oh, you took that extra space?" This year, Mz. Banshee was not even teaching in the one art room Mzzz. Fly was and she reprimanded her; that was her tone of speaking and how it sounded to Fly, that she moved her stuff on the bookshelf and not to do so. Fly only moved stuff so her students could have easy access to markers and colored pencils. She took a picture. And she continued to not let Mzzz. Fly do anything or get her a corkboard after three years of asking or let her move the teacher desk to a better location for student interaction to teach Dongleshop demos better and she really loved to tell Mzzz. Fly she would not be in that particular art room the following year nor would she ever teach the Widgetry Class or have a club. She was criticized to death and for what? Did it make Mz. Banshee feel better about herself, did it make her feel more powerful and in control, or was it just revenge theory?

She put several calls into the union president, but never heard back for a while as she was thinking of taking action in the form of a grievance, chronically breaking of the Teacher's Contract and intentionally doing so. Like, isn't there a document in place called the Constitution for a reason? And why did current national leadership not know what it was pertaining? That's what so many teachers from the previous school would have done run right to the teacher's union and get things changed—it seemed a lot faster than going via upper administration, which Fly absolutely did not trust. She continued to not get a response as he had once sat there at the large Round Table elbow to elbow, and once again, she would be doomed by the Boy's Club.

Mz. Banshee, as Mr. P.A.U.L. once had, tried to trap Fly into doing noncontractual items like suggesting having a bake sale to sell cupcakes even though she had a hissy fit last year about the cupcakes and that Fly did not even have the authority to do so since she did not have a club. That would be falsely making money with nowhere to deposit it. She would make attempts to sabotage by going to speak with Fly while she was proctoring state exams and duties to make it appear she was not doing her job. She made Fly take eighth graders on a senior field trip and then scheduled it during semester testing week. Between lowered inspection scores, lack of club advisership, denying field trips and special experiences for her students, and dismissing the school-wide committees Fly was a part of, she tried stripping away any possibility for Mzzz. Fly to ever become Teacher of the Year one day. Then one random day, Mz. Banshee removed Mzzz. Fly from her duty to go to the classroom to count the field trip money in front of her because some money went missing the year before, and Fly felt immediately like she was falsely accusing her once again of doing something she did not do. When Fly realized the sabotage, she quickly said, "I'll do this in front of the secretary. I have a duty right now and the other teacher is left alone with a hundred students." And Fly stormed out. It was probably the part-time teacher that she held the blatant double-standard for; she let that teacher do anything. Was Suzy the little preppy girl from her birthday party long ago with the penciled-in black eye haunting her from her past?

Mz. Banshee did not realize she constantly had really bad ideas from the tilting and overlapping the computer screens which she was probably trying to set Fly up to accuse her if they broke to blocking the emergency exits with furniture to in the third year, moving Fly's desk so that Mz. Banshee was always looking at her. Celeste and Fly were watching a reality TV show and the mother-in-law was wearing a ridiculously large-brimmed sun hat to which she could not view anything because she actually did not choose to see what was going on with her son and his fiancée. She was bitter and abrasive. The woven yellow straw brim must have been at least six inches all the way around the full perimeter of this lady's head. Celeste bluntly stated, "What kind of hat is that? It's like a million blind spots."

The following week, Fly was at kickboxing, which also repulsed Mz. Banshee with the bare exposed feet and germs, but who cared at that point as Fly could do nothing right, and she felt a pain on her rear as she was doing the Russian twists. Fly endured a lot of pain for such a long time now, but this one was urgent, localized, and needed immediate attention.

What now? thought Fly. She had to take another two days off for the minor surgical procedure and came back to work on Thursday. At least, it did not happen on the weekend where no doctors were in the office and had to go to the emergency room. She's gone in on New Year's Eve, Chanukah, Fourth of July so far, so she may challenge herself to hit all of the holidays, she joked to the nurse the last time admitted. She tried to hit St. Patrick's Day this time but settled for the Year of the Rat, the birth year of those who are clever and adapt quickly to new environments. She had so many doctors look at her derriere she thought if she were a butt model, she'd be rich. One time, Fly's husband had to get a hernia removed and the nurses were coming in and out asking questions and getting him ready for the procedure. Fly was sitting there in the room for one of the few times he was the one who needed medical moral support. The next nurse came in and asked, "Excuse me, sir, may I see your..." and with that he dropped his drawers, raised his gown, and flashed his privates, once again thinking nothing of it. She unexpectedly gasped, eyes large as saucers, and said, "Sir, I only need to see your insurance card!" A few minutes later, when he was under anesthesia, Fly could hear all the nurses quietly giggling for a long time. It had truly made their day. What a free show!

That morning, Fly opened her school email only to read yet another ridiculous e-scream message command from Mz. Banshee about how she should call her at a specific time and how she needed to organize her substitute plans a different way...than how she had been doing so for over twenty years? Maybe Mz. Banshee should have gotten to school on time to realize Mzzz. Fly was absent, maybe she should have used texting not iPutzes or her flip phone and how personalized did she want the absence notification? What did she want her teachers to drive to her house at 5:00 a.m. and knock on the door personally, stating they were going to be out sick, then hobble away after they were told to also contact the subs and explain everything to them. Was it bad enough Fly had to throw out all of her coloring worksheets that dealt with art concepts such as color theory or art word searches that the students always exclaimed they loved doing as a treat and didn't realize they were learning vocabulary? Mzzz. Fly was disgusted and wrote a scathing two-page written complaint to Principal Ave about all of the discriminatory and retaliatory behaviors she had been subjected to this school year and was fed up. Please stop. A "hope you feel better soon!" as the attendance person had emailed might have been nicer, kinder, better. Principal Ave emailed her back to make an appointment for Monday anytime to discuss the ongoing issues.

Fly had a Dongleshop student who the week before said his dad worked in the city fire department, and there was some sort of virus going around and something about Asia. Fly just said, "That's why I always have extra hand sanitizer around the art room and computers." But more of Fly's students were buzzing about this virus that was fast and furious, and Fly had not been watching the news because she was in so much pain. The hallways were buzzing with a nervous energy and Fly thought that she better bring a few bags of things, her computers, chargers, grade book, and XL Binders she might need as word of possible cleaning of the buildings was going to happen. One of Fly's students said the substitute who was Una Bruja yelled at him furiously because he sneezed, and she told him to leave the room immediately. Fly was shocked since the student as well as that teacher were usually very well mannered. That Thursday, Fly had hobbled back into the building where at the end of the school day, there was an announcement that "out of an abundance of caution all of the school buildings would be closed for forty-eight hours." So that Friday and Monday, there was going to be no school for deep cleaning and so Fly left and said to Mz. Banshee on her way out, "See you next Tuesday!"

Friday the thirteenth, March 2020. The halls were empty. Not a sound nor scream.

Mother Nature was super pissed off at all of us, and everyone was about to get a very big time out in detention and possibly suspension. She could not weep anymore and lashed out with intense fury. There is a global pandemic and the schools were closed until that Tuesday, then the next Tuesday, then the next, and then the next month, and after a few more weeks, no one ever returned. That certainly put the "F" in Friday. Fly never had to go back to that wretched workplace ever again. There were no meets online, just posted assignments. Fly never had that meeting with Principal Ave and still had not heard from Super DaNile about transferring yet. April, May, June. It had been six months and not a word from anyone about the requested transfer, so once again, pandemic or not, Fly was disgusted at the systematic discrimination of woman in the workplace. Explicit bias at its finest. Not even hidden. Her personnel superintendent and union president ignoring her pleas for help. She thought maybe all of these years they thought she was reporting Bigfoot sightings and just ignored in disbelief of the elusive creature as there was no other explanation she could ponder.

The quarantine experience was like yesterday is the same as today and will be the same as tomorrow for most people. It's when you wake up in the morning and you intend for the day to go a certain way with, perhaps a to-do list on a magenta Post-It pad, but unexpected actions set forth against or upon you thwart your good intentions of daily life with a particular and peculiar pattern of behaviors that are unwarranted and unwanted. It was the biggest blind spot no one expected to creep up into their vision. Humanity's sight. Everyone was witnessing something unprecedented and that had been on the sidelines, invisible, in our blind spot. Both Celeste and Fly thrived during the early pandemic days, but they were lucky enough to not know anyone close who had the virus. They were a pretty isolated family unit to begin with. Celeste, who was supposed to graduate high school, was not taking the attitude of being in that sucky senioritis state that they were all missing out on their senior experience, rather she was prolific with creativity making art out of everything she found around the house. She scavenged as no stores were open for paint and other art supplies. She painted on her car windows, the back yard fence, and sculpted out of recycled materials and repurposed vases, jars, and junk drawer items. The 9/11 babies had been cursed to become the pandemic Class of 2020. She was happy to be away from school and safe in her home away from the atrocities of the bullies housed in her high school that year. Even Celeste's artwork had been censored by the superintendent in February which never made it to exhibition and it was a black and white photograph of Fly's torn-up torso and they could not figure out why they would want to censor reality. Her hands intensely gripped her torso as if holding it all together and embracing the scars as they told her story. Fly even began working on sculptures which were sparkly blinged-out boxes inspired by her father's hot-rod airbrushed flame job cremation box he was buried in. She felt obligated to make as many beautiful boxes as she could to signify the loss of life the world was enduring. She could make one for every life lost if she could, even if symbolically.

After about a month, Fly decided to email her governor so she could shed some light on at least one pandemic positive; if you were bullied in school, you were not anymore.

Date: April 23
Topic: Human Rights
Subject: Bullying and Harassment in State Public School System- Students and Teachers
Dear Governor,

Why bother you with a message about bullying and harassment in public schools in the middle of a pandemic? Since March 13, the bullying and harassment as a teacher and former department administrator from two different coworkers in the public school district I teach in has suddenly ceased. As a DASL advocate for students, I wonder why bullying and harassment is not against the law in this state for all employees, not just that of a protected class (which I am) and why there are few systems in place to document, report, and have penalties for tenured staff that treat others with bullying tendencies, discrimination, and hatred (I

am not talking about sexual harassment here).
With the stay-at-home regulations, I understand
home lives may be challenging to students and
their parents, but in the public schools, students,
and employees have been freed of this heinous
behavior with remote teaching and learning. We
can no longer encounter the daily and repetitive "schoolyard" bully because of distancing.
Thank you, Governor. Unless you have actually
experienced this, I would not think it would be
something that one would consider the stats,
so I am happy to teach my awesome students
remotely and avoid the predator adults and
coworkers in my public school district. I have met
twice my senator about my concerns and have
had labor attorneys from upstate to downstate
and the city supporting my federal claim of
continued retaliation from my district. After this
is all over, I hope laws regarding bullying and
harassment in the workplace will be addressed,
like with DASL for students, for all (employees)
to be able to go to work and go about their
livelihood free from retaliation, manipulation,
anger, revenge, and violence and to be able
to have necessary human rights for productive
and peaceful working environments. Thank you,
and by the way, you rock!

She never heard back, but at least it was out there in cyber
space or in a data base somewhere in the state capital. The
family of three lay in the safety of their backyard. The clouds
moved and shifted. Shape shifting into various dimensions, and
you could see whatever you wanted to see in them. Celeste
saw a hot dog with chips, but Fly saw a lobster in one passing until it dissipated and faded into nothingness. Fly's husband
saw Big Mac, clearly, they were missing fast-food. Fly laid there
on her lounge chair in the back yard on her period "off" so to
speak, on the anniversary of her father's passing and the clouds
told her what to do.

Virtual Girl

Mz. Coupon Suzy Bad Boss Banshee tried to keep getting the last word in through the computer, but Fly wouldn't let her. She watched a lot of shows on TV that talked about cyberbullying and such and you could just turn the electronic devices off or pretend there was a power outage or something. The Great American Glitch, she preferred. Everyone is glitching! Fly and her husband both thought social media to be the demise of American culture, and if one watched the news, you would see that it can be used as a powerful tool of persuasion and No Good News in rapid thoughtless Twipps. Tuk-Tuk was the worst replacement of information as kids thought it to be factual as if these videos contained real information as in encyclopedias. Mz. Banshee even censored just had she done with the showcase and the Basquiat painting Fly had printed out, albeit remotely, two of her students artworks for a virtual gallery and you guessed it: the African-American girl fighting for her rights with an American flag across her mouth and the transgender student artwork which glorified the feminine figure. Fly just gagged and complied, hoping not to stir the pot and just get out of there. Then, Mz. Banshee must have stewed over the last inspection report response letter from last fall for an entire six months before she submitted a counter-counter claim response-response letter, which sent an automated time-stamped email notification to Fly via the web evaluation system. This was not allowed, but luckily, Fly had the wits to screenshot and print it before somehow, by the time she reported it to her union president and Principal Ave, Mz. Banshee had deleted it, even though it would remain eternally a ghost in her mailbox.

Fly thought of Madonna's song "Material Girl," but instead, she changed the lyrics as she sang along "You know that we are living in a Virtual World and I am just a Virtual Girl." Always the optimist, Fly thought of all the pandemic positives there were, and she grabbed her pack of Small Mart pens and jotted them in the lilac legal pad she would never use again, hoping she could cease the negative interactions that took place with her schoolyard bullies.

I have worn a bra only three times in a few weeks, I have only worn a watch twice, I can exercise every day, rain or shine, I ordered my own kickboxing bag for the basement, my biggest questions in the morning are: "coffee or tea?" and "black or gray leggings?" I have time to get quotes on tree removal and fencing. Oh, and I do not have to deal the pressures of workplace negativity. I don't have to hear "livin' the life" every day. I only wash my hair a few times a week so it's getting healthy. I haven't worn makeup in a while and decided to embrace the Year of No Lipstick, no war paint, even though I am sporting mascne no one can actually see it anyway! There has been not one discipline issue, detention, ISS, curse, inappropriate conversations, talking back, toss of the art supplies, breaking of materials, hallway fights to break up, dodging kids being pushed, bells ringing, fear of school violence or guns, report card comments that don't apply like "poor social skills," "destruction of materials" "inappropriate behavior," "excessive absences." Class size: zero. They are all sleeping under their covers and playing video games. One student emailed that he could not do the digital art assignment because his computer "had an attitude" several times, and it was all okay. He was so stressed by typing to him it was okay, he said he felt it was like an elephant was lifted off his chest. It was a drawing, no stress. There were positive emails from parents about remote teaching and how art helped their children get through the pandemic.

The only mandatory interactions were email correspondence and just two virtual meetings for work. There was one virtual department meeting where Mz. Banshee acted like she cared about everyone's safety. Too late, Fly was super safe now, and she was feeling a power surge coming on. Everyone looked like crap, but Fly put makeup and lip gloss on and arranged nice lighting nonetheless. The others talked for about thirty minutes, and Fly just quietly listened just as she had in the last in person department meeting with the rubber room discussion, fake smoking, and dolls. She still had her invisibility powers so decided to use them as she had nothing to add to the conversation and no one spoke to her. She still had not heard anything about any transfer, so was just focused on getting through this last dreadful meeting. They were about to wrap it up when Mzzz. Fly's classes were the only ones not addressed in the agenda as to how to finalize grading so when Fly said, "I have a question," and asked about calculating semester courses, Mz. Banshee squinted her eyes, peered blindly into the computer tilting her head back and forth as if she could not see Mzzz. Fly in the screen and asked, "What? I can't hear you. Oh, you are cutting out." Celeste stood directly on the back side of the laptop, so she could hear every word. She asked her mom, "What the heck kind of a meeting is this?" in which Fly responded after she hit the red disconnect button how ridiculous of a meeting that was and they laughed it off. Then came the annual report meeting where Mzzz. Fly was going to be alone in the computer with Mz. Director Coupon Suzy Banshee. A notification came up on her email "Happening Now..." and she started sweating, hands shaking, heart palpitating, and felt a lump in her throat as if she was going to vomit. But since she was still waiting to hear from administration, Fly declined the meet and emailed Banshee that she could not meet because she was waiting to hear from her union president.

Fly's phone rang, and it was Principal Ave giving her the Good News that while she would be missed, she would be transferred to her initially requested building even though Super DaNile did not want to approve the move. Fly could not understand that side comment and why he was so opposed to Fly's requests after everything she had been through. Fly and her husband drove to the dreaded school on the allotted day to swap out laptops and packed up their cars with all of her unwanted stuff and did the midnight move right out of there and left everything as if she were never there. She threw out all of the school theme-colored clothing she had purchased in attempts to fit in.

Over the summer, Fly made a "Wellness Visit" to Dr. Mendit which was a first. Fly was like a celebrity when she walked through the office doors, as Kiki gathered around her stating, "You're our success story!" and swiftly escorted her to the examination room with no wait. Fly would always have a small section of colitis and was unaware she would soon develop Crohn's. She knew she was not ever going to be completely out of the woods with this terrible disease, but she had a great medical team that could help her maintain her health with proper support and medical advancements, and she was beginning to see sunlight burst through the tree line in all directions around her. She knew she was feeling better than before her diagnosis that upheaved her life and that of her caregivers, her family. Anyway, she was still bionic in her husband's eyes, and no matter which direction the disease took her, he kept reminding her about sipping those mint juleps that were waiting for them in the future.

Fly made the time to read a book that her mother had mailed to her, and it made a profound change in her life and her vision on the grander scheme of the world. She knew she had heard about hundreds of school girls somewhere in Nigeria being kidnapped and she thought, *Who in their right mind would want to kidnap so many teenage girls?* Fly thought her one teenage daughter was enough drama and hormones. To teach nearly one hundred annually is a challenge. But to steal hundreds? Teenage girls are the same no matter what decade or country a teenager is from they are all similar. Teenagers are teenagers and they are growing physically, hormonally, emotionally, and educationally maturing. They are quirky, funny, sad, annoying, serious, lonely, introverted, extroverted, awkward, and invincible. The essence of the story in Fly's opinion is that there needs to be a reformation of the human rights in education. Kidnapping girls and taking them from their schools where they were trying to learn and become educated and better themselves was the ultimate denial and violation of educational rights. When the book store re-opened from the shutdown, she bought a copy and in a glittery, sparkly gift bag, gave a copy to Principal Ave with a sincere thanks for helping to get her sparkle returned. Fly walked out of that building never to return, or so she thought, as she left a trail of sparkles in her wake filling the stagnant school air with shine and hope for enlightenment.

Fly pondered for those few years what she ever did to deserve being treated the way she was. She searched and searched and could not find an answer neither simple or complex. From her perspective, her facet of that kaleidoscope, this was truly an X-File. Unusual, unexplainable, and swiftly ended unexpectedly just as soon as it began. Unless one was a trained therapist, a person who specializes in bullying and harassment, or some kind of a supersleuth, Fly did not know if one will ever fully understand what drives a person to act so terribly to another. And it is not that simple, the worst is the daily repeated over and over and over actions, the ones that are unnerving and unpredictable. It is hidden and unexplained torture. It is jealously, anger, rage, revenge, superiority complex. It is just far more simple to be kind. Fly looked at her sparkly plaque her niece had given to her, and she proudly displayed in her home office that said, "All I Want is a Pedicure and World Peace!"

America the Beautiful—American Mayhem

Where do you stand on the apology and forgiveness debate? Forgiveness is 50/50. Closure is needed, but can one ever get there? How can one easily forgive someone for an unthinkable act? Will you just walk away and maintain the wrongdoing, hold a grudge, then let it go?

A news reporter interviewed loved ones of those killed senselessly in mass shootings from coast to coast. Forgive or not?

Those that choose not to forgive look like the problem makers or mean and not understanding. No, we do not have to sympathize with the oppressors and the ones who choose not to be humane and decent. Forgiveness is a personal choice.

Word Wall

> "freedom" noun fre•dem
>   1.   the power or right to act, speak, or think as one wants without hindrance or restraint
>   2.   a political right
> synonyms: autonomy, independence, liberty, self-determination, self-governance, sovereignty

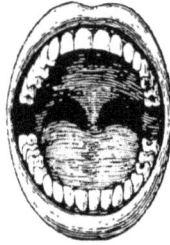

Notable Quotables

The time is always right to do what is right.
—Martin Luther King Jr.

Learn from yesterday, live for today, hope for tomorrow.
The important thing is not to stop questioning.
—Albert Einstein

Lesson #10

This school year, Fly learned that it takes an extraordinary event to finally be set free.

Workplace Rights

Worry-free
Organized
Respectful
Kind
Peaceful/ Professional
Livelihood
Accountable
Career building
Equitable

Rightful
Inclusive
Genuine
Tolerance
Humanitarian
Safe

Get Guts

Act Out!

Activity: Create an inspiration board. This can be an actual physical collage of things that inspire, motivate, and make you happy or you can create it digitally using any app of choice. You can post cards you have received, fortune cookie sayings, printouts that you admire, bookmarks, quotes, photographs, or any memorabilia you wish. Keep it in a place where you can walk by it on occasion to keep you balanced and grounded to yourself. You can share your inspiration board with others so they can get to know you better. Jot some ideas and notes on the following page.

Summary
Lead Your Own Way

This September is a gift!

Fight for the things you care about. But do it in
a way that will lead others to join you.

—Ruth Bader Ginsburg

Life is like a camera
Focus on what's important
Capture the good times
Develop from the negatives
And if things don't work out
Just take another shot

— Ziad K. Adbelnour

Cue the Music:
"Burning Gold" by Christina Perri
"You Learn" by Alanis Morissette
"Learn to Fly" by Foo Fighters
Bonus: "I Won't Back Down" by Tom Petty

What Great Teachers Do

Ms. Fly was preparing her supplies and samples for her students not yet in attendance. A pile of paintings in a portfolio gets stuck in the elevator door, but the elevator was stopped in between floors. She hit the Up button, but it kept going sucking the artwork into the shaft. Giving up on retrieving the teacher samples, she walked down the hall to her office, her own personal cubicle space. She looked out of the floor to ceiling glass window toward the city from the thirty-eighth floor. The cold gray skyline was interrupted by quickly passing dark and light ribbon clouds undulating in and out reflected in the mirrored and cement cityscape. Some departments were ordered to evacuate, so Ms. Fly made her way to get her things together when she decided to double-check with Una Bruja, and at that very moment, Suzy Banshee popped out from behind the tall metal filing cabinet and stuck her hand on the back of Fly's neck to tuck her shirt tag back in. A fleeting moment of being Little Red Riding Hood emerged from her gut sending a chill through her body. Feeling instantly and intensely violated, Fly told her outright this time, "Don't touch me!" Suzy justified her action by stating that her clothing tag was sticking out and it bothered her. Fly lashed back for once with words, not memos and emails. "You don't know what you're getting into," Fly said. As Fly picked up her schoolbag, Banshee snarled her lip and snarkily asked, "Where do you think *you're* going? No one is going anywhere," as if they were children being scolded.

The music director walked by and nonchalantly asked, "What are you all still doing here?" as Banshee argued that they were not evacuating as the clouds out the window view began to start swirling counterclockwise, fading in and out. She stormed away toward the elevator; she entered and turned around to glare one last time at Mzzz. Falayyya as the doors glided closed to obscure her anger and rage. It was as if the captain left the ship to sink with their passengers aboard. Never get into an elevator during a potential power outage.

Just then, Fly and Bruja glanced at each other in sheer panic after peering out the large glass window, instantly knowing what was about to happen, but almost unable to move quite fast enough to jump to safety. One danger was gone yet another emerged. For a moment the office was dead silent as the sky darkened in ominous hues. The lights flickered out as Fly ran to her office, strapped her purse around her body, so she would at least have her cell phone on her. The roar of the twister was coming closer like a freight train at full speed. The sky turned olive green, then dark brown, and the building began to sway. She buried her body in the love seat, and as the tornado rampaged and raged sideways outside her glass window, it suddenly imploded, shooting shards of glistening ice like shrapnel in all directions. In seconds, it ripped through, and then just as fast, it was gone. Just then after only one deep breath in, the building Fly was in began to lean into a graceful fall to the north, the very same direction from which the danger came from. She clung onto the couch for dear life, knowing the probable outcome of slow impending doom and death.

The buildings around the city all at once began to lean and tumble like a line of dominoes. Fly goes blank from intense fear for a few seconds, flies out the blown-out window, and in slow motion, lands a few miles away on the edge of a pool on a green grassy spread when she asked the stranger where she was. She had softly landed in a sunny and vibrant plush land completely unscathed. The colors were bright and the water was clear. She woke up in a sweat, but it took her a very long time to open her eyes. She remembered that a stranger helped her up and congratulated her on becoming the Teacher of the Year and led her toward the sunlit horizon walking, walking into the distance together hand in hand until they vanished under a magnificent rainbow.

Y2K, 9/11, hurricanes, wild fires, tornadoes, superstorms, a pandemic. Americans have been through a lot and persevere somehow. No matter how one has been personally affected by these uncontrollable disasters, each and every one of us can control how we act toward one another. You don't have to look far for some famous sayings that can be implemented today! "Be a rainbow in someone else's cloud" (Maya Angelou), "It's nice to be important, but it's more important to be nice" (unknown), and "A kind word is like a spring day" (Russian proverb).

Post-pandemic, the statistics about teaching are startling. Fifty-five percent of schoolteachers want to quit the profession cold turkey and 41 percent have a side hustle to get by. It was mid-July and that school year was a distant nightmare as Fly and her husband sleep in and turn on the news only to hear a morning newscaster state in a long drawn-out, unamused, monotone voice, "Welcome to the second half of the worst… year…ever…"

It was the first day of a new school year and the person in the car in front of Fly paid it forward by buying her coffee at the Sack of Donuts Shop Drive-thru. The cashier said it was "a thing" and that people were doing it a lot lately. She thought that it was a really good sign about the upcoming months and, in return, paid it forward to someone else the next day. The drive over the bridge on the first day of school was quietly sublime. The sun rose gently, reflecting off the still, unchurned river below, flowing smoothly in a never-ending current. The colors were awe-inspiring, the warm pinks, salmons, and yellows mixed with the cool turquoise, lavenders, and blue hues of the water. As she exited the bridge and made the turn to cruise the barren stretch of highway, she changed the radio from calm Coffee House tunes and cranked it up to "Thnks fr th Mmrs." She sang along to the ultimate good riddance song, "Thanks for the memories even though they weren't so great!" as she accelerated, anxious to start the new school year. Ms. Fly walked into her new school and was given a gift bag with a present, and stunned, Fly asked her new fearless leader, "What did I do to deserve a gift?" After being beaten to death in both body and spirit repeatedly for a decade, she was welcomed and appreciated in this new space. The gift was a coffee mug with T.E.A.M. in script: Together Everyone Achieves More.

Ms. Fly asked her new boss if there was a back room or somewhere in case she needed to cry, and taken aback, she replied, "Well, I hope there will be no reason for you to cry!" The greatest gift of all was a happy working environment as she was greeted with a warm welcome by the new colleagues, new teachers, new supervisor, and new principal in her new workplace. The supervisor told her that the new principal loved her smile and positive attitude, and masked, Ms. Fly asked, "How would he know what my smile looks like?" And they chuckled that he could just tell. Ms. Fly was happy in her new school albeit being half remote teaching and learning and half in-person, it was one of the best but most challenging school years she had in a very long time. All workplaces should be as such. She made an effort to participate in every committee and program pertaining to training and educating on diversity and equity in hopes that there one day would be a more unified and equitable culture in schools for everyone, free from biases, bullying, and discrimination. Free to be oneself and be the best each individual can be, to be a productive part of society in a peaceful school environment with people who exhibit compassion and care. She participated in the school parade where she felt as if she had been with these new colleagues forever. They let her lead the parade with her convertible as the students and parents cheered for the retired teacher that sat on the back seat as she drove the route.

Fly began to put some pieces of the puzzle together as she journeyed through her new and welcomed school year. To her, it was like she was looking at a large six-foot Italian submarine party style hero that feeds a lot of people, but there were parts that were missing over the years. She had the whole bottom bun, which was the timeline, and she had a lot of meat, lettuce, and tomatoes. There were parts of the hero that were missing, such as the pickles, olives, and dressing, but then some parts started to fill in. There was a retirement announcement via email that September, and when it glorified Super DaNile's life in education, there it was: he was a varsity coach in the same sport that Mr. P.A.U.L. was in so that pat on the back made sense now. The letter also alluded to the fact that as the district was downsizing, the personnel responsibilities would go to the District Lawyer Codswallop which was 200 percent worse than Super DaNile! If a woman had a harassment or sexual harassment complaint, they will now have to go to the lawyer in charge of only protecting the district's self-interests? It is preposterous and disgusting in today's day and age.

She was asked to become a mentor and put in to get approved for training. The only way Coupon Suzy Banshee could get to Fly now was by not approving her until after the event and also had to be told to do so by Fly's new fearless leader. She was so sick of the games that Fly contacted the EEOC again and the administrator indicated that what the district had done since the last Charge of Discrimination was indeed illegal and actionable. However, there was the money factor as well as he ended the conversation, indicating that with a second Charge, they would most likely escalate the retaliation. Hopeless, vicious cycle. As she participated in the workshop, she was reading and discussing the given district case studies with the other hand-picked master teacher colleagues. In the packet, there was a full page case study entitled "The Resistant Novice." Names were changed to protect the guilty. It had to be P.A.U.L. sabotaging the mentor experience and gave every excuse in the book as to why he could not do things.

> Case Study #9: Dick is a high schoolteacher and assistant coach who had two years teaching experience at another school before being hired. (The trainer mentioned he was let go for some reason.) This district requires all first year teachers, regardless of prior experience, to work with a mentor teacher. Bill, a highly respected and personable veteran teacher, finds Dick resistant to being mentored.
>
> Bill has observed each of Dick's classes once and has noticed a pattern of rote, textbook teaching with students working individually at their own pace. His presentations to the whole class tend to be hurried, with no time for questions or clarification. If students raise their hands or say they don't understand, he replies, "This is easy stuff. You should be able to get it right away. Check your notebook a bit if you don't understand."
>
> During independent learning time, Dick as an assistant coach reviews game highlights and strategies with another coach. He berates students for interrupting him.

Bill has attempted numerous times to schedule a conference with Dick to talk about his observations. Dick always has a reason he's unable to meet: practice, committee meeting, parent meetings. He has even stated to Bill that since he is an experienced teacher, he has no need for a mentor.

Discussion questions for the group to solve the problem were outlined below the passage.

She was validated and thrilled to finally be in a positive, peaceful, and productive working environment in her new school. Sometimes, no one will get you to where you want to be, and like a Drum Major, you have to be the leader, but at the same time lead your own way. This summary of the lessons lived and learned includes ways that toxic schools can be de-contaminated, schoolyards cleaned up and schoolyard bullies rehabilitated. Policies and procedures for human rights in the workplace need to be created, advocated for, and moved to legislation.

Learn to Fly

Sometimes, you have to go north in order to go south. Fly never understood when her husband would drive to a location, he would always end up going up and around and then all the way back down to get there. She would always disagree that was not the right path and could have just gone directly straight to get there. She now understood that sometimes, you have to go all the way around the destination and circle back to finally get to where you need to be.

But just then, the stranger from before came back, the rainbow faded, and the skies turned dark once again as she fell into the cold, dark waters below the bridge that had twisted and contorted from the storm. Echoing in her mind and muffled underwater, she was singing a phrase, "Mark my word, my story will be heard..." as she felt like she was draped in cement and shlepping a baggage full of books and computers through quicksand. Heavy, drowning, being pulled down into the cold water, and humiliated by insignificant others. It was a hot August day before the next school year, and they blindsided her by pulling the rug out from under her newly grounded feet. They forced a man-made tsunami upon her at the last minute; took her seniority away due to her disability leave; changed her teaching schedule; stole her beloved Widgetry Classes and students from her; stole her teacher desk; added two new preps; and then worse, punished her by placing her half of the day back with Banshee. Her hair stood on end, feeling impending doom. But knowing no one else heard Banshee's ear-piercing shrieks, Fly soared to new strengths and every day donned herself in banshee-slaying gold, salt, and fire, banishing the floating apparition to the far depths of the misty school corridor, leaving Fly alone to simply teach.

As she cleared out her widgetry lab that summer driving back over the bridge home, Whitesnake's hit came on the radio, and she wailed along, tears streaming down her warm cheeks in numbness and disbelief. "Here I go again on my own. Goin' down the only road I've ever known." Just then, with her car packed with over twenty-five years' worth of personal widgetry teaching items, she rounded the bend of the bridge, and a rainbow burst appeared to her left. She whispered to herself, "Hi, Dad." They did it to her a third time. Fool her once, shame on them. Fool her twice, shame on her. Fool her thrice, three strikes, she's out. She walked and walked over three hundred miles from classroom to classroom and school to school trying to smile teaching her students in a post-pandemic world despite her physical ailments. She just kept going because the students told her art was the favorite part of their day.

But then, she used every last ounce of strength to pull herself to shore, drenched and gasping for breath crawling on her hands and knees onto the sandy beach, which was only a few steps until she reached a thicket wood. She drifted with eyes closed at first listening very cautiously to figure out which direction would pull her as she was being scratched and torn up by branches of thorn bushes. Would she travel north, south, east, west, or in another direction? A blackbird singing in the dark skies guided her to the left fork in the road. She circled and circled in the woods following the calls of the blackbird and kept ending up in the very same location over and over again in a seemingly never-ending cycle. Both wings were broken.

Regardless, the tweeting blackbird finally broke free and flew into the night sky as she finally opened her eyes and looked up into the bright stars following its flight. Alone in the darkness, she put one hand in her pocket and felt a fortune cookie paper, a compass, and her last pen from the warehouse pack. The fortune read, "Only a person who risks is free." Her mom gave it to her as a sign of perseverance and courage. So with that, Warrior Fly rubbed her courage bracelet, gripped her half-heart necklace that lay on her warm beating chest, and stood stoically like a sculpture mimicking *The Karate Kid*'s crane pose. She slowly lifted her leg as she stretched her winged arms up, balanced that last empty pen on her foot, and took a deep breath in and exhaled as she crane-kicked it straight out into the universe with all her might. KO! Knock out, bullying. Warrior Fly was scratched and scarred, crumpled, beaten down, and stomped on but pulled herself out of the wreckage and sang, "Yes, I am the warrior. And victory is mine!"

Instantly, she woke up in a puddle of sweat and in a moment arose as she heard blackbirds chirping in the distance as she peered out the window with the sunrise rising from the east. No sullen Sundays and alarms. No one long Sunday night in August. No more somber Septembers. Peaceful, quiet, and calm. She put on her robe and walked to the kitchen and brewed two simple coffees. Light and sweet. Nothing more. Nothing less. She opened a piece of mail from the US Capitol Hill about the Healthy Workplace Bill and, with her mighty pen, completed the RSVP card to attend and testify at the federal level. Then, she walked to the narrow beach shoreline in the backyard and always waited for that "moment to arise," as she could hear Celeste slowly strumming the cords on her guitar in her mind. Fly and her husband placed their hot coffees in their kayaks and paddled away into the beautifully peaceful and serene quiet landscape where the calm waters of the lake gently touched the soft shores of the tree-lined mountains of retirement. The clouds gave shapes to what they wanted to see or how they wanted to be seen. The colors glistened with salmon, pink, turquoise, and magenta hues that only nature could create. They drifted across the lake in no specific direction and went with the flow as they reminisced about the tasty mint juleps they enjoyed on the porch the night before during sunset thinking about nothing but that moment.

Cures

So what do we do about schoolyard bullies? What can be done? Start small, think big. Fight to get that one little sparkle back and create a field of sparkles.

Fly walked down the hallway at the end of the school year and overheard two teachers talking. One said her eye had been twitching for a while, but now had moved to the other eye. They laughed knowing full well it was teaching stress, as another colleague said he was experiencing general malaise. There is always going to be some level of eye twitching in the workplace, first day of school jitters, end of year pressures, but to identify the triggers, make changes and add some self-care, workers can get through anything. And as Ms. Fly signed year-books filled with photos of seniors, "Good Riddance" blared over the school sound system. "It's somethin' unpredictable, but in the end, it's right. I hope you had the time of your life."

Fly has found some cures along her journey, but the pandemic was a clear-cut cure for these vile behaviors across America, setting things on a positive trajectory. Fly found some short-term cures along the way: summer, spring, and winter vacations, people retiring, learning to hide, learning to fight, using a thousand Band-Aids, finding exit strategies, using up sick days, and pleading for help. Fly watched as Hoda and Jenna discussed how it could be if they flipped the script and teachers got paid what actors did. And even though no matter how hard, Fly always pushed forward relentlessly to fight the two steps forward, three steps back struggle. While she would still always have to deal with her physical body and try to keep it healthy for herself, there was a broader battle that has escalated, bringing women fifty steps backward. Women's inherent human rights to make choices about their bodies have been threatened, and Americans can now freely roam the streets armed with weapons as if it was the Medieval Times. This all trickles down into the classroom. America needs to emerge from the darkness and division, with a revival, a new age Renaissance where we can once again celebrate enlightened life and embrace the human spirit. How can we make Anytown, USA, our public schools, your district, their classrooms, and everyone's schoolyards safe? There is a lot of work to be done to clean up our toxic schools, but if we all do our part, anything is possible.

List of things that need to be done:

- meaningful bullying awareness and education
- awareness and advocacy of systemic problems
- empathy and understanding in schools
- effective use of policies and procedures in schools
- clear complaint forms reviewed by neutral contact point
- methods for school district accountability
- human rights and equity in education
- workplace equity and diginity
- promote professionalism and respect in the workplace
- school violence policies and consequences
- healthy workplace legislation
- workplace rights laws and policies
- safer and healthier schools
- school reformation
- give teachers incentive to teach!
- increased pay for teaching workload
- student anti-bullying laws in all states
- humanitarian efforts
- social changes/society education
- affordable legal counsel
- stricter gun control laws
- violent offender warning signs awareness
- accessibility to mental health
- educate with character building for students
- provide family education programs
- community involvement and inclusion
- everyone can be kind in the workplace

Each time a man stands up for an ideal, or acts to improve the lot of others, or strikes out against injustice, he sends forth a tiny ripple of hope, and crossing each other from a million different centers of energy and daring, those ripples build a current that can sweep down the mightiest walls of oppression and resistance.

—Robert Kennedy

Do You Have the Guts to Make a Change?

Act Out!

Life is a long, bumpy road, but that makes for an exciting ride. It's okay to map out your future, but do it in pencil.

—Jon Bon Jovi

Journal Entry: Natasha Bedingfield once said, "Drench yourself in words unspoken. Live your life with arms wide open. Today is where your book begins. The rest is still unwritten." Take the next page and begin to write your story or anything that comes to mind. Let it all out. You might want to draw, doodle, write a poem or a song, there is no right or wrong. When done, you can keep your personal expressions safely nestled here. Make your story known by discussing your narrative with family, friends, or work colleagues. Which direction would you like your story to go? How does it end? Use more paper as needed.

Acknowledgments

I would like to express gratitude for those who have impacted my life and story and have shown unlimited kindness and compassion.

Selected Sources
and Inspirations

Adichie, Chimamanda Ngozi. *We Should All Be Feminists*. New York, NY: Anchor Books, 2014.

Arnold, Tedd. *Super Fly Guy*. New York, NY: Cartweel Books, Scholastic, 2006.

Asner, Anne-Marie Baila. *Shmutzy Girl*. USA: Matza Ball Books, 2004.

Benson, Richard. *F in Exams: The Very Best Totally Wrong Test Answers*. San Francisco, CA: Chronicle Books, 2011.

Brunke, Dawn Baumann. *The Spirit Animal Directory*. New York, NY: Chartwell Books, Quarto Publishing, 2015.

Bosher, Kaminski and Vacca. *The School Law Handbook*. Alexandria, VA: Association for Supervision and Curriculum Development, 2004.

Carlson, Gretchen. *Be Fierce*. New York, NY: Center Street-Hatchette Book Group, 2017.

Cleary, Kristen Maree. *Native American Wisdom*. New York, NY: Fall River Press, 1995.

Coloroso, Barbara. *The Bully, the Bullied and the Bystander* (Board of Ed. Policy). USA: William Morrow and Company, 2003.

Crawford, Susan. *Beyond Dolls and Guns*. Portsmouth, NH: Heinemann, 1996.

Danielson, Charlotte. *Enhancing Professional Practice: A Framework for Teaching*, 2nd ed. Alexandria, VA: Association for Supervision and Curriculum Development, 1996, 2007.

Davis, Charlotte. *Enhancing Professional Practice*. Alexandria, VA: Association for Supervision and Curriculum Development, 2007

Eisner, Elliot. *The Arts and the Creation of Mind, 10 Lessons the Arts Teach*. Alexandria, VA: Yale University Press, National Art Education Association, 2002.

Exley, Helen. *Art Lovers Quotations*. New York: Exley Publications, 1994.

Exley, Helen, *To the World's Best Mother*, New York: Exley Publications, 1992.

Fey, Tina. *Bossypants*. New York, NY: Reagan Arthur Books, 2011.

Haynes, Betsey. *The Against Taffy Sinclair Club*. New York, NY: A Bantam Skylark Book, 1978.

James, Aaron. *Ass-holes: A Theory*. New York, NY: Anchor Books, 2014.

Kaling, Mindy. *Is Everyone Hanging Out Without Me? (And Other Concerns)*. New York, NY: Crown Archetype, 2011.

Kelly, David W. *How to Talk Your Way Out of a Traffic Ticket*. Los Angeles, CA: CCC Publications, 1989.

Locks, Renee. *Live with Intention 2017 Date Book*. USA: Brush Dance, 2015.

London, Peter. *No More Second Hand Art: Awakening the Artist Within*. Boston, MA: Shambhala, 1989.

Nolte, Dorothy Law. *Children Learn What They Live: Parenting to Inspire Values*. New York, NY: Workman Publishing Co., 1998.

Norris, Pamela. *Sound the Deep Waters: Women's Romantic Poetry in the Victorian Age*. Boston, MA: Little, Brown and Co., 1991.

O'Brien, Sarah. *Whack-A-Zombie*. New York, NY: Running Press, 2008.

Posserello, Jodie Ann. *The Totally Awesome Val Guide*. Los Angeles, CA: Price, Stern, Sloan, 1982.

Pritchette, Price. *You2*. Dallas, TX: Pritchette LP, 2012.

Richards, Shola. *Making Work Work*. New York, NY: Sterling Ethos, 2016.

RuPaul. *Lettin It All Hang Out: An Autobiography*. (autographed) New York, NY: Hyperion, 1992.

Schulke, Flip, and Schudel, Matt. *Muhammed Ali*. New York, NY: St. Martin's Griffin, 1999.

Sesay, Isha. *Beneath the Tamarind Tree*. New York, NY: Dey St., 2019.

Schaef, Anne Wilson. *Meditations for Women Who Do Too Much*. San Francisco, CA: Harper and Row, 1990.

Silverstein, Shel. *Where the Sidewalk Ends*. New York, NY: Harper and Row, 1974.

Stevenson, Robert Louis. *The Strange Case of Dr. Jekyll and Mr. Hyde*. New York, NY: Dover Thrift Editions, 1991 (1886).

Tiger, Caroline. *How to Behave: A Guide to Modern Manners*. Philadelphia, PA: Quirk Books, 2011.

Wayne, Jimmy. *Walk to Beautiful*. Nashville, TN: W Publishing Group, an imprint of Thomas Nelson, 2014.

Whitaker, Todd. *What Great Teachers Do Differently: 14 Things that Matter Most* and Study Guide. Larchmont, NY: Eye on Education, 2004.

Zawacki, Neil. *How to Be a Villain: Evil Laughs, Secret Lairs*. San Francisco, CA: Chronicle Books, 2003.

References

Retro Rewind:

Tarallo, Mark. "A Brief History of Bullying," 2017. https://www. asisonline.org/security-management-magazine/articles/ 2017/05/a-brief-history-of-bullying/

"988" Suicide Hotline, 2022. https://www.health.com/news/ 988-suicide-hotline-number

The Crumpled Paper:

The Crumpled Paper Activity

https://purposefocuscommitment.com/wisdom-story-les-son-about-bullying-crumpled-piece-paper/

https://ripplekindness.org/crumpled-paper-wrinkled-heart-bul-lying-activity/

Chapter 1:

American Federation of Teachers. https://www.aft.org/

Meador, Derrick. "Pros and Cons of Teacher Tenure," February 28, 2018. https://www.thoughtco.com/what-is-teacher-tenure-3194690

Brittanica, 2011. https://teachertenure.procon.org/

Chapter 2:

Kelley, Raina. "The Social Significance of Zombies," 2010. https:// www.newsweek.com/social-significance-zombies-221328

Holohan, Meghan. "The Real-Life Neuroscience Behind Zom-bies," February 9, 2022. https://www.mentalfloss.com

Stockton, Chrissy. "10 Things that Passive-Aggressive People Do (That Normal People Don't)," 2014. https://thoughtcatalog. com/

Rachel's Challenge. https://rachelschallenge.org

History.com, Columbine Shooting, 2009, updated 2022. https://www.history.com/topics/1990s/columbine-high-school-shootings

Sandy Hook Promise, https://www.sandyhookpromise.org

Chapter 3:
Pay It Forward https://payitforwardday.com/
Mason, Jessica. "'Release the Kraken' Doesn't Mean What You Think it Does, Trumpsters" 2020. https://www.themarysue.com/
Vinney, Cynthia. "What are Different Types of Bullying?" 2021. https://www.verywellmind.com/what-are-the-different-types-of-bullying-5207717
Young, S. L., "How to Get Away with Workplace Bullying," January 25, 2015, https://www.huffpost.com/entry/how-to-get-away-with-work_b_6216532

Chapter 4:
Corley, Kirsten. "13 Ways Narcissists Turn the Tables Around and Manipulate You." 2017. https://thoughtcatalog.com
Maurer, Roy. "FBI: Over 80 Percent of Active Shooter Incidents Occur at Work," 2015. https://www.shrm.org/
"going postal," 2022. https://www.urbandictionary.com/define.php?term=going%20postal
Simon, Robb. "Will the Blue or White Dress Debate ever be Solved?" 2017. https://metro.co.uk/2017/04/07/has-the-blue-or-white-dress-debate-finally-been-solved-6560599/
CBS Mornings. "Is this Dress Blue and Black or White and Gold," February 27, 2015. https://www.cbsnews.com/news/blue-black-white-gold-dress-color-debate-goes-viral/
Hersh, Casey. "Resistance Training: Autoimmune Disease: *Costco Connection*, 2019.
Say Something Anonymous Reporting System, 1-844-5-SayNow, https://www.schoolsafety.gov/resource/say-something-anonymous-reporting-system

Chapter 5:
Crohn's and Colitis Foundation of America. https://www.crohnscolitisfoundation.org/
Findatopic.com. "Famous Alien Scene was Inspired by Crohn's," 2022. https://www.findatopdoc.com/Healthy-Living/famous-alien-scene-was-inspired-by-crohn-s

Justice. "Leave a Little Sparkle Wherever You Go: Quote Meaning," November 21, 2020. https://successismoney.com/leave-a-little-sparkle-wherever-you-go/

Chapter 6:

NCIS.fandom.com. "Judgement Day Part 1 (final episode)," Season 5, https://ncis.fandom.com/wiki/Judgment_Day_Part_1_(episode)

LaCapria, Kim. "The United States Has the Highest Maternal Mortality Rate of Any Developed Country." June 27, 2022. https://www.truthorfiction.com/the-united-states-has-the-highest-maternal-mortality-rate-of-any-developed-country/

Nelson, Jennifer. "Gender Bias: Disparities in Health Care do Exist" *Costco Connection*, May 2019.

Hoyert, Donna. "Maternal Mortality Rates in the United States" Centers for Disease Control, 2020. https://www.cdc.gov/nchs/data/hestat/maternal-mortality/2020/maternal-mortality-rates-2020.htm

Legal Dictionary. "Hostile Work Environment." November 30, 2015. https://legaldictionary.net/hostile-work-environment/

Gomez, Jasmine. "Inside Job: The State of Your Gut Impacts Your Wellness." *Women's Health*, February 2021

Americans with Disabilities Act, https://www.ada.gov

Chapter 7:

Frida Kahlo: Paintings, Biography, Quotes https://www.frida-kahlo.org/the-wounded-deer.jsp

United States Census. "Anniversary of Americans with Disabilities Act Fun Facts" 2017. https://www.census.gov/programs-surveys/sis/resources/fun-facts/anniversary-of-ada.html

Tresca, Amber. "Is IBD Covered Under the ADA?" 2020. https://www.verywellhealth.com/is-ibd-covered-under-the-ada-1942917

National Kindness Day https://nationaltoday.com/world-kindness-day/

Crohn's and Colitis Foundation of America, "Employment and Inflammatory Bowel Disease Fat Sheet," https://www.crohnscolitisfoundation.org/sites/default/files/legacy/assets/pdfs/employment-and-inflammatory.pdf

Chapter 8:
US Equal Opportunity Employment Commission https://www.
    eeoc.gov/facts-about-retaliation
Time's Up https://timesupnow.org/
    https://www.dailydot.com/irl/what-is-times-up-movement/
Gorgon, Sherri. "What is the #MeToo Movement?" 2022.
    https://www.verywellmind.com/what-is-the-metoo-move-
    ment-4774817

Chapter 9:
Durkin, Erin. "Women's March 2019: Thousands to Protest Across
    U.S.," *US News*, January 19, 2019. https://www.theguardian.
    com/us-news/2019/jan/19/womens-march-2019-protests-
    latest-event
Mazarine. "Wow, I'm Really Angry. What is Internalized Oppres-
    sion?" January 31, 2011.
        https://wildwomanfundraising.com/women-beating-
            women-2/
Inspirational Stories: The Power of Words, Frank Tyger Profession-
    alism quote https://www.inspirationalstories.com/quotes/
    frank-tyger-professionalism-is-knowing-how-to-do-it/#:~:-
    text=Frank%20Tyger%20Quotes%3A%20Professionalism%20
    is%20knowing%20how%20to,off%20the%20main%20
    road%2C%20by%20trying%20the%20untried
Pritchett, Price, "You2, A High Velocity Formula for Multiplying
    Your Personal Effectiveness in Quantum Leaps," https://
    www.pritchettyou2.com/product/you2
    https://www.stopbullying.gov/resources/laws

Chapter 10:
P.S. I Love You http://psiloveyouday.net
Walker, Tim. "It's Time for a Raise." NEA Today, June 2022.
Wike, Erin, "20 Leadership Qualities that Make a Great Leader
    (With Tips)," August 26, 2022.
        https://www.indeed.com/career-advice/career-develop-
            ment/leadership-qualities-that-make-a-great-leader
        https://chinesenewyear.net/zodiac/rat/
Eisner, Elliot, "Ten Lessons the Arts Teach," February 1, 2016

National Art Education Association, "10 Lessons the Arts Teach," February 1, 2016. https://www.arteducators.org/advocacy-policy/articles/116-10-lessons-the-arts-teach
https://www.merriam-webster.com

Ziad K. Adbelnour, "Economic Warfare: Secrets of Wealth Creation in the Age of Welfare Politics," https://www.goodreads.com/quotes/1012037-life-is-like-a-camera-focus-on-what-s-important-capture
https://supernatural.fandom.com/wiki/Banshee

Schoolhouse Rock, "I'm Just a Bill"
https://www.msn.com/en-us/news/politics/that-daylight-saving-time-bill-passed-because-a-bunch-of-senators-just-weren-t-paying-attention/ar-AAVcwdG

About the Author

Zana K. Elin has over twenty-five years' experience in the field of education in both teaching and administration. She has a Bachelor of Fine Arts in Photography from Rhode Island School of Design, a Graduate Degree in Art Education from Teachers College, Columbia University, and a Graduate Degree in Educational Administration and Leadership and Certificate of Advanced Graduate Study in Administration from Massachusetts College of Liberal Arts. She has exhibited her artwork professionally and likes to use her artistic integrity in every facet of her life. She lives and teaches in suburban America.

About the Artist

The selected works of art were created during the artist's middle and high school life and freshman foundation art courses. Violet Elin is a student of life and is passionate about a wide diversity of art and music media from illustration to photography and poetry to songwriting.

www.ingramcontent.com/pod-product-compliance
Lightning Source LLC
Chambersburg PA
CBHW041801280326
41926CB00103B/4763